Learning C++
A Hands-On Approach

Eric Nagler

De Anza College
University of California,
Santa Cruz Extension

West Publishing Company
Minneapolis/St. Paul   New York   Los Angeles   San Francisco

Trademarks

ANSI is a registered trademark of American National Standards Institute.

AT&T is a registered trademark of AT&T.

Borland C++ is a registered trademark of Borland International, Inc.

CompuServe is a registered trademark of CompuServe, Inc.

Turbo C++ is a registered trademark of Borland International, Inc.

Watcom is a registered trademark of Watcom Systems, Inc.

X3J16 is a technical committee that operates under X3 procedures and policies. X3 is an Accredited Standards Committee that operates under the procedures of ANSI.

WEST'S COMMITMENT TO THE ENVIRONMENT

In 1906, West Publishing Company began recycling materials left over from the production of books. This began a tradition of efficient and responsible use of resources. Today, up to 95% of our legal books and 70% of our college and school texts are printed on recycled, acid-free stock. West also recycles nearly 22 million pounds of scrap paper annually—the equivalent of 181,717 trees. Since the 1960s, West has devised ways to capture and recycle waste inks, solvents, oils, and vapors created in the printing process. We also recycle plastics of all kinds, wood, glass, corrugated cardboard, and batteries, and have eliminated the use of Styrofoam book packaging. We at West are proud of the longevity and the scope of commitment to the environment.

Production, Prepress, Printing and Binding by West Publishing Company.

 PRINTED ON 10% POST CONSUMER RECYCLED PAPER

COPYRIGHT © 1993 by   WEST PUBLISHING CO.
610 Opperman Drive
P.O. Box 64526
St. Paul, MN 55164–0526

Library of Congress Cataloging-in-Publication Data

Nagler, Eric P.
       Learning C++ : a hands-on approach / Eric P. Nagler.
           p. cm.
       Includes index.
       ISBN 0–314–02464–6 (soft)
       1. C++ (Computer program language)   I. Title.
QA76.73.C15N33   1993
005.13'3--dc20   93-16017
                                CIP

Table of contents

Acknowledgments

An undertaking of this magnitude cannot be done without the help of a great many other people. I would like to express my gratitude to all of the manuscript reviewers who offered their insights on how to make this text work:

- Thomas J Ahlborn, West Chester University
- Edmund I Deaton, San Diego State University
- H E Dunsmore, Purdue University
- Carl F Eckberg, San Diego State University
- John J Forsyth, Michigan State University
- Peter Isaacson, University of Northern Colorado
- Bob Koss, Robert Koss & Associates
- Grant Larkin, De Anza Community College
- Daniel Masterson, Utah Valley Community College
- Robert A McDonald, East Stroudsburg University
- Mike Michaelson, Palomar College
- Allan Miller, College of San Mateo
- Richard J Reid, Michigan State University
- Arline Sachs, Northern Virginia Community College
- Jerrold Siegel, University of Missouri at St. Louis
- Al Stevens, Dr. Dobbs' Journal

A special thanks goes to Bob Koss, Allan Miller, and Timothy Butterfield for their helpful comments in a technical review of the manuscript. In addition, I wish to thank the technical staff at Borland International and the people who participate in the Borland forums on CompuServe for answering many of my questions. In particular, Gary Blaine has helped me fill in a lot of details with his intricate knowledge of the C and C++ languages.

The design of this book was done with help from Barbara Smyth and Tess Lujan of Apple Computer, Inc.

Finally, I would like to acknowledge the faith and patience that have been placed in me for the past several years by Richard Mixter and Melanie Shouse of West Educational Publishing. I pray that their efforts will be rewarded.

About the author...

Eric Nagler received his B.A. in mathematics from the University of Michigan in 1963, went to work for the federal government as a computer programmer, and has been working in the field of data processing ever since. He first started teaching computer languages in 1980, and C++ in 1990. He is currently on the staff of De Anza College in Cupertino and the University of California Santa Cruz Extension, and teaches C++ at both institutions and at various companies in the San Jose, California Bay Area.

Introduction

This book presents a complete introductory course in the C++ programming language. It is designed to be used either on your own or in a classroom setting, in which case it serves as your notes for the various topics about which the instructor will be talking.

Prerequisites

In order to get the maximum benefit from this book, you should have a thorough working knowledge of the C language. This means, in particular, that your knowledge of C syntax, the various constructs, structures, arrays, functions, pointers, etc. is current. A knowledge of advanced C programming is helpful but not mandatory.

Unfortunately, some people believe that C++ is just C with a couple of extra keywords and the ability to write classes. They could not be more wrong. In terms of difficulty, I have polled many of my former students and overwhelmingly they agree that the material covered in C++ was a lot more difficult than they had anticipated. I would estimate that it is at least twice as hard to move from C to C++ as it is to go from another language, say Pascal, to C.

Details, details

The level of detail in this book goes beyond what most other books on C++ have to say on any particular topic. This means that in a classroom the amount of note-taking that you will have to do should be kept to a minimum. The advantage to this approach to learning is that (1) if you are constantly taking notes, you are not devoting complete attention to what the instructor or another student is saying, and (2) it is very easy to copy code incorrectly, thereby resulting in a program that either will not compile or has a bug. Instead, you may want to keep a marking pen handy to highlight certain passages. Nevertheless, at the end of each chapter there are several blank pages that you may use to jot down any new material that may come up.

Nothing explains like an example

There are over 500 examples of C++ programs (or parts of programs) that are included in this book. The reason that there are so many is simply my belief that nothing can explain a C++ concept as well as a good example with the output shown. In fact, many of the examples in this book were created as a direct result of questions asked by students in previous classes. Please note that some programs are deliberately created so that they will either not compile, not link, or not produce the correct output. These situations are noted at the start of each example and in the accompanying text. In the case of a compilation or link error, you will find the message that the Borland compiler/linker yields. Of course, you may experience different messages on your computer, depending upon the particular compiler you are using, the memory model, options selected, etc. To gain the maximum benefit, each example should be compiled and executed (where applicable), either in the classroom itself or on your own at home or at work. By doing so, you are then free to play "what if" games with each example in order to try things with the program that may not be 100% clear. An old saying goes, "The only way to learn programming is to program". It has never been more true than it is with C++.

How to obtain the examples on diskette

All of the examples in this book are available on diskette. An order form may be found in the back. Be sure to specify the size and density of the diskette you want.

Other sources of information

I would also like to note that no matter how good a given book on C++ may be, no single book can possibly teach you everything that you might want or need to know. Therefore, I highly encourage you to purchase as many books on C++ as you can afford so that you may see what a variety of authors have to say on a given topic. Then you should contrast and compare their views (and perhaps even find inconsistencies). There are also several good magazines on the market that deal exclusively with the C++ language, such as The C++ Report, The C++ Journal, and Inside Turbo C++.

What about object-oriented programming?

I also assume that many of you are studying C++ because you have heard that it has the capability to do object-oriented programming, which currently is the hot buzz word in the computer industry. The reason that C++ has become so popular is that it is a natural extension of the C language, which in and of itself has become widely used. Therefore, people feel it is quite natural to migrate into C++ once they have mastered C. This is fine, except that you should be aware that there are many other object-oriented languages in use today, such as Object Pascal, Smalltalk, Modula 2, Objective-C, and Eiffel.

The transition from C to C++ can logically be categorized into three phases. Phase 1 would be the use of C++ as a "better C". This might entail the usage of reference variables, the new style of commenting, new ways to dynamically allocate memory, function overloading, etc. Phase 2 would involve the creation of classes and data encapsulation. Phase 3 would introduce derivation and polymorphism to make full use of C++ as an object-oriented programming language (OOPL). Please be aware that while certain areas of object-oriented design will be mentioned (indeed, it's impossible to ignore), a complete course in object-oriented programming, including analysis, design, implementation, message passing, client-server relationships, and so forth, is beyond the scope of this book.

Where things now stand

The semi-official standard for the C++ language is set by AT&T and documented in The Annotated C++ Reference Manual (ARM), written by Bjarne Stroustrup and Margaret Ellis. The X3J16 Technical Committee, which started its work in 1989, is currently hammering out a C++ standard to which all compilers must eventually conform, but this will not be completed for several more years. The examples in this book (with the exception of Chapter 18) have been tested with Borland C++, version 3.1, which implements AT&T version 3.0. The examples in Chapter 18 have been tested with Watcom C/C++[32], which implements AT&T version 3.0 with exception handling.

Nobody is perfect

If you encounter any errors in this book, grammatical or technical, I would appreciate hearing from you. I can be contacted at the following address:

Eric Nagler
P O Box 2483
Santa Clara, California 95055-2483

CompuServe ID: 76711,521
From Internet: 76711.521@compuserve.com

Chapter 1

Moving from C to C++

The C++ language was invented by Bjarne Stroustrup of AT&T Bell Laboratories in the early 1980's as an extension of the C language. This means that, in theory, you can take your existing C programs and compile them successfully using a C++ compiler. Unfortunately, it's not quite that simple, as there are some subtle differences that you must be aware of. In addition, C++ adds some very useful misc. features to C that are covered in this chapter.

Source program names

Because a C++ compiler can accommodate both the C and C++ languages, it must have a way to determine the type of code that it is processing. Since most C programs have an extension of .C, if a program having this extension is encountered by the Borland compiler, it will assume that you want to do a C compilation. On the other hand, if the extension is .CPP, then the compiler assumes that you want to do a C++ compilation. If you are doing a command-line compilation, the option -P will force the compiler to do a C++ compilation regardless of the program's extension.

It is up to you to ensure that the compiler you are using interprets your code in the way you intend.

Commenting a program

The C style method of commenting a program is still valid. That is, a C comment begins with the token /* and ends with the token */. Anything between these two tokens is ignored by the compiler, and the comment may extend for more than one line. While some C compilers support the nesting of this style of comment, you should be very careful because the ANSI standard does not provide for nested comments, and your program may then not compile successfully using a different compiler.

A better method would be to use the statements #if 0 and #endif to force the preprocessor to bypass large amounts of code. For example, this program comments out the two C style comments using the aforementioned preprocessor statements.

Example 1.1

```
#include <stdio.h>

int main(void)
{
   #if 0
   /* Your first C program */
   /* printf() is a function call */
   printf("Hello world\n") ;
   #endif
   printf("Hello C++\n") ;

   return 0 ;
}
```

The output is:

```
Hello C++
```

In addition, C++ defines a new comment token that consists of two forward slashes (*//*). Whenever the compiler encounters this token, it will ignore everything that follows *to the end of the line, including the start of a C style comment*. However, the token // itself is ignored if it is encountered as part of a C style comment.

This example shows how you can commingle the two comment styles.

Example 1.2

```
int main()
{
   /*  C comment     */

   //  C++ comment

   /*  C comment — // is ignored
         (cont.)   */

   //  C++ comment — /* is ignored
}
```

Here is a rather unusual way to determine if you are doing a C or C++ compilation *without* resorting to the use of a preprocessor variable (assuming that your C compiler does *not* support the C++ style of commenting). See if you can figure out how the compiler parses the declaration of the variable cplusplus in both types of compilation.

Example 1.3

```
#include <stdio.h>

int main(void)
{
   int cplusplus = 1 //**/ 2
    ;   /* Semicolon by itself */
   if(cplusplus == 1)
     puts("C++ compilation") ;
   else
     puts("C compilation") ;

   return 0 ;
}
```

If you compiled and ran this program using a C compiler, the comment /**/ is ignored and the message c compilation would appear. However, if you compiled and ran using a C++ compiler, the message c++ compilation would appear. Can you explain why?

Needless to say, your program should always use enough comments to explain to the reader (and to yourself!) what it is trying to accomplish.

> ☞ The preprocessor symbol __cplusplus (two leading underscores) will always be on whenever you are compiling a C++ (not C) program.

ANSI function prototyping

You *must* use ANSI-style function prototyping in your programs. This means that the declaration or definition of a function must:

■ precede the actual call of that function;

■ specify the correct number of the arguments;

■ specify the correct types of the formal arguments that match the types of the actual arguments. If a type does not match exactly, it is an error only if the compiler *cannot* do implicit type conversion.

Arguments passed in to ellipsis will undergo default promotions, e.g., char to int, and float to double.

Recall that a function *definition* consists of the complete function itself, and if it precedes the call to that function, it negates the need for a function *declaration* (prototype).

For example, this program does *not* include the header file `stdio.h`, yet it still compiles in C. However, the missing prototype for the function `printf()` causes a compilation error in C++.

Example 1.4   *(Will not compile!)*

```
int main()
{
   printf("Hello World\n") ;

   return 0 ;
}
```

The compiler error message is:

```
Function 'printf' should have a prototype
```

Function argument declarations

If you define a non-class function using the "old" C style as defined by Kernighan and Ritchie, it will still compile and run in C++, but a warning message will be issued. This "old" style consists of declaring the formal argument names on separate lines following the function definition line, and before the opening brace.

In C++ you should use the ANSI standard style to declare your functions. This implies that the declarations for the formal arguments are contained totally in the parameter list between the parentheses. For example:

Example 1.5

```
void f(number) // wrong way
int number ;
{
   // Function body
}

void f(int number) // right way
{
   // Function body
}
```

Note that this rule does *not* apply to a class's member functions; they *must* use ANSI style as shown above.

In addition, a missing return type in front of a function name still implies type `int`, but why not be explicit and always write it if that is your intent?

Functions taking no arguments

In C++, if a function `f()` is called with no arguments, you may declare it either as `f()` or `f(void)`. The C++ purists insist on using `f()`, as they maintain that `f(void)` is only allowed for the sake of compatibility with C programs. Note, however, that in C `f()` means that the function takes *any number of arguments* (and does not qualify as a prototype), which is not the same meaning as C++.

To illustrate, the following example compiles as a C program, but not as a C++ program.

Example 1.6   ***(Will not compile!)***

```
void f ()
{
   // Function body
}

int main ()
{
   f (1) ;
   return 0 ;
}
```

The compiler error message is:

```
Extra parameter in call to f ()
```

Placement of variable declarations

In C, whenever you write a block of code, the variables must be declared at the beginning before any executable statements. If you want to create a new variable, you must start a new block (scope) by writing an open brace ({).

For example, in this program, a number (n1) is declared and printed, after which the same operation is performed on another integer (n2). Because n2 is declared after the call to the printf() function, a new block is required. This is OK provided that n2 does not need to be referenced outside the block (since it is an auto variable and will go out of scope when the block ends).

Example 1.7

```
#include <stdio.h>

int main(void)
{
   int n1 = 1 ;
   printf("n1 = %d\n" , n1) ;
    {
       int n2 = 2 ;
       printf("n2 = %d\n" , n2) ;
    }

   return 0 ;
}
```

The output is:

```
n1 = 1
n2 = 2
```

The only other approach would be to declare n2 at the same time that n1 is declared.

However, in C++ this restriction disappears because declaration statements are treated the same as executable statements. This means that declaration and executable statements may be freely commingled.

Here is a repeat of Example 1.7 now written in C++.

Example 1.8

```
#include <stdio.h>

int main()
{
   int n1 = 1 ;
   printf("n1 = %d\n" , n1) ;
   int n2 = 2 ;
   printf("n2 = %d\n" , n2) ;

   return 0 ;
}
```

The output is:

```
n1 = 1
n2 = 2
```

One advantage is that this allows you to declare a variable closer to its actual usage in the program. In addition, when you get to the point of creating user-defined objects, you must first have on hand the values that are to be used in the creation process. Therefore, it's mandatory that you have the capability to freely mix the two types of statements. On the other hand, some people may prefer to have all of the variables declared in only one place, i.e., at the beginning of a function.

Note also that a variable *cannot* be declared in the conditional part of a `while` or `if` construct:

Example 1.9   *(Will not compile!)*

```
int main()
{
   if(int number == 1) {}
   while(int number == 1) {}
}
```

The compiler error message is:

```
Expression syntax
```

Variable declaration within a `for` loop

C++ goes one step further and allows you to declare the counting variable of a `for` loop as part of the initialization step.

Example 1.10

```
for(int i = 0 ; i < 10 ; ++i)
{
   // Body of loop
}
```

Note that when this `for` loop ends, the variable `i` *is still in scope*, just as it is if you had declared it prior to the `for` loop. This means that if you want to write another loop using `i` in the same scope, you *cannot* declare it again.

In addition, note that you may declare two such counting variables in the initial part of a `for` loop.

Example 1.11

```
for(int i = 0 , j = 0 ; i < 10 ; ++i , ++j)
{
   // Body of loop
}
```

Initialization of global variables

In C global variables may be initialized only to constant values. In C++ they may be initialized to the value of an expression, provided that the expression can be computed. This capability is required so that global objects can be properly initialized. For example, this code is invalid in C, and valid in C++.

Example 1.12   ***(Will not compile in C!)***

```
#include <stdio.h>

int x = puts("Ready to start") ;
int main()
{
   puts("In main()") ;

   return 0 ;
}
```

In C the compiler error message is:

```
Illegal initialization
```

In C++ the output is:

```
Ready to start
In main()
```

If the variable x at global scope had not been present at all, or had been assigned instead of initialized, then the program would not have compiled.

Initialization of arrays

In C the addresses of all of the initializers in an array declaration must be known to the compiler. An array of pointers-to-characters is a good example because the compiler knows the address of each string in global memory. In other words, the strings are *not* placed on the stack when main() is called.

The following program works just fine in both C and C++:

Example 1.13

```
#include <stdio.h>

int main(void)
{
   const char* array[] = { "Some" , "string" , "data" } ;
   const int size = sizeof(array) / sizeof(const char*) ;
   int i ;
   for(i = 0 ; i < size ; ++i)
      puts(array[i]) ;

      return 0 ;
}
```

The output is:

```
Some
string
data
```

On the other hand, the following somewhat similar program does *not* compile in C because the compiler has no idea where the (auto) integers will be on the stack at execution time. C++, however, does not impose this restriction, but instead computes the addresses of the initializing elements at execution time.

Example 1.14   *(Will not compile in C!)*

```
#include <stdio.h>

int main(void)
{
   int n1 = 1 , n2 = 2 ;
   const int* array[] = { &n1 , &n2 } ;

   const int size = sizeof(array) / sizeof(const int*) ;
   int i ;
   for(i = 0 ; i < size ; ++i)
      printf("array[%d] = %d\n" , i , *array[i]) ;

   return 0 ;
}
```

In C the compiler error message is:

```
Illegal initialization
```

In C++ the output is:

```
array[0] = 1
array[1] = 2
```

Character constants

In C all character constants are stored in 2 bytes. Therefore, the `sizeof` a character constant, e.g., 'A', is 2. But in C++ the `sizeof` operator applied to type `char` or to a variable of type `char` is 1.

Recursive call to `main()`

In C you can set up a recursive call in `main()` to itself. In C++ this will not compile.

Example 1.15   ***(Will not compile!)***

```
#include <stdio.h>

int main(void)
{
   printf("An endless loop\n") ;
   main() ;

   return 0 ;
}
```

The compiler error message is:

```
Cannot call 'main' from within the program
```

Assignment of pointers of type `void*`

In C, you may assign a pointer of type `void*` to any other pointer without having to use an explicit cast. In C++, to ensure that you know what you are doing, the cast is mandatory. For example, the function `malloc()` returns a pointer of type `void*`. Therefore, this program compiles in C but not in C++.

Example 1.16   **(Will not compile!)**

```
#include <stdlib.h>

void f(void)
{
   char* ptr = malloc(10) ;
}
```

In C++ the compiler error message is:

```
Cannot convert 'void *' to 'char *'
```

In order to compile successfully in C++ you have to write an explicit cast:

Example 1.17

```
#include <stdlib.h>

void f()
{
   char* ptr = (char*)malloc(10) ;
}
```

One implication of this restriction is that in C++ you should get into the habit of using the constant 0 (zero) whenever you would ordinarily use the macro NULL. C++ guarantees that a constant expression that evaluates to 0 will be converted to a pointer whenever it is assigned, compared, or used to initialize a pointer type. The only exception is when 0 is passed as an unchecked argument (e.g., as the second argument in a `print()` statement). In this case the 0 requires a cast to a pointer type.

Using the tag name as the type name

In C if you have a structure definition called `person`, and later wish to create an instance of this definition called `student`, you may write:

Example 1.18

```
struct person
{
   char name[25] ;
   long ssn ;
} ;

struct person student ;
```

However, you can shorten this process by using a `typedef`:

Example 1.19

```
typedef struct
{
   char name[25] ;
   long ssn ;
} person ;

person student ;
```

Fortunately, in C++ this is no longer necessary because the tag name of a structure also serves as the type name. That is, in C++ you may write:

Example 1.20

```
struct person
{
   char name[25] ;
   long ssn ;
} ;

person student ;
```

As you can see, there is no longer a need to `typedef` the structure. This change also applies to the keywords `enum` and `union`, and to the new keyword `class` in C++.

The `const` keyword

By definition, in ANSI C a variable declared with the modifier `const` is one that cannot be modified. In C a variable may be declared `const` without being initialized (and thereby serving no useful purpose), whereas in C++ all constant variables *must* be initialized.

When dealing with pointers, the situation is a little more confusing because now there are two objects involved: the pointer itself and the object to which the pointer points. If the word `const` is immediately in front of the pointer, then the pointer itself cannot be changed. However, this has nothing to do with the object being pointed at.

Example 1.21

```
char* const ptr = "ABC" ;

// Error — cannot assign to a constant
ptr = "DEF" ;

// OK
*ptr = 'Z' ;
```

On the other hand, if the word `const` is immediately in front of the object being pointed at, then this object cannot be changed. Similarly, this has nothing to do with the pointer itself.

Example 1.22

```
const char* ptr = "ABC" ;

// OK - pointer is being changed
ptr = "DEF" ;

// Error — cannot assign to a constant
*ptr = 'Z' ;
```

Of course, you may write the keyword `const` in both places.

Example 1.23

```
const char* const ptr = "ABC" ;

// Error — cannot assign to a constant
ptr = "DEF" ;

// Error — cannot assign to a constant
*ptr = 'Z' ;
```

The big difference between how C and C++ handle constants is that in C++ the primitive (built-in) type constant values are kept in a separate compiler-only table and substituted into the code as literal constants, very similar to how `#define` works. In C the value of a `const` is not determined until execution time.

One good use of the way C++ handles const variables is when you need to specify the dimension of some array. Of course, in C this would cause a compilation error because, as was just stated, the variable does not get its value until execution time. For example:

Example 1.24

```
void f ()
{
  const int dim = 10 ;
  int array[dim + 1] ;
}
```

works in C++ but not in C. On the other hand:

Example 1.25

```
void f ()
{
  int temp = 10 ;
  const int dim = temp ;
  int array[dim] ;
}
```

does *not* work in C++ (and, obviously, not in C) because there is no way that the compiler can determine the value of `dim` since the value of `temp` is not determined until execution time.

In C++ whenever you would normally use a #define to symbolically declare a value, use the const keyword. It preserves type checking, and the variable follows the normal scoping rules.

For example, this program using a #define will not compile because the #define, although written within the function f(), affects the remainder of the program, including the max in main().

Example 1.26   ***(Will not compile!)***

```
#include <stdio.h>

void f()
{
  #define max 10
  printf("max = %d\n" , max) ;
}

int main()
{
  f() ;
  double max = 10.0 ;
  printf("max = %f\n" , max) ;

  return 0 ;
}
```

The compiler error message is:

```
Declaration terminated incorrectly
```

Changing the #define to a const gives the right answer because now the definition is localized to the function.

Example 1.27

```
#include <stdio.h>

void f()
{
   const int max = 10 ;
   printf("max = %d\n" , max) ;
}

int main()
{
   f() ;
   double max = 10.0 ;
   printf("max = %f\n" , max) ;

   return 0 ;
}
```

The output is:

```
max = 10
max = 10.000000
```

Linkage of `const` variables

By default, `const` values in C at file scope have *external* linkage. This means that the linker sees them and may use them in a file that has an `extern` declaration. In C++, the default is *internal*. If a `const` declaration appears in a header file, then multiple inclusions of the header file in a project will not cause the linker to produce a duplicate definition error message.

Example 1.28

```
// Internal in C++, external in C
const int x = 1 ;

// External in both C++ and C
extern const int x = 1 ;

// Internal in both C++ and C
static const int x = 1 ;
```

Initialization of static data members

The initialization of static data members that have function scope is handled dynamically, so that the initializing value can be deferred until execution time. In C this value must be known to the compiler.

In the following example (which does not compile in C) the static member j is initialized with the first value of i and is never initialized again.

Example 1.29

```
#include <stdio.h>

int main()
{
   for(int i = 0 ; i < 3 ; ++i)
    {
      static int j = i ;
      printf("j = %d\n" , j) ;
    }

   return 0 ;
}
```

In C the compilation error message is:

```
Expression syntax
```

The output in C++ is:

```
j = 0 ;
j = 0 ;
j = 0 ;
```

Output of the increment and decrement operators

In C the output of the increment and decrement operators is an 'rvalue'. This means that you cannot concatenate successive calls. In C++, however, if prefix is used, then the output is an 'lvalue', meaning that it can indeed be modified. (The output from using postfix is an 'rvalue'.)

For example, the following program does not compile in C, but works just fine in C++.

Example 1.30   *(Will not compile in C!)*

```
#include <stdio.h>

int main()
{
    int i = 0 ;
    ++(++i) ;
    printf("i = %d\n" , i) ;

    return 0 ;
}
```

In C the compilation error message is:

```
Lvalue required in function main
```

In C++ the output is:

```
i = 2
```

C and C++ keywords

Here are all of the keywords used in C and C++. Those in bold-face type are specific to C++.

Table 1.1

asm	auto	break	case
catch	char	**class**	const
continue	default	**delete**	do
double	else	enum	extern
float	for	**friend**	goto
if	**inline**	int	long
new	**operator**	**private**	**protected**
public	register	return	short
signed	sizeof	static	struct
switch	**template**	**this**	**throw**
try	typedef	union	unsigned
virtual	void	volatile	**wchar_t**
while			

A C program that uses any of the C++ keywords as identifiers will not compile under C++. The keywords catch, throw and try are reserved for a feature called "exception handling" that will be part of AT&T version 4.0. (Exception handling is the topic of Chapter 18.)

In addition, the X3J16 Technical Committee has proposed that the following keywords be added to the language definition, so it is probably a good idea to avoid using them as identifiers:

Table 1.2

and	and_eq	bitand	bitor
compl	not	not_eq	or
or_eq	xor	xor_eq	

■ Exercise #1

Write a C++ program that allocates an array of size integers on the heap, where size has been declared as a constant. Then declare a variable called value and prompt the operator to enter a number into value which is subsequently used to fill each element of the array. Finally, print the array using a for loop and the same counting variable that was used to fill the array. Be sure to include some C++ style comments.

■ Exercise #2

Given the global structure type:

```
typedef struct
{
    char name[20] ;
    long ssn ;
    int grades[5] ;
    float average ;
} STUDENT ;
```

write a `main()` function that:

■ Creates an object of type STUDENT;

■ Passes the *address* of this object to a function called `GetData()` ;

■ Passes this object *by value* to a function called `WriteData()`.

Then write the function `GetData()` (using ANSI-style function prototyping) that:

■ Receives the address of the structure object as its one formal argument;

■ Prompts the terminal operator and receives the `name` field;

■ Prompts the terminal operator and receives the `ssn` field;

■ Prompts the terminal operator and loops 5 times to receive all entries in the `grades` array;

■ Computes the floating point average of the 5 grades and stores it into the field `average`;

■ Returns control back to `main()`.

Finally, write the function `WriteData()` (using full ANSI-style function prototyping) that:

■ Prints a title line to identify the NAME, SSN, and AVERAGE;

■ Prints the `name`, `ssn`, and the `average` (to an accuracy of 2 decimal positions);

■ Returns control back to `main()`.

Notes

Notes

Chapter 2

Reference variables

A reference variable in C++ is a new type that provides the means by which an alias to another variable can be created. What is an alias? Just another name for something or someone. This means that whenever the alias is used, the action is really taking place on the object to which the alias refers. While a reference variable is conceptually similar to a pointer variable in that they both refer, or point, to some other object, a reference variable is a "hidden" pointer because unlike a pointer variable, it does not have its own unique address.

The benefit of using reference variables

One of the great benefits of using reference variables is that in many cases they can replace function calls that are "pass by address" with calls that are "pass by reference". This syntax does not involve your having to manually generate the address of a variable, nor do you have to create a pointer variable in which to receive the address. As a result, it is much easier to code functions and function calls. This is similar to how Pascal handles the case when an actual argument in some function call needs to be modified. That is, declaring the formal argument as `var` in the function achieves the same effect as a reference variable.

How to create a reference variable

A reference variable in C++ is created by appending an ampersand (`&`) to the end of some existing type field. Example 2.1 shows how to create some new reference types. If you wish, you may have whitespace between the primitive type and the ampersand.

Example 2.1

```
// Type reference to int
int&

// Type reference to char
char&

// Type reference to float
float&

// Type reference to pointer to int
int*&
```

Do not confuse this usage of the ampersand with the case when it is used to generate the address of some object, or used as the bitwise 'and' operator.

Example 2.2

```
// 'object' is type reference to int
int& object

// Take the address of 'object'
&object

// Bitwise 'and' of the 'object' and 1
object & 1
```

Creation of reference variables and initialization

When a reference variable is created it must *always* be initialized with the name of some other existing variable. This makes sense because otherwise you would be saying, "some variable is an alias for". For what? Example 2.3 shows an invalid declaration, followed by a valid one.

Example 2.3

```
// Invalid. What is 'number' an alias for?
int& number ;

// Valid. 'number' is an alias for 'num'
int num ;
int& number = num ;
```

In the valid case, since number is just an alias for num, then whenever number is referenced, num is really the variable being used. Note also that once a reference variable is initialized with some existing variable, it cannot be reassigned to some other variable as long as it (the reference variable) remains in scope.

If a reference variable is an alias for still another reference variable, then it really refers to the variable for which the first reference variable is an alias. Stated another way, the two reference variables are aliases for the same variable in memory. Example 2.4 illustrates this because n2 and n3 really are just aliases for n1.

Example 2.4

```
#include <stdio.h>

int main()
{
   int n1 = 1 ;
   printf("n1 = %d\n" , n1) ;

   // n2 is an alias for n1
   int& n2 = n1 ;
   printf("n2 = %d\n" , n2) ;

   // n3 is an alias for n2, which really means that n3 is
   // an alias for n1
   int& n3 = n2 ;
   printf("n3 = %d\n" , n3) ;

   return 0 ;
}
```

The output is:

```
n1 = 1
n2 = 1
n3 = 1
```

You may also create a *constant* reference variable. In this case you may not modify the object for which the variable is an alias by using the variable. However, the object itself may still be changed. You will soon see why constant references are useful in a function's formal argument list.

Example 2.5

```
int num ;
const int& number = num ;

// Invalid
++number ;

// Valid
++num ;
```

Note that you may not create a non-constant reference to a constant value because a reference sets up an 'lvalue', and this implies that somehow you are now able to change the constant. The only type of reference that you can create for a constant value is a constant reference.

Example 2.6

```
// Invalid
const int x = 0 ;
int& ref_x = x ;

// Valid
const int y = 0 ;
const int& ref_y = y ;
```

Address of a reference variable

To prove that reference variables are not separate entities in memory with their own addresses, if you take the address of one, all you will get is the address of the variable for which it is an alias. In the following program the address of n2 is the same as the address of n1.

Example 2.7

```
#include <stdio.h>

int main()
{
   int n1 ;
   printf("&n1 = %p\n" , &n1) ;

   int& n2 = n1 ;
   printf("&n2 = %p\n" , &n2) ;

   return 0 ;
}
```

The output is:

```
&n1 = FFF4
&n2 = FFF4
```

Reference variables used as formal arguments

The declaration of reference variables up to now has not really served a very useful purpose. After all, if a variable and an alias for that variable are both defined within the same scope, then why bother to use the alias? Why not just use the name of the variable itself?

The real usefulness of a reference variable occurs when it is created in a scope that is *different* than the scope of the variable for which it is an alias. For example, a function sets up a brand new scope whenever it is called. If a reference variable is used as a formal argument, then it merely becomes an alias for the corresponding actual argument. This means that whenever the formal argument is used within the body of the function, *the actual argument in the calling function is the one that is really being manipulated.*

What good is this? Suppose that changes to the actual argument need to be made by the function. In C this implies that you must pass the *address* of the actual argument to the function (using the address operator for a non-array argument), so that the function can then receive the argument in some pointer variable, and by using dereferencing, it can then make changes to the actual argument. At best, this situation has always been a rich source of confusion for C programmers because of the way in which the formal arguments must be declared and used. Obviously, reference variables provide a much cleaner alternate method.

Passing primitive types — no modification

First, consider primitive types. These are types that are "built in" to each and every C and C++ compiler. When you pass arguments of these types into functions, you have two options: (1) by value, and (2) by address. Let's start with the pass-by-value case. When the function `f()` is called, a *copy* of `num` is put onto the stack and used to initialize the formal argument `number`. Then the function simply prints the value of `number`.

Example 2.8

```
#include <stdio.h>

void f(int number)
{
   printf("number = %d\n" , number) ;
}

int main()
{
   int num = 0 ;
   f(num) ;

   return 0 ;
}
```

The output is:

```
number = 0
```

Now let's re-write the function `f()` so that a pass-by-reference instead of a pass-by-value is used. Now the formal argument `number` is simply a constant alias for the actual argument `num`, so that when `number` gets printed, in reality a copy of the variable `num` is being passed to `printf()`. Note that the reference variable is declared `const` to ensure that the actual argument `num` cannot be modified by the function.

Example 2.9

```
#include <stdio.h>

void f(const int& number)
{
   printf("number = %d\n" , number) ;
}

int main()
{
   int num = 0 ;
   f(num) ;

   return 0 ;
}
```

The output is:

```
number = 0
```

Does this mean that it is always more advantageous to use a pass-by-reference instead of a pass-by-value? No, because in this case it really buys you nothing. It's just as efficient to pass the actual value of a primitive type as it is to create an alias in the function. So the rule is: when a primitive type variable needs to be used in a function, and no changes need to be made to that variable, pass it in by value.

Passing primitive types — function modification

It becomes a completely different story, however, when the function must *alter* the value of a variable in the calling routine. Let's change the example again so that the function adds 1 to the value of num. First, here is the solution written in C.

Example 2.10

```
#include <stdio.h>

void f(int* ptr_num)
{
   // Add 1 to 'num'
   ++(*ptr_num) ;
}

int main()
{
   int num = 0 ;
   f(&num) ;
   printf("num = %d\n" , num) ;

   return 0 ;
}
```

The output is:

```
num = 1
```

While this code works in C++ just as well, a reference variable provides a much more elegant way to accomplish the same result. So now let's change the program one last time so that it is written in C++ using a reference variable.

Example 2.11

```
#include <stdio.h>

void f(int& number)
{
   // Add 1 to 'num'
   ++number ;
}

int main()
{
   int num = 0 ;
   f(num) ;
   printf("num = %d\n" , num) ;

   return 0 ;
}
```

The output is:

```
num = 1
```

Avoiding a double dereference by using reference variables

Sometimes in C the address of a pointer variable needs to be passed into a function. In this case the function argument needs to be declared as "pointer to pointer" in order to access the original variable that was being pointed at in the first place. Here is a program written in C that uses a function to access the variable `ptr` in `main()` and make it point to some string literal. Because `ptr` is a pointer type, and must be modified by the function, it is passed in as "pointer-to-pointer".

Example 2.12

```
#include <stdio.h>

void f(char* *ptr_ptr)
{
   *ptr_ptr = "Hello C++" ;
}

int main()
{
   char* ptr ;
   f(&ptr) ;
   printf("ptr = \"%s\"\n" , ptr) ;

   return 0 ;
}
```

The output is:

```
ptr = "Hello C++"
```

A better solution is to create a reference variable for the pointer. For example, since the type of the pointer variable `ptr` is `char*`, then a reference to it would be type `char*&`. Therefore, in order to use the actual value of the variable `ptr` from within the function, no dereferences are required.

Example 2.13

```
#include <stdio.h>

void f(char*& ptr_ptr)
{
   ptr_ptr = "Hello C++" ;
}

int main()
{
   char* ptr ;
   f(ptr) ; // No & required
   printf("ptr = \"%s\"\n" , ptr) ;

   return 0 ;
}
```

The output is:

```
ptr = "Hello C++"
```

Inexact matches between actual and formal arguments

In this program the integer `num` is being passed by reference into the function `f()`, but it is received as a reference-to-float, *not* a reference-to-int. Borland C++ gives you a warning message that you may not get the intended results. (Other compilers will probably give a fatal error.)

Example 2.14

```
#include <stdio.h>

void f(float& number)
{
   // 'num' is NOT being changed
   ++number ;
   printf("number = %0.2f\n" , number) ;
}

int main()
{
   int num = 1 ;
   f(num) ;
   printf("num = %d\n" , num) ;

   return 0 ;
}
```

The output is:

```
number = 2.00
num = 1
```

Note that the value of num did *not* get changed by the function. In order to pass an argument by reference and have the function modify the actual value, there can be no temporary variables created in the process. In other words, if you pass an int by reference, and create a floating point reference to it, then the compiler will convert the int into a temporary float variable, and then make reference to this temporary float via the formal argument. Therefore, if you attempt to modify this float, you would only be modifying the temporary float instead of the actual int argument itself.

Syntax of call by value vs. call by reference

You should note that one possible drawback to the pass-by-reference method is that the actual function call is identical to that of a call that is pass-by-value. And sometimes, it is identical to a pass-by-address (if the variable is the name of an array). In other words, if you see a code fragment such as:

Example 2.15

```
int num = 0 ;
f (num)  ;
```

then num is possibly being passed by reference or by value. The only way to know for sure is to look at the function declaration or definition. For this reason, some people suggest that when primitive types need to be modified in a function, you should always use the C style of passing by address, so that someone reading your code knows that modification of the variable could possibly occur.

Making a reference to a structure

In addition to creating references to primitive (and pointer) types, you may also create references for structures. This has the benefit of passing a hidden pointer to the structure object instead of passing the entire structure object on the stack (which can be quite inefficient). In addition, if you want to ensure that the structure object is a "read-only" object in the sense that it cannot be modified by a function, then its declaration must be a *constant* reference. You do this by preceding the reference type with the keyword const.

In this example the object Author is passed to the function change() by reference in order to fill the data field name. Then it is passed by constant reference to the function print() in order to display the name.

Example 2.16

```
#include <stdio.h>

struct person
{
  char* name ;
} ;

// Non-constant reference to allow changes to occur
void change(person& p)
{
  p.name = "Bjarne Stroustrup" ;
}

// Constant reference to disallow changes
void print(const person& p)
{
  printf("%s is the author of C++\n" , p.name) ;
}

int main()
{
  person Author ;
  change(Author) ;
  print(Author) ;

  return 0 ;
}
```

The output is:

```
Bjarne Stroustrup is the author of C++
```

Making a reference to an array

Although not particularly useful, you may create a reference to an entire array, as shown in the following example.

Example 2.17

```
#include <stdio.h>

const int dim = 3 ;
typedef int array[dim] ;

void f(array& ref)
// Without a typedef...
// void f(int (&ref)[dim])
{
  for(int i = 0 ; i < dim ; ++i)
    printf("[%d] = %d\n" , i , ref[i]) ;
}

int main()
{
  array ar = {0 , 1 , 2} ;
  f(ar) ;

  return 0 ;
}
```

The output is:

```
[0] = 0
[1] = 1
[2] = 2
```

Returning from a function by reference

In Chapter 7 you will learn how a function can return a value by reference, and the usefulness of this technique.

■ Review questions

1) Explain what a reference variable is.

2) Why would you use a reference variable?

3) What are the advantages and disadvantages of reference variables in comparison to pointers?

4) Why can't a reference variable be "reassigned" to another variable after being created?

5) Why do reference variables have to be initialized?

6) What happens when a value is passed into a function by reference and the type of the reference variable is incompatible with the argument?

7) What is the difference between passing a structure object into a function by reference vs. by constant reference?

8) In Example 2.10 the expression `++(*ptr_num)` is used. By way of comparison, can you determine the meaning of the following expressions?

```
++*ptr_num
(*ptr_num)++
*++ptr_num
*ptr_num++
*(ptr_num++)
```

■ Exercise #1

Write a function called `swap1()` that uses pointer variables to swap the content of 2 integer variables in the calling routine. Then write another function called `swap2()` that does the same thing, but now uses reference variables. Finally, write a `main()` function to test both functions.

■ Exercise #2

Write a program that declares a string pointer initialized to some value, and then proceeds to put the characters into reverse order. Do not create a temporary string. This means that the first character gets swapped with the last character, the second with the next-to-last, etc. Be sure to use reference variables in a `for` loop to refer to the two ends of the string.

■ Exercise #3

Given the `main()` function:

```
int main()
{
    int array[] = { 5 , -6 , 21 , 15 , -8 } ;
    const int length = sizeof(array) / sizeof(int) ;
    int max , min ;
    find(array , length , max , min) ;
    printf("max = %d\n" , max) ;
    printf("min = %d\n" , min) ;

    return 0 ;
}
```

write the function `find()` that finds the maximum and minimum values in the array. Be sure to use reference variables only where applicable.

■ Exercise #4

Write a program that computes the number of quarters, dimes, nickels, and pennies that are contained within a specified amount of money. For example, given $1.18, the answer would be 4 quarters, 1 dime, 1 nickel, and 3 pennies. Given $0.31, the answer would be 1 quarter, 1 nickel and 1 penny.

Use the following structure to describe a coin type:

```
struct COIN
{
    int denom ;        // 1 or 5 or 10 or 25
    long count ;       // Count of occurrences
    char* single ;     // Text for 1 occurrence, e.g., "penny"
    char* multiple ;   // Text for more than 1 occurrence, e.g.,
                       // "pennies"

} ;
```

In the `main()` function:

■ Create a 4-element array of structures, and call upon the function:

```
void initialize(COIN*) ;
```

■ to initialize each element with its appropriate values. Note that the `count` field for all coins and the `multiple` field for the nickel structure may be left uninitialized.

■ Set up a `for` loop that will generate test amounts in the range 0 to 51 (representing the values $0.00 to $0.51). Create `const` values to describe the starting and ending ranges of the `for` loop (as opposed to hard-coding the values in the `for` loop).

■ For each test amount, create another `for` loop that traverses the array of structures and, for each element, calls upon these two functions:

```
void change(int& , COIN&) ;
void print(const COIN&) ;
```

The first argument in `change()` is the money amount (as a reference to an `int` to avoid rounding problems associated with floating point numbers) and the second is a reference to an array element. The argument in `print()` is the array element passed in by constant reference.

■ Do not print any output for a coin whose `count` is zero.

Notes

Notes

Notes

Chapter 3

Default function arguments

In C, whenever a function is written, then under the rules of ANSI prototyping it must *be called with the same number of actual arguments that are specified by the formal argument list (ignoring variable length argument lists, such as found in the function* `printf()`*). C++, however, provides the capability to define* default function argument *values. This means that when a function uses default arguments, the actual function call has the* option *to specify new (overriding) values, or use the default values.*

The benefit of default arguments

In many cases a C++ function needs to be *overloaded* so that it can be called with no arguments, one argument, two arguments, etc. Normally this would entail having to write separate function bodies that can accommodate the varying number of arguments, but by using default function arguments, only one such function needs to be written.

For example, you may want to construct a complex number that requires both a real and an imaginary part. There are three ways in which this can be done: (1) by specifying no arguments whatsoever, in which case both the real and imaginary parts of the number will default to some fixed value, (2) by specifying only the real part, in which case the imaginary part will default to some fixed value, and (3) by specifying both the real and the imaginary parts. Normally this scenario would require three distinct types of construction, but by employing the power of default function arguments, only one such type of construction needs to be written. Exactly how this is accomplished will be discussed in detail in Chapter 6.

Mandatory and default arguments

A function's formal argument list now contains two types of formal arguments: mandatory and default. The order of these arguments is easy to remember — the mandatory arguments, if present, are written first, followed by any default arguments. A function may thus contain all mandatory arguments, all default arguments, or some combination thereof.

When the function is called, you must first specify all of the mandatory actual arguments, if present, in the order in which they are declared. Next, you may override the default arguments, if any, but only in the order in which they were declared. That is, if there are 3 default arguments, then you may override the first, the first and the second, or all 3. You *cannot* override the first and the third, or just the second, or just the third. (If this were not so, then how would the compiler know which formal argument to match with an actual argument?) You also cannot simply write a comma to "skip over" a default argument because Bjarne Stroustrup felt that having an empty argument list was too subtle and made it more difficult to detect errors.

How to specify default arguments

If you are *declaring* a function, then you can specify a default argument value by writing:

- The type of the formal argument;

- The formal argument name (always optional);

- An '=' sign;

- The default value itself as an expression that does not contain any of the function's formal arguments.

For example, consider these misc. function declarations:

Example 3.1

```
// OK - 1 default argument
void print1(int = 0) ;

// OK - 1 mandatory and 1 default argument
void print2(int , char = '\0') ;

// OK - 2 default arguments
void print3(int = 0 , char = '\0') ;

// Error - mandatory argument after the default argument
void print4(int = 0 , char) ;
```

When you write the function definition, it is written just as you normally would. For example, for the first declaration above the function definition would be written:

Example 3.2

```
// Declaration
void print(int = 0) ;

void f()
{
   // Call print()
}

// Definition
void print(int number)
{
   printf("%d\n" , number) ;
}
```

Of course, you may want to *define* the function before you use it. In this case the definition implies the declaration, so you must specify the default arguments in the function definition line. To do this, simply add the formal argument name after you write the type. Thus, the function above may be defined as:

Example 3.3

```
// Definition
void print(int number = 0)
{
   printf("%d\n" , number) ;
}

void f()
{
   // Call print()
}
```

☞ It is very important to note these two items when using default function arguments: (1) If you are going to first declare a function and then define it, be sure to specify the default argument values in the declaration, not the definition. While this may seem obvious to you now, it's not so obvious when you start to write class member functions that take default arguments. (2) Never respecify the default value in the function definition if they were already specified in the function declaration. This is still true even if the values are the same.

Here is a program that needs to do exponentiation, i.e., raise a number to a certain power. However, let's assume that most of the time the number has to be squared, so it makes sense to use a default value of 2 for the exponent in the function power() that will do the computation.

Example 3.4

```
#include <stdio.h>

// Function declaration. The second argument defaults to the
// value 2
long power(int , int = 2) ;

int main()
{
   printf("Enter the base: ") ;
   int base ;
   int result = scanf("%d" , &base) ;
   if(result == 1)
    {
       // Use the default value
       printf("%d squared is %ld\n" , base , power(base)) ;
       // Override the default
       printf("%d cubed is %ld\n" , base , power(base , 3)) ;
    }
   else
       printf("Input error\n") ;

   return 0 ;
}

long power(int base , int exp)
{
   return (exp == 0) ? 1L : base * power(base , exp - 1) ;
}
```

If you entered 3 for the base, then the output would be:

```
3 squared is 9
3 cubed is 27
```

Here is the same example, but now the function `power()` is defined first. Therefore, this is the one and only opportunity for you to specify the default value.

Example 3.5

```
#include <stdio.h>

// Function definition. The second argument defaults to the
// value 2
long power(int base , int exp = 2)
{
  return (exp == 0) ? 1L : base * power(base , exp - 1) ;
}

int main()
{
  printf("Enter the base: ") ;
  int base ;
  int result = scanf("%d" , &base) ;
  if(result == 1)
   {
     // Use the default value
     printf("%d squared is %ld\n" , base , power(base)) ;
     // Override the default
     printf("%d cubed is %ld\n" , base , power(base , 3)) ;
   }
  else
     printf("Input error\n") ;

  return 0 ;
}
```

The output is the same as that of Example 3.4.

As another example, suppose you need to write a function whose job is to clear some buffer area. In all probability the number of bytes to be cleared will remain the same, and you probably will want to clear the area to some predetermined character, such as a blank. Therefore, these two parameters should be specified as the default function arguments. The address of the buffer area is the one mandatory argument.

Example 3.6

```c
#include <stdio.h>
const int size = 20 ;

// Function to clear the buffer. The last 2 arguments have
// defaults

void clear_buffer(char* ptr , char ch = ' ' , int length = size)
{
   for(int i = 0 ; i < length ; ++i)
      *ptr++ = ch ;
   *ptr = '\0' ;
}

int main()
{
   char buffer[size + 1] ;

   // Use the default values
   clear_buffer(buffer) ;
   printf("\"%s\"\n" , buffer) ;

   // Override only the character
   clear_buffer(buffer , '?') ;
   printf("\"%s\"\n" , buffer) ;

   // Override the character and the size
   clear_buffer(buffer , '*' , 10) ;
   printf("\"%s\"\n" , buffer) ;

   return 0 ;
}
```

The output is:

```
"                    "
"????????????????????"
"**********"
```

Structures used as default arguments

The default value in a function declaration may involve a structure object. For example, if an instance of a structure is defined in the global space, it may be used as the default, as shown in the following program:

Example 3.7

```
#include <stdio.h>

struct employee
{
  long ssn ;
  char* name ;
} ;

employee manager = { 999999999L , "Manager" } ;

void display(const employee& = manager) ;

int main()
{
  employee worker = { 11111111L , "Worker" } ;
  display() ;
  display(worker) ;

  return 0 ;
}

void display(const employee& emp)
{
  printf("SSN = %ld\n" , emp.ssn) ;
  printf("Name = %s\n" , emp.name) ;
}
```

The output is:

```
SSN = 999999999
Name = Manager
SSN = 111111111
Name = Worker
```

Expressions used as default arguments

The default value in a function may also consist of some expression, even if the expression itself contains a function call. Any arguments are evaluated at the point of the expression declaration. That's why, in the following example, the value of the global variable a is used, not the one local to main().

Example 3.8

```c
#include <stdio.h>

// Global definition
int a = 1 ;

int f ()
{
   return 1 ;
}

int g (int x = f () + a)
{
   return x ;
}

int main ()
{
   int a = 2 ;
   int answer = g () ;
   printf ("answer = %d\n" , answer) ;

   return 0 ;
}
```

The output is:

```
answer = 2
```

Default function arguments will be discussed again in Chapter 5 in the context of class member functions, and also in Chapter 6 in regard to constructor functions.

■ Review questions

1) Why are default function arguments useful?

2) What's the difference between a mandatory and a default function argument?

3) Why must default function arguments be specified last in a function's argument list?

■ Exercise #1

Write a function that takes 3 input arguments: (a) a starting number, (b) an ending number, and (c) a number representing the number of integers to be output per line. This latter value should default to 5. Display all of the numbers in the specified range in the format specified by the third argument.

Then write a `main()` function that tests the function by:

■ Reading in three integer numbers (start, end, and number-per-line) within a `while` loop. If end-of-file is entered, then the program should terminate;

■ Ensuring that three valid integers were read, i.e., no garbage;

■ Ensuring that the starting number is less than or equal to the ending number;

■ Ensuring that the number-per-line is greater than or equal to 1;

■ Calling the function using all three actual arguments;

■ Calling the function using only the first two arguments;

■ Returning to the top of the `while` loop for more data.

■ Exercise #2

Write a function that prints a specified number of blank lines on the screen. This number should default to 1. If it's zero or negative, assume the number 1. Then write a program to test the function.

■ Exercise #3

Write a function called `read()` that reads input from the keyboard using `getchar()` until either (1) some terminating character has been read, or (2) end-of-file has been encountered. The function takes two arguments: (1) a pointer to a character buffer area, and (2) the terminating character, which defaults to a newline. Then write a main line driver program to test the function using both the default terminating character and some other terminating character. Print the buffer area after each call to the function to ensure that the proper characters are being read in.

■ Exercise #4

Given the `main()` function:

```
int main()
{
    int array[] = { 4 , 6 , -3 , -9 , 10 } ;
    const int length = sizeof(array) / sizeof(int) ;

    puts("Originial sequence:") ;
    print(array , length) ;
    puts("Ascending sequence:") ;
    sort(array , length) ;
    print(array , length) ;
    puts("Descending sequence:") ;
    sort(array , length , 'D') ;
    print(array , length) ;

    return 0 ;
}
```

write the function `sort()` that sorts the array into either ascending or descending sequence and then prints it. By default, the function should use ascending sequence. Be sure to use the `swap()` routine from Chapter 2, Exercise #1. In addition, write a `print()` function that iterates through the array and displays each element.

Notes

Notes

Chapter 4

Dynamic memory allocation

Because of the introduction of user-defined types, C++ provides a new way in which dynamic memory is allocated. This method takes advantage of the constructor and destructor functions (discussed in Chapter 6) and simplifies how you make the actual request. Consequently, you should now have very little need to rely upon the functions `malloc()` *and* `free()`.

Memories are made of this

First, let's do a short review of the three different ways that memory is utilized by your program:

■ All global and static variables are found in a region known as static memory. These variables "live" throughout the running of your program, and are automatically initialized to zero.

■ The creation of automatic (keyword `auto`) variables at function or block scope occurs in an area known as the stack. This is just a "scratch pad" working area for variables that are constantly being created and destroyed. As each variable is created, it is said to be "pushed" onto the stack, and when it goes out of scope, it gets "popped" off the stack. In addition, whenever you call upon a function, the formal arguments and any auto variables that the function may need are pushed onto the stack, and when the function exits, these variables are popped from the stack.

■ You may allocate memory at execution time from an area known as the heap, or free memory. In tiny, small, and medium memory model programs, the heap is about 62K bytes long. Such memory is always unnamed, and therefore is addressed by a pointer that contains the starting address. Note that this memory is still reserved even when the function in which it is allocated terminates.

It is this third area, the heap, with which this chapter will deal, and how the memory management techniques in C++ differ from those in C.

Dynamic memory allocation in C

Let's take a moment to review how memory is allocated dynamically in C. There are 3 functions that handle this: `malloc()`, `calloc()` and `realloc()`.

■ `malloc()` takes one argument: an unsigned integer value (of type `size_t`) representing the number of bytes that is to be obtained. In order to ascertain this exact number of bytes, the `sizeof` keyword is typically used, especially where structure objects are involved. If the function successfully finds the requested amount of contiguous space, it returns an address of type `void*` that points to the first byte of this space. If an error occurred, or no more space is available, then the address zero (NULL) is returned.

■ `calloc()` takes two arguments: a number representing how many elements are to be allocated, and an argument specifying the size of each element. In addition, all of the allocated space is automatically initialized to zero.

■ `realloc()` takes two arguments: a pointer to existing space, and a number representing the total amount of new space. The data from the existing space is copied into the new space, the existing space is deallocated, and the pointer to the new space is returned.

C++ keyword new

Like the `malloc()` function in C, the `new` operator in C++ is used to allocate contiguous, unnamed memory at execution time. Unlike `malloc()`, however, the `new` operator no longer needs to use the `sizeof` keyword to specify the exact number of bytes needed. Instead, you merely request the number of instances (or variables) of a particular type. The fact that different types occupy different amounts of storage is handled automatically by the compiler. In reality, the `new` keyword calls upon the function `operator new()` to obtain storage. A first argument of `sizeof(T)` is automatically supplied when allocating an object of type `T`.

In its simplest form, you would write the keyword `new` followed by whatever type of data you want to allocate. For example:

Example 4.1

```
// An expression to allocate a single char
new char

// An expression to allocate a single int
new int

// An expression to allocate a single double
new double

// An expression to allocate a single pointer to a float
new float*
```

The output of the function call to `new()` is almost identical to the output of `malloc()`, i.e., a pointer to the space that is allocated (if successful), or the address zero if the space could not be found or some kind of error was detected. The difference is that while `malloc()` always returns a pointer of type `void*`, the `new()` operator returns a pointer of the type of object being allocated. The pointer variable you create to hold the address being returned must, therefore, be consistent with the type of object being allocated.

☞ C++ does not provide functions analogous to `realloc()` and `calloc()`. Therefore, should you want to emulate what these functions do, you will have to write your own versions.

Memory for a single instance of a primitive type

To get memory using the new operator for a single instance of some primitive type, write the keyword new followed by the type. Then initialize (or assign to) a pointer with the resultant address. For example:

Example 4.2

```
// One char
char* ptr_char = new char ;

// One int
int* ptr_int = new int ;

// One double
double* ptr_double = new double ;

// One pointer to a float
float** ptr_ptr_float = new float* ;

// One pointer-to-function taking no arguments and returning
// an int
int (**ptr_func)() = new (int(*)()) ;

// The preceding example with a typedef
typedef int (*ptr)() ;
ptr* ptr_func = new ptr ;
```

Here is a complete program that allocates space for some primitive types, stores data into this space, and then prints the data.

Example 4.3

```
#include <stdio.h>

int main()
{
   char* ptr_char = new char ;
   if(ptr_char != 0)
    {
       *ptr_char = 'A' ;
       printf("%c\n" , *ptr_char) ;
    }

   int* ptr_int = new int ;
   if(ptr_int != 0)
    {
       *ptr_int = 65 ;
       printf("%d\n" , *ptr_int) ;
    }

   float* ptr_float = new float ;
   if(ptr_float != 0)
    {
       *ptr_float = 1.234 ;
       printf("%f\n" , *ptr_float) ;
    }

   float** ptr_ptr_float = new float* ;
   if(ptr_ptr_float != 0)
    {
       *ptr_ptr_float = new float ;
       if(*ptr_ptr_float != 0)
        {
           **ptr_ptr_float = 5.678 ;
           printf("%f\n" , **ptr_ptr_float) ;
        }
    }

   return 0 ;
}
```

The output is:

```
A
65
1.234000
5.678000
```

The following example uses the new operator to determine the size of free memory (the heap) and the minimum size of each chunk of memory when allocation is desired. Note the loop that will run until the heap has been exhausted.

Example 4.4

```c
#include <stdio.h>

int main()
{
  // Save the starting address
  char* start = new char ;

  // Exhaust the heap
  long loops = 0L ;
  char *end , *ptr ;
  while((ptr = new char) != 0)
   {
     ++loops ;
     end = ptr ;
   }

  printf("Starting address = %p\n" , start) ;
  printf("Ending address = %p\n" , end) ;
  printf("You looped %ld times\n" , loops) ;
  long bytes = (long)end - (long)start ;
  printf("Heap consists of %ld bytes\n" , bytes) ;
  printf("Each loop grabbed %0.2f bytes\n" ,
          (float)bytes/loops) ;

  return 0 ;
}
```

The output in a small memory model is:

```
Starting address = 0864
Ending address = FDBC
You looped 7851 times
Heap consists of 62808 bytes of memory
Each loop grabbed 8.00 bytes of memory
```

☞ The output of Example 4.4 shows that Borland C++ allocates a minimum of 8 bytes of storage from the heap each time operator new() is called. This value very well may be different for other compilers.

How to initialize a primitive type

Primitive types allocated from the heap via `new` can be initialized with some user-specified value by enclosing the value within parentheses immediately after the type name. Here is an example that compares an allocation for an `int` from both the heap and the stack:

Example 4.5

```
// An 'int' from the heap initialized to 65
int* ptr_int = new int(65) ;

// An 'int' from the stack or global space initialized to 65
int number = 65 ;
```

Here is Example 4.3 again, but now each element is initialized at the time it is allocated.

Example 4.6

```
#include <stdio.h>

int main()
{
   char* ptr_char = new char('A') ;
   if(ptr_char != 0)
      printf("%c\n" , *ptr_char) ;

   int* ptr_int = new int(65) ;
   if(ptr_int != 0)
      printf("%d\n" , *ptr_int) ;

   float* ptr_float = new float(1.234) ;
   if(ptr_float != 0)
      printf("%f\n" , *ptr_float) ;

   float** ptr_ptr_float = new float*(new float(5.678)) ;
   if(ptr_ptr_float != 0)
      printf("%f\n" , **ptr_ptr_float) ;

   return 0 ;
}
```

The output is:

```
A
65
1.234000
5.678000
```

Memory for an array of a primitive type

In all probability your program will need to allocate not just one object, but rather an array of objects of some type. To get memory for an array of some primitive type using `new`, write the keyword `new` followed by the number of array elements enclosed within square brackets (*not* parentheses!). This number can be either a constant or some expression whose value is determined at execution time (but see the restrictions associated with multidimensional arrays). Note that the return type and value are identical to that of a single instance.

If the number of elements specified is zero, then it is treated the same as 1. If the number of elements is hard-coded and in error (e.g., negative), it is up to the particular compiler as to how it is handled. If the value is determined to be invalid at execution time, then the address zero is returned to indicate this error condition.

Note that it is not possible to initialize the individual elements of an array created when using `new`. The best you can do is assign into them after the creation has occurred.

Here are some examples of allocating an array of some primitive type:

Example 4.7

```
// An array of 1 char
char* ptr_char = new char[1] ;

// An array of 5 floats
float* ptr_float = new float[5] ;

// An array of 5 pointers to char
char** ptr_ptr_char = new char*[5] ;

// An array of 5 pointers-to-function taking no arguments
// and returning an int
int (**ptr_func)() = new (int(*[5])()) ;
```

```
// The preceding example with a typedef
typedef int (*ptr_func)() ;
ptr_func* ptr = new ptr_func[5] ;
```

☞ **The allocation of a single object and the allocation of an array of one object are not the same. This has important ramifications when the delete operator is used.**

To illustrate how an array of objects can be allocated at execution time, this program loops and asks the operator to specify the number of characters that are desired. Then an array consisting of the requested number of bytes is allocated.

Example 4.8

```
#include <stdio.h>

int main()
{
   printf("How many characters? ") ;
   int result ;
   long number ;
   while((result = scanf("%ld" , &number)) != EOF)
    {
       if(result != 1)
          printf("Input error!\n") ;
       else
        {
          char* ptr = new char[number] ;
          if(ptr == 0)
             printf("Allocation error\n") ;
          else
             printf("You allocated %ld characters at %p\n" ,
                     number , ptr) ;
       }

       fflush(stdin) ;
       printf("Next number: ") ;
    }

   return 0 ;
}
```

A sample run might appear as (the user input is underlined):

```
How many characters? 3
You allocated 3 characters at 076C
Next number: -1
Allocation error
Next number: 0
You allocated 0 characters at 0774
Next number: ^Z
```

 The function call `fflush(stdin)` will be used throughout this book whenever it's necessary to clear the system input buffer of extraneous characters. Be aware that this function is non-ANSI standard, and may not work on other systems or with other compilers.

The C++ keyword `delete`

The `delete` keyword in C++ is used to release the space that was reserved by `new`. It is analogous to the function `free()` in C, which takes as its one argument a pointer to the space.

 You should not commingle C and C++ styles of dynamic memory allocation. That is, if you `malloc()` some space, then you should `free()` it. Similarly, if you `new` some space, then you should `delete` it. Do not use `delete` with `malloc()`, nor `free()` with `new`.

How to delete a single instance from the heap

To delete a single instance from the heap, write the keyword `delete` followed by the name of the pointer that points to the heap space. For example:

Example 4.9

```
int* ptr = new int ;
delete ptr ;
```

If the value of `ptr` is the address zero, it is perfectly permissible to use `delete` since this situation is guaranteed *not* to cause an abort. This comes in handy in a program that initializes a pointer to 0, and then eventually terminates by deleting whatever space happens to be pointed at by this pointer. If the terminal operator is prompted for some number representing the amount of space desired, but immediately enters end-of-file, then the program will attempt to "delete" space at address zero.

In addition, AT&T version 2.1 ensures that you cannot delete space pointed at by a constant pointer.

 You should *never* attempt to release space via delete that was not allocated via new, and never attempt to release the same space twice. If you do, the results are unpredictable.

How to delete an array of instances from the heap

To delete an array of instances from the heap, write the keyword delete followed by empty brackets and the name of the pointer variable. For example:

Example 4.10

```
int* ptr = new int[10] ;
delete [] ptr ;
```

Note that prior to AT&T version 2.1, the number of elements in the array *must* be written between the brackets. If a Borland C++ compiler subsequent to (Borland) version 2.0 encounters this value, it will issue a warning message and ignore the number of elements.

Note that you must *never* commingle the allocation of a single instance with the deletion of an array of instances, and vice-versa. The easy way to remember this rule is this: if you used brackets in new, then use brackets in delete. If you didn't use brackets in new, then don't use brackets in delete.

In the following example the user is asked to enter some strings. The input is captured into a buffer area of some fixed length, after which it is copied onto the heap. Note that exactly the right amount of heap space is allocated to store each string. A fixed-length array of pointers-to-char is used to keep track of the address of each string. After all strings have been entered, they are then printed and their heap space released via delete.

Example 4.11

```
#include <stdio.h>
#include <string.h>

int main()
{
   const int max = 256 ;
   char buffer[max] ;
   const int dim = 3 ;
   char* array[dim] ;
   int index = 0 ;
   printf("Enter your string: ") ;

   while(fgets(buffer , max , stdin) != 0)
    {
       if(index == dim)
          printf("Too many strings!\n") ;

       else
        {
          char* ptr = new char[strlen(buffer) + 1] ;
          array[index++] = ptr ;
          strcpy(ptr , buffer) ;
        }

       printf("Next string: ") ;
    }

   printf("\nThe strings:\n") ;
   for(int i = 0 ; i < index ; ++i)
    {
       printf("%s" , array[i]) ;
       delete [] array[i] ;
    }

   return 0 ;
}
```

A sample run might appear as:

```
Enter your string: This
Next string: is
Next string: a
Next string: test
Too many strings!
Next string: ^Z

The strings:
This
is
a
```

In the following example the `main()` function defines a type 'pointer-to-pointer-to-char' that will be used to point to an array of 'pointers-to-char'. This array will grow dynamically on the heap as new strings are entered by the user, the space to hold them is allocated from the heap, and the heap addresses are stored into the array. To complicate things, the tasks of filling, printing and deleting the array have been separated into functions. Note the use of the reference type in the function get() to avoid a triple dereferencing situation.

Example 4.12

```
#include <stdio.h>
#include <string.h>

int get(char**&) ;
void put(char** , int) ;
void del(char** , int) ;

int main()
{
  char** pointer = 0 ;
  int counter = get(pointer) ;
  put(pointer , counter) ;
  del(pointer , counter) ;

  return 0 ;
}

int get(char**& ptr)
{
  const int dim = 256 ;
  int index = 0 ;
  printf("Enter a string: ") ;
  char buffer[dim] ;
```

```
   while(fgets(buffer , dim , stdin) != 0)
    {
       char* string = new char[strlen(buffer) + 1] ;
       strcpy(string , buffer) ;
       char** temp = new char*[index + 1] ;
       for(int i = 0 ; i < index ; ++i)
           temp[i] = ptr[i] ;
       temp[index++] = string ;
       delete [] ptr ;
       ptr = temp ;
       printf("Next string: ") ;
    }
   return index ;
}

void put(char** ptr , int counter)
{
   printf("\nThe strings:\n") ;
   for(int i = 0 ; i < counter ; ++i)
       printf("%s" , ptr[i]) ;
}

void del(char** ptr , int counter)
{
   for(int i = 0 ; i < counter ; ++i)
       delete [] ptr[i] ;
   delete [] ptr ;
}
```

A sample run might appear as (the user input is underlined):

```
Enter a string: This
Next string: is
Next string: a
Next string: test
Next string: ^Z

The strings:
This
is
a
test
```

How to allocate and delete multidimensional arrays

Instead of allocating space for a 1-dimensional array, you can allocate space for an array of any dimension. For example, to allocate space for a 2-dimensional 3 x 5 array of `int`'s, you would write:

Example 4.13

```
int rows = 3 ;
const int cols = 5 ;
int (*ptr) [cols] = new int[rows] [cols] ;
```

The preceding example requires a bit of explanation. First, the elements of a 2-dimensional array are just a collection of 1-dimensional arrays (the rows). Consequently, the parentheses surrounding the expression `*ptr` are *mandatory* in order to create just *one* pointer that points to the first 1-dimensional array which is 5 integers long (the number of columns). In other words, the array above consists of *3 elements*, not 15. To prove this, if you were to add 1 to the content of `ptr`, its address would increase by 10 bytes (5 * sizeof int). This represents the start of the second 1-dimensional array (row 1, column 0), *not* the second `int` (row 0, column 1).

Second, when allocating an array from the heap using `new`, *all* dimensions must be known by the compiler *except* the first. That's why the `rows` could be determined at execution time, but the `cols` must be constant so that the compiler knows its value. This means that for a 2-dimensional array, you *cannot* write a program that prompts the operator for the number of rows and columns, and then proceeds to allocate this array on the heap using `new`. The best you can do is to prompt *only* for the number of rows. (Note: Exercise #6 in Chapter 8 asks you to write a program that circumvents this problem.)

When it is time to delete the array from the heap, the format of the `delete` statement is that same as that of a 1-dimensional array. In other words, the number of columns does *not* need to be specified.

The following program prompts the operator for the number of rows to be allocated in a 2-dimensional array allocated from the heap. The number of columns has been fixed at 3.

Example 4.14

```
#include <stdio.h>
#include <stdlib.h>

// Number of columns must be known to the compiler
const int cols = 3 ;

void read(int(*)[cols] , int) ;
void print(int(*)[cols] , int) ;

int main()
{
   printf("How many rows? ") ;
   int rows , result ;
   while((result = scanf("%d" , &rows)) != EOF)
    {
       if(result != 1 || rows < 0)
          printf("Input error\n") ;
       else
        {
          int (*ptr)[cols] = new int[rows] [cols] ;

          // Fill the array
          read(ptr , rows) ;

          // Print the array
          print(ptr , rows) ;

          // Delete the array
          delete [] ptr ;
        }

       fflush(stdin) ;
       printf("How many rows? ") ;
    }

   return 0 ;
}

// Fill the array
void read(int(*ptr)[cols] , int rows)
{
   for(int i = 0 ; i < rows ; ++i)
      for(int j = 0 ; j < cols ; ++j)
       {
          printf("Row %d , column %d : " , i , j) ;
          scanf("%d" , &ptr[i] [j]) ;
       }
}
```

```
// Print the array
void print(int(*ptr)[cols] , int rows)
{
   printf("\nThe array\n\n") ;
   for(int i = 0 ; i < rows ; ++i)
    {
      for(int j = 0 ; j < cols ; ++j)
         printf("%3d" , ptr[i] [j]) ;
      printf("\n") ;
    }
   printf("\n") ;
}
```

A typical run of the program would yield the following results:

```
How many rows? 2
Row 0 , column 0 : 0
Row 0 , column 1 : 1
Row 0 , column 2 : 2
Row 1 , column 0 : 3
Row 1 , column 1 : 4
Row 1 , column 2 : 5

The array:

0  1  2
3  4  5
```

How to detect memory leakage

When writing large programs that are constantly allocating and releasing memory from the heap, it is very easy to "forget" to release some of the space. If a particular function has this bug, and is executed many times, then it is quite possible that your program will run out of heap space before it finishes.

If you suspect that your program has this problem, then the following function called `HeapSize()` (stored in the file `heapsize.h`) might prove useful. It returns the number of bytes on the heap that are currently in use. By checking this value at both the start and end of your program, or a particular function, you can easily detect if some memory is not being released.

Example 4.15

```
#ifndef HEAPSIZE_H
#define HEAPSIZE_H

#include <stdio.h>
#include <stdlib.h>
#include <alloc.h>

long HeapSize()
{
  heapinfo info ;
  int result ;
  if((result = heapcheck()) != _HEAPOK)
   {
     printf("Corrupted heap: %d\n" , result) ;
     exit(1) ;
   }

  long size = 0L ;
  info.ptr = 0 ;
  while(heapwalk(&info) == _HEAPOK)
   {
     if(info.in_use)
     size += info.size ;
   }
  return size ;
}

#endif
```

Here is a test of the `HeapSize()` function. Note that the space for the array of characters is never released, thereby accounting for the difference is heap sizes between the starting and ending values.

Example 4.16

```
#include "heapsize.h"

int main()
{
   printf("Heap size = %ld\n" , HeapSize()) ;
   int* ptr_int = new int ;
   printf("Heap size = %ld\n" , HeapSize()) ;
   char* ptr_char = new char[100] ;
   printf("Heap size = %ld\n" , HeapSize()) ;
   delete ptr_int ;
   printf("Heap size = %ld\n" , HeapSize()) ;

   return 0 ;
}
```

The output is:

```
Heap size = 516
Heap size = 524
Heap size = 628
Heap size = 620
```

☞ The Borland function coreleft() in the small data models
returns (as an unsigned int) the amount of unused memory
between the top of the heap and the stack. If heap memory is
fragmented, then this figure is not a true representation of the
amount of heap space left.

How to make a reference to the heap space

If desired, you may create a reference to an object allocated from the heap space. To
do this, you must dereference the pointer coming back so that you reference the
instance itself. Note that the delete must use the address operator to generate the
address of the instance. For example:

Example 4.17

```
#include <stdio.h>

int main()
{
    int& ref_int = * (new int(65)) ;
    printf("Value = %d\n" , ref_int) ;
    delete &ref_int ;

    return 0 ;
}
```

The output is:

```
Value = 65
```

■ Review questions

1) How is the `new` operator different from `malloc()`?

2) What is the advantage of using `new` rather than `malloc()`?

3) How do you initialize an instance allocated from the heap?

4) How do you allocate an array of instances from the heap?

5) Why can't you initialize each element of an array of instances allocated from the heap?

6) What is the difference between deleting a single instance and an array of instances?

7) How would you allocate a 3-dimensional array of doubles from the heap?

■ Exercise #1

Write a program that asks the user to specify the size of an integer array. Then allocate this array from the heap via `new` and prompt the operator for all of the values. Then print the array and release the space it occupies.

■ Exercise #2

Write a program that uses `new` and `delete` to dynamically allocate exactly enough free memory to hold string input data. That is, instead of allocating a fixed array of characters from the stack (which may be too big or too small), you will receive one character at a time (using the function `getchar()`) and continually allocate, copy, and release space so that the physical and logical lengths of the input buffer area are always the same. When the newline character is encountered, print the string and release the space. Then prompt for the next string. If and when end-of-file is entered, terminate the program.

Notes

Notes

Chapter 5

Introduction to C++ classes

The ability to create a class in C++ is probably the most important enhancement that was made to the C language. As a matter of fact, C++ was originally called 'C with classes'. In the realm of top-down procedural design, the focus is on the function. In the realm of data structures, the focus is on the data. But in the realm of object-oriented programming, the focus is on the class and how it can be used to model real world abstract types.

Thinking about structures

Let's start by thinking about a structure object in C. It consists of individual data elements whose types may be different. For example, a circle can be abstracted by envisioning a center point and a radius (using Cartesian coordinates), and can then be defined by using an appropriate structure type to describe these data elements. Here is one way to do it:

Example 5.1

```
typedef struct
{
   int x , y ;
} Point ;

typedef struct
{
   Point center ;
   int radius ;
} Circle ;
```

In order to perform operations on a circle object (an instance of the Circle structure), you need global functions that have knowledge of the object, which is usually passed by address in order to avoid the overhead of passing by value and to allow the functions to make changes to the object. For example, here are two functions that can move a Circle object and compute its area.

Example 5.2

```
void move(Circle* c)
{
   /* Code to move the circle */
}

double compute_area(const Circle* c)
{
   /* Code to compute and return the area */
}
```

Note the loose connection between the global functions `move()` and `compute_area()` and the circle object itself. That is, they live in different scopes which means that the object somehow has to be "passed" to the function. In addition, there is nothing to prevent a new function from modifying the circle object in some disastrous way, such as storing a negative radius. And things just keep getting worse. Suppose that you change your mind and decide that it would be better to represent the circle object using polar coordinates (a radius and an angle) instead of Cartesian coordinates. Now all the functions in a big project that have abstracted a circle using Cartesian coordinates will have to be painstakingly modified.

Looked at from another viewpoint, it should be obvious that the `Circle` object is completely passive in nature; it has no life of its own and is essentially "brain-dead". Thus, any messages ("move", "compute area", "draw", "report your coordinates", etc.) that you may wish to send to it are completely ignored, because there is nothing inherent within the `Circle` structure to obey these messages. That's why you need to write global functions. A program written in C therefore consists of a series of global functions designed in some top-down fashion that pass primitive data and structure objects back and forth in order to get the problem solved. This is also known as *procedural* programming.

The implication is that modeling a `Circle` object with a structure in C is not good because in the "real" world, objects are not dependent upon outside "forces" to make them "do something", and should not have to be tossed around like ping-pong balls. Instead, objects contain *within themselves* the wherewithal to perform the necessary actions to accomplish some goal or task. As another example, consider an automobile. It inherently "knows" how to start, stop, turn left, turn right, speed up, slow down, etc., provided it receives the appropriate message. These operations are "built in", and no external forces are required. (If they were, we would all literally be pushing and steering our cars down the road!)

A first look at encapsulation

The big difference between C and C++ in how a structure object is handled is that in C++ the object can contain *functions* as well as data elements. Thus, by sending messages to the object, it will respond in some predetermined way. Combining member data and the functions that operate upon this data into one composite type is called *data encapsulation*. That is, the data and functions are encapsulated (packaged together) in one nice, neat bundle called a C++ structure. The result is that an object no longer needs to be dependent upon any "outside" (global) functions to alter its state or behavior since these functions are already part of the object itself. That is, it can receive messages (function calls) and act upon these messages via its methods (function bodies). The structure object may also send messages to other structure objects.

This is what the `Circle` structure looks like after the global functions `move()` and `compute_area()` have been encapsulated with the data members `center` and `radius`. Note carefully that the functions no longer need to take a pointer to a `Circle` object in their formal argument lists because they are in direct communication with the data that comprises the abstraction of the `Circle` object itself. In addition, recall from Chapter 1 that there is no longer a need for a `typedef` because `Point` and `Circle` are inherently valid type names.

Example 5.3

```
struct Point
{
   int x , y ;
} ;

struct Circle
{
   Point center ;
   int radius ;

   void move()
    {
       /* Code to move the circle */
    }

   double compute_area()
    {
       /* Code to compute and return the area */
    }
} ;
```

A structure vs. a class

A *class* in C++ is identical to a structure in C++; the major difference lies in the default access category of its members. (This difference, and why classes are preferred to structures, will be discussed shortly.) Consequently, the big change from C to C++ lies in the enhancements that were made to what a structure can contain and what it can do. From here it is a minor step to go from a structure to a class.

What is a type in C++?

Before continuing the discussion of structures and classes, it's important to understand the concept of a *type* in C. When you buy a C++ compiler, it comes with some built-in, or primitive, data types, such as `int`, `char`, `float`, `double`, etc. These types in and of themselves do not do you any good until you *instantiate* them, i.e., create variables of a particular type.

So what is the actual definition of a type? *A type in C++ defines a range of values, and the operators that act upon these values.* For example, the type `int` (assuming 2 bytes) defines the integer values in the range -32768 to +32767, and the corresponding operators + , - , / , * , and %.

Notice how much more flexible a type in C++ is as opposed to a "derived" type in C such as a structure, array, or pointer. You cannot define new operators for these types, and as a result they really are inferior to the built-in types.

The purpose of a class

The concept of a *class* allows you to define a new type of data according to the needs of the problem to be solved, and to define operators to act upon those types. (This is also called *abstract data typing*, or ADT.) For example, a string in C is not one of the pre-defined types; instead, it is made up of various characters followed by the null character. It logically follows that the operators '=', '+', '-', etc., have absolutely no meaning with regard to string handling, which is why you need a function such as `strcpy()` in order to copy one string into another, as opposed to using the '=' operator.

But with C++ it's now possible to define a new type (which is really a class) called `string` (or whatever name you may want to give it) that contains the data and requisite operators (functions) to accomplish the normal tasks associated with string handling. Therefore, the user of the class no longer needs to be concerned with the intricacies of the `string.h` library functions, and instead merely has to manipulate `string` objects just like objects of the primitive types. In point of fact, we will be doing exactly this in Chapter 8.

There are many reasons to use classes in your C++ programs. For example, they encapsulate design decisions that might involve machine dependencies, e.g., how a floating point number is represented internally. In addition, classes represent well known data structures or algorithms that are of general use when writing programs, such as complex numbers and dates. They also allow the user to write in a more convenient notation by using infix rather than functional notation to imply concepts such as addition, assignment, etc. Finally, classes have the capability to provide automatic construction and destruction of their variables.

Components of a class

A class can contain these different types of information:

- Member data (also called instance variables) consisting of these types:
    - Nonstatic
    - Static
- Member functions (also called methods) consisting of these types:
    - Nonstatic, consisting of these types:
        - Typical "named" functions
        - Overloaded operator functions
        - Conversion functions
    - Static

A structure in C may not have a data member declared as static. However, this is perfectly legal in C++. Static data members and static function members will be discussed in Chapter 7.

Also note that a class may contain no data and functions whatsoever, data only, functions only, or both data and functions.

How to write a class definition

A class definition is very similar to the way in which you write a structure definition, with the keyword `class` replacing the keyword `struct`. Also, the structure tag is now called the class name. If desired, you may also create an instance of the class at file scope by writing its name after the closing brace and before the semicolon.

For example, a very high-level view of some class called `integer` would appear as:

Example 5.4

```
class integer
{
  // all class members
} ;
```

Note that this definition (like a structure definition) reserves *no memory* and is usually located at file scope so that all functions within a program can have access to it. Also, as with a structure definition, no (direct) initialization of the data members is possible for the simple reason that no memory exists that can store the value of a hypothetical initialization statement. This means that you *cannot* write:

Example 5.5   *(Will not compile!)*

```
class integer
{
  int number = 0 ;
} ;
```

The compiler error message is:

```
Cannot initialize a class member here
```

By the way, note that the creation of a structure or class is called a *definition*, whereas a structure or class *declaration* involves writing only the keyword `struct` or `class`, followed by the name, and then a semicolon. For example:

Example 5.6

```
// This is a class declaration
class integer ;

// This is a class definition
class integer
{
  // all class members
} ;
```

A forward declaration of a class name would be needed when, for example, the name is used as an argument to a function, and the complete class definition has not yet been encountered by the compiler. Such a declaration tells the compiler that the type is indeed valid.

Data hiding

One of the key ingredients of the C++ language is the *principle of data hiding*. (Actually, this is a misnomer, as a better term would be "data inaccessibility". You can still look at a class definition and see the data members.) What it means is that the data member portion of a class is *inaccessible* to those functions that are not part of the class. The advantage of data hiding is that once a class has been written, debugged and placed into a library, there is no danger of a non-class function accessing the data and perhaps modifying the state of the class object in some unexpected or erroneous way. Put another way, the class object is guaranteed to be correctly manipulated by the member functions of its own class. For example, if a class member function is designed to display the object in a certain way, then such behavior will always work properly, and the user has no need to write some global function to accomplish this task. If the user of the class accidentally or intentionally tries to violate the principle of data hiding by directly addressing a class data member, then the compiler will output an error message.

You should also be aware that how a class is represented internally is not really your concern. For example, how a floating point number is represented internally (IEEE or some other format) does not really matter to you. All that you want is the ability to manipulate floating point numbers and get the correct result. Similarly, in C++ is a class that abstracts a rectangle represented internally by four points or by a center point, a width and a height? It makes absolutely no difference if you're the user of the class.

How to manipulate a class object

You might very well be asking yourself, "If I, as the user of a class, cannot access the data members of that class, then how do I make changes to any object or instance of that class?" The answer is that you will always access the (public) member functions of that class in order to accomplish your task. These member functions will, in turn, access the data members for you.

Think of the data and function members of a class as living together in the same "house". Thus, they have unlimited access to each other. You, on the other hand, do not live in that house, but still need to communicate with one or more of the data members. Therefore, you must ring the doorbell and send your message to an occupant (a data member) through the sentinel (a member function) who answers. This message, will then be carried out by the sentinel, and whatever results there are will be reported back to you.

Access specifiers

The principle of data hiding, and the preceding scenario, are all very nice, except that inherently it means nothing to the compiler. In other words, you are responsible for explicitly telling the compiler which class members obey the principle of data hiding, and which do not. This is done by using access specifiers within the class definition.

There are three different access specifiers:

- private

- public

- protected

The first possibility is the specifier called `private`. This is the default specifier for a class, so that all members written first automatically are `private`. The rule with `private` class members is that they may be accessed *only* by the member functions of that class. (Note: friend functions also have access to the `private` members of a class, and will be discussed in Chapter 7.) Consequently, you use the `private` keyword to enforce the principle of data hiding. Unless you have an excellent reason for not doing so, *all* data members of a class should be `private`. Some member functions may be `private` if you do not want them to be accessible to non-class functions. Also note that a class member function may access the `private` members of some other instance of the same class. This other instance would probably be passed into the member function as a formal argument.

The second access specifier is called `public`. Unlike a class, this is the default for a structure definition in order to be compatible with a C program that is compiled using C++. The rule with `public` class members is simple: they may be accessed by both member and non-member functions. This is the means by which you can communicate with a class — by sending messages to the `public` member functions.

The third access specifier, `protected`, pertains to the member functions of some new class that will be inherited from a base class. As far as non-member functions are concerned, `private` and `protected` are one and the same. This specifier will be discussed in detail in Chapter 10.

How to write an access specifier

To write an access specifier, within the class definition (ideally on a separate line and clearly visible) use the appropriate keyword followed by a colon before the class members to which the specifier applies. For example, we can expand the definition of the `integer` class to include the access specifiers:

Example 5.7

```
class integer
{
    private:    // optional
  // All private members here

    public:
  // All public members here
} ;
```

If `integer` had been defined as a structure instead of a class, then the `private` keyword would have been mandatory. A class or structure may repeat an access specifier any number of times, and use them in any order.

Categories of class member functions

The data members of a class describe the state of some object created, or instantiated, by that class. The member functions of a class are designed to operate upon these data members, and can typically be categorized in three different ways:

■ *Manager Functions*. These functions are used to perform "initialization", "clean up", and other fundamental chores associated with the class. They will be discussed in Chapters 6, 8 and 9.

■ *Accessor Functions*. These are constant functions that return information about an object's current state. To ensure that these functions do not make any kind of modification to the data members, you must add the keyword `const` after the formal argument list. This will be discussed later in this chapter.

■ *Implementor Functions*. These are the functions that make modifications to the data members. This is how the state of an object can be changed. These functions are also known as *mutators*.

Implementation hiding

Another key ingredient in the design of a class in C++ is that of *implementation hiding*. When you send a message to an instance of some class, it is carried out by the class's *method*. This is just object-oriented terminology for a member function definition. Exactly *how* this is done is really not your concern. After all, why should it be? You are simply interested in having that message carried out, and the correct results obtained. Therefore, when you use a class that someone else has written, you will not normally be able to see the actual member function definitions within the class definition.

The principle of implementation hiding is not particularly new or unique to C++. To return to the analogy of a floating point number, when you add two such numbers together, you send the message "add" to the type `float` and the correct result is output. Exactly how the two numbers are added is not really your problem; it just happens.

The big advantage in this design is that the author of the class is free to change the implementation of the methods, and your code will not have to be modified. Instead, all that you will be required to do is re-link your object code.

Consequently, when you intend to use a class that someone else has written, you will only need to know the following:

■ Whether or not the class can be instantiated (see Chapter 11);

■ If the class can be instantiated, the various ways in which instances can be created. That is, what arguments, if any, are required in order to perform proper initialization;

■ The names of the member and friend functions, including any overloaded operator functions or conversion functions;

■ What, if anything, each function returns;

■ What the arguments of each function are, including which arguments have default values, and what those default values are;

■ Which functions, if any, are declared static;

■ Which functions, if any, are declared virtual;

■ Which functions, if any, throw exceptions, and what are the kinds of exceptions being thrown (see Chapter 18);

A class that is correctly documented will always provide this information.

How to write a class using implementation hiding

In order to write a class and enforce the principle of implementation hiding, you must write the declaration of the member function within the scope of the class definition. For example, here the declaration for the class `integer` contains the declaration of the member function `store()`.

Example 5.8

```
class integer
{
    private:
  int number ;

    public:
  // A member function that stores its argument into the private
  // data member 'number'
  void store(int) ;
} ;
```

This class is now complete enough for someone to use since the compiler only needs to encounter the declaration of any function in order to yield a successful compilation.

Once again, note that the order of the members and access specifiers within a class definition are irrelevant. For example, the class `integer` could just as well have been written as:

Example 5.9

```
class integer
{
    public:
  // A member function that stores its argument into the private
  // data member 'number'
  void store(int) ;

    private:
  int number ;
} ;
```

Some people like to list the members in the order of increasing accessibility, i.e., first `private`, then `protected`, then `public`. On the other hand, since the user of the class is only interested in its `public` interface, then that should be the first portion of the class that the user sees.

When the linker gains control, it will, of course, look for all of the function definitions. If these definitions are in some object library, the linker will automatically extract them and use them to satisfy your function calls. On the other hand, you may choose to supply one or more function definitions as part of your source code. Optionally, you could supply these function definitions in a separate compilation unit.

Let's see how you go about writing your function definitions. At first, you might be tempted to write the member function `store()` just like a global function:

Example 5.10

```
// The WRONG way to write a member function that stores its
// argument into the private data member 'number'
void store(int n)
{
   number = n ;
}
```

The compiler cannot compile this "member" function because it has no way to determine that `store()` is, in fact, a member of the class `integer`. What you have done is create a *global* function called `store()`. (Incidentally, the function itself will not compile even as a global function because `number` has never been defined.) Therefore, it is your responsibility to give the function `store()` *class scope* for the class `integer`.

The scope resolution operator — binary form

The task of associating an externally defined member function with its proper class is done by using a new operator in C++ called the scope resolution operator. This operator, consisting of the token ':', does exactly what its name implies — it unambiguously resolves the scope of a function or data member. When used to resolve a class scope, it is preceded with the name of the class and followed by some class member name.

Therefore, to resolve the scoping of the member function `store()`, you must write:

Example 5.11

```
// A member function that stores its argument into the
// private data member 'number'
void integer::store(int n)
{
   number = n ;
}
```

Note that even if a member function is defined outside the class definition, it *always* has complete and unlimited access to the class's `private` member data. That is, it still has class scope insofar as the compiler is concerned.

 The scope resolution operator is also used when referring to the name of a public enumerated type or an enumerated type value that is defined at class scope

The scope resolution operator — unary form

If the scope resolution operator is used in its unary form, it is preceded by nothing and followed by the name of some item (data or function) which is to be resolved at *file scope*. For example, in the function `store()` the number being accessed is the one at file scope, not class scope.

Example 5.12

```
// A global definition of 'number'
int number = 0 ;

class integer
{
     private:
   int number ;

     public:
   void store(int) ;
} ;

// A member function that stores its argument into the global
// variable 'number'
void integer::store(int n)
{
   ::number = n ;
}
```

Note that the class name and scope resolution operator could be used *within* the context of a class definition, but in this case it's completely redundant (unless it is being used to override scoping precedence). Here is a case where it is necessary to use it in order to refer to the `number` declared at class scope, *not* the one at function scope.

Example 5.13

```
class integer
{
    private:
  int number ;

    public:
  void store(int) ;
} ;

// A member function that stores its argument into the private
// data member 'number'
void integer::store(int n)
{
  int number = 0 ;
  integer::number = n ;
}
```

Note that it is also possible to use a class data member name as a formal argument name in a class member function. However, you are now required to use the scope resolution operator with the class data member name to differentiate it from the formal argument.

Example 5.14

```
class integer
{
    private:
  int number ;

    public:
  void store(int) ;
} ;

// A member function that stores its argument into the private
// data member 'number'
void integer::store(int number)
{
  integer::number = number ;
}
```

Because functions and data can be declared at different scoping levels (global, class and function), the documentation of the names of the data and functions usually includes the scope resolution operator in order to avoid any ambiguity as to which one is being referred to.

How to create a library class using implementation hiding

What follows is the complete sequence of events that would be typical for creating a class while enforcing the principle of implementation hiding:

■ Write the class definition and make a header file with this definition in it. Give this file the same name as the class, with the suffix `.h`. (Some C++ compilers may require you to use the suffix .hpp.) To avoid duplicating the code that is passed to the compiler, use preprocessor directives. For example, the following class definition for `integer` will get compiled just once no matter how many times the file `integer.h` is included in your source program:

Example 5.15

```
// File integer.h

#ifndef integer_h
#define integer_h

class integer
{
     private:
   int number ;

     public:
   void store(int) ;
} ;

#endif
```

■ Define the member functions, and put them into a file. Give this file the same name as the class, using the suffix `.CPP`. Also, be sure to include the header file for the class. Thus:

Example 5.16

```
// File integer.cpp

#include "integer.h"

// A member function that stores its argument into the private
// data member 'number'
void integer::store(int n)
{
    number = n ;
}
```

■   Compile this file into object form and put it into a library file.

■   Write your `main()` program and other functions. Be sure to include the header file for the class. Compile this program into object form.

Example 5.17

```
#include <stdio.h>
#include "integer.h"

int main()
{
    // Instantiate and use the class 'integer'
}
```

■   Finally, link your object program with the member functions from the object library.

On the other hand, there are some situations where the compiler *must* see the source code for the member functions when it compiles your program. This entails the use of inline functions, and will be discussed later in this chapter.

How to instantiate a class

After a class has been defined, you may then create *instances* or *objects* of the class in the normal fashion, i.e., just like the primitive types. This process is called *instantiation*. For example, to create an instance `in` of some class called `integer`, you would write:

Example 5.18

```
integer in ;
```

To create several instances, you would write:

Example 5.19

```
// Keyword 'class' not needed
integer in1 , in2 , in3 ;

// This also works
class integer in1 , in2 , in3 ;
```

Classes may be instantiated on the stack, in which case their storage specification is `auto`. As with the primitive types, they will exist until the scope in which they are defined terminates. You may also instantiate a class object in the global space, so that it is created before the `main()` function gains control, and is destroyed after the `main()` function terminates. Finally, you may instantiate a class object on the heap via the `new` operator, in which case it is your responsibility to destroy it with the `delete` operator.

While not particularly useful, C++ also allows either a primitive or user-defined type to be instantiated using what is termed "functional notation." This implies that the instance name is included within parentheses immediately after the type name. This instance may also be initialized. For example, these are all valid declarations:

Example 5.20

```
float(f) ;
double(g) = 1.2 ;
integer(in1) ;
integer(in2) = 1 ;
```

How to access class members via instances

Recall that the only members of a class that you may legally call upon are those that have been declared `public`. This normally implies the function members of the class. To do this, you must use the direct member operator (dot notation), just like a structure.

In the following program, an instance `in` of class `integer` is created, after which the public member function `integer::store()` is called to store the number 5 into the private class member `integer::number`. Finally, the `public` member function `integer::get()` is called to return the value of the `private` member `integer::number` so that it can be displayed.

Example 5.21

```
#include <stdio.h>

class integer
{
    private:
  int number ;

    public:
  void store(int) ;
  int get() ;
} ;

void integer::store(int n)
{
  number = n ;
}

int integer::get()
{
  return number ;
}

int main()
{
  // Define an instance of the class
  integer in ;

  // Store a number
  in.store(5) ;

  // Retrieve the number and print it
  printf("%d\n" , in.get()) ;

  return 0 ;
}
```

The output is:

5

For the sake of comparison, here is how the same program would appear if it were written in C. Note how the instance in needs to be an explicit argument in the calls to the global functions store() and get().

Example 5.22

```
#include <stdio.h>

typedef struct
{
   int number ;
} integer ;

void store(integer* ptr , int n)
{
   ptr->number = n ;
}

int get(const integer* ptr)
{
   return ptr->number ;
}

int main()
{
   /* Define an instance of the class */
   integer in ;

   /* Store a number */
   store(&in , 5) ;

   /* Retrieve the number and print it */
   printf("%d\n" , get(&in)) ;

   return 0 ;
}
```

The output is:

5

How to create an array of class instances

There is certainly no problem in creating an array of class instances. Here is Example 5.21 again, but now an array of instances is being created. Note the use of the const keyword in declaring the size of the array.

Example 5.23

```
#include <stdio.h>

class integer
{
     private:
   int number ;

     public:
   void store(int) ;
   int get() ;
} ;

void integer::store(int n)
{
   number = n ;
}

int integer::get()
{
   return number ;
}

int main()
{
   const int dim = 5 ;
   integer array[dim] ;

   for(int i = 0 ; i < dim ; ++i)
    {
      array[i].store(i) ;
      printf("%d\n" , array[i].get()) ;
    }

   return 0 ;
}
```

The output is:

```
0
1
2
3
4
```

Allocating a user-defined instance from the heap

Memory for a single instance of a user-defined class can be obtained from the heap in the same fashion as that of a primitive type. That is, you write the keyword `new` followed by the class type. The address that is returned (assuming success) is of type "pointer-to-class-type".

In this example the space for the instance of `integer` comes from the heap instead of the stack. Of course, to access the public member functions of the class, you must use the indirect member operator (->).

Example 5.24

```
#include <stdio.h>

class integer
{
     private:
   int number ;

     public:
   void store(int) ;
   int get() ;
} ;

void integer::store(int n)
{
   number = n ;
}

int integer::get()
{
   return number ;
}

int main()
{
   integer* ptr = new integer ;
   if(ptr == 0)
      puts("No more heap space") ;
   else
    {
      ptr->store(5) ;
      printf("%d\n" , ptr->get()) ;
      delete ptr ;
    }
```

```
        return 0 ;
    }
```

The output is:

```
5
```

Allocating an array of user-defined instances from the heap

An array of some user-defined type can be created just like an array of some primitive type. In order to release the space occupied by the array, the `delete` operator for an array must be used.

Here is a repeat of Example 5.23, but now the array of instances is located on the heap instead of the stack.

Example 5.25

```
#include <stdio.h>
#include <stdlib.h>

class integer
{
    private:
  int number ;

    public:
  void store(int) ;
  int get() ;
} ;

void integer::store(int n)
{
  number = n ;
}

int integer::get()
{
  return number ;
}
```

```
int main()
{
   int dim = 5 ;
   integer* ptr = new integer[dim] ;
   if(ptr == 0)
    {
       puts("No more heap space") ;
       exit(1) ;
    }

   for(int i = 0 ; i < dim ; ++i)
    {
       ptr[i].store(i) ;
       printf("%d\n" , ptr[i].get()) ;
    }

   delete [] ptr ;

   return 0 ;
}
```

The output is:

```
0
1
2
3
4
```

The topic of how `delete` affects user-defined types is discussed further in Chapter 6 in conjunction with the destructor function.

Inline functions

Envision a C program which reads disk records containing employee information. If this is a payroll application, as each employee record is read, the data is probably processed via a series of function calls, e.g., a call to print the entity data, a call to compute the salary, a call to compute the taxes to be withheld, etc. Each one of these calls inherently contains overhead that must be part of your overall program. In other words, it takes code space and time to push actual arguments onto the stack, call the function, push some return value onto the stack, and finally pop all of those values.

C++ provides the *inline function* mechanism by which these explicit function calls can be avoided. An inline function by definition is a function whose code gets substituted in lieu of the actual call to that function. That is, whenever the compiler encounters a call to that function, it merely replaces it with the code itself, thereby saving you all of that overhead. Such a function can be either a member of a class or a global function. Inline functions work best when they are small, straightforward bodies of code that are not called from too many different places within your program (which could then significantly increase the size of your code).

Even if you request that the compiler make a function into an inline function, the compiler *may or may not* honor that request. It depends on the type of code the function contains. For example, Borland C++ will not inline any function that contains a loop, static data member, or aggregate initializer list. If this turns out to be the case, a warning message will be issued. In fact, the AT&T C++ Reference Manual specifies nothing about the conditions under which the compiler may choose to honor or ignore the inline request. Your best approach, of course, is to consult the documentation of the particular C++ compiler that you are using.

Obviously, in order for the compiler to make this code substitution, it must have access to it. This simply means that the source code constituting the function body must be part of the project or program that you are compiling. Of course, the disadvantage with inline functions is that if the code itself ever needs to be modified, then all programs that use the function would then have to be recompiled. Furthermore, an inline function is a violation of implementation hiding.

How to write a global inline function

First, let's get away from member functions for a moment and consider a global function. To make a request that this function be inline:

- Precede the return type of the function with the keyword `inline`
- Write the function body (the definition, not just the declaration) before any calls to that function.

Here is a program that uses an inline function to compute and return the absolute value of its input argument.

Example 5.26

```
#include <stdio.h>

inline int abs(int x)
{
   return x < 0 ? -x : x ;
}

int main()
{
   for(int i = -2 ; i < 2 ; ++i)
    {
      int value = abs(i) ;
      printf("Absolute value of %+d = %+d\n" , i , value) ;
    }

   return 0 ;
}
```

The output is:

```
Absolute value of -2 = +2
Absolute value of -1 = +1
Absolute value of +0 = +0
Absolute value of +1 = +1
```

When the call to the `abs()` function is encountered, the compiler, instead of making a function call, generates this assembly code:

Example 5.27

```
          or      si,si
          jge     short @1@114
          mov     ax,si
          neg     ax
          jmp     short @1@142
@1@114:
          mov     ax,si
@1@142:
```

If the `inline` keyword is removed, the assembly code would then be:

Example 5.28

```
        push    si
        call    near ptr @abs$qi
```

Obviously, now an actual function call is being made.

How to write an inline class member function

In addition to global functions, you may request that nonstatic member functions of a class be inlined. The "normal" method of doing this is to simply define the function within the scope of the class definition. In this case the inline request is made automatically, so the keyword `inline` does not need to be written.

Here the member function `integer::store()` is an inline member function because it is completely defined within the context of the class definition.

Example 5.29

```
class integer
{
   int number ;

     public:
   // This is an inline function
   void store(int n)
    {
      number = n ;
    }
} ;
```

☞ Functions inlined within the class definition are not "evaluated" by the compiler until the entire class scope has been processed. That's why, if they are defined first, they can refer to members defined later, or even compute the `sizeof` the class.

The only problem with this class is that now it has been "cluttered up" with the actual definition of the `integer::store()` function. Strictly speaking, the user really does not care how the function is implemented, just what its declaration is.

A better approach is to move the function definition outside the class and use the scope resolution operator to give it class scope. However, without writing anything else, the function definitely will *not* be inlined by the compiler. For example:

Example 5.30

```
class integer
{
   int number ;

      public:
   void store(int) ;
} ;

// This is NOT an inline function
void integer::store(int n)
{
   number = n ;
}
```

In order to make the inline request to the compiler, you must write the keyword `inline` in front of both the function declaration *and* its definition.

Example 5.31

```
class integer
{
   int number ;

      public:
   inline void store(int) ;
} ;

// This is an inline function
inline void integer::store(int n)
{
   number = n ;
}
```

A few words of explanation are in order here. While Example 5.31 shows the correct way to define an inline function, the usage of the keyword `inline` in front of the *declaration* (within the class definition) is not always necessary. This is the case when the *definition* (still preceded by the keyword `inline`) is encountered by the compiler before it is ever called. Now there is no problem because the inlining will still occur.

In the following program the function `integer::increment()` will be inlined because it is defined before being called within the function `integer::store()`.

Example 5.32

```
#include <stdio.h>

class integer
{
   int number ;

      public:
   void store(int) ;
   void increment() ;
} ;

inline void integer::increment()
{
   ++number ;
}

inline void integer::store(int n)
{
   number = n ;
   // increment() defined first
   increment() ;
}

int main()
{
   integer in ;
   in.store(5) ;

   return 0 ;
}
```

On the other hand, it is easy to make a mistake and reverse the order of the member functions so that `integer::increment()` is defined *after* `integer::store()`. This means that `integer::increment()` is now being called *before* the compiler knows that it should be inlined.

Example 5.33

```
#include <stdio.h>

class integer
{
  int number ;

     public:
  void store(int) ;
  void increment() ;
} ;

inline void integer::store(int n)
{
  number = n ;
  // increment() called before being defined
  increment() ;
}

inline void integer::increment()
{
  ++number ;
}

int main()
{
  integer in ;
  in.store(5) ;

  return 0 ;
}
```

Fortunately, Borland C++ is smart enough to handle this situation and inline both functions. On the other hand, other C++ compilers may generate an assembly language `call` instruction when the call to `increment()` is encountered, and then complain when they see the actual definition of the `increment()` function preceded by the word `inline`. The reason is that you have provided conflicting information to the compiler. After all, how is it supposed to replace the `call` instruction with the actual code "after the fact"?

The solution to this potential error is to make sure that the `inline` keyword appears in front of the function *declaration* for `increment()` within the class definition. Now any C++ compiler that failed to compile Example 5.33 will successfully compile Example 5.34.

Example 5.34

```
#include <stdio.h>

class integer
{
   int number ;

     public:
   void store(int) ;
   // Keyword inline used here
   inline void increment() ;
} ;

inline void integer::store(int n)
{
   number = n ;
   // Call is always OK
   increment() ;
}

inline void integer::increment()
{
   ++number ;
}

int main()
{
   integer in ;
   in.store(5) ;

   return 0 ;
}
```

☞ In Borland C++, if you specify the option -v (to turn debugging information on), then all functions will not be inlined.

Design considerations for inline functions

When should a member function be requested to be made inline, and when should it definitely *not* be made inline? Whenever possible, you should make your member functions inline by including them within the class definition in the header file, or preferably outside the class definition preceded by the keyword `inline` (and still within the header file) Admittedly, this will increase the compilation time (since there's more source code present), but the program will probably run a lot faster.

There is a danger however, in making an inline request that is *not* honored by the compiler. If this happens, and the function is included in a header file, then multiple inclusions of this header file by two different source files will result in a duplicate definition error by the linker. To correct this problem, put the function into its own separate source file, and include it just once during the compilation process. Another approach would be to precompile the function into object form and make it visible to the linker.

If you were to "snoop around" in the header files that any C++ compiler provides, you will see lots of code that resembles the previous examples. Also, constructor and destructor functions, which are the subject of Chapter 6, are excellent candidates for inlining.

Default function arguments with class member functions

Recall the discussion of default function arguments from Chapter 3. Class member functions may also have default arguments just like non-member functions. If the function is defined within the scope of the class definition, then obviously this is the (one and only) place to specify the default value(s).

Example 5.35

```
#include <stdio.h>

class integer
{
   int number ;

      public:
   void store(int n = 0)
   {
      number = n ;
   }

   int get()
   {
      return number ;
   }
} ;

int main()
{
   // Create an instance
   integer in ;
```

```
   // Store the default value
   in.store() ;
   printf("%d\n" , in.get()) ;

   // Store an explicit value
   in.store(5) ;
   printf("%d\n" , in.get()) ;

   return 0 ;
}
```

The output is:

```
0
5
```

If the member function is defined outside the class definition, then the default value(s) must be specified in the function declaration, *not* the definition. This makes sense because normally you don't even have access to the source code containing the implementation of the member functions (the methods), so how is the compiler going to know that your function call expects to use one or more default arguments? On the other hand, you always have access to the member function declarations that must be part of the class definitions, so this is where the default argument(s) must be written.

Example 5.36

```
#include <stdio.h>

class integer
{
   int number ;

      public:
   void store(int = 0) ;
   int get() ;
} ;

inline void integer::store(int n)
{
   number = n ;
}

inline int integer::get()
{
   return number ;
}
```

```
int main()
{
    // Create an instance
    integer in ;

    // Store the default value
    in.store() ;
    printf("%d\n" , in.get()) ;

    // Store an explicit value
    in.store(5) ;
    printf("%d\n" , in.get()) ;

    return 0 ;
}
```

The output is:

```
0
5
```

In Chapter 6 you will see how default function arguments can greatly simplify the writing of constructor functions.

Enumerated types with classes

A class may contain a definition of an enumerated type. Note that when member functions are written outside the class definition, the enumerated type name does not have to be scoped with the class name except when it is used in the return type of the function.

For non-member functions to gain access to the actual values of the enumerated type, the type itself must be made public. Note that Borland C++ incorrectly requires that the enumerated type be public when that type is scoped and used in the return type of a function defined outside the class definition.

In the following program the data member of the class takes on the enumerated type Boolean, and its value can be only False or True.

Example 5.37

```
#include <stdio.h>

class integer
{
    public:
  enum Boolean { False , True } ;
  void set_number(Boolean) ;
  Boolean get_number() ;

    private:
  Boolean number ;
} ;

void integer::set_number(Boolean n)
{
  number = n ;
}

integer::Boolean integer::get_number()
{
  return number ;
}

int main()
{
  integer in ;
  integer::Boolean value = integer::False ;
  in.set_number(value) ;
  printf("number = %d\n" , (int)in.get_number()) ;
  value = integer::True ;
  in.set_number(value) ;
  printf("number = %d\n" , (int)in.get_number()) ;

  return 0 ;
}
```

The output is:

```
number = 0
number = 1
```

Under the AT&T 2.0 implementation of C++, an enumerated type has global scope. Therefore, if two or more classes happen to have an enumerated type with the same name, then your program will not compile. Fortunately, however, under AT&T 2.1 an enumerated type retains its class scope, so that an instance of this type must have its name fully qualified.

Constant class member functions

Recall that, other than the manager functions, there are only two kinds of class member functions — those that make modifications to the state of an object, and those that merely report on the state. The latter kind of function is called an *accessor function*. In other words, these functions merely *access* the data, as opposed to doing any modification on the data.

Stated another way, any instance that calls upon an accessor function is considered to be constant by the function, and therefore by definition cannot be changed.

The C++ compiler has no inherent way to distinguish a mutator function from an accessor function, but you can make this difference explicit. To make a member function into an accessor function, append the keyword `const` *after* the formal argument list in *both* the definition and declaration (if present). Note that the use of the `const` keyword in this context is valid *only* for nonstatic class member functions. In other words, you cannot append the `const` keyword after a global function or a static member function (static member functions will be discussed in Chapter 7).

Here is a repeat of Example 5.21, but now both functions have been inlined and the function `integer::get()` has been declared to be constant.

Example 5.38

```
#include <stdio.h>

class integer
{
      private:
    int number ;

      public:
    void store(int) ;
    int get() const ;
} ;
```

```
inline void integer::store(int n)
{
  number = n ;
}

inline int integer::get() const
{
  return number ;
}

int main()
{
  // Define an instance of the class
  integer in ;

  // Store a number
  in.store(5) ;

  // Retrieve the number and print it
  printf("%d\n" , in.get()) ;

  return 0 ;
}
```

The output is:

```
5
```

Now let's modify the function `integer::get()` so that one is added to the data member `number` before it is returned.

Example 5.39   *(Will not compile!)*

```
#include <stdio.h>

class integer
{
    private:
  int number ;

    public:
  void store(int) ;
  int get() const ;
} ;

inline void integer::store(int n)
{
  number = n ;
}
```

```
inline int integer::get() const
{
   // Cannot modify number
   return ++number ;
}

int main()
{
   // Define an instance of the class
   integer in ;

   // Store a number
   in.store(5) ;

   // Retrieve the number and print it
   printf("%d\n" , in.get()) ;

   return 0 ;
}
```

The compiler error message is:

```
Cannot modify a const object in function integer::get()
const
```

This program no longer compiles because you promised the compiler that the function `integer::get()` would make no changes to the data members, and then proceeded to violate that promise.

From now on, you should get into the habit of writing the keyword `const` after all member functions that are deemed by you to be accessor functions.

Constant instances

If an instance itself of a user-defined class is declared to be `const`, the implication is that *all* data members of the instance are also `const`, and therefore cannot be changed. Note, however, that this restriction does *not* preclude the possibility of *initializing* the data members. How this is done will be discussed in Chapter 6.

For example, a class may consist of all pointer data members that are initialized to point to specific locations of some hardware device. Once these addresses are established, there is no need to ever change them. Or something as familiar as a playing card may be created whose state is determined by its suit and value. Once this has been done, it should never be changed.

If you attempt to call a mutator function with a constant instance, the compiler will complain. Therefore, by implication the *only* type of member function that a constant instance may explicitly call upon is a *constant* function.

Summary of const vs. non-const instance and function

Because the possibilities of calling constant and non-constant functions with both constant and non-constant instances can be confusing, here is a summary:

- A constant instance may always call an accessor function declared constant because the function guarantees not to make any modifications.

- A constant instance may not call a mutator function because the function conceivably could try to make modifications to the instance (but this is only a warning in Borland C++).

- A non-constant instance may always call an accessor function declared constant. However, the instance is considered to be constant insofar as the function is concerned.

- A non-constant instance may always call a mutator function in order to make changes to the state of the instance.

Constant references to instances of user-defined classes

Recall from Chapter 2 in the discussion of reference variables that a structure object can be passed by reference into a function. This is better than passing the object by value, because then the entire structure object would have to be copied onto the stack. In addition, if you wish to ensure that the object cannot be modified by the function, you may pass it by constant reference.

This principle is just as valid for classes as it is for structures. In the following example a member function called copy() has been added to the class integer. This function takes as its one argument a constant reference to an existing integer object, and proceeds to copy this object into the invoking object of the function call itself. Because the argument is a constant reference, any changes to it (in1) via the reference variable (n) are not allowed by the compiler.

Example 5.40

```
#include <stdio.h>

class integer
{
    int number ;

      public:
    void store(int) ;
    int get() const ;
```

```
      void copy(const integer&) ;
} ;

inline void integer::store(int n)
{
   number = n ;
}

inline int integer::get() const
{
   return number ;
}

inline void integer::copy(const integer& n)
{
   number = n.number ;
}

int main()
{
   integer in1 , in2 ;
   in1.store(1) ;
   in2.copy(in1) ;
   printf("in1 = %d\n" , in1.get()) ;
   printf("in2 = %d\n" , in2.get()) ;

   return 0 ;
}
```

The output is:

```
in1 = 1
in2 = 1
```

You should now experiment with this program by modifying the function `integer::copy()` so that it modifies the member `n.number`.

From now on, whenever you pass an instance of a class into a function by reference, be sure to pass it by *constant reference* if you have no intention of making modifications to it. In point of fact, some C++ compilers may complain if you don't use a constant reference, and then pass in a *temporary* instance. The rationale is that by *not* using constant reference, you are implying that the function may make changes to the instance, and this makes no sense when dealing with temporary instances, because they are going to disappear real quick!

A containing relationship

Up to now the only type of data members within a class have been primitive types, e.g., int, float, etc. But there is nothing that forbids you from having a class definition that contains an instance of some other class. This relationship between a class and an instance of another class is called a *containing relationship* because one class literally contains an instance of the other class. In OOP terminology, this is also referred to as a "has-a" relationship because the containing class "has a(n)" instance of the other class.

Note that the private members of the contained instance are still inaccessible to the member functions of the containing class. But the public functions of the contained instance may be accessed by the functions of the containing class simply by writing the instance name and the dot operator.

For example, the class exponen contains two instances of the class integer. Its purpose is to raise the first integer to the power of the second integer. In order to access the data member number of each of the contained instances, the functions of exponen must call upon the member functions of class integer.

Example 5.41

```
#include <stdio.h>
#include <math.h>

class integer
{
   int number ;

     public:
   void store(int) ;
   int get() const ;
} ;

inline void integer::store(int n)
{
   number = n ;
}
```

```cpp
inline int integer::get() const
{
  return number ;
}

class exponen
{
  integer in1 , in2 ;

    public:
  void store(int , int) ;
  int get1() const ;
  int get2() const ;
  double power() const ;
} ;

inline int exponen::get1() const
{
  return in1.get() ;
}

inline int exponen::get2() const
{
  return in2.get() ;
}

inline void exponen::store(int n1 , int n2)
{
  in1.store(n1) ;
  in2.store(n2) ;
}

inline double exponen::power() const
{
  return pow(get1() , get2()) ;
}

int main()
{
  exponen ex ;
  ex.store(5 , 3) ;
  printf("%d to the power %d = %0.0f\n" ,
            ex.get1() , ex.get2() , ex.power()) ;

  return 0 ;
}
```

The output is:

```
5 to the power 3 = 125
```

Nesting of class definitions

If desired, you may literally define one class definition within another class definition. To illustrate this concept, here is the preceding example now with the class integer totally defined within the scope of the class exponen.

Example 5.42

```
#include <stdio.h>
#include <math.h>

class exponen
{
   class integer
    {
      int number ;
         public:
      void store(int) ;
      int get() const ;
    } ;
   integer in1 , in2 ;

      public:

   void store(int , int) ;
   int get1() const ;
   int get2() const ;
   double power() const ;
} ;

inline void exponen::integer::store(int n)
{
   number = n ;
}

inline int exponen::integer::get() const
{
   return number ;
}

inline int exponen::get1() const
{
   return in1.get() ;
}
```

```
inline int exponen::get2() const
{
   return in2.get() ;
}

inline void exponen::store(int n1 , int n2)
{
   in1.store(n1) ;
   in2.store(n2) ;
}

inline double exponen::power() const
{
   return pow(get1() , get2()) ;
}

int main()
{
   exponen ex ;
   ex.store(5 , 3) ;
   printf("%d to the power %d = %0.0f\n" ,
                     ex.get1() , ex.get2() , ex.power()) ;

   return 0 ;
}
```

The output is:

```
5 to the power 3 = 125
```

Initializing classes with pointer data members

Very often a class will contain a pointer as one of its data members. Since using an uninitialized pointer will lead to disastrous results, it is your responsibility to allocate space on the heap and have this pointer point to this space.

To illustrate this, the data member `number` has been changed to a pointer. In addition, two new member functions have been added: `initialize()` is responsible for allocating space for the pointer on the heap, and `del()` is responsible for releasing this space.

Example 5.43

```
#include <stdio.h>

class integer
{
    private:
  int* ptr ;

    public:
  void initialize() ;
  void store(int) ;
  int get() const ;
  void del() ;
} ;

inline void integer::initialize()
{
  ptr = new int ;
}

inline void integer::store(int n)
{
  *ptr= n ;
}

inline int integer::get() const
{
  return *ptr ;
}

inline void integer::del()
{
  delete ptr ;
}

int main()
{
  // Define an instance of the class
  integer in ;

  // Get space for the pointer
  in.initialize() ;

  // Store a number
  in.store(5) ;

  // Retrieve the number and print it
  printf("%d\n" , in.get()) ;
```

```
    // Release the space
    in.del() ;

    return 0 ;
}
```

The output is:

```
5
```

Caution: In the `initialize()` function do *not* declare the variable `ptr` since this will have the effect of hiding the variable `integer::ptr`.

As an enhancement of the previous example, now an *array* of `int`s is being allocated from the heap.

Example 5.44

```
#include <stdio.h>

class integer
{
    private:
  int* ptr ;

    public:
  void initialize(int) ;
  void store(int , int) ;
  int get(int) const ;
  void del() ;
} ;

inline void integer::initialize(int d)
{
  ptr = new int[d] ;              ,
}

inline void integer::store(int index , int value)
{
  ptr[index] = value ;
}

inline int integer::get(int index) const
{
  return ptr[index] ;
}
```

```
inline void integer::del()
{
   delete [] ptr ;
}

int main()
{
   const int dim = 5 ;

   // Define an instance of the class
   integer in ;

   // Get space for an array
   in.initialize(dim) ;

   // Store the index as the value
   for(int i = 0 ; i < dim ; ++i)
      in.store(i , i) ;

   // Retrieve the numbers and print them
   for(i = 0 ; i < dim ; ++i)
      printf("%d\n" , in.get(i)) ;

   // Release the space
   in.del() ;

   return 0 ;
}
```

The output is:

```
0
1
2
3
4
```

☞ Caution: If a member function returns a pointer data member, it is recommended that the return type is preceded by the keyword const so that whoever calls upon the function cannot modify the data to which the pointer points.

You could reasonably be asking yourself if you always have to remember to code functions similar to `initialize()` and `del()` every time your class has at least one pointer data member, and to execute them for each instantiation. While they must still be coded, these tasks can be set up to be executed automatically. How this is done is the subject of the next chapter on constructor and destructor functions.

Class declaration vs. definition

Earlier in this chapter a distinction was made between a class *declaration* and its *definition*. Look at Example 5.6 to refresh your memory on this.

A class declaration would be needed in the case where another class needs to refer to the first class as a function argument. The compiler only needs to be told that the class name is valid. This can be done with a declaration. For example:

Example 5.45

```
class A ;
class B
{
   void f(A&) ;
   // Remainder of class
} ;
```

Another case is where the second class declares a pointer or reference to the first class.

Example 5.46

```
class A ;
class B
{
   A* ptr ;
   A& ref ;
   // Remainder of class
} ;
```

Note, however, that if you try to create an actual instance of class A, then the compiler will complain because it always needs to know the size of the class it is currently compiling. Since the complete definition of class A has yet to be seen by the compiler, you must ensure that the definition of class A occurs *before* the definition of class B.

Example 5.47

```
class A
{
   // Members in the class
} ;

class B
{
   A instance ;
   // Remainder of class
} ;
```

From a design standpoint, it is usually better to declare pointers or references to other classes (Example 5.46), as this creates what is termed a "loose" coupling between the classes, whereas using the "has-a" relationship (Example 5.47) creates a much tighter coupling.

■ Review questions

1) In what ways does a class differ from a structure? In what ways are they similar?

2) Why can't you initialize data members within a structure or a class?

3) What is the difference between private and public access rights?

4) What are the two types of member functions?

5) How does a class declaration differ from a class definition?

6) How does a function declaration differ from a function definition?

7) What is the scope resolution operator, and when do you need it?

8) When would you define a member function *inside* the class definition?

9) When would you define a member function *outside* the class definition?

10) What is an inline function?

11) What does it mean when a class member function terminates with the word `const`?

12) Why would you pass an instance of a class into a function by reference instead of by value?

13) How do you prevent a function from modifying an instance of a class passed in by reference?

■ Exercise #1

Write a class called `A_clock` that simulates the keeping of time. Use 3 private data members: `hours`, `minutes`, and `seconds`. Your class should be able to:

■ `set()` the starting time. To do this, use three formal arguments representing the hours, minutes, and seconds.

■ `increment()` the time by one second.

■ `display()` the time. The function should take an argument with a default value of zero to imply military time. If this value is something other than zero, display the time in standard AM and PM notation. For example, 4 minutes and 31 seconds past 7 PM should be displayed as either 19:04:31 or 7:04:31 PM, and 5 minutes past midnight should be displayed as either 00:05:00 or 12:05:00 AM.

Declare all three functions within the class definition, and then define them as inline functions. To test your class, use the following `main()` function:

```
int main()
{
    A_clock BigBen ;
    BigBen.set(23 , 59 , 00) ;
    for(int i = 0 ; i < 100 ; ++i)
    {
        BigBen.increment() ;
        BigBen.display() ;
        BigBen.display(1) ;
    }

    return 0 ;
}
```

■ Exercise #2

Write a class called `Date` that keeps track of the current date. Use 3 private data members: `month`, `day`, and `year`. Your class should be able to:

■ `set()` the starting date. To do this, use three formal arguments representing the month, day and year.

■ `increment()` the day by 1. If the current month has overflowed, increment to the next month. If the current year has overflowed, increment to the next year. You may ignore leap year.

■ `display()` the date in MM/DD/YYYY format. Print a blank line preceding each new month.

Define the following table in the global space to tell you the number of days in a month:

```
int days_array[] =
{
   31 , 28 , 31 , 30 , 31 , 30 ,
   31 , 31 , 30 , 31 , 30 , 31
} ;
```

To test your class, use the following `main()` function:

```
int main()
{
   Date today ;
   today.set(01 , 01 , 1993) ;
   for(int i = 0 ; i < 370 ; ++i)
   {
      today.increment() ;
      today.display() ;
   }

   return 0 ;
}
```

■ Exercise #3

Write a program that reads in string input from the user, reverses the case of the letters, and then echoes the string back to the user.

Start by creating a class called `in_out` to handle these tasks. It needs:

■ One data member: a character buffer 80 bytes in length (as represented by a `const` value).

■ A function called `read()` (defined *inside* the class definition) that uses the C function `fgets()` to read in the characters. The function should return 'true' if end-of-file is found, 'false' otherwise.

■ A function called `convert()` (defined *outside* the class definition) that converts all lower case letters to upper case, all upper case letters to lower case, and does not modify any non-letters.

■ A function called `print()` (defined *inside* the class definition) that outputs the contents of the buffer.

■ In addition, include an enumerated type called `Boolean` that defines the values 'false' and 'true'.

To test your class, use the following `main()` function:

```
int main()
{
    in_out io ;
    printf("Enter some data: ") ;
    while(!io.read())
    {
        io.convert() ;
        io.print() ;
        printf("Next data: ") ;
    }

    return 0 ;
}
```

■ Exercise #4

Given the following class definition that is designed to emulate an array of integers:

```
class array
{
    int* ptr ;
    int length ;
    void realloc(int) ;

        public:
    // all function declarations
} ;
```

and the `main()` function:

```
int main()
{
    const int dim = 5 ;
    array a ;
    a.initialize(dim) ;
    a.print() ;

    for(int i  = 0 ; i < a.get_length() ; ++i)
        a.store(i , i) ;
    a.print() ;

    a.increment() ;
    a.append(6) ;
    a.print() ;

    a.reverse() ;
    a.print() ;

    a.trunc() ;
    a.print() ;
```

```
        a.del() ;

        return 0 ;
    }
```

write the member function definitions for the class `array`.

■ The *private* function `realloc()` gets heap space according to the value of its input argument. Of course, it must ensure that the existing heap space is copied into this new space, the old space is released, the `length` field is set accordingly, and `ptr` points to the new space.

■ The function `initialize()` stores the value of its input argument into `length` and allocates that many integers from the heap. It then sets each element to the value 0.

■ The accessor function `get_length()` returns the value of `length`.

■ The function `store()` stores its second argument into the array position indicated by the first argument.

■ The function `increment()` adds 1 to each element in the array.

■ The function `append()` calls upon the function `realloc()` to increase the size of the array by 1. It then appends its input argument to the end of the array.

■ The function `reverse()` reverses the order of elements in the array.

■ The function `trunc()` calls upon the function `realloc()` in order to truncate the last element in the array.

■ The function `print()` outputs each array element with its index position.

■ The function `del()` releases the heap space.

■ Exercise #5

Write a class called `parser` that can:

■ Read in string input from the user;

■ Parse the line one word at a time. That is, isolate and store the next word in the line;

■ Return a pointer to the currently parsed word;

■ Return where in the line the first character of the word is located relative to the start of the line.

A word is defined to consist of letters, numbers, and underscores. Letters are case sensitive.

To test the class, write a `main()` function that merely reads in strings and outputs the words one at a time showing where the first character is in the line.

Notes

Notes

Chapter 6

Constructor and destructor functions

Since C++ supports the concept of user-defined classes and the subsequent instantiations of these classes, it is important that initialization of these instantiations be performed so that the state of any object does not reflect "garbage". One of the principles of C++ is that objects know how to initialize and cleanup after themselves. This automatic initialization and clean up is accomplished by two member functions — the constructor and the destructor.

What is a constructor function?

By definition, a *constructor function* of some class is a nonstatic member function that automatically gets executed whenever an instance of the class to which the constructor belongs comes into existence. The execution of such a function (assuming that it has been written properly) guarantees that the instance variables of the class will be initialized properly.

Why constructors and destructors are needed

Let's suppose that you have a class called `employee` that is abstracted as follows:

Example 6.1

```
class employee
{
    long ssn ;
    char* name ;
} ;
```

then every time a new `employee` is instantiated, the constructor must take the responsibility for allocating space for the `name` on the heap and establishing the correct social security number. This is exactly what the constructor function will do for you.

The destructor function is just the opposite of the constructor. It is automatically called whenever an instance of the class `employee` is about to go out of existence. Its principal purpose is to release the space on the heap that the `name` field points to, and perform any other cleanup chores.

Why the constructor function is unique

A constructor function is different from all other nonstatic member functions in a class because it is *not* called using some instance of the class, but instead is used to *initialize* the variables of whatever instance is being created. In other words, it is called "before the fact" (the "fact" in this case being the complete instantiation of an object).

Note that a constructor function can be overloaded to accommodate many different forms of initialization for instances of the class. In addition, the execution of the constructor does *not* reserve memory for the instance itself. The compiler generates the code to do this, either in static memory, on the stack, or on the heap, after which control is handed over to the constructor to do the initialization of the data members.

Syntax rules for writing constructor functions

Here are the syntax rules for writing a constructor function:

- Its name, by definition, must be the *same* as that of the class to which it belongs.

- It is declared with *no return type* (not even `void`). However, it will implicitly return a temporary copy of the instance itself that is being created.

- It cannot be declared `static`, `const` or `volatile`.

- It should have public or protected access within the class. (Protected access will be discussed in Chapter 10.) Only in some rare circumstances should it be declared private.

For example, here are some typical declarations for constructors that might be written for the `employee` class. Note the use of function overloading that is occurring here.

Example 6.2

```
class employee
{
     public:
   employee() ;
   employee(long) ;
   employee(long , const char*) ;
} ;
```

 In this particular situation the use of default function arguments would allow you to combine these three constructors into one constructor, but there are many cases where this simply cannot be done.

When the constructor function is called

An instance of some class `employee` comes into existence and causes the constructor function to be invoked when:

- A global or static local variable of class `employee` is defined (the constructor is called before `main()` starts).

- An auto variable of class `employee` is defined within a block and the location of its definition is reached.

- A temporary instance of class `employee` needs to be created.

- An instance of class `employee` is obtained from free memory via the `new` operator.

143

- An instance of some class is created that contains, as a data member, an instance of class `employee`.

- An instance of some class derived from class `employee` is created (see Chapter 10).

An instance of the class `employee` also comes into existence when it is created via initialization from an existing instance, or when it gets passed into or out of a function *by value*. This particular type of constructor will be discussed later in this chapter.

Note that the creation of a pointer or reference to an instance of some class does *not* cause the constructor function of that class to be called for the simple reason that an instance itself is *not* being created. Also, in C++ there is no such thing as a constructor function for a primitive type (`int`, `char`, etc).

Destructor function

As stated earlier, a destructor function gets executed whenever an instance of the class to which it belongs goes out of existence. The primary usage of a destructor function is to release space on the heap that the instance currently has reserved. By having a destructor function in your program you are relieved of having to remember to execute a "cleanup" member function each time a class instance goes out of scope. Note, however, that if you terminate your program abnormally, for example, with an `exit()` call, then the destructor function will be called *only* for global instances, and not for auto instances. Primitive types do not have a destructor function.

Syntax rules for writing a destructor function

The rules for writing a destructor are:

- Its name is the same as that of the class to which it belongs, except that the first character of the name must be a tilde (~).

- It is declared with *no return type* (not even `void`) since it cannot ever return a value.

- It cannot be declared `static`, `const` or `volatile`.

- It takes no input arguments, and therefore cannot be overloaded.

- It should have public access in the class declaration.

Note that a destructor function may be called explicitly. Calling a destructor in this manner allows you to release the resources for an object in preparation for the allocation of new resources, e.g., releasing heap space because a larger chunk of space is now needed. Although earlier versions of Borland C++ required that the destructor name be fully qualified, Borland C++ 3.1 allows you to call a destructor directly.

For example, here is how the declaration for a destructor for the class `employee` would be written:

Example 6.3

```
class employee
{
    public:
   ~employee() ;
} ;
```

When a destructor function is called

The destructor function for some class `employee` is called:

- After the end of `main()` for all static, local to `main()`, and global instances of class `employee`.

- At the end of each block containing an `auto` variable of class `employee`.

- At the end of each function containing an argument of class `employee`.

- To destroy any unnamed temporaries of class `employee` after their use.

- When an instance of `employee` allocated on the heap is destroyed via `delete`.

- When an object containing an instance of class `employee` is destroyed.

- When an object of a class derived from class `employee` is destroyed.

Order of invocation

When the declaration for an instance is encountered in a program at file scope, it is stored into global, or static, memory and the constructor function is called. When an instance is encountered within a function or block scope, it is pushed onto the stack and the constructor function is called. At the end of the function or block, the last instance created is popped off the stack first, and the destructor function is called. And after the `main()` function terminates, the destructor function for all global instances is called. Therefore, it is obvious that the order of constructor and destructor calls follows a strict Last-In-First-Out (LIFO) pattern.

> ☞ There may be some exceptions to this rule insofar as temporary instances are concerned. In this case the compiler is free to destroy them whenever it deems fit to do so.

The default constructor and destructor

If you fail to write a constructor and destructor function (as has been the case up to now), the compiler automatically supplies them for you. These functions have public access within the class and essentially do nothing useful. If you were to code these functions yourself, this is what they would look like:

Example 6.4

```
class employee
{
     public:
  employee() ;
  ~employee() ;
} ;

inline employee::employee() {}
inline employee::~employee() {}
```

Of course, you may choose to define either or both functions completely within the scope of the class definition.

From this point on the term "default constructor" will be used quite frequently. Quite simply, it refers to the constructor that takes no arguments, whether it is supplied automatically by the compiler or is written by you. Note that a constructor that takes all default arguments serves as the default constructor.

For example, in Chapter 5 we had to write initialization functions in order to establish the starting values of the data members of each class instance. Instead of such an initializing function, the following program uses the constructor function to set the value of the private data member ssn to zero. Note that the member functions are defined within the class definition.

Example 6.5

```
#include <stdio.h>

class employee
{
  long ssn ;

    public:
  employee()
   {
     puts("Constructor") ;
     ssn = 0L ;
   }

  ~employee()
   {
     puts("Destructor") ;
   }

  long get_ssn() const
   {
     return ssn ;
   }
} ;

int main()
{
  puts("In main()") ;

  // Create the instance 'Tom' and call the constructor
  // automatically
  employee Tom ;

  // Verify that the constructor worked
  printf("ssn = %ld\n" , Tom.get_ssn()) ;

  puts("Leaving main()") ;

  return 0 ;
}
```

The output is:

```
In main()
Constructor
ssn = 0
Leaving main()
Destructor
```

Here is the same example, but now the constructor and destructor functions are written outside the class definition and the instance Tom is created at global scope. The implicit call to the constructor function to initialize Tom is reminiscent of Example 1.12 in which a global variable is initialized as the result of a function call.

Example 6.6

```
#include <stdio.h>

class employee
{
   long ssn ;

      public:
   employee() ;
   ~employee() ;
   long get_ssn() const ;
} ;

inline employee::employee()
{
   puts("Constructor") ;
   ssn = 0L ;
}

inline employee::~employee()
{
   puts("Destructor") ;
}

inline long employee::get_ssn() const
{
   return ssn ;
}

employee Tom ;

int main()
{
   puts("In main()") ;
   printf("ssn = %ld\n" , Tom.get_ssn()) ;
   puts("Leaving main()") ;

   return 0 ;
}
```

The output is:

```
Constructor
In main()
ssn = 0
Leaving main()
Destructor
```

The constructor and destructor for a single instance on the heap

When a single instance of a user-defined class is allocated on the heap via the `new` operator, the constructor is called automatically. However, since you are responsible for releasing the space on the heap via a `delete` operator, this is the only way in which the destructor will get called.

Assuming that an appropriate class `employee` has been defined, in this example the space for the instance of `employee` comes from the heap instead of the stack or the global area. Note the use of `delete` to release the space.

Example 6.7

```c
int main()
{
   employee* ptr = new employee ;
   if(ptr != 0)
    {
      printf("ssn = %ld\n" , ptr->get_ssn()) ;
      delete ptr ;
    }
   else
      puts("Out of heap space") ;

   return 0 ;
}
```

Constructors taking one argument

The problem with the preceding examples is that the constructor function has been coded so that it stores a zero social security number into every instance that gets created. Obviously this is not correct. Instead, what is needed is a method to pass different social security numbers into the constructor function so that the various instances will be unique. This can be done by declaring the constructor with a formal argument list just like any other function.

For example, the following code declares and then defines a constructor for class `employee` that takes a long integer as its one formal argument.

Example 6.8

```
class employee
{
   long ssn ;

     public:
   employee(long) ;
} ;

inline employee::employee(long n)
{
   ssn = n ;
}
```

In this situation, the creation of the instance `Tom` can be written in two different ways. The first method uses the equals sign, and resembles the way you have been doing it in C. For example:

Example 6.9

```
employee Tom = 123456789L ;
```

The second method is the C++ style of initialization, and involves writing an argument list immediately following the name of the instance being created, as though you were calling a function. For example:

Example 6.10

```
employee Tom(123456789L) ;
```

It should be obvious that if you construct an instance and supply a single argument, but fail to write a constructor function that accepts a single argument in its formal argument list, the compiler will complain.

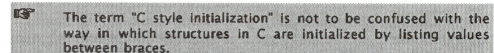 The term "C style initialization" is not to be confused with the way in which structures in C are initialized by listing values between braces.

Let's change the constructor function so that it can accept a `long` integer argument and instantiate the class using both the C and C++ styles of initialization.

Example 6.11

```cpp
#include <stdio.h>

class employee
{
    long ssn ;

      public:
    employee(long) ;
    ~employee() ;
    long get_ssn() const ;
} ;

inline employee::employee(long n)
{
    puts("Constructor") ;
    ssn = n ;
}

inline employee::~employee()
{
    puts("Destructor") ;
}

inline long employee::get_ssn() const
{
    return ssn ;
}

int main()
{
    puts("In main()") ;
    employee Tom = 123456789L ;
    printf("ssn = %ld\n" , Tom.get_ssn()) ;

    employee Dick(987654321L) ;
    printf("ssn = %ld\n" , Dick.get_ssn()) ;
    puts("Leaving main()") ;

    return 0 ;
}
```

The output is:

```
In main()
Constructor
ssn = 123456789
Constructor
ssn = 987654321
Leaving main()
Destructor
Destructor
```

 Using C style initialization, the compiler is free to first create a temporary instance of the class, and then copy this instance into your object name. Using C++ style initialization, the compiler guarantees that no such intermediate step will occur. That is, the object will be initialized "directly". Therefore, given a choice, you should always prefer the C++ style of initialization.

Where to go wrong

Since the creation of an instance of some class `employee` that takes a single argument can be written:

Example 6.12

```
// Correct -- pass 1 argument
employee Tom(123456789L) ;
```

you might be tempted to say that the creation of an instance that takes no argument can be written by simply removing the expression within the parentheses, like this:

Example 6.13

```
// Wrong! -- a function declaration
employee Tom() ;
```

This is wrong, and no instance will be created. Why? Because the syntax of empty parentheses tells the compiler that you are *declaring a function* called `Tom` that takes no arguments and returns an instance of class `employee` by value. Therefore, you must be sure to write:

Example 6.14

```
// Correct -- call the default constructor
employee Tom ;
```

without the parentheses.

Constructor function overloading

Suppose that your program needs to create an instance of class employee that takes no arguments, and also an instance that takes one argument. Certainly you need to write a constructor function that takes one formal argument. However, you might then think that you could use the default constructor supplied by the compiler to accommodate the instance with no arguments. Unfortunately, this will not work because the compiler is now saying, "OK, if you want to participate in the constructor game, that's fine with me, so I'll bow out completely and take my default constructor with me. Therefore, it's up to you to supply a default constructor".

Note that this program will not compile because there is no default constructor function to accommodate the instance Tom.

Example 6.15   *(Will not compile!)*

```
#include <stdio.h>

class employee
{
  long ssn ;

    public:
  employee(long) ;
  ~employee() ;
  long get_ssn() const ;
} ;

inline employee::employee(long n)
{
  puts("Constructor") ;
  ssn = n ;
}

inline employee::~employee()
{
  puts("Destructor") ;
}
```

```
inline long employee::get_ssn() const
{
  return ssn ;
}

int main()
{
  puts("In main()") ;
  employee Tom ;
  printf("ssn = %ld\n" , Tom.get_ssn()) ;
  puts("Leaving main()") ;

  return 0 ;
}
```

The compiler error message is:

```
Could not find a match for 'employee::employee()'
```

The solution, of course, is to add a default constructor function. Note that now you have two constructor functions, which constitutes an example of function overloading. This poses no problem to the compiler as it can distinguish between them by the difference it detects in the formal argument list.

Example 6.16

```
#include <stdio.h>

class employee
{
  long ssn ;

    public:
  employee() ;
  employee(long) ;
  ~employee() ;
  long get_ssn() const ;
} ;

inline employee::employee()
{
  puts("Default constructor") ;
  ssn = 0L ;
}
```

```
inline employee::employee(long n)
{
  puts("Constructor") ;
  ssn = n ;
}

inline employee::~employee()
{
  puts("Destructor") ;
}

inline long employee::get_ssn() const
{
  return ssn ;
}

int main()
{
  puts("In main()") ;
  employee Tom ;
  printf("ssn = %ld\n" , Tom.get_ssn()) ;
  puts("Leaving main()") ;

  return 0 ;
}
```

The output is:

```
In main()
Default constructor
ssn = 0
Leaving main()
Destructor
```

Constructors taking two or more arguments

Let's add a salary field and an appropriate accessor function to our employee class, so that now the data members in the definition appear as:

Example 6.17

```
class employee
{
   long ssn ;
   double salary ;

      public:
   // Member functions
} ;
```

In order to create an instance of the class and properly initialize the two data members, you may still use either the C or the C++ style of initialization. First, for the C style, the arguments must be enclosed between parentheses and preceded by the class name.

Example 6.18

```
employee Tom = employee(123456789L , 45000.00) ;
```

The C++ style is similar to the constructor that takes one argument, and is the preferred method of coding:

Example 6.19

```
employee Tom(123456789L , 45000.00) ;
```

Again, it is up to you to supply a proper constructor function to handle this type of creation.

> ☞ Caution: If you use the C style of initialization, do not forget to write the class name in front of the parentheses. For example
>
>   employee Tom = (123456789 , 45000.00) ;
>
> is wrong and will invoke the constructor taking just one argument.

In this example two employees are created, Tom using the C style, and Dick using the C++ style.

Example 6.20

```c
#include <stdio.h>

class employee
{
  long ssn ;
  double salary ;

    public:
  employee() ;
  employee(long , double) ;
  ~employee() ;
  long get_ssn() const ;
  double get_salary() const ;
} ;

inline employee::employee()
{
  puts("Default constructor") ;
  ssn = 0L ;
  salary = 0.0 ;
}

inline employee::employee(long n , double s)
{
  puts("Constructor") ;
  ssn = n ;
  salary = s ;
}

inline employee::~employee()
{
  puts("Destructor") ;
}

inline long employee::get_ssn() const
{
  return ssn ;
}

inline double employee::get_salary() const
{
  return salary ;
}
```

```
int main()
{
   puts("In main()") ;

   employee Tom = employee(123456789L , 45000.00) ;
   printf("ssn = %ld\n" , Tom.get_ssn()) ;
   printf("salary = %0.2f\n" , Tom.get_salary()) ;
   employee Dick(987654321L , 46000.00) ;
   printf("ssn = %ld\n" , Dick.get_ssn()) ;
   printf("salary = %0.2f\n" , Dick.get_salary()) ;

   puts("Leaving main()") ;

   return 0 ;
}
```

The output is:

```
In main()
Constructor
ssn = 123456789
salary = 45000.00
Constructor
ssn = 987654321
salary = 46000.00
Leaving main()
Destructor
Destructor
```

How to create a temporary instance

It is always possible to create a temporary instance of a class by writing the class name followed by parentheses, within which the constructor arguments, if any, are specified. If there are no arguments to be used in the constructor of the instance, the parentheses must still be written. The constructor function will then be called when the temporary instance is created.

You have already seen an example of this usage of a temporary in the C style initialization of an object that requires 2 or more arguments. Another situation occurs when you have the individual data members of a class available, and need to combine them to form a new instance of the class. In other words, if a function called `create()` receives both the social security number and a salary as its two input arguments, then it can return a new `employee` object by creating a temporary thusly:

Example 6.21

```
employee create(long n , double s)
{
   return employee(n , s) ;
}
```

Later on in this chapter you will see another occurrence of a temporary class object when you have to initialize an array of objects.

> ☞ If the temporary instance calls upon the default constructor, i.e., no arguments are specified between the parentheses, then you may have to write an explicit default constructor. In other words, the compiler-supplied default constructor may not handle this particular situation which, according to Bjarne Stroustrup, is not the proper behavior.

Implicit type conversion

The constructor of a class that takes one argument is unique in the sense that it will get called automatically whenever a conversion to the class type needs to be done from a single argument. This frequently occurs when a function argument consists of a class type (usually received by reference) and the actual argument is some primitive type. In this situation the compiler will automatically call upon the constructor function that takes one argument in order to create a temporary instance of the class which it can then use as the actual argument for the function call.

In the following example after the instance Tom is created using the default constructor, it calls upon the member function copy() with an argument that represents the Social Security Number (a long). Notice, however, that the argument in the copy() function expects to receive a constant reference to an instance of the employee class instead. Therefore, the compiler will automatically invoke the constructor function that accepts one argument in order to create a temporary employee instance that will become the argument for the function call.

Example 6.22

```
#include <stdio.h>

class employee
{
  long ssn ;

    public:
  employee() ;
  employee(long) ;
  ~employee() ;
  long get_ssn() const ;
  void copy(const employee&) ;
} ;

inline employee::employee()
{
  puts("Default constructor") ;
  ssn = 0L ;
}

inline employee::employee(long n)
{
  puts("Constructor") ;
  ssn = n ;
}

inline employee::~employee()
{
  puts("Destructor") ;
}

inline long employee::get_ssn() const
{
  return ssn ;
}

inline void employee::copy(const employee& e)
{
  ssn = e.ssn ;
}
```

```
int main()
{
   employee Tom ;
   Tom.copy(123456789L) ;
   printf("ssn = %ld\n" , Tom.get_ssn()) ;

   return 0 ;
}
```

The output is:

```
Default constructor
Constructor
Destructor
ssn = 123456789
Destructor
```

Constructor functions taking default arguments

Earlier you saw an example of a class in which the constructor was overloaded so that one version took no arguments, and the other one argument. While this works, it causes you to write extra code because it doesn't take advantage of the concept of default function arguments that you learned in Chapter 3.

For example, in this program only one constructor function is needed because it takes all default arguments. Now it is possible to instantiate the class with either no arguments, one argument (the social security number), or two arguments (the social security number and the salary). In the cases where the social security number and the salary are not explicitly given, they will default to the value zero.

Example 6.23

```
#include <stdio.h>

class employee
{
  long ssn ;
  double salary ;

    public:
  employee(long = 0L , double = 0.00) ;
  ~employee() ;
  long get_ssn() const ;
  double get_salary() const ;
} ;

inline employee::employee(long n , double s)
{
  puts("Constructor") ;
  ssn = n ;
  salary = s ;
}

inline employee::~employee()
{
  puts("Destructor") ;
}

inline long employee::get_ssn() const
{
  return ssn ;
}

inline double employee::get_salary() const
{
  return salary ;
}

int main()
{
  // Instantiate with no arguments
  employee Tom ;
  printf("ssn = %ld\n" , Tom.get_ssn()) ;
  printf("salary = %0.2f\n" , Tom.get_salary()) ;

  // Instantiate with 1 argument
  employee Dick(123456789L) ;
  printf("ssn = %ld\n" , Dick.get_ssn()) ;
  printf("salary = %0.2f\n" , Dick.get_salary()) ;
```

```
    // Instantiate with 2 arguments
    employee Harry(987654321L , 45000.00) ;
    printf("ssn = %ld\n" , Harry.get_ssn()) ;
    printf("salary = %0.2f\n" , Harry.get_salary()) ;

    return 0 ;
}
```

The output is:

```
Constructor
ssn = 0
salary = 0.00
Constructor
ssn = 123456789
salary = 0.00
Constructor
ssn = 987654321
salary = 45000.00
Destructor
Destructor
Destructor
```

The copy constructor

In both C and C++ using primitive types, it is possible to initialize a new variable with one of the same type that already exists. In C this can be done with primitive types and with structures. In the latter case, each member of the existing structure is copied into the corresponding member of the structure being created.

Moving into the world of C++, if a new class instance is created by initializing it with some existing instance, then this process is called "memberwise initialization" because, like C, each data member of the new instance is initialized via a copy of the corresponding data member of the existing instance. This is identical to how the initialization of a structure object works. However, in C++ it's not quite as simple as in C because the initialization process is more complex, e.g., when pointer data members are involved. Therefore, it follows that a constructor function is needed.

In particular, the constructor to handle the creation and initialization of a class instance via an existing instance is called the *copy constructor*.

When the copy constructor is called

The copy constructor for some class employee is called when:

■ An instance of class employee is created from an existing instance of class employee.

■ A function is called and an argument of class `employee` is passed by value.

■ An unnamed temporary variable is created to hold the return value of a function returning an instance of class `employee`.

> ☞ Note that in all probability the instantiation of a class instance from a *temporary* instance of that class will *not* invoke the copy constructor. Instead, the only constructor call will be for the creation of the temporary instance.

Like the default constructor, if you do not write a copy constructor, then the compiler will automatically provide one for you. Then what happens is that each data member in the existing instance will get copied into the corresponding data member of the new instance. This memberwise copy is recursive in the sense that if a data member is also an instance of some other class, then all of its data members are also copied. In other words, all such data members down to the primitive types are copied.

In the following example the instance `Dick` is created via initialization from the existing instance `Tom`. Note that the class is using the compiler-supplied copy constructor.

Example 6.24   *(Produces run-time error!)*

```
#include <stdio.h>
#include <string.h>

class employee
{
  long ssn ;
  double salary ;
  char* name ;

    public:
  employee(long = 0L , double = 0.00 , const char* = "") ;
  ~employee() ;
  long get_ssn() const ;        ,
  double get_salary() const ;
  const char* get_name() const ;
} ;
```

```cpp
inline employee::employee(long n , double s , const char* nm)
{
  puts("Constructor") ;
  ssn = n ;
  salary = s ;
  name = new char[strlen(nm) + 1] ;
  strcpy(name , nm) ;
}

inline employee::~employee()
{
  puts("Destructor") ;
  delete [] name ;
}

inline long employee::get_ssn() const
{
  return ssn ;
}

inline double employee::get_salary() const
{
  return salary ;
}

inline const char* employee::get_name() const
{
  return name ;
}

int main()
{
  // Instantiate Tom
  employee Tom(123456789L , 45000.00 , "Tom") ;
  printf("ssn = %ld\n" , Tom.get_ssn()) ;
  printf("salary = %0.2f\n" , Tom.get_salary()) ;
  printf("name = %s\n" , Tom.get_name()) ;

  // Instantiate Dick from Tom
  employee Dick(Tom) ;
  printf("ssn = %ld\n" , Dick.get_ssn()) ;
  printf("salary = %0.2f\n" , Dick.get_salary()) ;
  printf("name = %s\n" , Dick.get_name()) ;

  return 0 ;
}
```

The output is:

```
Constructor
ssn = 123456789
salary = 45000.00
name = Tom
ssn = 123456789
salary = 45000.00
name = Tom
Destructor
Destructor
Null pointer assignment
```

Note the message `Null pointer assignment` in the last output line. The reason is that since the *default* copy constructor function is being called to initialize the instance `Dick`, all of the data members of `Tom` are copied into `Dick`, including the pointer data member `Tom.name`. Therefore, both `Tom.name` and `Dick.name` now point to the same space on the heap. When the instance `Dick` goes out of scope, its destructor function is automatically called, which then releases the space on the heap that `Dick.name` points to. Then, when the instance `Tom` goes out of scope, its destructor function is automatically called and will attempt to release the space on the heap that `Tom.name` points to, which no longer exists because the destructor for `Dick` already released it!

A similar situation would have occurred if you had first created the instance `Dick` and then assigned the instance `Tom` into it. While the solution to the assignment problem involves the concept of operator function overloading, and won't be discussed until Chapter 8, the problem of creating a bug-free copy constructor can be solved right now.

How to write your own copy constructor

As the preceding example illustrated, sometimes you may use a default copy constructor, and sometimes you may not. The general rule is that whenever there are pointer data members as part of the class definition, then you must write your own copy constructor. So let's see how it is done.

Because a copy constructor function must "know" about the existing instance in order to copy the data members, it must take this instance as its one formal argument. The individual data members of this existing instance may then be accessed by using the formal argument name and the direct member operator. Obviously this existing instance should *never* be modified by the copy constructor function, so the keyword `const` should be used in the function signature. Therefore, if you are going to write your own copy constructor, it must take the form:

Example 6.25

```
// Declaration
employee(const employee&) ;

// Definition
inline employee::employee(const employee& e)
{
   // perform initialization
}
```

After you have written your own copy constructor, then for a code fragment such as:

Example 6.26

```
employee Tom ;

// C style initialization
employee Dick = Tom ;

// C++ style initialization
employee Dick(Tom) ;
```

the existing instance (Tom) becomes the formal argument (passed in by constant reference), and its data members are accessed using the formal argument name with the direct member operator. The object being initialized (Dick) becomes the implicit invoking instance for the constructor call. You then access the data members of Dick as you would in any other member function.

Here is the corrected version of Example 6.24 in which a copy constructor has now been added.

Example 6.27

```
#include <stdio.h>
#include <string.h>

class employee
{
   long ssn ;
   double salary ;
   char* name ;

     public:
    employee(long = 0L , double = 0.00 , const char* = "") ;
   employee(const employee&) ;
   ~employee() ;
   long get_ssn() const ;
   double get_salary() const ;
   const char* get_name() const ;
} ;

inline employee::employee(long n , double s , const char* nm)
{
   puts("Constructor") ;
   ssn = n ;
   salary = s ;
   name = new char[strlen(nm) + 1] ;
   strcpy(name , nm) ;
}

inline employee::employee(const employee& e)
{
   puts("Copy constructor") ;
   ssn = e.ssn ;
   salary = e.salary ;
   name = new char[strlen(e.name) + 1] ;
   strcpy(name , e.name) ;
}

inline employee::~employee()
{
   puts("Destructor") ;
   delete [] name ;
}

inline long employee::get_ssn() const
{
   return ssn ;
}
```

```
inline double employee::get_salary() const
{
   return salary ;
}

inline const char* employee::get_name() const
{
   return name ;
}

int main()
{
   employee Tom(123456789L , 45000.00 , "Tom") ;
   printf("ssn = %ld\n" , Tom.get_ssn()) ;
   printf("salary = %0.2f\n" , Tom.get_salary()) ;
   printf("name = %s\n" , Tom.get_name()) ;
   employee Dick = Tom ;
   printf("ssn = %ld\n" , Dick.get_ssn()) ;
   printf("salary = %0.2f\n" , Dick.get_salary()) ;
   printf("name = %s\n" , Dick.get_name()) ;

   return 0 ;
}
```

The output is:

```
Constructor
ssn = 123456789
salary = 45000.00
name = Tom
Copy constructor
ssn = 123456789
salary = 45000.00
name = Tom
Destructor
Destructor
```

Initialization vs. assignment

A constructor function is a special function for another reason that so far has been ignored. This reason involves the distinction between the processes of *initialization* and *assignment* that was already discussed.

Consider a constructor function for some class employee that is written as:

Example 6.28

```
class employee
{
   long ssn ;

      public:
   employee(long = 0L) ;
} ;

inline employee::employee(long n)
{
   ssn = n ;
}
```

Since the constructor contains an *assignment* statement, it must first *create* the variable ssn and then *assign* the value n to it. This is equivalent in C to writing the code:

Example 6.29

```
   long ssn ;
   ssn = n ;
```

in which the variable ssn must first be created before it can be assigned whatever happens to be in the variable n. Since there are no intervening statements between the definition of ssn and the assignment of n into it, the end result is achieved correctly — ssn contains the same value as n.

The point is simply this: the constructor in the class employee is *not* doing true initialization of the data member ssn. While it may appear to be a trivial distinction, there are several situations in which assignment simply does not work.

The base/member initialization list

To perform true initialization (not assignment) for a class data member, C++ provides extended syntax for the constructor function (and *only* the constructor function). After the argument list has been written, this extended syntax, called the *base/member initialization list*, is then specified:

- A single colon;
- The class data member to be initialized;

- A parenthesized list of one or more initializing values, each one separated by a comma. These values may be constants or expressions or even the output of a function call;
- A comma, and repeat of items 2 and 3 if another data member is to be initialized.

For the initialization of a primitive type, specify just one value between the parentheses. For the initialization of a user-defined type, you may specify any number of arguments, depending upon what the constructor for the member's class is expecting.

Thus, in order to initialize the data member `ssn` in the class `employee`, the definition would be written:

Example 6.30

```
class employee
{
   long ssn ;

     public:
   employee(long n = 0L) : ssn(n) {}
} ;
```

Or, if you wanted only to declare the constructor function in the class definition, you would write:

Example 6.31

```
class employee
{
   long ssn ;

     public:
   employee(long = 0L) ;
} ;

inline employee::employee(long n) : ssn(n) {}
```

Any other work that the constructor needs to do would then be done in the body of the function, i.e., between the braces.

Therefore, a constructor function can be thought of as being comprised of two executable sections:

- The initialization part, which is the action that occurs within the member initialization list, and

■   The assignment part, which is the action that occurs within the body of the function.

The initialization part always occurs first, and is immediately followed by the assignment part.

When the base/member initialization list is mandatory

There are some situations that absolutely require you to use the base/member initialization list. The first case occurs when an instance variable of a class is declared to be constant. Recall that in C++ *all* constants must be initialized and you cannot assign into a constant.

For example, suppose you decide that the Social Security number of an `employee` should never be changed once it gets initialized. To ensure this condition, you would simply make it a constant class data member of the class by writing:

Example 6.32

```
class employee
{
   const long ssn ;

      public:
   employee(long = 0L) ;
} ;
```

Since C++ mandates that all constants must be initialized, you might be tempted to write:

Example 6.33   *(Will not compile!)*

```
class employee
{
   const long ssn = 0L ;

      public:
   employee(long = 0L) ;
} ;
```

The compiler error message is:

```
Cannot initialize a class member here
```

Of course, this results in a compilation error because no C-style initialization is allowed within a structure or class definition for the simple reason that no memory has been reserved for an instance of the structure or class.

So, in order to initialize the data member `ssn` you might next try doing this:

Example 6.34   *(Will **not** compile!)*

```
class employee
{
   const long ssn ;

      public:
   employee(long = 0L) ;
} ;

inline employee::employee(long n)
{
   ssn = n ;
}
```

The compiler error message is:

```
Cannot modify a const object in function
employee::employee(int)
```

The compiler error message explains quite clearly what you are incorrectly trying to do.

Of course, the solution to this little dilemma is to use the member initialization list because that's exactly what it's for — to provide member initialization. Thus, in this class the constant data member `ssn` can now be properly initialized with whatever value is passed in to the constructor as an argument.

Example 6.35

```
class employee
{
   const long ssn ;

      public:
   employee(long = 0L) ;
} ;

inline employee::employee(long n) : ssn(n) {}
```

The second case where the member initialization list must be used is when the class contains reference variables. As with constants, C++ mandates that all reference variables must be initialized. Let's suppose that you want to be able to refer to the Social Security number using all capital letters. This is what you would have to do:

Example 6.36

```
class employee
{
   const long ssn ;
   const long& SSN ;

      public:
   employee(long = 0L) ;
} ;

inline employee::employee(long n) : ssn(n) , SSN(ssn) {}
```

Assignment to constant class members

If a class contains a `const` data member, then by implication any instance of that class cannot have its corresponding data member modified. This means that you cannot assign one class instance into another class instance of the same type because that implies the modification of the constant data member.

For example, in the following program after `Tom` and `Dick` get instantiated, `Tom` is assigned into `Dick` implying that all of the data members of `Tom` are to be copied into `Dick`. However, the compiler rightfully complains that it cannot do this. (The solution is to overload the assignment operator for the `employee` class. How this is done is described in Chapter 8.)

Example 6.37   *(Will not compile!)*

```
#include <stdio.h>

class employee
{
   const long ssn ;

      public:
   employee(long = 0L) ;
} ;
```

```
inline employee::employee(long n) : ssn(n) {}

int main()
{
   employee Tom(123456789L) , Dick ;
   Dick = Tom ;

   return 0 ;
}
```

The compiler error message is:

```
Compiler could not generate operator= for class 'employee'
```

An array as a data member

The C++ language does not provide any syntax by which you can *initialize* the individual elements of an array which has been declared within a class. The best you can do is *assign* to each element in the body of the constructor function.

For example, here is a constructor that assigns its input argument to each element of the array. Note the use of an enumerated type to provide the array dimension.

Example 6.38

```
class employee
{
   enum {limit = 10} ;
   int array[limit] ;

      public:
   employee(int = 0) ;
} ;

employee::employee(int n)
{
   for(int i = 0 ; i < limit ; ++i)
      array[i] = n ;
}
```

Order of member initialization

Since the initialization of one class data member may be dependent upon the initialization of another member, it's important to know the order in which the members get initialized. There are two theoretical ways in which this could be done: (1) the declaration order, or (2) the order of the members in the member initialization list. In point of fact, it's the declaration order that governs.

For example, in the following `employee` class the data member `ssn` is guaranteed to be initialized before `salary` because it appears first.

Example 6.39

```
class employee
{
   long ssn ;
   double salary ;

      public:
   employee(long = 0L , double = 0.0) ;
} ;

inline
employee::employee(long n , double s) : salary(s) , ssn(n) {}
```

Contained class instances

In Chapter 5 you saw how one class definition can contain an instance of another class. Because only the containing class will be instantiated, the problem is how to invoke the constructor function for the contained instance and pass to it any arguments that it may need in order to initialize itself. In other words, *both* constructors must somehow get control in order to perform proper initialization of the containing class.

The solution, as you may have suspected, is to use the member initialization list of the constructor function of the containing class. The syntax to initialize the contained instance is almost identical to that of initializing a primitive type data member of the containing class. That is, simply write the name of the contained instance followed by a parenthesized list of arguments. The difference here is that you may write more than one expression between the parentheses for the simple reason that the constructor function for the contained instance may very well be expecting more than one argument.

You should also note that if you fail to explicitly initialize the contained instance, the compiler will automatically invoke the default constructor of the contained class, so be careful!

For example, let's create a class called `company` that contains a single instance of the `employee` class (this is a very small company!). In addition, let's add a data member to the `company` class to accommodate the company name.

Example 6.40

```
class company
{
   employee Tom ;
   char* company_name ;

      public:
   // Function declarations
} ;
```

Now it becomes the responsibility of the constructor function of the `company` class to receive the actual name of the company as well as the arguments for the instance `Tom`, and invoke the constructor for `Tom` in its member initialization list. Here is a complete program to test the contained instance. For the sake of convenience, the `company` class also contains a `print()` function that is designed to output the company name as well as the data members of the `employee` class.

Example 6.41

```
#include <stdio.h>
#include <string.h>

class employee
{
   long ssn ;
   double salary ;
   char* name ;

      public:
   employee(long = 0L , double = 0.0 , const char* = "") ;
   employee(const employee&) ;
   ~employee() ;
   long get_ssn() const ;
   double get_salary() const ;
   const char* get_name() const ;
} ;
```

```cpp
inline employee::employee(long n , double s , const char* nm)
      : ssn(n) , salary(s) , name(new char[strlen(nm) + 1])
{
   strcpy(name , nm) ;
}

inline employee::employee(const employee& e)
                  : ssn(e.ssn) , salary(e.salary) ,
                   name(new char[strlen(e.name) + 1])
{
   strcpy(name , e.name) ;
}

inline employee::~employee()
{
   delete [] name ;
}

inline long employee::get_ssn() const
{
   return ssn ;
}

inline double employee::get_salary() const
{
   return salary ;
}

inline const char* employee::get_name() const
{
   return name ;
}

///////////////////////////////////////

class company
{
   employee Tom ;
   char* company_name ;

     public:
   company(const char*, const employee&) ;
   ~company() ;
   void print() ;
} ;
```

```
inline company::company(
  // Company name
  const char* cn ,
  // Employee instance
  const employee& e)
  // Initialize 'Tom'
  : Tom(e) ,
  // Initialize company name
  company_name(new char[strlen(cn) + 1])
{
    // Copy stack to heap
    strcpy(company_name , cn) ;
}

inline company::~company()
{
  delete [] company_name ;
}

inline void company::print()
{
  printf("company = %s\n" , company_name) ;
  printf("name = %s\n" , Tom.get_name()) ;
  printf("ssn = %ld\n" , Tom.get_ssn()) ;
  printf("salary = %0.2f\n" , Tom.get_salary()) ;
}

int main()
{
  employee temp(123456789L , 45000.00 , "Tom") ;
  company Borland("Borland" , temp) ;
  Borland.print() ;

  return 0 ;
}
```

The output is:

```
company = Borland
name = Tom
ssn = 123456789
salary = 45000.00
```

Don't forget that the instance `Borland` of class `company` is limited to accessing only the public member functions of its own class. If it wants to access the public member functions of the `employee` class, it must do so through an instance of, or pointer to, the `employee` class. That's why the function `company::print()` had to be invoked in order to call upon the functions `employee::get_name()`, etc.

Constructors and destructors with an uninitialized array of user-defined instances

An uninitialized array of class instances can be created just like any other primitive type of array, e.g., int , float, etc. In this case, since no initialization is specified, the default constructor is called for each instantiation. Also, as each instance goes out of scope, the destructor function is called.

Example 6.42

```
#include <stdio.h>

class employee
{
    public:
  employee() ;
  ~employee() ;
} ;

inline employee::employee()
{
  puts("Constructor") ;
}

inline employee::~employee()
{
  puts("Destructor") ;
}

int main()
{
  employee staff[2] ;

  return 0 ;
}
```

The output is:

```
Constructor
Constructor
Destructor
Destructor
```

Constructors and destructors with an initialized array of user-defined instances

As with an array of primitive types, you may specify initializers when declaring an array of class instances. As a quick review, let's see how it's done with a primitive type. The actual values are listed between braces and separated by commas. Remember that the dimension of the array does not need to be written. In addition, any uninitialized element is automatically set to binary zero. That is, under ANSI C it is *not* possible to partially initialize an array; it's an all-or-nothing situation.

When the array consists of instances of some class, it should be obvious that if you provide initial values, then a constructor function that accepts these values as formal arguments must be written. In addition, for any uninitialized array element, the compiler will attempt to invoke the default constructor, so this particular constructor must also be written.

> ☞ Under some implementations of AT&T 2.0, a constructor with all default arguments does *not* serve as the default constructor when initializing an array of instances. Therefore, you must explicitly write a default constructor.

Note that when you write the values that each array element will take on, it is mandatory that you use the syntax for creating a temporary class instance. That is, you must write the class name followed by the arguments enclosed within parentheses. To invoke the default constructor, write nothing between the parentheses. The only exception to this rule is when there is only one argument specified for each instance. In this case implicit type conversion may be used on the argument, so that the class name does not need to be written.

In the following example an array of class `employee` is created and initialized four different ways.

Example 6.43

```
#include <stdio.h>
#include <string.h>

class employee
{
  long ssn ;
  double salary ;
  char* name ;

     public:
  employee(long = 0L , double = 0.00 , const char* = "") ;
  employee(const employee&) ;
  ~employee() ;
  long get_ssn() const ;
  double get_salary() const ;
  const char* get_name() const ;
} ;

inline
employee::employee(long n , double s , const char* nm)
      : ssn(n) , salary(s) , name(new char[strlen(nm) + 1])
{
  strcpy(name , nm) ;
}

inline employee::employee(const employee& e)
                  : ssn(e.ssn) , salary(e.salary) ,
                    name(new char[strlen(e.name) + 1])
{
  strcpy(name , e.name) ;
}

inline employee::~employee()
{
  delete [] name ;
}

inline long employee::get_ssn() const
{
  return ssn ;
}

inline double employee::get_salary() const
{
  return salary ;
}
```

```
inline const char* employee::get_name() const
{
  return name ;
}

int main()
{
  employee staff[] =
   {
     employee() ,                           // #0
     123456789L ,                           // #1
     employee(123456789L , 45000.00) ,      // #2
     employee(123456789L , 45000.00 , "Tom")   // #3
   } ;

  const int size = sizeof(staff) / sizeof(employee) ;
  for(int i = 0 ; i < size ; ++i)
   {
     printf("ssn = %ld\n" , staff[i].get_ssn()) ;
     printf("salary = %0.2f\n" , staff[i].get_salary()) ;
     printf("name = %s\n\n" , staff[i].get_name()) ;
   }

  return 0 ;
}
```

The output is:

```
ssn = 0
salary = 0.00
name =

ssn = 123456789
salary = 0.00
name =

ssn = 123456789
salary = 45000.00
name =

ssn = 123456789
salary = 45000.00
name = Tom
```

An array of constant data members

If you ever need to declare an array of constant data members in some class, you come face to face with a real dilemma. On the one hand, C++ insists that all constants be initialized. On the other hand, it will not let you initialize the individual elements of an array.

One possible solution is to declare the array as non-constant in one class, and then use an instance of this class as a constant data member in another class.

The following program shows how this can be done.

Example 6.44

```
class employee
{
   enum {dim = 3} ;
   int array[dim] ;

      public:
   employee(int n1 , int n2 , int n3)
    {
       array[0] = n1 ;
       array[1] = n2 ;
       array[2] = n3 ;
    }
} ;

class Employee
{
   const employee e ;

      public:
   Employee(int n1 = 0 , int n2 = 0, int n3 = 0)
           : e(n1 , n2 , n3) {}
} ;

int main()
{
   Employee Tom(1 , 2 , 3) ;

   return 0 ;
}
```

How to initialize a user-defined type on the heap

Like a primitive type, a single instance of a user-defined type created on the heap can also be initialized by specifying some value or values between parentheses. For example:

Example 6.45

```
employee* ptr = new employee(123456789L , 45000.00 , "Tom") ;
delete ptr ;
```

If you wish to allocate an instance of some user-defined type and invoke the default constructor, you may write empty parentheses after the class name, or eliminate the parentheses entirely. For example, to create a single instance of class `employee` and then release the space, you would write:

Example 6.46

```
employee* ptr = new employee() ;  // or
employee* ptr = new employee ;
delete ptr ;
```

Arrays of instances allocated on the heap

Like an array of some primitive type, an array of class instances allocated on the heap does not have any syntax by which each instance can pass one or more arguments to a constructor. Therefore, the default constructor will automatically be called for each array element. Of course, the only way to eliminate the space occupied by these instances is to use the `delete` operator on the resulting pointer.

This is how an array of 10 instances of class `employee` would be allocated and released:

Example 6.47

```
employee* ptr = new employee[10] ;
delete [] ptr ;
```

☞ Don't forget that if you are using a version of C++ that supports AT&T release 2.0, then you must designate the array dimension between the square brackets.

As a simple test, this program allocates space on the heap for an (empty) class `employee` and then deletes the space.

Example 6.48

```
#include <stdio.h>

class employee
{
    public:
  employee() ;
  ~employee() ;
} ;

inline employee::employee()
{
  puts("Constructor") ;
}

inline employee::~employee()
{
  puts("Destructor") ;
}

int main()
{
  int dim = 3 ;

  employee* ptr = new employee[dim];
  delete [] ptr ;

  return 0 ;
}
```

The output is:

```
Constructor
Constructor
Constructor
Destructor
Destructor
Destructor
```

Here is another example using a 2-dimensional array.

Example 6.49

```
#include <stdio.h>

class employee
{
     public:
   employee() ;
   ~employee() ;
} ;

inline employee::employee()
{
   puts("Constructor") ;
}

inline employee::~employee()
{
   puts("Destructor") ;
}

int main()
{
   int rows = 3 ;
   const int cols = 2 ;
   typedef employee PTR[cols] ;
   PTR* ptr = new PTR[rows] ;
   delete [] ptr ;

   return 0 ;
}
```

The output is:

```
Constructor
Constructor
Constructor
Constructor
Constructor
Constructor
Destructor
Destructor
Destructor
Destructor
Destructor
Destructor
```

Early releases of Borland C++ abort the program on a "Null pointer assignment" when it is time to call the destructor function. This occurred only in the case of a multidimensional array of user-defined instances, and has been corrected in Borland C++ 3.1.

Function style cast vs. a declaration

Recall from earlier in this chapter that a temporary instance of a user-defined class can always be created by writing the class name followed by a parenthesized list of arguments. However, sometimes this syntax comes into direct conflict with the syntax for declaring (not instantiating) an object of the particular class type. This can be seen in the following example in which the creation of an instance of class Y needs an instance of class X.

Example 6.50   **(Will not compile!)**

```
class X
{
     public:
  X(int = 0) {}
} ;

class Y
{
     public:
  Y(const X& = 0) {}
  void f () {}
} ;

int main ()
{
  int n = 1 ;
  Y y (X (n)) ;
  y.f () ;

  return 0 ;
}
```

The compiler error message from the call to function f () is:

```
Structure required on left side of . or .* in function main()
```

The problem is that y is *not* an instantiation of class Y, but instead the name of a function that takes X as its one argument by value and returns a Y by value. To get around this dilemma, either remove the X before n or use C style initialization.

A word about inline constructors and destructors

Constructor and destructor functions, as we have already seen, can be coded as either inline or non-inline functions. Since they are typically short, straightforward bodies of code, in all probability they should be inline. But because they get called so frequently, is this a good idea? That is, won't the replication of the code itself take up too much memory? After all, constructors get called for declarations, implicit type conversions, allocation from the heap, and destructor functions get called at the end of a scope or when `delete` is called. In addition, the code for an inline constructor or destructor in a derived class contains the code for the inline constructor or destructor in the base class. The only way to determine if this is too much code generation is by experimentation.

Trapping error conditions

By now you are probably asking yourself what you should do if a constructor function cannot do its job properly. For example, suppose space from the heap needs to be allocated, and none is left, or an input argument to the constructor turns out to be invalid. Then what? Bjarne Stroustrup and Margaret Ellis have proposed a method to handle these situations called "exception handling", which is described in The Annotated C++ Reference Manual (ARM). The X3J16 Technical Committee is currently defining the details of how it should work, and will probably adopt their proposal without too much change. Chapter 18 covers exception handling in great detail, but you must be using a C++ compiler that implements AT&T version 4.0.

In the meantime, consider this simple class:

Example 6.51

```
#include <string.h>

class employee
{
   char* name ;

      public:
   employee(const char* = "") ;
   ~employee() ;
} ;
```

```
inline employee::employee(const char* n)
        : name(new char[strlen(n) + 1])
{
  if(name != 0)
     strcpy(name , n) ;
  else
   {
     // Now what???
   }
}

inline employee::~employee()
{
  delete [] name ;
}
```

The problem, of course, is what you should do if the pointer name contains 0.

There are two possible approaches you can take to handle errors in constructor functions. The first is quite simple — display an error message and perform an exit() call back to the operating system. Here is the previous example with this code:

Example 6.52

```
#include <string.h>
#include <stdlib.h>

class employee
{
  char* name ;

    public:
  employee(const char* = "") ;
  ~employee() ;
} ;

inline employee::employee(const char* n)
        : name(new char[strlen(n) + 1])
{
  if(name != 0)
     strcpy(name , n) ;
  else
   {
     puts("Out of heap space") ;
     exit(1) ;
   }
}
```

```
inline employee::~employee()
{
   delete [] name ;
}
```

If you don't want to exit the program, your other option is to set some kind of error flag in the class, provide an accessor function for this flag, and hope that the user of the class checks the flag after instantiating the class. This in effect shifts the responsibility for handling the error to the user of the class as opposed to the designer of the class. For example:

Example 6.53

```
#include <stdio.h>
#include <string.h>
#include <stdlib.h>

class employee
{
   int error ;
   char* name ;

      public:
   employee(const char* = "") ;
   ~employee() ;
   int check_error() const ;
} ;

inline employee::employee(const char* n)
                  : name(new char[strlen(n) + 1]) , error(0)
{
   if(name != 0)
      strcpy(name , n) ;
   else
      error = 1 ;
}

inline employee::~employee()
{
   delete [] name ;
}

int employee::check_error() const
{
   return error ;
}
```

```
int main()
{
  employee Tom("Tom") ;
  if(Tom.check_error())
   {
     printf("Constructor failed - call the programmer\n") ;
     exit(1) ;
   }
  // proceed normally
  return 0 ;
}
```

■ Review Questions

1) What is the purpose of the constructor and destructor functions?

2) Why don't the constructor and destructor functions have return types?

3) What is the default constructor?

4) Why would you overload a constructor function?

5) What is the copy constructor and when is it used?

6) In what order are class data members initialized?

7) What is the difference between initialization and assignment?

8) When do you need to initialize (not assign) class data members?

9) How are constructor arguments passed to a contained instance?

10) In a copy constructor is it really necessary for the existing instance to be passed into the function by reference? Wouldn't a pass by value still work, even though it may not be as efficient?

11) How do you allocate a single instance of a class on the heap? How do you initialize this instance?

12) How do you allocate an array of instances of a class on the heap? Why can't you initialize these instances at the same time?

■ Exercise #1

Create a class called driver that contains:

■ Data members for the name (type char*) and age (type int);

■ A constructor function that uses the member initialization list to initialize age and then allocates space on the heap for the name;

■ A copy constructor function;

■ A print() function that displays the name and age;

■ A destructor function that releases the space on the heap;

Then create a class called `automobile` that contains:

- An instance of the class `driver`;
- Data members for the `make` (type `char*`) and `year` (type `int`) of the automobile;
- A constructor function that uses the member initialization list to initialize the `driver` and `year` members;
- A `print()` function that calls upon `driver::print()` and then displays the `make` and `year`.

Finally, write a `main()` function that instantiates the `driver` class and the `automobile` class. The latter instantiation passes the `driver` instance to the constructor function.

Exercise #2

Write a program that proves that the order in which the data members of a class are declared governs the order in which they are initialized.

Exercise #3

Given the class declaration for a complex number:

```
class complex
{
   float real , imag ;

      public:
   complex(float = 0.0 , float = 0.0) ;
   complex(const complex&) ;
   float get_real() const ;
   float get_imag() const ;
   void increment() ;
   void accumulate(const complex&) ;
   void print() ;
} ;
```

and the `main()` function:

```
int main()
{
   complex c1 , c2(1.1) , c3(2.2 , 3.3) ;
   c1 = add(c2 , c3) ;
   c1.increment() ;
   complex c4(c1) ;
   complex c5 = add(c4 , 6.2) ;
   c5.accumulate(c1) ;
   complex c6 = multiply(c4 , c5) ;

   c1.print() ;
   c2.print() ;
```

```
        c3.print() ;
        c4.print() ;
        c5.print() ;
        c6.print() ;
        return 0 ;
    }
```

and the output:

```
4.30 + 3.30i
1.10 + 0.00i
2.20 + 3.30i
4.30 + 3.30i
14.80 + 6.60i
41.86 + 77.22i
```

write:

- A default and a copy constructor function.

- Two accessor functions.

- The function `complex::increment()` that adds 1 to the real portion of the invoking instance.

- The function `complex::accumulate()` that adds the real and imaginary portions of the explicit argument into the real and imaginary portions of the invoking instance, respectively.

- The function `complex::print()` that displays a complex number.

- The global function `add()` that adds two complex numbers together and returns the sum as a new complex number.

- The global function `multiply()` that multiplies two complex numbers together and returns the product as a new complex number.

Exercise #4

Rewrite Chapter 2, Exercise #4 so that the COIN structure is now a class. Eliminate the `initialize()` function and replace it with a constructor function that initializes the `value`, `single`, and `multiple` fields. In addition, make `change()` and `print()` into member functions. The `main()` function instantiates an array of type COIN with each element specifying the appropriate data to be passed to the constructor.

Exercise #5

Write a program that simulates the movement of an elevator. Start by creating a class called `button` that abstracts a push button located inside the elevator. Use an enumerated type to represent its state — either pressed or not pressed. Write implementor functions to change the state, and an accessor function to retrieve the state. If a button is pressed that is already in the pressed state, then display an error message.

Next, write a class called `elevator` that contains the following data members:

■ A pointer to an array of `button` objects.

■ An integer representing which floor the elevator is currently on.

■ A *constant* integer representing the top floor for the elevator. Its value comes from the one formal argument in the `elevator` constructor function. Assume that the bottom floor is always number 1.

Write member functions for the `elevator` class that allow the user to press any number of valid buttons. Assume that button number 0 means that it is time to close the elevator doors. When this happens, the elevator must move to a floor that has a corresponding button pressed. When this floor is reached, stop and prompt for more buttons. When determining which floor to go to next, give priority to any floor that is higher than the floor the elevator is currently on. If the user enters end-of-file from the keyboard, terminate the program.

Be sure to output messages so that the movement and direction of the elevator can easily be traced.

To "slow down" the elevator as you watch the program run, you can use the DOS function `sleep()` (prototyped in the file `dos.h`) whose one argument is an integer that represents the number of seconds that the program will pause.

A typical `main()` function to set the elevator in motion would appear as follows:

```
int main()
{
    const int top = 9 ;  // Top floor
    elevator Otis(top) ;
    Otis.prompt() ;

    return 0 ;
}
```

A sample run might produce the following output:

```
Enter the floor from 1 to 9, 0 to close the doors, EOF to quit: 2
Next floor: 5
Next floor: 0
The doors are closing
Elevator going up!
   Now on floor 2
The doors are open
Next floor: 4
Next floor: 0
The doors are closing
Elevator going up!
   Passing floor 3
   Now on floor 4
The doors are open
Next floor: 1
Next floor: 0
```

```
The doors are closing
Elevator going up!
   Now on floor 5
The doors are open
Next floor: 0
The doors are closing
Elevator going down!
   Passing floor 4
   Passing floor 3
   Passing floor 2
   Now on floor 1
The doors are open
Next floor: ^Z
Elevator being destroyed
```

■ Exercise #6

Write a program that allows the user to create a data base of people, list the data base, and perform a simple search routine.

Start by creating a class called `person` whose interface is as follows:

```
class person
{
    char* name ;

        public:
    person(const char*) ;
    ~person() ;
    int search(const char*) ;
    void print() ;
} ;
```

■   The function `search()` prints the person's name if the string input argument is contained anywhere within the name, and returns 'true'. If the argument cannot be found, then the function returns 'false'.

■   The function `print()` displays the name.

Next, create a class called `people` whose interface is as follows:

```
class people
{
    person** array ;
    int length ;
    void prompt() ;

        public:
    people() ;
    ~people() ;
    void menu() ;
    void add() ;
    void list() ;
```

```
    void search() ;
} ;
```

- The function `prompt()` displays the choices to the user as follows:

```
    'A' -- Add a person
    'L' -- List all persons
    'S' -- Search
    EOF -- Quit
```

- The function `menu()` prompts the user to enter the menu choice, validity checks the answer, and calls the proper member function. Exit the function if end-of-file is entered.

- The function `add()` prompts the user for a name and allocates a new `person` object from the heap space to hold this name. The address for this `person` is then appended to the end of the existing `array`, the space for which must be dynamically allocated.

- The function `list()` calls upon the function `person::print()` for each person in the data base.

- The function `search()` prompts the user to enter a string value. It then calls upon the function `person::search()` for each person in the data base. If the search string cannot be found in at least one person, then this function must output an appropriate error message.

A suggested `main()` function would be:

```
int main()
{
    people all ;
    all.menu() ;

    return 0 ;
}
```

Notes

Notes

Chapter 7

More class features

In Chapters 5 and 6 you learned how to write a class definition, encapsulate member data and functions, specify access categories, create instances of the class, and write constructor and destructor functions. However, there are many more features of C++ classes with which you must be familiar before moving on to such topics as function overloading, inheritance, virtual functions, and object-oriented programming.

The special pointer `this`

When several instances of a class come into existence, it naturally follows that each instance has its own separate copy of the member variables. If this were not the case, then for obvious reasons it would be impossible to create more than one instance of a class. On the other hand, even though the class member functions are encapsulated with the data members inside the class definition, it would be very inefficient in terms of memory usage to replicate all of these member functions and store the code for them within each instance. Consequently, only *one* copy of each member function per class is stored in memory, and must therefore be shared by *all* of the instances of the class.

But this poses a big problem for the compiler: How can any given member function of a class know which *instance* it is supposed to be working on? In other words, up to now in a class member function you have simply been referring to the members directly without regard to the fact that when the instantiations occur each (nonstatic) data member will have a different memory address. In other words, all the compiler knows is the *offset* of each data member from the start of the class.

This is not a particularly new problem for a C++ compiler, because in C the comparable situation exists with a structure. The difference, however, is that when a function needs to refer to a data member of a structure, you always use either the direct member operator with some structure object, or the indirect member operator with a pointer of the structure type that points to some structure object. Then the relative address of the particular data member within the structure definition is added to the base address of the object in order to yield the absolute address of the data member. However, in C++ you do not write any instance name or pointer to instance when coding member functions. But, as with a C structure, the address of some class object must still be made available.

The solution to this dilemma is that, in point of fact, each nonstatic member function does have access to a *pointer* variable that *points* to the instance being manipulated. In the case of constructor and destructor functions, the variable points to the instance being created and destroyed. (The reason that the function must be nonstatic will be discussed later.) Fortunately, this pointer variable is supplied to each nonstatic member function *automatically* when the function is called, so that this burden is *not* placed upon you.

This pointer variable has the special name `this` (which is a reserved word in C++). Even though the `this` pointer is implicitly declared, you always have access to it and may use the variable name anywhere you deem appropriate. Remember: like any other formal argument, the `this` pointer has absolutely no meaning outside the scope of a nonstatic member function.

How the pointer `this` works

To explain more fully how the pointer `this` works, let's start by creating a simple class called `integer` and perform some trivial operations with it:

Example 7.1

```
#include <stdio.h>

class integer
{
   int number ;

      public:
   integer(int = 0) ;
   void increment(int) ;
   int get() const ;
} ;

inline integer::integer(int n) : number(n) {}

inline void integer::increment(int n)
{
   number += n ;
}

inline int integer::get() const
{
   return number ;
}

int main()
{
   integer in(1) ;
   in.increment(3) ;
   printf("number = %d\n" , in.get()) ;

   return 0 ;
}
```

The output is:

```
number = 4
```

Now let's re-write the same program in C using a structure instead of a class. In addition, we will combine the structure name with the name of the global functions to imply that there is some kind of relationship between the two. The structure instance `in` gets passed in to the global functions by address, and received in a formal argument called `This`:

Example 7.2

```c
#include <stdio.h>

typedef struct
{
   int number ;
} integer ;

void integer_increment(integer* const This , int n)
{
   This->number += n ;
}

int integer_get(const integer* const This)
{
   return This->number ;
}

int main()
{
   integer in = { 1 } ;
   integer_increment(&in , 3) ;
   printf("number = %d\n" , integer_get(&in)) ;

   return 0 ;
}
```

The output is:

```
number = 4
```

In point of fact, the preceding example very closely resembles the code that the C++ compiler would produce as a result of the process called "name mangling". The goal is to create unique function names within a single scope (class or global), and within that scope to be able to differentiate between overloaded functions having the same name. Note, however, that the argument name `This` has been used instead of the "real" name `this` so that it can be compiled either as a C or C++ program.

Note carefully the declaration of the pointer variable `This` as the first formal argument in the two (simulated) member functions. Its value will be the address of the invoking instance `in`. The `const` keyword directly preceding the argument `This` means that the content of `This` itself cannot be modified. In the function `integer_get()` the first `const` keyword means that the structure object itself (`in`) cannot be modified by the function. Note that this is actually the definition of an accessor function declared `const` in C++.

Remember: In a C++ program, since the pointer variable `this` contains the address of the invoking instance, when you refer to some nonstatic data member of the class within a nonstatic member function, the compiler will *automatically* precede the data member name with `this` and the indirect member operator (->). If you wish, you may write this code explicitly, but there is really no reason to do so.

Dereferencing the pointer `this`

Since the pointer `this` always points to the invoking instance of a nonstatic member function call, if you were to write the expression `*this` then you would be obtaining the invoking object itself. What good does this (!) do you? For one thing, sometimes a nonstatic member function needs to make a copy of the invoking instance so that it can modify the copy without affecting the original instance. For some class `integer`, all you would have to write is:

Example 7.3

```
integer temp(*this) ; // or
integer temp = *this ;
```

Of course, this statement will invoke the copy constructor to properly initialize the new instance. In Chapter 8 you will see other reasons to use `*this` in a nonstatic member function.

Function chaining

Suppose that you have an unruly child named Johnny who has not been particularly good lately. You might say to him, "Johnny, I want you to go to your room, pick up your clothes, make your bed, and wash your hands". In this sentence note that poor Johnny was mentioned by name only *once*, and yet four different concatenated "messages" were sent to him. Contrast this with saying, "Johnny, I want you to go to your room". "Johnny, pick up your clothes". "Johnny, make your bed". "Johnny, wash your hands". Certainly the latter method is more "choppy" and just doesn't sound as smooth as the former method.

Since user-defined instances in C++ are just emulations of real world objects, it naturally follows that messages sent to them should be able to be concatenated in much the same fashion as were the messages sent to Johnny. That is, it should be possible to write an instance name just *once* followed by a series of messages.

In point of fact, the syntax in C++ allows this to happen. The technique is called function chaining or function concatenation. All you have to do is write the statement as follows:

```
instance.message1().message2().message3();
```

The "trick" is to make sure that each method that carries out a message returns the invoking instance (`*this`) by reference (sometimes constant reference). Since this instance then represents the value of the function itself, it may be used as the (implicit) invoking instance of the next function call *without your having to write it again explicitly.*

For example, here is a typical member function `integer::increment()` that conforms to this rule:

Example 7.4

```
integer& integer::increment(int n)
{
  // Perform computations
  return *this ;
}
```

Note the return type of `integer&`. When you do this, a *temporary reference variable* of the type of the class is created that then becomes an *alias* to the invoking instance. Think of it as creating the statement:

Example 7.5

```
integer& temp(*this) ;
```

Now assume that `in` is the invoking instance of the function `integer::increment()`. Then, since `*this` really refers to `in`, the statement is equivalent to:

Example 7.6

```
integer& temp(in) ;
```

And since `temp`, which represents the value of the function call, is just an alias for `in`, the instance `in` itself becomes the output of the function and may be used as the invoking instance of a subsequent member function call.

In the following example, the class `integer` uses function chaining to invoke the `increment()` twice before calling the `print()` function.

Example 7.7

```
#include <stdio.h>

class integer
{
   int number ;

      public:
   integer(int = 0) ;
   integer& increment(int) ;
   void print() ;
} ;

inline integer::integer(int n ) : number(n) {}

inline integer& integer::increment(int n)
{
   number += n ;
   return *this ;
}

inline void integer::print()
{
   printf("number = %d\n" , number) ;
}

int main()
{
   integer in(1) ;
   in.increment(2).increment(3).print() ;

   return 0 ;
}
```

The output is:

```
number = 6
```

You should also note that a return by reference creates an 'lvalue' for the object to which the alias refers. Thus, it is probably not a good idea to return a reference to a private data member of a class, although in some situations this can prove to be very useful. If you need to return by reference in order to create a non-modifiable value instead, then precede the return type with the keyword `const`.

In Chapter 8 you will see how function chaining and return by reference are required in order to properly write an overloaded assignment operator as well as other overloaded operators.

Static class data members

Recall that in C if a variable in some function has been declared to be `static`, then (1) it "lives" in the global space from the start of the program until the end, and (2) it is automatically initialized with a value of zero (unless you override with some other value). However, static variables defined within a function still only have function scope, so that they may not be accessed by any other function.

Even though you cannot declare a member of a C structure to be static, in C++ this is perfectly permissible with class data members. If, in fact, a class data member is declared to be `static`, it means that:

■ It still obeys the rules of data member access (private vs. public);

■ Only a single copy of the data member exists, and it will be shared by all of the instances of the class. That is, the static member becomes *global* to all instances of the class;

■ It still cannot be accessed by a non-member function (unless it is public);

■ It is completely independent of any and all class instantiations that may or may not occur;

■ It is created and initialized before the `main()` function gains control.

Since static class data members are instance-independent, and are only *declared* within the scope of the class definition, you are then responsible for providing the *definition*. This is done by providing a definition in the *global* part of the program after the class definition. This is the case for all static members, `private`, `protected`, and `public`. By default, the value for this definition is zero, as it is in C, for arithmetic types, and the address zero for pointer types.

When writing the definition, you must *not* repeat the word `static`. However, you must repeat the type of the variable, followed by the class name, scope resolution operator, and variable name.

For example, in the class `integer` the variable `counter` has been declared to be `static`.

Example 7.8

```
class integer
{
   // static declaration
   static int counter ;
} ;

// static definition
int integer::counter = 0 ;
```

Note that a static data member may actually be an instance of some other class. In this case the constructor for the class of which the static is an instance will automatically get called when the definition of the static occurs, which is before the `main()` function begins.

One good usage of a class static variable would be to keep count of the number of instantiations of the class. Therefore, in this program the constructor function simply adds 1 to a `static` counter each time it gains control.

Example 7.9

```
#include <stdio.h>

class Keep_count
{
   // static declaration
   static int counter ;

     public:
   Keep_count() ;
   void print() ;
} ;

// static definition
int Keep_count::counter = 0 ;

inline Keep_count::Keep_count()
{
   ++counter ;
}

inline void Keep_count::print()
{
   printf("counter = %d\n" , counter) ;
}
```

```
int main()
{
    Keep_count kc1 , kc2 , kc3 ;
    kc1.print() ;

    return 0 ;
}
```

The output is:

```
counter = 3
```

If the static data member happens to be a user-defined type, then its constructor function will be called when it gets instantiated in the global space. Here is the preceding example, but now the static member counter is type integer.

Example 7.10

```
#include <stdio.h>

class integer
{
    int number ;
        public:

    integer(int = 0) ;
    integer& increment() ;
    int get() const ;
} ;

inline integer::integer(int n) : number(n) {}

integer& integer::increment()
{
    ++number ;
    return *this ;
}

inline integer::get() const
{
    return number ;
}
```

```
class Keep_count
{
   // static declaration
   static integer counter ;

      public:
   Keep_count() ;
   void print() ;
} ;

// static definition
integer Keep_count::counter(0) ;

inline Keep_count::Keep_count()
{
   counter.increment() ;
}

inline void Keep_count::print()
{
   printf("counter = %d\n" , counter.get()) ;
}

int main()
{
   Keep_count kc1 , kc2 , kc3 ;
   kc1.print() ;

   return 0 ;
}
```

The output is:

```
counter = 3
```

Static class member functions

Since C++ requires an instance of the class to invoke a *nonstatic* member function, and since static class members are instance-independent, it doesn't quite make sense to use this type of member function to display the variable counter in Example 7.9. To solve this dilemma, C++ provides the syntax to define a *static* member function of a class.

The characteristics of a static member function are as follows:

■ While it is a member function, there is *never* a this pointer as the first formal argument. By implication, the function can manipulate *only* static data members of the class;

- It cannot be declared as an accessor function, i.e., with the keyword const following the argument list;

- Since it is instance-independent, it can be called "directly" by using the class name and scope resolution operator (assuming that it is public);

- It may be called via some instance of the class, or even by an uninitialized pointer of the class type, but this is not recommended.

To make a member function static, precede its return type with the keyword static. If you are both declaring and defining the function, then use the keyword only in the declaration. Remember: because there is no this pointer, you *cannot* access nonstatic data members, nor call upon nonstatic member functions.

Here is the Example 7.9 again, but now the print() function has been made static. Note carefully how this function is called, and how it can now be called *before* any instantiations are done.

Example 7.11

```
#include <stdio.h>

class Keep_count
{
   static int counter ;

      public:
   Keep_count() ;
   static void print() ;
} ;

int Keep_count::counter = 0 ;

inline Keep_count::Keep_count()
{
   ++counter ;
}

inline void Keep_count::print()
{
   printf("counter = %d\n" , counter) ;
}

int main()
{
   Keep_count::print() ;
   Keep_count kc1 , kc2 , kc3 ;
   Keep_count::print() ;

   return 0 ;
}
```

The output is:

```
counter = 0
counter = 3
```

Another use of a class that needs a static data member occurs when this member must be an instance of some other class that should be instantiated *only once* regardless of the number of instantiations of the containing class. For example, here is a class called `Random` (stored in the file `random.h`) whose job is to seed the random number generator and return a random number in some range specified by the user. Note that there are no data members in this class, so that any instantiations do not have a state.

Example 7.12

```
#ifndef RANDOM_H
#define RANDOM_H

#include <stdlib.h>
#include <time.h>

class Random
{
    public:
  Random() ;
  unsigned get_random(int) const ;
} ;

inline Random::Random()
{
   srand((unsigned)time(0)) ;
}

inline unsigned Random::get_random(int n) const
{
   return rand() % n ;
}

#endif
```

Such a class would be very useful in gambling situations when the seeding of the random number generator should be transparent to the user.

For example, here is a class called `die` (stored in the file `die.h`) that emulates a die that you would use in games of chance. For complete flexibility, the number of sides on the die has not been "hard-coded", so that instead the actual number is specified by an argument to the constructor function. Of course, this value defaults to 6,

213

which has been specified by a static constant. Note also that an instance of the `Random` class called `rn` has been declared `static` in the class so that only *one* such instance will ever exist even though the class `die` itself will get instantiated more than once. The constructor for the instance `rn` will be called even before the `main()` function is entered. Finally, the function `die::toss()` has been declared to return a `die` by reference so that function chaining can occur.

Example 7.13

```
#ifndef DIE_H
#define DIE_H

#include "random.h"

class die
{
    private:
  static const int def_value ;
  const int sides ;
  int* faces ;
  int face_up ;
  static Random rn ;

    public:
  die(int = def_value) ;
  ~die() ;
  die& toss() ;
  int get_value() const ;
} ;

inline die::~die()
{
  delete [] faces ;
}

inline die& die::toss()
{
  face_up = faces[rn.get_random(sides)] ;
  return *this ;
}

inline int die::get_value() const
{
  return face_up ;
}

#endif
```

The file `die.cpp` provides the definitions for the static declarations and for the out-of-line constructor function. If it is not pre-compiled, then it must be included in a project just *once* in order to avoid a duplicate definition error from the linker.

Example 7.14

```
// The file "die.cpp"

#include "die.h"

// static definitions
const int die::def_value = 6 ;
Random die::rn ;

// Out-of-line constructor function
die::die(int s) : sides(s <= 0 ? def_value : s) ,
                  faces(new int[sides])
{
   for(int i = 0 ; i < sides ; ++i)
     faces[i] = i + 1 ;
}
```

Here is a program that uses the `die` class to create a pair of dice. Then this pair is rolled six times and the resulting values shown.

Example 7.15

```
#include <stdio.h>
#include "die.h"

#include "die.cpp"

int main()
{
   die die1 , die2(-1) ;
   for(int i = 0 ; i < 6 ; ++i)
    {
       int value1 = die1.toss().get_value() ;
       int value2 = die2.toss().get_value() ;
       int total = value1 + value2 ;
       printf("%d + %d = %d\n" , value1 , value2 , total) ;
    }

   return 0 ;
}
```

Some typical output would be:

```
4 + 1 = 5
2 + 5 = 7
5 + 5 = 10
5 + 3 = 8
3 + 6 = 9
4 + 1 = 5
```

In the world of object-oriented programming, static class data members are very useful to maintain the state of a single instance even though the class may be instantiated many times. The advantage of having more than one class with multiple instantiations is that a single message can be used to affect the object in different ways. This topic is covered in more detail in Chapter 11.

The size of a class

If you ever need to compute the size of a class, you may use the sizeof operator. This will tell you how much space any instance of the class is occupying in the global space, on the stack, or on the heap. Just be aware that the only members that are considered are *nonstatic data* members. In other words, functions and static data members are *not* counted for the simple reason that they are *not* replicated for each instantiation. In addition, the size of a class is guaranteed to be greater than zero. In other words, all instantiated objects will have a size of at least one byte.

 This definition of the size of a class will be modified slightly in Chapter 11 when virtual functions are introduced.

Friend functions

As you know, because of encapsulation and data hiding, the only functions that have unrestricted access to a class's private members are the member functions of that particular class. Any attempt by a non-member function to directly access these data members (read or write) will result in a compilation error.

However, there are several circumstances under which a *non-member* function must have access to these private members. The easy way to do this would be to change the access category from private to public, but then this completely violates the whole concept of encapsulation and data hiding. So what can you do?

This dilemma can be solved by declaring the function in question to be a *friend* of the class in which the private data members are located. That is, *the class in which the private members are located bestows friendship upon the function*, not the other way around. In this fashion, the friend function then has access to *all* of the class's members, including the private ones. Remember, the function itself *cannot* choose to become a friend of a class ("I choose to be your friend; therefore, I now have complete and unlimited access to your private members"), because this would make no sense and violate the principle of data hiding.

There are three situations in which a class may grant friendship:

- To a non-member function;
- To another class (implying that all of the member functions of that class are friend functions);
- To a particular member function of another class.

How a friend function may access the private members

Because a friend function is always a *non-member* function of the class that bestows the friendship, it *cannot* be called via some instance of the class. Consequently, there is no `this` pointer that the compiler can use to get at the individual members of the class. So the logical question then becomes, how can the friend function refer to the individual members of the class that gave it friendship?

The first answer is to always call the function with at least one argument consisting of an instance of the class which bestowed the friendship. This argument is usually passed into the function by address or reference. (It could be passed in by value if you only needed to access a private or protected data member.)

The second answer is to create an instance of the class that bestowed the friendship within a class that has this friendship. Then this instance may be used with the direct member operator to access the private members.

If the friend function needs to gain direct access to a static member of the class, then this member must be preceded by the class name and scope resolution operator.

Note that friend functions may also be inline functions. That is, if the friend function is defined within the scope of the class definition, then the inline request to the compiler is automatically made. If the friend function is defined outside the class definition, then you must precede the return type with the keyword `inline` in order to make the request.

How to write a friend function

As just stated, a friend function may be either declared or defined within the scope of a class definition. In both cases you must precede the return type with the keyword `friend` to tell the compiler that this function is *not* a member function. Note that the access category in which this declaration appears is *completely irrelevant*. If you only declare the friend function within the class definition, then obviously you must define it outside the class, but *do not* repeat the keyword `friend`.

To repeat: the keyword `friend` (like the keyword `static`) can appear *only* within the context of a class definition.

Here is an example in which a friend function is being used to output the value of the private data member called `number`.

Example 7.16

```
#include <stdio.h>

class integer
{
   int number ;

      public:
   integer(int n = 0) : number(n) {}

   // friend function declaration
   friend void print(const integer&) ;
} ;

// friend function definition
inline void print(const integer& in)
{
   printf("number = %d\n" , in.number) ;
}

int main()
{
   integer in = 1 ;
   print(in) ;

   return 0 ;
}
```

The output is:

```
number = 1
```

A friend function with two instances of a class

Sometimes a function needs to have access to two or more instances of some class. If this function were to be a member function, then one of the instances would serve as the invoking instance, while the others would be explicit arguments. This doesn't quite make sense. After all, the objects are "equal", and should be treated "equally" insofar as the function is concerned. The solution is to create a friend function in which *all* instances become the explicit arguments.

A good example would be a function that is designed to add two instances of some class. From a very high level viewpoint, any such add function takes in two arguments, does some processing, and yields a new argument of the same type. Since the two input arguments are "balanced" and may be sent to the function in either order (under the commutative rule of arithmetic), both arguments should be explicitly written. And since the function will most likely need to gain access to the private parts of the class to which the arguments belong, this function should be a friend function.

In the following example, the friend function `add()` is used to add two complex numbers and return a new instance. Both instances of the `complex` class are used as explicit arguments to the function.

Example 7.17

```
#include <stdio.h>

class complex
{
   float real ;
   float imag ;

     public:
   complex(float = 0.0 , float = 0.0) ;
   void print() ;
   // friend function declaration
   friend complex add(const complex& , const complex&) ;
} ;

inline complex::complex(float r , float i) : real(r) , imag(i) {}

inline void complex::print()
{
   printf("%0.2f%+0.2fi\n" , real , imag) ;
}

// friend function definition
inline complex add(const complex& c1 , const complex& c2)
{
   return complex(c1.real + c2.real , c1.imag + c2.imag) ;
}
```

```
int main ()
{
    complex c1 (1.1 , 2.2) , c2 (3 , 4) ;
    complex c3 = add (c1 , c2) ;
    c3.print () ;
    complex c4 (2 , -7.1) ;
    c3 = add (c3 , c4) ;
    c3.print () ;

    return 0 ;
}

The output is:

4.10+6.20i
6.10-0.90i
```

☞ Sometimes it is possible to avoid the friend declaration if the global function can use accessor functions to retrieve the private data members of the class.

Granting friendship to another class

To grant friendship to another class, write the keyword `friend` followed by the class's name. The keyword `class` is optional. Note that this declaration also implies a forward declaration of the class to which the friendship is being granted. The implication of this declaration is that *all* of the member functions of the friend class are friend functions of the class that bestows the friendship.

In this linked list example the class `node` is granting friendship to the class `list` because the member functions of `list` need to have direct access to the private data members `node::data` and `node::next`.

Example 7.18

```
#include <stdio.h>

class node
{
    int data ;
    node* next ;
    // private constructor
    node (int = 0) ;
    friend class list ;
} ;

inline node::node (int n) : data (n) , next (0) {}
```

```
class list
{
   node* head ;
   node* tail ;

      public:
   list() ;
   ~list() ;
   list& add(int) ;
   void print() ;
} ;

inline list::list() : head(0) , tail(0) {}

// Delete all nodes from the list
list::~list()
{
   node* p = head ;
   while(p != 0)
    {
       node* temp = p->next ;
       delete p ;
       p = temp ;
    }
}

// Add a new node to the list
list& list::add(int value)
{
   // Get space
   node* n = new node(value) ;

   // If this is the first node to be created, its
   // address becomes the head
   if(!head)
      head = n ;
   // Otherwise, it's not the first node and the tail must
   // point to the node being added
   else
      tail->next = n ;

   // The new node is now the tail
   tail = n ;

   return *this ;
}
```

```
// Print the data from all of the nodes in the list
void list::print()
{
  node* p = head ;
  while(p != 0)
    {
      printf("%d\n" , p->data) ;
      p = p->next ;
    }
}

int main()
{
  list my_list ;
  my_list.add(1).add(2).add(3) ;
  my_list.print() ;

  return 0 ;
}
```

The output is:

```
1
2
3
```

Granting friendship to a member function of another class

If you want class A to grant friendship to one or more individual member functions of class B, then you must code the classes and their member functions in this manner:

- Forward declare class A;

- Define class B and declare (*not* define) the member functions;

- Define class A in which you declare the friendship for the member functions of class B. Of course, you must qualify the names of these functions using the class name B and the scope resolution operator.

- Define the member functions of class B;

Here is a repeat of the previous example showing steps 1-3, but now the node class (class A) is granting friendship specifically to the function list::~list(), list::add(), and list::print() of the list class (class B).

Example 7.19

```
#include <stdio.h>

class node ;

class list
{
   node* head ;
   node* tail ;

      public:
   list() ;
   ~list() ;
   list& add(int) ;
   void print() ;
} ;

class node
{
   int data ;
   node* next ;

      public:
   node(int = 0) ;
   friend list::~list() ;
   friend list::add(int) ;
   friend list::print() ;
} ;

// Definitions of all member functions of class list follow
```

Two classes having the same friend

Sometimes two or more classes need to grant friendship to the same non-member function. This would be the case when the non-member function needs to refer to an instance of each class, implying that it needs access to the private members of both classes. To do this:

■   Forward declare all of the classes except one;

■   Define the remaining class in which you declare the friend function;

■   Define the remaining classes in which you repeat the friend declaration;

■   Define the friend function.

In this example, the function add() needs to gain access to the private members of two different classes (floating and integer) in order to add the members together.

Therefore, the function takes as formal arguments instances of both classes by constant reference.

Example 7.20

```
#include <stdio.h>

// Forward declaration needed
class floating ;

class integer
{
   int number ;

      public:
   integer(int = 0) ;

   // Give friendship to add()
   friend float add(const integer& , const floating&) ;
} ;

inline integer::integer(int n) : number(n) {}

class floating
{
   float fl ;

      public:
   floating(float = 0.0) ;

   // Give friendship to add()
   friend float add(const integer& , const floating&) ;
} ;

inline floating::floating(float f) : fl(f) {}

// The friend function defined
float add(const integer& i , const floating& f)
{
   return (i.number + f.fl) ;
}

int main()
{
   integer int_number(1) ;
   floating float_number(0.234) ;
   printf("%0.2f\n" , add(int_number , float_number)) ;

   return 0 ;
}
```

The output is:

```
1.23
```

Declaring pointers to class members

Suppose you have a class that contains various public functions to do a variety of tasks. Instead of executing these tasks as they are encountered, you need to queue them up in an array or linked list for execution at a later time. One way to "remember" which member function is to be called would be to store the address of that function in an array or linked list. Then, later on in the program, the array or linked list would be traversed and the appropriate function executed.

Obviously, what is needed in this scenario is the ability to create a pointer to a class member, usually a nonstatic function. Just as you can declare pointers to non-class variables and functions, it is possible to declare pointers to the individual function members of a class. The syntax, however, is a little different than what you are accustomed to using. The main difference is that such a pointer must always be qualified with the name of the class to which it pertains. This implies that a pointer-to-function of some class A can never be the same type as a pointer-to-function of some class B, even if the functions themselves take the same argument list and have the same return type.

Ignoring classes for the moment, a pointer to a function called `ptr_function` that takes a `float` as its one argument and returns an `int` would be declared as:

Example 7.21

```
int (*ptr_function)(float) ;
```

If you wish, you may use a `typedef` to simplify the creation of more than one variable:

Example 7.22

```
typedef int (*PTR)(float) ;
PTR ptr_function ;
```

If you have a function `f()` that does indeed take a `float` and return an `int`, you may store its address into the pointer variables. Since the name of a function yields the address of that function, the `&` operator is optional.

Example 7.23

```
int f(float) ;
ptr_function = f ;
```

Now let's do the same thing for a class member function. First, in order to create a pointer-to-member-function variable of some class `integer`, you must qualify the pointer name with the class name and scope resolution operator.

Example 7.24

```
int (integer::*ptr_function)(float) ;
```

Once again, you may use a `typedef`:

Example 7.25

```
typedef int (integer::*PTR)(float) ;
PTR ptr_function ;
```

To take the address of a class member function called `integer::f()`, you must qualify the function name with the class name and scope resolution operator. In addition, the member must have public access. Note that unlike non-member functions, the AT&T 2.1 spec calls for the use of the address operator. Now you may write:

Example 7.26

```
ptr_function = &integer::f ;
```

Don't forget that in order to store the address of `integer::f()` into these pointers, there must be an exact match on:

■ The type and number of formal arguments;

■ The return type of the function;

■ The class name.

Invoking functions using pointers to class members

Creating a pointer-to-member-function is only half the story. In order to provide a `this` pointer, all nonstatic member functions of a class still need to be invoked by an instance or pointer of the class to which they belong. However, in this case a new C++ operator is needed.

- If you want to use an instance of the class to call the member function through the pointer, then the instance must be followed with the operator '`.*`' (dot-star).

- If you want to use a pointer of the class to call the member function through the pointer, then the pointer must be followed with the operator '`->*`' (arrow-star).

- Be sure to enclose the instance or pointer name, the operator itself, and the function name in one set of parentheses. This is then followed by the actual argument list.

Note the similarity to calling non-member functions using the dot or arrow operators, only now you add an asterisk.

Here is a simple program that uses pointers to class members.

Example 7.27

```
#include <stdio.h>

class integer
{
    public:
  int f(float n)
   {
      printf("number = %2.2f\n" , n) ;
      return n ;
   }
} ;

int main()
{
  // Create pointer to function
  int (integer::*ptr_function)(float) ;

  // Use a typedef
  typedef int (integer::*PTR)(float) ;
  PTR ptr_func ;

  // Store address of function f() into both pointers
  ptr_function = ptr_func = &integer::f ;

  // Create an instance
  integer in ;

  // Call function f() directly
```

```
        int n1 = in.f(1.1) ;
        printf("n1 = %d\n" , n1) ;

        // Call the function f() using the instance and the
        // pointer
        int n2 = (in.*ptr_function)(2.2) ;
        printf("n2 = %d\n" , n2) ;
        int n3 = (in.*ptr_func)(3.3) ;
        printf("n3 = %d\n" , n3) ;

        // Store the address of the instance into a pointer to
        // the instance
        integer* ptr_integer = &in ;

        // Call function f() using the pointer to the instance
        // and the pointer to function
        int n4 = (ptr_integer->*ptr_function)(4.4) ;
        printf("n4 = %d\n" , n4) ;
        int n5 = (ptr_integer->*ptr_func)(5.5) ;
        printf("n5 = %d\n" , n5) ;

        return 0 ;
}
```

The output is:

```
number = 1.10
n1 = 1
number = 2.20
n2 = 2
number = 3.30
n3 = 3
number = 4.40
n4 = 4
number = 5.50
n5 = 5
```

Here is another example, but now a member function takes as an argument a pointer to another member function. In order to call the function that the pointer points at, the invoking instance, as specified by the this pointer, must be used.

Example 7.28

```
#include <stdio.h>

class integer
{
        public:

   // f1 is a function that takes 2 arguments:
   //     1) A pointer to a member function that takes an
   //        int as its one argument, and returns void
   //     2) An int

   void f1(void(integer::*ptr)(int) , int n)
    {
     // Call the function pointed at by ptr, using 'n' as
     // the one argument
     (this ->* ptr)(n) ;
    }

   // f2 is a function that takes an int as its one argument,
   // and returns void

   void f2(int n)
    {
       printf("integer::f2 called with %d\n" , n) ;
    }
} ;

int main()
{
   integer in ;

   // Call f1() passing it 2 arguments:
   //   1) The address of f2
   //   2) The constant 1

   in.f1(&integer::f2 , 1) ;

   return 0 ;
}
```

The output is:

```
integer::f2 called with 1
```

229

If the member function is declared `static`, then for purposes of declaring a pointer to it, you must treat it as a non-member function. For instance, in this example the member function `integer::f()` is static.

Example 7.29

```
#include <stdio.h>

class integer
{
    public:
  static int f(float n)
   {
      printf("number = %2.2f\n" , n) ;
      return n ;
   }
} ;

int main()
{
  // Create pointer to function
  int (*ptr_function)(float) ;

  // Store address of function into pointer to function
  ptr_function = &integer::f ;

  // Call the function directly
  int n1 = integer::f(1.2) ;
  printf("n1 = %d\n" , n1) ;

  // Call the function using an instance and a pointer to
  // function
  int n2 = (*ptr_function)(3.4) ;
  printf("n2 = %d\n" , n2) ;

  return 0 ;
}
```

The output is:

```
number = 1.20
n1 = 1
number = 3.40
n2 = 3
```

Unions

Recall from C that a union is a kind of structure whose members all begin at offset zero and whose size is sufficient to hold the largest member. In other words, all members of a union occupy the same memory location once the union is instantiated.

In C++ a union may have member functions, including constructors and a destructor (but no virtual functions are allowed). It is illegal to have as a member of a union an instance of another class that contains either a constructor, destructor, or user-defined assignment operator. In addition, a member of a union cannot be declared `static`.

A union may be anonymous. This means that it declares an unnamed object within the scope of a class. The members of this union must have names distinct from the other names within the class and may be referenced directly. The access of the members of an anonymous union may not be `private` or `protected`. Also, unlike a "normal" union, an anonymous union may not have function members.

Consider the following situation. You wish to examine the bits of a floating point number (stored in IEEE format) in order to display them in some meaningful representation. The problem here is that the bitwise operators cannot be used on floating point data types. Therefore, by using an anonymous union containing both a `float` and a `long`, you can "trick" the compiler into thinking that it is really operating upon a `long` data type, whereas in fact it is really operating upon the `float`.

The following example shows how this can be done.

Example 7.30

```
#include <stdio.h>
#include <math.h>

const int bits = 8 ;
const int size = bits * sizeof(float) ;

class IEEE
{
  // Private member data
  int sign_bit , exp , digit ;
  double man ;
  unsigned long mask ;
  const int sign_start ;
  const int exp_start , exp_end ;
  const int man_start ;
```

```
    // Private member functions
    void sign() ;
    void exponent(int) ;
    void mantissa(int) ;
    void results() ;

    // Anonymous union
    union
     {
        float fl ;
        long number ;
    } ;

      public:
    IEEE(float = 0.0) ;
    int input() ;
    void print() ;
} ;

inline IEEE::IEEE(float n)
        : fl(n) , exp(0) , man(0.0) , mask(1L << size - 1) ,
          sign_start(0) , exp_start(1) , exp_end(8) ,
          man_start(9) {}

int IEEE::input()
{
  printf("Enter the float value: ") ;
  return scanf("%f" , &fl) ;
}

void IEEE::print()
{
  for(int i = 0 ; i < size ; ++i)
   {
      digit = (number & mask) ? 1 : 0 ;
      if(i == sign_start)
         sign() ;
      else if(i >= exp_start && i <= exp_end)
         exponent(i) ;
      else
         mantissa(i) ;
      number <<= 1 ;
   }
   results() ;
}

void IEEE::sign()
{
  printf("%d" , digit) ;
  sign_bit = digit ;
}
```

```
void IEEE::exponent(int i)
{
   if(i == exp_start)
    {
      printf("-") ;
      exp = 0 ;
    }
   printf("%d" , digit) ;
   exp = (exp * 2) + digit ;
}

void IEEE::mantissa(int i)
{
   if(i == man_start)
    {
      printf("-") ;
      man = 0.0 ;
    }
   printf("%d" , digit) ;
   man += digit / pow(2 , i - 8) ;
}

void IEEE::results()
{
   double result ;
   printf("\n\nExponent: %d\n" , exp) ;
   printf("Mantissa: %.10f\n" , man) ;
   result = (1 + man) * (pow(2 , exp - 127)) ;

   if(sign_bit == 1)
      result = -result ;
   printf("Original value: %0.15f\n\n" , result) ;
}

int main()
{
   IEEE number ;
   int r ;
   while((r = number.input()) != EOF)
    {
      if(r == 0)
        puts("Non-numeric input") ;
      else
        number.print() ;
      fflush(stdin) ;
    }

   return 0 ;
}
```

A typical run would be:

```
Enter the float value: -1.2
1-01111111-00110011001100110011010

Exponent: 127
Mantissa: 0.2000000477
Original value: -1.200000047683716

Enter the float value: 8.0
0-10000010-00000000000000000000000

Exponent: 130
Mantissa: 0.0000000000
Original value: 8.000000000000000

Enter the float value: ^Z
```

■ Review Questions

1) Explain how the pointer `this` works.

2) What is `*this`?

3) Explain how nonstatic member function calls can be concatenated together.

4) What is a static data member of a class? Why would you use one?

5) What is a static member function?

6) Why can't a static member function access a nonstatic member of a class?

7) What is a friend function, and why is it needed?

8) How is friendship granted by a class?

9) Why does a friend function need to take as an input argument at least one instance of the class bestowing the friendship?

10) Explain how a pointer to a member function works.

11) Explain how a union works.

■ Exercise #1

Given the following class definition that emulates a fractional number:

```
class fraction
{
      private:
  long num ;   // numerator
  long den ;   // denominator

      public:
  // All member and friend functions
} ;
```

declare within the function definition and define outside the definition:

■ An inline constructor that accepts zero, one or two arguments. The numerator defaults to zero, while the denominator defaults to 1. If one argument is specified, assume that it represents the numerator. Use only the member initialization list to construct the instance. If the denominator is equal to zero, change it to a 1.

■ An inline copy constructor. Use only the member initialization list to construct the instance.

■ A function called print() that displays the fraction in its reduced form. In order to do this, call upon the global function gcd() that will return the greatest common denominator of its two input numbers:

```
long gcd(long x , long y)
{
    return (x == 0) ? y : gcd(y % x , x) ;
}
```

■ A friend function called add() that returns the sum of two fractions.

■ A friend function called subtract() that returns the difference of two fractions.

■ A friend function called multiply() that returns the product of two fractions.

■ A friend function called divide() that returns the quotient of the first fraction divided by the second fraction.

■ An inline function called inc() that adds 1 to the invoking instance. Be sure to use the add() function and to allow for function chaining.

Use the following main() function:

```
int main()
{
   fraction f1 , f2(2L , 0L) ;
   fraction f3(f2) ;
   f1.print() ;
   f2.print() ;
   f3.print() ;
   f3 = add(f3 , fraction(-5 , 4)) ;
   f1 = add(f2 , f3) ;
   f1.print() ;
```

```
        f1 = sub(f2 , f3) ;
        f1.print() ;
        f1 = mult(f2 , f3) ;
        f1.print() ;
        f1.inc().inc().print() ;
        f1 = div(f2 , f3) ;
        f1.print() ;

        return 0 ;
    }
```

The output should be:

```
0/1
2/1
2/1
11/4
5/4
3/2
7/2
8/3
```

■ Exercise #2

Write a class called `date` whose purpose is to convert a month and day into the absolute day of the year, ranging from 1 to 365. Ignore leap year, but be sure to check the month and day for valid data. As part of the class, include a static table that contains the number of days in each of the 12 months. Then write a program to test your class.

■ Exercise #3

Create a class called `dice` that contains a variable number of instances of the `die` class, defaulting to the number 2. The member functions should provide the capability to roll the dice, obtain the value of any individual die, and obtain the total of all dice.

Then test the class by rolling the dice 100,000 times to generate statistics on the number of occurrences of each of the 11 possible totals. For example, part of your output should show that the number 7 occurs once out of every 6 rolls.

■ Exercise #4

Write a program that plays a dice game called C Raps. (Note: Any resemblance to the dice game craps is purely coincidental.) This game consists of 3 sub-games, any one of which you may choose to play.

■ Pass Line — In this game you roll the dice (called the come-out roll) and look at the total. If this total is equal to 7 or 11, then you win the amount of the bet. If the total is equal to 2, 3 or 12, then you lose the bet. Any other total of the dice becomes the "point", and you continue to roll the dice until you either (a) roll the point total again, in which case you win the amount of the bet, or (b) roll a total of 7, in which case you lose the amount of the bet. If the total of the dice is not 7 and not equal to the point, then you roll again, and continue to roll, until either condition (a) or (b) is met. Note that once the point has been determined, it does not change for subsequent rolls of the dice.

■ Field Bet — In this game you roll the dice just once. If this total is 3, 4, 9, 10 or 11, then you win the amount of the bet. If the total is 2, then you win double the bet. If this total is 12, then you win triple the bet. For any other total of the dice (5, 6, 7, or 8), you lose the amount of the bet.

■ Any 7 — In this game you roll the dice just once. If this total is equal to 7, then you win quadruple the bet. For any other total of the dice, you lose the amount of the bet.

Before the start of each sub-game, display the amount of money in your bankroll. Then display a prompt to enter an (integer) bet. If this bet amount is a non-integer, or greater than what is currently in the your bankroll, or is less than or equal to zero, display an error message and re-prompt.

To determine which sub-game you wish to play, display a menu of choices, as follows:

```
(P)ass Line
(F)ield bet
(A)ny 7
(E)xit
```

Play continues until you either choose Exit, or run out of money. At this time display either your net gain, net loss, or a break-even message for this session at the C Raps table.

Start by creating a class called Bankroll that controls the manipulations of the bankroll amount and the bet. The definition should closely resemble the following:

```
class Bankroll
{
    int balance ;
    int bet ;

      public:
    Bankroll(int) ;
    void prompt_for_bet() ;
    int get_bet() const ;
    int get_balance() const ;
    void add(int) ;
    void subtract(int) ;
} ;
```

Next, create a class called `dice` (from Exercise #3). Finally, create a class called `c_raps` that contains private instances of the `dice` class and the `bankroll` class. The member functions to play the 3 types of games should be private. The only public member functions are the constructor, destructor, and `prompt()`.

The `main()` function should appear as follows:

```
int main()
{
    const int start = 100 ; // Starting bankroll amount
    c_raps game(start) ;
    game.prompt() ;

    return 0 ;
}
```

Be sure to test the program thoroughly, including all possible error conditions that can occur, such as betting too much money, making a negative or non-integer bet, choosing an invalid sub-game, etc. Also, at the very minimum show the results of winning on the come-out roll, losing on the come-out roll, winning by making the point, losing by failing to make the point, winning the field bet, losing the field bet, winning any 7, and losing any 7. Also, show the 3 possible end-of-game situations (win, lose, and draw). When showing a dice total, be sure to show the values of the individual dice.

■ **Exercise #5**

Write a class called `card` that contains two private *constant* data members: `suit` and `pips`. Then write three accessor functions: `get_pips()` that returns the value of `pips`, `get_suit()` that returns the value of `suit`, and `display()` that translates the suit and pips into meaningful verbiage, e.g., "The Four of Hearts". Also write a friend function called `equal()` that returns 'true' if its two input card instances are equal.

Next, write a class called `deck_of_cards` whose private data members consist of a 52-position array of pointers to card and an integer called `cards_in_use` that reflects the number of cards that have been dealt. Also include an instance of the random number generator class. The constructor function must allocate space for the cards themselves from the heap, and provide the proper initialization for a standard deck. The `suit` should range from 0 to 3, and the `pips` should range from 0 to 12. Write a mutator function that shuffles the deck and optionally displays a message, an accessor function that obtains a pointer to the next card in the deck, and an accessor function that returns the number of cards that have been dealt.

To test all classes, write a program that instantiates the deck of cards, shuffles it, and deals out all 52 cards. Also, prove that all 52 cards have been dealt.

Exercise #6

Using the classes `card` and `deck_of_cards` that were developed in Exercise #5, write a program that empirically determines the chances of obtaining at least one exact match if the top cards of two decks are turned over one at a time until both decks are completely dealt. Be sure to use a friend function called `equal()` to do the comparison of the cards. Run 10,000 tests to obtain a good statistical average.

Exercise #7

Using the classes `card` and `deck_of_cards` that were developed in Exercise #5, write a program that plays a game called Simple Bridge. In this game four players, North, South, East and West, each receive 13 cards. Each hand is valued according to the following scheme:

```
Ace            4 points
King:          3 points
Queen:         2 points
Jack:          1 point
Anything else: 0 points
```

You must create a new class called `hand` that contains an array of 13 cards, and a count of the number of cards currently in use. You should have member functions to initialize the hand, store a card into the next available array element, display the entire hand, and get the point total of the hand.

The `main()` function should contain an instance of the `deck_of_cards` class and a 4-element array consisting of the `hand` class. Elements 0 and 2 of this array comprise the North-South team, and elements 1 and 3 comprise the East-West team. After dealing out the four hands, show each hand followed by the total points in that hand. Then add the North-South points together, and the East-West points together, and show these totals. Whichever team has the higher total should be declared the winner of the hand.

Exercise #8

Using the classes `card` and `deck_of_cards` that were developed in Exercise #5, write a program that plays the card game Blackjack (also known as "21"). You, as the player, will be competing against the computer (the dealer). The player starts with some initial amount of money as the bankroll.

In this game you are dealt 2 cards, and the dealer 2 cards, but you are only able to see one of the dealer's cards. The object of the game is to draw cards from the deck so that the total of the cards comes as close to 21 as possible without going over 21. Each card counts at its own face value, except that picture cards count as 10 and aces count as either 1 or 11. To determine what value to give to an ace, use this rule: if the total of all cards is less than 12, then add 10 to the total.

If your or the dealer's original 2 cards total 21, then that hand ends immediately with a winner (called Blackjack), unless both of you have 21, in which case it is a draw and no money is exchanged. Any other time that a total of 21 is reached, it is *not* considered to be a Blackjack.

You have the first choice to receive additional cards ("hits"). If you go over 21, then you lose your bet and that hand is over. If you choose to receive no more cards ("stand"), then the dealer *must* draw cards until the total reaches 17 or higher. If the dealer goes over 21, then you win the hand. Otherwise, the dealer's total is compared against your total, and whoever has the higher total wins. If the totals are equal, then it is a draw.

If your first 2 cards total either 10 or 11, then you have the option to "double down", which means that the amount of the bet is automatically doubled (assuming that the money is in the bank account), and you will receive *exactly one more card*, after which it becomes the dealer's turn. (In this case it is impossible for you to go "bust".) Of course, you may choose *not* to double down, in which case you have the normal option to hit or stand.

Start by creating a class called `hand` that contains:

- An array of instances of the `card` class (15 such cards should suffice).
- A count of cards in use for the hand.
- A constructor function that outputs the message "Welcome to the blackjack table, sucker!" if the dealer's hand is being constructed.
- A constructor function that outputs the message "Shut up and deal!" if the player's hand is being constructed.
- A destructor function that outputs the message "Better luck next time" if the dealer's hand is being destructed.
- A destructor function that outputs the message "No tip for you, buddy" if the player's hand is being destructed.
- Various member functions, as needed.

Next, create a class called `blackjack` that contains:

- An instance of the class `deck_of_cards`.
- Two instances of the `hand` class, one for the dealer, and one for the player.
- A constructor function that initializes the bankroll amount and the two hands.
- A destructor function that outputs the message "Anyone for bridge?"
- Various member functions, as needed.

■ Exercise #9

Given the following class definitions:
```
const int max = 100 ;
class node
{
   int* ptr ;
   long size ;
   node() ;
   friend class memories ;
} ;

class memories
{
   node array[max] ;

      public:
   memories() ;
   int* malloc(long) ;
   int* realloc(int* , long) ;
   void free(int*) ;
   void report() ;
} ;
```

write the member functions of the classes node and memories that emulate the corresponding functions in C (assuming that only variables of type int are used). The array must keep track of all of the memory obtained. Be sure to check for all error conditions, e.g., space on the heap not available, attempting to reallocate or free space that is not in use, etc.

Then write a main() function that tests the various functions.

■ Exercise #10

Using the parser class that you wrote in Chapter 5 Exercise #5, write a program that produces an alphabetized cross reference listing of all of the words contained in a line of input data.

To keep track of each unique word encountered, start by creating a class called one_word as follows:
```
class one_word
{
   friend class all_words ;
   char* word ;
   int* positions ;
   int counter ;
} ;
```

The data member `word` will point to a word whose space must be allocated on the heap. The data member `positions` will point to an array of integers whose space must also be allocated on the heap. The first time a word is encountered, exactly 1 integer must be allocated, the content of which will be the relative position of the start of the word. If and when the same word is found, then a new array of integers must be allocated, the length of which is one more than what currently exists. You must then copy the existing array into the newly allocated array, fill the last element with the location of the latest occurrence of the word, and release the obsolete space. The data member `counter` will keep count of the length of the array of integers. Note that friendship is given to the class `all_words`.

Next, create a class called `all_words` as follows:

```
class all_words
{
   one_word array[100] ;
   parser p ;
   int index ;
   // etc.
} ;
```

The key data members in this class are an instance of the `parser` class called `p` and an array of the class `one_word`. The data member `index` keeps track of the number of entries in the array.

A suggestion for the `main()` function follows:

```
int main()
{
   all_words words ;
   words.initialize() ;
   puts("Enter your data: ") ;
   while(words.new_string() != 0)
   {
      words.initialize() ;
      while(words.next_word() != 0)
         words.store_word() ;
      words.sort() ;
      words.print() ;
      puts("Next data: ") ;
   }
   return 0 ;
}
```

If, for example, the line of data is "Row, row, row your boat", then the output would be:

Word	Count	Positions
"Row"	1	0
"boat"	1	19
"row"	2	5 10
"your"	1	14

■ Exercise #11

Modify your answer to Exercise #10 so that when the `parser` class reads in a line of data, it echoes it to the screen preceded by a line number. Also, take into account the fact that a line may contain C and C++ style comments. *All such comments are to be ignored when parsing out the words.* In other words, if you encounter the token "/*", then you ignore everything that follows until the token "*/" appears. If you encounter the token "//", then you ignore everything from that point to the end of the line unless you are already ignoring characters due to the "/*" token having been encountered.

In addition, a word now has both a line number and a column number. To create one unique (long) number that reflects both values, multiply the line number by 100 and then add the column number. For example, line 34 and column 21 would be represented by the value 3421. To convert this number back into a line and column, divide by 100 — the quotient is the line number and the modulus is the column.

Notes

Notes

Chapter 8

Function overloading

Because the concept of function overloading is so fundamental in the C++ language, it has been impossible to ignore up to now. The first real usage of it came in Chapter 6 when you saw how it was possible to write more than one constructor function in a class. With the power of function overloading you can write more than one function having the same name. This frees the user of your program from having to learn about many different function names that essentially do the same task.

Scoping rules

You should note that function overloading can occur only within a single scope. In other words, if you have a global function called `::f()`, and a function with the same name in some class `integer` called `integer::f()`, then this does *not* constitute function overloading because the two functions exist at different scoping levels. The same situation is true for two classes that happen to contain functions with the same name.

Argument matching

If two or more functions exist with the same name in the same scope, then the determination as to which function is actually called at run-time depends on the number and type(s) of the argument(s) that are supplied in the actual call of the function. *The return type of the function is ignored in this determination.* The compiler goes through a process known as "argument matching", which involves an algorithm that matches the actual arguments in the function call against the argument list of all the functions with that same name. The compiler will then choose the function that best matches the actual argument(s) from among all of the functions by that name that are in scope and for which a set of conversions exists so that the function could possibly be called. Put another way, the compiler will do this:

- Using the first actual argument, it will look for all functions that could possibly be called, according to the 5 rules listed below, and select those functions that constitute the best match. Call these functions set #1. It will then repeat the process for the second argument. Call these functions set #2. It will repeat the process again for all subsequent arguments.

- Next, from all of the sets that have been created, the compiler will take the intersection, and if there is exactly one function in the intersection, then that is the one that will be chosen. If no such function exists, then the call is ambiguous, and the compiler will yield a fatal error message.

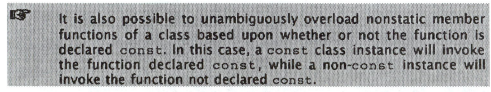

It is also possible to unambiguously overload nonstatic member functions of a class based upon whether or not the function is declared `const`. In this case, a `const` class instance will invoke the function declared `const`, while a non-`const` instance will invoke the function not declared `const`.

Argument matching rules

The basis of choosing an overloaded function unambiguously resides in the process called "argument matching". This is a 5-step process. A succeeding step is entered only if all preceding steps have failed to produce a match. The steps are as follows:

- Exact matches and trivial conversions
- Match using promotions
- Match using standard conversions
- Match using user-defined conversion functions
- Match using ellipsis

Here is a more detailed description of each step.

Exact matches and trivial conversions

In this step the compiler will look for an exact match between the actual arguments of the function call and the formal argument list in the declaration, doing a trivial conversion if necessary. A "trivial conversion" occurs when the arguments need to be converted according to the following table:

Table 8.1

From	To
T	T&
T&	T
T[]	T*
T	const T
T	volatile T
T*	const T*
T*	volatile T*
T&	const T&
T&	volatile T&
F(arguments)	(*F)(arguments)

where T is some type and F is a function name. The last case represents a function name being converted to a pointer-to-function taking the same set of arguments.

Here is an example of exact matching. The first two calls are exact matches. The next two involve trivial conversions. The last illustrates a constant object matching unambiguously with an accessor function.

Example 8.1

```
#include <stdio.h>

class A
{
     public:
   void print(char)
    {
       puts("char") ;
    }

   void print(int)
    {
       puts("int") ;
    }

   void print(int& , char&)
    {
       puts("int& , char&") ;
    }

   void print(const char , const int)
    {
       puts("const char , const int") ;
    }

   void print(int) const
    {
       puts("int const") ;
    }
} ;

int main()
{
   A a ;
   const A b ;
   char ch = 'A' ;
   int number = 65 ;

   // char
   a.print(ch) ;

   // int
   a.print(number) ;

   // const char , const int
   a.print(ch , number) ;

   // int& , char&
   a.print(number , ch) ;
```

```
    // int const
    b.print(number) ;

    return 0 ;
}
```

The output is:

```
char
int
const char , const int
int& , char&
int const
```

Match using promotions

In this step the compiler will perform argument promotion. This involves:

Table 8.2

From	To
char	int
short int	int
float	double

If several functions can be matched using promotion only, then the function with the least number of promotions will be chosen.

Example 8.2

```
#include <stdio.h>

class A
{
    public:
  void print(double)
   {
     puts("double") ;
   }

  void print(int)
   {
     puts("int") ;
   }
} ;

int main()
{
  A a ;
  // Promote 'char' to 'int'
  char ch = 'A' ;
  a.print(ch) ;

  // Promote 'short int' to 'int'
  short int si = 1 ;
  a.print(si) ;

  // Promote 'float' to 'double'
  float fl = 1.0F ;
  a.print(fl) ;

  return 0 ;
}
```

The output is:

```
int
int
double
```

The following example constitutes an ambiguous situation. Without function overloading, the double could be converted into either a float or a char. But with overloading, there is no single unambiguous match, so it will not compile.

Example 8.3   *(Will not compile!)*

```
#include <stdio.h>

class A
{
    public:
  void print(float)
   {
      puts("float") ;
   }

  void print(char)
   {
      puts("char") ;
   }
} ;

int main()
{
  A a ;
  double d = 1.23 ;
  a.print(d) ;

  return 0 ;
}
```

The compiler error message is:

```
Ambiguity between 'A::print(float)' and 'A::print(char)'
```

Here is another ambiguous situation. In the following program the first argument 'A' is of type char, so print(char , unsigned) is an exact match according to rule #1, and it constitutes set #1. The second argument consisting of the integer is an exact match for print(double , int) so this function constitutes set #2. Since the intersection of the two sets is empty, the program will not compile.

Example 8.4   *(Will not compile!)*

```
#include <stdio.h>

class A
{
    public:
  void print(char , unsigned)
   {
     puts("char , unsigned") ;
   }

   void print(double , int)
   {
     puts("double , int") ;
   }
} ;

int main()
{
  A a ;
  char ch = 'A' ;
  int number = 65 ;
  a.print(ch , number) ;

  return 0 ;
}
```

The compiler error message is:

```
Ambiguity between 'A::print(char,unsigned int)' and
'A::print(double,int)'
```

Now let's change the preceding example to add the function `print(char,int)`. The first argument matches both `print(char,unsigned)` and `print(char,int)`, so both of these functions constitute set #1. The second argument matches both `print(double,int)` and `print(char,int)` so these two functions constitute set #2. Since the intersection of these two sets yields the common function `print(char,int)`, this is the one chosen.

Example 8.5

```
#include <stdio.h>

class A
{
    public:
  void print(char , unsigned)
   {
      puts("char , unsigned") ;
   }

   void print(double , int)
    {
       puts("double , int") ;
    }

   void print(char , int)
    {
       puts("char , int") ;
    }
} ;

int main()
{
   A a ;
   char ch = 'A' ;
   int number = 65 ;
   a.print(ch , number) ;

   return 0 ;
}
```

The output is:

```
char , int
```

Match using standard conversions

Standard conversion involves the conversion of one primitive type into another primitive type. Of course, significance may be lost, but if the compiler can do it unambiguously, it will. It also involves the conversion of a pointer to a derived class into a pointer to its base class (discussed in Chapter 10) and the conversion of a pointer of any type into type `void*`.

For example, in this program the integer number will match the function `print(double)`, and the address of number and the address of a string buffer will match the function `print(void*)`.

Example 8.6

```
#include <stdio.h>

class A
{
    public:
  void print(double)
   {
     puts("double") ;
   }

  void print(void*)
   {
     puts("void*") ;
   }
} ;

int main()
{
  A a ;
  int number ;
  char string[] = "A" ;

  a.print(number) ;
  a.print(&number) ;
  a.print(string) ;

  return 0 ;
}
```

The output is:

```
double
void*
void*
```

Match with user-defined conversion functions

A user-defined conversion function is a member function that the compiler can automatically call upon in order to convert from one type into another type. There are two types of such functions, with a constructor function being the first type.

(The second type of user-defined conversion function is the operator conversion function, and will be discussed in Chapter 9.)

In the following program, note the call of the function `A::assign()`. What the program is attempting to do is call this function (which expects an object of type `A`) with an object of type `int`. Obviously the compiler has no inherent way in which it knows how to do this.

Under the rules of argument matching, rule #1 does not apply because an `int` does not match an `A`. That is, there is no exact match. Rules #2 and #3 also do not apply, but rule #4 succeeds because the compiler can use the constructor function in order to convert from type `int` into type `A`, and it can then use the resulting temporary object that the constructor produces as the actual argument to the `A::assign()` function.

Example 8.7

```
#include <stdio.h>

class A
{
   int number ;

      public:
   A(int = 0) ;
   void assign(const A&) ;
   void print() ;
} ;

inline A::A(int n)  : number(n)
{
   puts("Constructor") ;
}

inline void A::assign(const A& a)
{
   number = a.number ;
}

inline void A::print()
{
   printf("number = %d\n" , number) ;
}
```

```
int main ()
{
  A a(1) ;
  a.assign(2) ;
  a.print() ;

  return 0 ;
}
```

The output is:

```
Constructor
Constructor
number = 2
```

Match with ellipsis

Ellipsis (3 dots) are used to accept a variable number of arguments. This is exactly how `printf()` and `scanf()` take their second arguments.

In this program the integer argument cannot match `print(const char*)` under rules #1 through #4, so under rule #5 it will match `print(...)`.

Example 8.8

```
#include <stdio.h>

class A
{
    public:
  void print(const char*)
   {
     puts("const char*") ;
   }

  void print(...)
   {
     puts("ellipsis") ;
   }
} ;
```

```
int main()
{
  A a ;
  a.print(5) ;

  return 0 ;
}
```

The output is:

```
ellipsis
```

Type-safe linkage

The concept of function overloading presents a problem to the linker because it must be able to associate any particular function call with its corresponding library code. In other words, since there could be many functions in the library having the same name, it is not enough for the linker to identify a function simply by using only its name. Instead, the number and types of function arguments must also be factored in.

The linker solves this problem by a process known as "name mangling" in which the unique identity of each function is, in fact, some combination of the function name and its arguments. The only problem now is that this mangled name no longer matches any C-style library functions, since they have nothing to do with C++, and therefore do *not* have their names mangled. Nevertheless, they must still be available for usage in any C++ program.

To resolve this dilemma, you may "escape" from using the C++ name mangling technique by using a special form of the `extern` keyword. The declaration tells the compiler *not* to perform name mangling on the specified functions. There are three ways in which this declaration can occur:

Example 8.9

```
// Form #1 -- a single function declaration
extern "C" void f(int) ;

// Form #2 -- more than one function declaration
extern "C"
{
  void f(int) ;
  void g(char) ;
  // more declarations
}
```

```
// Form #3 -- an entire header file
extern "C"
{
   #include <stdio.h>
}
```

Typically such declarations are found in the header files already provided for you. But because a C program cannot make such a declaration, a test for the preprocessor symbol __cplusplus must be made. As mentioned in Chapter 1, this symbol is defined in every C++ compiler. Therefore, the code might be:

Example 8.10

```
#ifdef __cplusplus
extern "C" {
#endif

void f(int) ;
void g(char) ;
// etc.

#ifdef __cplusplus
}
#endif
```

To illustrate name mangling, consider this program in which it would appear that there is no need to include <string.h> because a prototype for the function strlen() has been written. It compiles just fine, but fails to link.

Example 8.11   *(Will not link!)*

```
#include <stdio.h>
// Prototype
size_t strlen(const char*) ;

int main()
{
   printf("%d\n" , strlen("ABC")) ;

   return 0 ;
}
```

The linker error message is:

```
Undefined symbol strlen(const char near*)
```

If you were to look at the assembled code, you would see that the call to `strlen()` has been compiled into: `call near ptr @strlen$qpxzc` where `$q` denotes the start of the argument list, `p` means 'near *', `x` means 'const', `z` means 'signed', and `c` means 'character'. On the other hand, note that the call to `printf()` (which was not mangled) has been compiled into: `call near ptr _printf`.

To fix the problem, use the `extern` declaration for the `strlen()` function prototype.

Example 8.12

```
#include <stdio.h>

extern "C"
{
   size_t strlen(const char*) ;
}

int main()
{
   printf("%d\n" , strlen("ABC")) ;

   return 0 ;
}
```

The output is:

```
3
```

A tracing class

Before getting into the details of how to write a string emulation class, it will prove advantageous to create a class called `trace` that will assist you in tracing through the various member functions being executed. When an instance of this class gets created, its state will be set to 0 (off), and can be changed to 1 (on) by calling the `change()` function. The `dump()` function has the capability to output a message and an address. This class is stored in the file `trace.h`.

Example 8.13

```
#ifndef TRACE_H
#define TRACE_H

#include <stdio.h>
#include <conio.h>

class trace
{
    public:
  enum STATUS { OFF , ON } ;
  trace(STATUS = OFF) ;
  void change(STATUS = OFF) ;
  void dump(const char* = "" , const void* = 0) ;

    private:
  STATUS state ;
} ;

inline trace::trace(STATUS s) : state(s) {}

inline void trace::change(STATUS n)
{
  state = n ;
}

inline void trace::dump(const char* message , const void* add)
{
  if(state == ON)
   {
     printf("\t%s" , message) ;
     if(add != 0)
        printf(" %p" , add) ;
     puts("\n\tPress a key...") ;
     getch() ;
   }
}

#endif
```

Overloading the string class — a case study

One of the most popular classes to define in C++ is the one that emulates a string literal in C. The reason is that a string is not a built-in type in C, and yet it is used all the time. Thus, to perform the various manipulations on string objects, you must call upon functions in the library `string.h` that perform operations such as copy, duplicate, compare, etc. In C++ this need is obviated by the use of function and operator overloading.

In order to represent the state of a string object, we will use two data members:

- The length of the string as an `int`
- A pointer to the string literal of type `char*`

A pointer to a character (`char*`) is used instead of a fixed-length character array so that memory can be allocated at run-time (via the operator `new`) and, therefore, have no restrictions placed upon the length of the string (too big or too small). The length field is not strictly mandatory since it can always be obtained from the string pointer via the `strlen()` function. However, it's probably a good idea to have it to avoid repeated calls to `strlen()`. We will also need to read the length of the string, so an accessor member function is provided.

The abstraction of the string class

In addition, to take advantage of the `trace` class, a static instance will be included (static because we want *all* instances of the `string` class to share the *one* instance of the `trace` class). The complete listing of the `string` class can be found in Appendix B.

Therefore, the skeleton for our `string` class is as follows:

Example 8.14

```
#include "trace.h"

class string
{
    private:
  static trace tracer ;

    protected:
  int length ;
  char* ptr ;
```

```
      public:
   static void debug(trace::STATUS = trace::OFF) ;
   int get_length() const ;

   // Other member and friend function declarations
} ;

trace string::tracer(trace::OFF) ;

inline void string::debug(trace::STATUS t)
{
   tracer.change(t) ;
}

inline int string::get_length() const
{
   return length ;
}
```

 The access specifier for these two data members is `protected`. **It is done this way in preparation for inheritance in Chapter 10. For now, you may think of** `protected` **as being the same as** `private`.

By default, the tracing information is suppressed. In order to toggle it on and off at any time in the `main()` function, simply execute these statements:

Example 8.15

```
string::debug(trace::ON) ;
string::debug(trace::OFF) ;
```

 Even though definitions should not be kept in a header file, they will be shown with their declarations for ease in understanding. The declarations and definitions are actually kept in two separate files: mystring.h and mystring.cpp.

Private member functions

Because the creation of each `string` instance involves (1) allocation of space on the heap, (2) copying the string literal, (3) setting the `length` data member accordingly, and because this will need to be done so frequently, a special *private* function called `copy()` in the `string` class will be used. This function will be used by the various overloaded constructor functions and the overloaded assignment operator to initialize the data members of a `string` object. The function is kept private because there is no need for any global function to call upon it.

Example 8.16

```
// Declaration
void copy(const char*) ;

// Definition
inline void string::copy(const char* s)
{
   length = strlen(s) ;
   ptr = new char[length + 1] ;
   strcpy(ptr , s) ;
}
```

In addition, we will want to create a `string` object from a single character, so the `copy()` function has been overloaded to accommodate this type of argument.

Example 8.17

```
// Declaration
void copy(char) ;

// Definition
inline void string::copy(char ch)
{
   length = 1 ;
   ptr = new char[2] ;
   ptr[0] = ch ;
   ptr[1] = '\0' ;
}
```

Furthermore, it will be useful to create a `string` object from an integer value. This implies allocating the required number of bytes from the heap, and setting the first byte to the null character.

Example 8.18

```
// Declaration
void copy(int) ;

// Definition
inline void string::copy(int len)
{
   length = len ;
   ptr = new char[length + 1] ;
   ptr[0] = '\0' ;
}
```

Of course, at various times it will be necessary to release the space on the heap that a particular string instance points to. This will be done in a member function called `release()`.

Example 8.19

```
// Declaration
void release() ;

// Definition
inline void string::release()
{
   delete [] ptr ;
}
```

Finally, later on when it's time to concatenate `string` objects, we will need a function that can concatenate two string literals and place the result into the heap space that the invoking instance has already allocated.

Example 8.20

```
// Declaration
void concat(const char* , const char*) ;

// Definition
inline void string::concat(const char* s1 , const char* s2)
{
   strcpy(ptr , s1) ;
   strcat(ptr , s2) ;
}
```

Now we are ready to start writing the manager functions of the `string` class.

Overloaded constructor functions

Because there are many different ways in which a `string` object can be initialized, the constructor functions for the `string` class must be overloaded to accommodate all of the various situations.

First, if a `string` object is created with no explicit initialization, then the default constructor (the one that can be called with no actual arguments) will be called. It makes sense that we should have the invoking instance point to an empty string literal whose length is zero. This can be done by passing an empty string literal to the `copy()` function. Note that under the rules of argument matching, the `copy()` function that expects a `const char*` argument will be called.

Example 8.21

```
// Declaration
string() ;

// Definition
inline string::string()
{
   tracer.dump("Default constructor" , this) ;
   copy("") ;
}
```

Second, because there is such a close relationship between a string literal (which is type `char*`) and the `string` class, it should be easy to create a `string` object based upon that literal. In this case a separate copy of the literal must be made so that it can be encapsulated as part of the class. Once again the `copy()` function will be used.

Example 8.22

```
// Declaration
string(const char*) ;

// Definition
inline string::string(const char* s)
{
   tracer.dump("char* constructor" , this) ;
   copy(s) ;
}
```

Third, it might be useful to be able to create a string instance from a single character.

Example 8.23

```
// Declaration
string(char) ;

// Definition
inline string::string(char ch)
{
   tracer.dump("char constructor" , this) ;
   copy(ch) ;
}
```

Fourth, here is a constructor that takes an `int` as its argument and calls upon the `copy()` function expecting an `int`. Note that a value less than zero will be changed to zero.

Example 8.24

```
// Declaration
string(int) ;

// Definition
inline string::string(int len)
{
   tracer.dump("int constructor" , this) ;
   copy(len < 0 ? 0 : len) ;
}
```

Finally, recall from Chapter 6 and the discussion on copy constructors that the compiler automatically supplies one for you if you fail to write one. This is fine if a class contains no pointer data members, but will cause a big problem if at least one pointer data member is present. The reason for this is that two or more pointer members may not point to the same space on the heap, and this is exactly what would happen if you used the default copy constructor. Therefore, it is now necessary to create one for the `string` class.

Example 8.25

```
// Declaration
string(const string&) ;

// Definition
inline string::string(const string& s)
{
    tracer.dump("Copy constructor" , this) ;
    copy(s.ptr) ;
}
```

Destructor function

When the `string` object goes out of scope, the destructor function must release the space on the heap that `ptr` points to. Otherwise, we will have a severe case of "memory leakage". The private member function `release()` will handle this.

Example 8.26

```
// Declaration
~string() ;

// Definition
inline string::~string()
{
    tracer.dump("Destructor" , this) ;
    release() ;
}
```

`print()` function

In order to display the state of any `string` object, we have to write a print function. This function should display the length of the string literal, the literal itself between double quotation marks, and an identifier that names the object. If the trace is turned on, then the address of the string literal (the content of the member `ptr`) on the heap will also be shown.

Example 8.27

```
// Declaration
void print(const char* = "") ;

// Definition
inline void string::print(const char* name)
{
   tracer.dump("Heap address" , ptr) ;
   printf("%s: \"%s\" %d\n" , name , ptr , length) ;
}
```

Here is a program that will run a test of all the previously defined functions.

Example 8.28

```
#include "mystring.h"
#include "mystring.cpp"

int main()
{
   string s1 ;
   s1.print("s1") ;

   string s2("ABC") ;
   s2.print("s2") ;

   string s3('Z') ;
   s3.print("s3") ;

   string s4(s3) ;
   s4.print("s4") ;

   return 0 ;
}
```

The output is:

```
s1: "" 0
s2: "ABC" 3
s3: "Z" 1
s4: "Z" 1
```

To test the trace class, here is a repeat of the previous example with the debugging feature turned on.

Example 8.29

```
#include "mystring.h"
#include "mystring.cpp"

int main()
{
  string::debug(trace::ON) ;

  string s1 ;
  s1.print("s1") ;

  string s2("ABC") ;
  s2.print("s2") ;

  string s3('Z') ;
  s3.print("s3") ;

  string s4(s3) ;
  s4.print("s4") ;

  return 0 ;
}
```

The output is:

```
      Default constructor FFF2
      Press a key...
      Heap address 1404
      Press a key...
s1: "" 0
      char* constructor FFFE
      Press a key...
      Heap address 140C
      Press a key...
s2: "ABC" 3
      char constructor FFEA
      Press a key...
      Heap address 1414
      Press a key...
s3: "Z" 1
      Copy constructor FFE4
      Press a key...
      Heap address 141C
      Press a key...
```

```
s4: "Z" 1
     Destructor FFE4
     Press a key...
     Destructor FFEA
     Press a key...
     Destructor FFEE
     Press a key...
     Destructor FFF2
     Press a key...
```

Assigning one string instance to another string instance

The final manager function that we need in the `string` class is one that can assign one `string` instance to another instance (every C programmer's dream!). In order to do this successfully, you must overload the assignment operator for the string class. Why is this necessary since the compiler automatically supplies a *default* assignment operator that is used to copy all of the data members? For much the same reason that we had to write an explicit copy constructor, i.e., without one the address in the pointer `ptr` would get copied into the corresponding `ptr` data member of the receiving instance and, as a result, the pointer would then be pointing to the same space on the heap. This could cause an abort when the destructor function attempts to release this space. Therefore, the default assignment operator that the compiler supplies in this situation obviously is *not* good enough, and therefore needs to be overloaded.

How operator function overloading is done

Before we can overload the assignment operator, we have to learn the rules and constraints that the compiler imposes upon us. In C and C++, many operators are already supplied that work with the built-in data types, such as '+' for both integers and floats. Of course, not all operators are valid with all types. For example, the '%' operator (modulus) is only valid for integers, not for floats. By extension, whenever a new class is created, you need the ability to create new operators specifically designed to operate upon the data members of that class. As a result, the usage of the `string` class becomes much more intuitive because now you can use familiar operators such as '=' to mean assignment, '+' to mean concatenation, etc. This is certainly better than having to "drag out" such old standbys as `strcpy()` and `strcat()` to perform these operations.

Even though most of the existing operators have no inherent meaning in regard to any user-defined class (e.g., '+' has no meaning when used with the `string` class), certain operators still work with any new class. For example, the '&' still yields the address of an instance of some class type, while the '=' (by default) causes all data members of one instance of a class to be assigned to the corresponding data members of another instance of that same class (just like the copy constructor). In addition, the direct member operator (dot) and `sizeof` operator are automatically valid.

Finally, whatever meaning you give to the operators should make sense to someone reading your code. For example, obviously you should not overload the '+' operator to mean any kind of subtraction.

Rules for overloading an operator

This list summarizes the most important things you need to know in order to do operator function overloading.

■ The only operators that you may overload are the ones from the C++ precedence chart (and not all of those are available). You may not arbitrarily choose a new symbol (such as '@') and attempt to "overload" it.

■ Start by declaring a function in the normal fashion, but for the function name use the expression:

```
operator@
```

where the symbol '@' generically represents the operator to be overloaded. You may leave one or more spaces before the '@'.

■ The pre-defined operator precedence rules *cannot* be rebuked. That is, you cannot, for example, make binary '+' have a higher precedence than binary '*'. In essence, you must live by the existing precedence now in the table of C++ operators (Appendix A). In addition, you cannot change the associativity of the operators.

■ The unary operators that you may overload are:

->	indirect member operator
!	not
&	address
*	dereference
+	plus
-	minus
++	prefix increment
++	postfix increment (AT&T version 2.1)
--	prefix decrement
--	postfix decrement (AT&T version 2.1)
~	one's complement
->*	indirect pointer-to-member

■ The binary operators that you may overload are:

()	function call
[]	subscript
new	create space
delete	destroy space
*	multiply
/	divide
%	modulus
+	add
-	subtract
<<	left shift
>>	right shift
<	less than
<=	less than or equal to
>	greater than
>=	greater than or equal to
==	equal to
!=	not equal to
&	bitwise AND
^	bitwise exclusive OR
|	bitwise OR
&&	logical AND
||	logical OR
=	assignment
*=	multiply and assign
/=	divide and assign
%=	modulus and assign
+=	add and assign
-=	subtract and assign
<<=	shift left and assign
>>=	shift right and assign
&=	bitwise AND and assign
|=	bitwise OR and assign
^=	bitwise exclusive OR and assign
,	comma

■ These operators *cannot* be overloaded:

.	direct member
.*	direct pointer-to-member
::	scope resolution
? :	conditional
sizeof	size of

■ No default arguments are allowed in overloaded operator functions.

■ As with the pre-defined operators, an overloaded operator may be unary or binary. If it normally is unary, then it *cannot* be defined to be binary. If it is normally binary, then it *cannot* be defined to be unary. However, if an operator can be both unary and binary, then it can be overloaded either way or both ways.

■ The operator function for a class may be either a nonstatic member or a nonmember function. A nonstatic member function automatically has one argument implicitly defined, namely the address of the invoking instance (as specified by the pointer variable this). Since a nonmember function has no this pointer, it needs to have all of its arguments explicitly defined.

■ At least one of the arguments to the overloaded function (implicit or explicit) must be an instance of the class to which the operator belongs. The reason for this rule is to "attach" the operator uniquely to the class for which it is being defined, and to avoid any ambiguity with the pre-defined operators and other classes which may also have this particular operator overloaded.

■ This table shows the correct number of implicit and explicit arguments for a member or nonmember function, either unary or binary:

Table 8.3

	Unary (1 argument)	Binary (2 arguments)
Member	1 implicit, 0 explicit	1 implicit, 1 explicit
Nonmember	0 implicit, 1 explicit	0 implicit, 2 explicit

☞ The function operator()() may take more than one explicit argument.

■ In the case of a binary member operator, where there is only one explicit argument written, the invoking instance is *always* assumed to be the one on the *left-hand side* of the operator. In other words, for the class string, if you created and initialized two instances:

    string s1 , s2 ;

and then assigned s2 to s1 using infix notation:

    s1 = s2 ;

the implication is that s1 becomes the invoking instance and s2 becomes the explicit argument. The same result can be obtained if the assignment statement is written using functional notation:

    s1.operator=(s2) ;

■ In the case of a binary member operator, no implicit type conversion is ever done on the 'lvalue'. This means that the 'lvalue' *must* be an instance of the class of which the overloaded operator is a member. However, you may write an explicit cast to create a temporary instance of the class (which should never be modified).

■ A nonmember function may also be declared as a friend function of the class if the function needs to gain access to the private (or protected) members. If, however, the accessor and mutator functions of the class can be used instead of granting friendship, then this is the preferred coding style because it enforces the principle of data hiding.

■ This table shows how the compiler translates your code from infix into functional notation given the various situations ('@' is assumed to be the operator being overloaded, and X and Y are the class instances):

Table 8.4

Operator	Type	Infix Notation	Functional Notation
Unary	Member	@X	X.operator@()
Unary	Member	X@[1]	X.operator@(0)
Binary	Member	X@Y	X.operator@(Y)
Unary	Nonmember	@X	operator@(X)
Unary	Nonmember	X@[1]	operator@(X , 0)
Binary	Nonmember	X@Y	operator@(X , Y)

[1] This postfix notation (in which the operator appears *after* the class instance) is valid *only* for the operators '++' and '--'. C++ compilers that support AT&T version 2.1 or later automatically generate an extra argument of type `int`. AT&T version 2.0 cannot distinguish between prefix and postfix usage. This topic is discussed in more detail later in this chapter.

■ These operators *must* be overloaded as *member* (not nonmember) functions:

    =   assignment
    ()   function call
    []   subscript
    ->   indirect member operator

■ While not strictly mandatory, you should overload all compound assignment operators ('+=', '-=', '*=', etc.) as member functions.

■ The operators `new` and `delete` may be overloaded as static member functions. `operator new` must take an argument of type `size_t` and return `void*`, while `operator delete` must take an argument of type `void*` and return `void`.

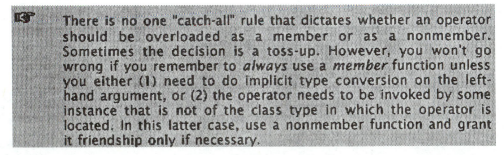

There is no one "catch-all" rule that dictates whether an operator should be overloaded as a member or as a nonmember. Sometimes the decision is a toss-up. However, you won't go wrong if you remember to *always* use a *member* function unless you either (1) need to do implicit type conversion on the left-hand argument, or (2) the operator needs to be invoked by some instance that is not of the class type in which the operator is located. In this latter case, use a nonmember function and grant it friendship only if necessary.

The overloaded assignment operator

Now that you know something about operator overloading, we can get back to the `string` class. This is the code necessary to overload the assignment operator. Remember: this *must* be done as a binary member function.

Example 8.30

```
// Declaration
string& operator=(const string&) ;

// Definition
inline string& string::operator=(const string& s)
{
   tracer.dump("operator=()" , this) ;
   // Check for self-assignment
   if(&s == this)
      tracer.dump("Self-assignment" , this) ;
   // Check for different lengths
   else if(length != s.length)
    {
      release() ;
      copy(s.ptr) ;
    }
   else
      strcpy(ptr , s.ptr) ;

   return *this ;
}
```

There are several interesting aspects to this function.

■ The return type of the function is `string&`. This allows for the possibility of function chaining, and corresponds to the return value of `*this` at the end of the function.

■ The function checks for self-assignment. This is mandatory when pointer variables are involved because if a `string` instance is assigned to itself, then `ptr` and `s.ptr` would be pointing to the same space on the heap. When the call to the function `release()` is made, the space for the existing string literal (pointed at by `s.ptr`) on the heap would then be released, and the `copy()` function could easily fail.

■ If the instance is not being assigned to itself, then a check is made to see of the lengths of the two instances are different. If so, new heap space is allocated; otherwise, the existing heap space is reused because now there is no need to allocate new heap storage.

Here is a test in which the `string` instance `s1` is assigned to the existing instances `s2` and `s3`.

Example 8.31

```
#include "mystring.h"
#include "mystring.cpp"

int main()
{
   string s1("ABC") , s2 , s3 ;
   s3 = s2 = s1 ;

   s1.print("s1") ;
   s2.print("s2") ;
   s3.print("s3") ;

   return 0 ;
}
```

The output is:

```
s1: "ABC" 3
s2: "ABC" 3
s3: "ABC" 3
```

Here is a test of the self-assignment check with the debugging information turned on.

Example 8.32

```
#include "mystring.h"
#include "mystring.cpp"

int main()
{
   string::debug(trace::ON) ;
   string s1("ABC") ;
   s1 = s1 ;
   s1.print("s1") ;

   return 0 ;
}
```

The output is:

```
        char* constructor FFF2
        Press a key...
        operator=() FFF2
        Press a key...
        Self-assignment FFF2
        Press a key...
        Heap address 1370
        Press a key...
s1: "ABC" 3
        Destructor FFF2
        Press a key...
```

An interesting aspect of the assignment operator is that in C the output is a non-modifiable value, whereas in C++ it is an 'lvalue'. This poses the question of whether the output of an overloaded assignment operator for a user-defined type should be modifiable or non-modifiable. In the function provided here, it is an 'lvalue', so it is modifiable to be consistent with the behavior of primitive types in C++. If you want to make it non-modifiable, so that the following (rather obscure) code produces a compilation error:

Example 8.33

```
(s3 = s2) = s1 ;
```

then add the keyword `const` to the return type so that it becomes `const string&`.

Implicit type conversion

In addition to assigning one `string` instance to another `string` instance, it makes sense to have the capability to assign a string literal (a `char*` object) to a `string` instance. Obviously, if you create an instance of the `string` class called `s` and then attempt to execute the following assignment statement:

Example 8.34

```
string s ;
s = "ABC" ;
```

then rule #1 of argument matching fails. That is, the overloaded `string::operator=()` *cannot* be invoked directly because the right-hand actual and formal arguments do not match (the actual argument is `char*`, and the formal argument is `const string&`). Rules #2 and #3 are irrelevant, so that in this situation the compiler will attempt to apply rule #4 and look for a user-defined conversion function with which it can convert a `char*` object into a `string` object. Does such a function already exist? Yes! It's the constructor function that takes a `const char*` object as the one formal argument. Therefore, the compiler will *automatically* use this constructor function to create a temporary `string` object that it can use to invoke the overloaded `string::operator=()` function.

In this program the string literal `"ABC"` is assigned to the `string` object s. Note the automatic calling of the constructor function.

Example 8.35

```
#include "mystring.h"
#include "mystring.cpp"

int main()
{
    string s ;
    s = "ABC" ;
    s.print("s") ;

    return 0 ;
}
```

The output is:

```
s: "ABC" 3
```

An alternate choice to implicit type conversion

The previous example showed how a user-defined conversion function can be automatically used by the compiler to save you the trouble of having to code functions that always satisfy rule #1 (exact match) of the rules for argument matching. The only disadvantage of this technique is that it takes a little longer to execute the program because in order to convert from a `char*` object to a `string` object, a "detour" has to be made through the constructor function. Is there a way to eliminate this detour? Yes, if you overload the assignment operator again to accept a `char*` object. In this fashion, the compiler would then detect an exact match between the actual argument and the formal argument. Such a function might appear as:

Example 8.36

```
// Declaration
string& operator=(const char*) ;

// Definition
inline string& string::operator=(const char* s)
{
   release() ;
   copy(s) ;
   return *this ;
}
```

It is up to you to determine if you want to employ this technique. It's a little more coding on your part, but the execution time is faster because the constructor function is no longer being called.

String concatenation

The next step in the process of overloading functions for the string class is to "add" two strings together. For our purposes we will assume that this implies a string concatenation operation. Since addition typically involves the binary '+' operator, it seems natural to overload it for the string class.

There are, however, some design considerations to be made here. First, should the function be a member or nonmember? The better choice would be to use a nonmember friend function. As stated earlier in the general rule about members vs. nonmembers, this has the advantage of allowing the left-hand argument to be a string literal (type char[]) or a character (type char) so that implicit type conversion can occur. In addition, if you coded it as a member function, then one of the string instances would have to be the invoking instance, and the other would have to be the explicit argument. This doesn't make sense because the arguments in an add operation are, in essence, equal. Therefore, both of them should be explicit arguments, thereby implying a nonmember function. Friendship is also granted so that the function can access the data members ptr and length.

Second, should the function literally emulate what strcat() does and modify the first argument? In this case the better answer would be no, because normally an add operation implies that neither argument is modified. Instead, they are simply combined to produce a brand new object.

Here is one way to do it. Note that the return type of the function is a string object *by value*. A reference cannot be used because you should never make an alias to an auto object, which is what the result of the function really is. Also, this give us our first chance to use the constructor taking an `int`, and the private member function `concat()`.

Example 8.37

```
// Declaration
friend string operator+(const string& , const string&) ;

// Definition
inline string operator+(const string& s1 , const string& s2)
{
   string::tracer.dump("binary operator+()") ;
   string new_string(s1.length + s2.length) ;
   new_string.concat(s1.ptr , s2.ptr) ;
   return new_string ;
}
```

As stated above, if you want to try to utilize rule #1 of argument matching, i.e., always go for an exact match, then the alternative solution would be to overload `operator+()` four more times in order to achieve an exact match under all possible concatenation circumstances.

Example 8.38

```
// Declaration
friend string operator+(const string& , const char*) ;
// Definition
inline string operator+(const string& s1 , const char* str)
{
   string::tracer.dump("binary operator+(string,char*)") ;
   string new_string(s1.length + (int)strlen(str)) ;
   new_string.concat(s1.ptr , str) ;
   return new_string ;
}

// Declaration
friend string operator+(const char* , const string&) ;
// Definition
inline string operator+(const char* str , const string& s1)
{
   string::tracer.dump("binary operator+(char*,string)") ;
   string new_string((int)strlen(str) + s1.length) ;
   new_string.concat(str , s1.ptr) ;
   return new_string ;
}
```

```
// Declaration
friend string operator+(const string& , char) ;
// Definition
inline string operator+(const string& s1 , char ch)
{
   string::tracer.dump("binary operator+(string,char)") ;
   char buffer[2] ;
   buffer[0] = ch ;
   buffer[1] = '\0' ;
   return s1 + buffer ;
}

// Declaration
friend string operator+(char , const string&) ;
// Definition
inline string operator+(char ch , const string& s1)
{
   string::tracer.dump("binary operator+(char,string)") ;
   char buffer[2] ;
   buffer[0] = ch ;
   buffer[1] = '\0' ;
   return buffer + s1 ;
}
```

Here is a test of the overloaded addition operator.

Example 8.39

```
#include "mystring.h"
#include "mystring.cpp"

int main()
{
   string s1("DEF") ;
   string s2('H') ;
   string s3("ABC" + s1 + "G" + s2 + 'I') ;
   s3.print("s3") ;

   return 0 ;
}
```

The output is:

```
s3: "ABCDEFGHI" 9
```

String concatenation — another approach

You know that in C the operator '+=' has the effect of adding the two operands together and then storing the result into the left-hand argument. If your intent in doing string concatenation is to modify the left-hand argument, then this operator would be a natural choice for you to use. Obviously, you must allocate new space on the heap for the resulting literal to avoid an overflow situation.

Here is what this operator would look like. Note how the function takes advantage of the overloaded '+' operator so that the detail code that '+=' implies does *not* need to be repeated. In addition, this implementation guarantees that the '+=' operator behaves in a manner that is completely consistent with that of the '+' operator.

Example 8.40

```
// Declaration
string& operator+=(const string&) ;

// Definition
inline string& string::operator+=(const string& s)
{
   tracer.dump("operator+=()\n") ;
   return *this = *this + s ;
}
```

Here is a test of this operator.

Example 8.41

```
#include "mystring.h"
#include "mystring.cpp"

int main()
{
   string s1('A') ;
   string s2("BC") ;
   s1 += s1 += s2 += 'D' ;
   s1.print("s1") ;
   s2.print("s2") ;

   return 0 ;
}
```

The output is:

```
s1: "ABCDABCD" 8
s2: "BCD" 3
```

Overloading an operator as both unary and binary

To demonstrate an operator being overloaded in both its unary and binary modes, here is the '+' operator now overloaded as a unary member operator. Of course, what the operator actually does is completely arbitrary, so let's just assume that its purpose is to ensure that all letters of the string literal are upper case. Note that this function does not modify the string object itself, but instead returns a new string object that contains the modification. This is somewhat consistent with how unary operators behave. If you really do want to modify the invoking object, then it's just a matter of storing the result back into the invoking object.

Example 8.42

```
// Declaration
string operator+() const ;

// Definition
string string::operator+() const
{
   tracer.dump("unary operator+()\n") ;
   string new_string(*this) ;
   for(int i = 0 ; i < length ; ++i)
      new_string.ptr[i] = toupper(new_string.ptr[i]) ;
   return new_string ;
}
```

As a test, this program uses the unary `operator+()` to create a new string. Then it modifies the original string by assigning back into it.

Example 8.43

```
#include "mystring.h"
#include "mystring.cpp"

int main()
{
   string s1("Unary +") , s2(+s1) ;
   s1.print("s1") ;
   s2.print("s2") ;

   s1 = +s1 ;
   s1.print("s1") ;

   return 0 ;
}
```

The output is:

```
s1: "Unary +" 7
s2: "UNARY +" 7
s1: "UNARY +" 7
```

Comparing two string instances

The next operation you might want to perform on instances of the string class would be to compare them against each other. This implies overloading the six relational operators. All comparisons will be case sensitive, although you could easily make them non-case sensitive. Once again, note that the functions are all nonmember friends to allow the left-hand operand (which could be type char* or type char) to be implicitly cast into a temporary string object.

Example 8.44

```
// Declaration
friend int operator==(const string& , const string&) ;
// Definition
inline int operator==(const string& s1 , const string& s2)
{
   string::tracer.dump("operator==()\n") ;
   return (!strcmp(s1.ptr , s2.ptr)) ;
}
```

```
// Declaration
friend int operator!=(const string& , const string&) ;
// Definition
inline int operator!=(const string& s1 , const string& s2)
{
   string::tracer.dump("operator!=()\n") ;
   return (strcmp(s1.ptr , s2.ptr)) ;
}

// Declaration
friend int operator<(const string& , const string&) ;
// Definition
inline int operator<(const string& s1, const string& s2)
{
   string::tracer.dump("operator<()\n") ;
   return (strcmp(s1.ptr , s2.ptr) < 0) ;
}

// Declaration
friend int operator>(const string& , const string&) ;
// Definition
inline int operator>(const string& s1 , const string& s2)
{
   string::tracer.dump("operator>()\n") ;
   return (strcmp(s1.ptr , s2.ptr) > 0) ;
}

// Declaration
friend int operator<=(const string& , const string&) ;
// Definition
inline int operator<=(const string& s1,  const string& s2)
{
   string::tracer.dump("operator<=()\n") ;
   return (strcmp(s1.ptr , s2.ptr) <= 0) ;
}

// Declaration
friend int operator>=(const string& , const string&) ;
// Definition
inline int operator>=(const string& s1 , const string& s2)
{
   string::tracer.dump("operator>=()\n") ;
   return (strcmp(s1.ptr , s2.ptr) >= 0) ;
}
```

Here is a test of the relational operators. The global function `compare()` receives two `string` instances by constant reference and compares them in the six different ways.

Example 8.45

```
#include "mystring.h"
#include "mystring.cpp"

void compare(const string& s1 , const string& s2)
{
  if(s1 == s2)
   {
     s1.print("s1") ;
     puts("==") ;
     s2.print("s2") ;
   }

  if(s1 != s2)
   {
     s1.print("s1") ;
     puts("!=") ;
     s2.print("s2") ;
   }

  if(s1 < s2)
   {
     s1.print("s1") ;
     puts("<") ;
     s2.print("s2") ;
   }

  if(s1 <= s2)
   {
     s1.print("s1") ;
     puts("<=") ;
     s2.print("s2") ;
   }

  if(s1 > s2)
   {
     s1.print("s1") ;
     puts(">") ;
     s2.print("s2") ;
   }

  if(s1 >= s2)
   {
     s1.print("s1") ;
     puts(">=") ;
     s2.print("s2") ;
   }
  puts("") ;
}
```

```
int main()
{
   string s1 = 'A' ;
   string s2 = "B" ;

   compare(s1 , s2) ;
   compare('a' , s1) ;

   return 0 ;
}
```

The output is:

```
s1: "A" 1
!=
s2: "B" 1
s1: "A" 1
<
s2: "B" 1
s1: "A" 1
<=
s2: "B" 1

s1: "a" 1
!=
s2: "A" 1
s1: "a" 1
>
s2: "A" 1
s1: "a" 1
>=
s2: "A" 1
```

Overloading operator[]()

As you know, in C the operator [] (square brackets) is typically used to represent indexing. That is, the value between the square brackets specifies which element of the designated array is to be referenced. Of course, if you were to attempt to apply the bracket operator to an instance of some user-defined class, the compiler would complain because it has no idea what you are trying to do. However, you may give it meaning for your class by overloading it. Typically this would be done for a class that contains an array or a pointer as a data member. The big advantage here is that having your own function allows you to do a validity check on the index value.

Recall that operator[]() must be a *binary member* (not friend) function of the class. In other words, there must be one explicit argument which is the index value itself.

First, let's look at how you would write it using both functional and infix notation. Suppose that s is an instance of class string. Then writing:

Example 8.46

```
// Functional notation
s.operator[](index)// or
// Infix notation
s[index]
```

causes s to become the invoking (implicit) instance for the function, and index to become the one explicit argument.

The resulting array element (in this case a character) can now be returned from the function *by value*, in which case you are "safe" because there is no way that the calling routine can modify the element. In effect, you have then created an accessor function, and the principle of data hiding has been maintained.

However, if you return *by reference*, you have created an 'lvalue' for the character and thereby given the calling routine access to that one array element, which could then be modified. Sometimes this is required, e.g., in the case of a class designed to emulate all of the functions you would want to perform on an array, including storing data into the array elements. While this task could be done by a named mutator function, the bracket operator provides a much more intuitive solution.

In the case of the string class, the [] operator function will be used to fetch a particular character from the array of characters pointed at by ptr. The following example shows one way to do it. Note that the character is being returned *by reference*, and that the input index value is validity checked. If it turns out to be invalid, the function sounds the alarm but must still return some character by reference and we have chosen the null byte. The reason, of course, is that the null byte cannot be part of a string literal and the calling routine can now check for it and take appropriate action. The variable dummy is static because you should never return a reference to an auto object. In addition, the null byte is assigned into dummy each time the if clause evaluates to 'true'. Do you see why? The reason is that since the function returns a reference, there is nothing to prevent the calling routine from modifying the variable dummy, so that its content cannot be guaranteed to be null every time the function gains control. The assignment statement takes care of this.

Example 8.47

```
// Declaration
char& operator[](int) const ;

// Definition
inline char& string::operator[](int index) const
{
   tracer.dump("operator[]()\n") ;
   if(index < 0 || index >= length)
    {
       putchar('\a') ;
       static char dummy ;
       dummy = '\0' ;
       return dummy ;
    }
   return ptr[index] ;
}
```

Here is a test of the overloaded `operator[]()` in which the `main()` function will cause each character of the string array to have its value increased by 1.

Example 8.48

```
#include "mystring.h"
#include "mystring.cpp"

int main()
{
   string s("C++ is fun") ;
   // Deliberate error at both ends of 'for' loop
   for(int i = -1 ; i <= s.get_length() ; ++i)
    {
       char& ch = s[i] ;
       if(ch != '\0')
           ++ch ;
    }
   s.print("s") ;

   return 0 ;
}
```

The output is:

```
s: "D,,!jt!gvo" 10
```

and the sound of two beeps.

This use of the overloaded `[]` for the `string` class is not the same as the use of `[]` when using an array of objects of the `string` class, in which the use of the brackets takes on its "normal" subscript meaning of identifying exactly which class instance is being referenced.

This is the same example as before, but now an array of `string` instances is used. The subscript `i` represents the particular `string` instance, and the subscript `j` represents the character of the string array being pointed at.

Example 8.49

```cpp
#include "mystring.h"
#include "mystring.cpp"

int main()
{
   string s[] = {"C++ is fun" , " to learn"} ;
   const int size = sizeof(s) / sizeof(string) ;

   for(int i = 0 ; i < size ; ++i)
    {
      for(int j = 0 ; j < s[i].get_length(); ++j)
       {
          char& ch = s[i][j] ;
          if(ch != '\0')
              ++ch ;
       }
      s[i].print("s[i]") ;
    }

   return 0 ;
}
```

The output is:

```
s[i]: "D,,!jt!gvo" 10
s[i]: "!up!mfbso" 9
```

Brackets vs. pointer notation

The use of brackets in C is just a convenience for you that avoids your having to use pointer dereferencing when accessing an array element. In other words, for some array s, these three lines should all yield the same result since they are equivalent:

Example 8.50

```
s[i] ;
*(s + i) ;
*(i + s) ;
```

Thus, it is incumbent upon you to allow the user of the string class to be able to write code using the latter two notations. As things stand now, the compiler would complain because it has no idea how to "add" a string object and an int. Therefore, the '+' operator must be overloaded again to accommodate both syntax forms. Here is an easy way to do it using the overloaded operator[]():

Example 8.51

```
// Declaration
friend char* operator+(const string& , int) ;

// Definition
inline char* operator+(const string& s , int i)
{
   string::tracer.dump("operator+(s , i)\n") ;
   return &s[i] ;
}

// Declaration
friend char* operator+(int , const string&) ;

// Definition
inline char* operator+(int i , const string& s)
{
   string::tracer.dump("operator+(i , s)\n") ;
   return &s[i] ;
}
```

The following program will test both forms of the dereferencing notation:

Example 8.52

```
#include "mystring.h"
#include "mystring.cpp"

int main()
{
  string s("ABCDE") ;
  for(int i = 0 ; i < s.get_length() ; ++i)
     ++(*(s + i)) ;

  for(int j = 0 ; j < s.get_length() ; ++j)
     printf("%c" , *(j + s)) ;
  puts("") ;

  return 0 ;
}
```

The output is:

BCDEF

> 👉   Because these two functions:
>
>   operator+(const string& , int) ;
>   operator+(int , const string&) ;
>
> constitute a match using a promotion if called with string and
> char types, it was mandatory to define the functions shown in
> Example 8.38 that take these two types as formal arguments.
> Otherwise, the functions in Example 8.51 would have been called
> to "add" two string instances together.

Overloading operator()()

In C the operator () (parentheses) is used to execute a call to some function. Once again, if this operator is applied to an instance of some class, it has no inherent meaning. However, like the operator [], you can give it meaning by overloading it as a *member* function. One thing unique about this particular operator, however, is that the number of explicit arguments is completely variable.

That leaves the question of what it means to treat an instance of the string class as the name of a function. One usage might be to emulate the function strncmp() in which two explicit arguments are needed: 1) the second string against which to do the comparison, and 2) the number of characters to compare.

Example 8.53

```
// Declaration
int operator () (const string& , int) const ;

// Definition
inline int string::operator () (const string& s , int len) const
{
   tracer.dump ("operator () () \n") ;
   return !strncmp (ptr , s.ptr , len) ;
}
```

The following program uses the overloaded `operator () ()` to compare an instance of the `string` class against various values and print the results of the comparison.

Example 8.54

```
#include "mystring.h"
#include "mystring.cpp"

int main ()
{
   string s ("ABCDE") ;
   puts (s ("AX" , 1) ? "Equal" : "Unequal") ;
   puts (s ('A' , 1) ? "Equal" : "Unequal") ;
   puts (s ("AX" , 2) ? "Equal" : "Unequal") ;
   puts (s ("ABC" , 3) ? "Equal" : "Unequal") ;
   puts (s ("ABCDEF" , 6) ? "Equal" : "Unequal") ;
   puts (s ("ABCDEF" , 5) ? "Equal" : "Unequal") ;

   return 0 ;
}
```

The output is:

```
Equal
Equal
Unequal
Equal
Unequal
Equal
```

Overloading the increment and decrement operators

In C the operators '++' (increment by 1) and '--' (decrement by 1) are unique in that they may appear on either side of the variable to which they apply. If the operator appears on the left, it implies prefix notation ("do the operation and then use the content of the variable") while on the right it implies postfix notation ("use the content of the variable and then do the operation"). You should never use the variable more than once in this context within a single statement; otherwise, you're just asking for trouble.

In all C++ compilers that implement AT&T version 2.0, the distinction between prefix and postfix notation for user-defined types is lost. That is, for the `string` class and an instance called s, the expressions s++ and ++s cannot be distinguished from each other because the compiler will generate exactly the same code for each one. However, starting with AT&T version 2.1, any postfix usage automatically generates an extra argument consisting of an integer 0. The actual value of this integer, of course, is meaningless, so that a formal argument name does not need to be written when the function is defined. Nevertheless, this extra argument allows both prefix and postfix versions of the operator to be present.

Thus, for the `string` class and some instance s, Table 8.5 shows the corresponding functional notation that is generated as a result of using the prefix version:

Table 8.5

Expression: ++s	AT&T 2.0	AT&T 2.1
Member	s.operator++()	s.operator++()
Nonmember	operator++(s)	operator++(s)

Table 8.6 show the corresponding functional notation that is generated as a result of using the postfix version:

Table 8.6

Expression: s++	AT&T 2.0	AT&T 2.1
Member	s.operator++()	s.operator++(0)
Nonmember	operator++(s)	operator++(s , 0)

You are then responsible for coding the function to do whatever you choose, e.g., adding 1 to some private data member. Although you could do so, it's probably not a good idea to write the function to emulate post-fix notation. In addition, since there is no good reason to overload the function as a nonmember, you should write it as a member function.

As an example, let's overload `operator++()` for the `string` class to mean that the value 1 should be added to each character in the string pointed at by `ptr`, and `operator--()` to mean the value 1 should be subtracted from each character.

Note the "trick" in the postfix functions in which a temporary instance is created and returned *by value*. It's the invoking instance that actually gets modified, but it's the temporary one that will be used as the subsequent invoking instance for the rest of the statement. Note also that the postfix version of the operator utilizes the prefix version to save on redundant coding and to make the two functions consistent in their behavior.

Example 8.55

```
// Declaration of prefix ++
string& operator++() ;
// Definition of prefix ++
string& string::operator++()
{
   tracer.dump("operator++()" , this) ;
   for(int i = 0 ; i < length ; ++i)
      ++ptr[i] ;
   return *this ;
}

// Declaration of prefix --
string& operator--() ;
// Definition of prefix --
string& string::operator--()
{
   tracer.dump("operator--()" , this) ;
   for(int i = 0 ; i < length ; ++i)
      --ptr[i] ;
   return *this ;
}
```

```
// Declaration of postfix ++
string operator++(int) ;
// Definition of postfix ++
string string::operator++(int)
{
  tracer.dump("operator++(int)" , this) ;
  string temp(*this) ;
  ++(*this) ;   // use prefix ++
  return temp ;
}

// Declaration of postfix --
string operator--(int) ;
// Definition of postfix --
string string::operator--(int)
{
  tracer.dump("operator--(int)" , this) ;
  string temp(*this) ;
  --(*this) ;   // use prefix --
  return temp ;
}
```

Now let's run a test on the overloaded increment function. Note that for the prefix operator, both s1 and s2 have the same value, but for the postfix operator, s4 has retained its initial value while s3 still got modified.

Example 8.56

```
#include "mystring.h"
#include "mystring.cpp"

int main()
{
  // Apply prefix operator
  string s1("ABC") , s2(++s1) ;
  s1.print("s1") ;
  s2.print("s2") ;

  // Apply postfix operator
  string s3("ABC") , s4(s3++) ;
  s3.print("s3") ;
  s4.print("s4") ;

  return 0 ;
}
```

The output is:

```
s1: "BCD" 3
s2: "BCD" 3
s3: "BCD" 3
s4: "ABC" 3
```

How to overload `new` and `delete`

The operators `new` and `delete` may be overloaded for the `string` class so that these functions gain control whenever a *single instance* of the class is allocated from the heap. The allocation of an *array* of `string` instances will always invoke the global operators `new` and `delete` (`::new()` and `::delete()`), as will the allocation of a single instance of some class if it has not been overloaded. This could be useful if you wanted to display your own message should an out-of-memory condition occur.

For example, here is a very simple case of overloading `new()` for the `string` class. The one input argument that is automatically passed to the function is the size of a `string` instance, denominated in bytes. The global function `::new()` is then used to obtain the space on the heap. (Remember that the size of a `char` is exactly one byte.)

Example 8.57

```
// Declaration
static void* operator new(size_t) ;

// Definition
void* string::operator new(size_t size)
{
   tracer.dump("operator new") ;
   void* temp = new char[size] ;
   if(temp == 0)
      puts("Out of heap space") ;
   return temp ;
}
```

☞ The X3J16 Technical Committee has adopted a proposal that allows a class to overload the functions operator new[]() and operator delete[]() so that control is retained whenever an array of the class type is allocated on the heap. However, no C++ compiler currently supports this feature.

Here is the `delete` operator for the `string` class is overloaded. The one argument that is passed to the function is a pointer to the `string` instance on the heap to be released. This is done by calling the global function `::delete()`.

Example 8.58

```
// Declaration
static void operator delete(void*) ;

// Definition
void string::operator delete(void* p)
{
   tracer.dump("operator delete") ;
   delete p ;
}
```

Here is a test of the overloaded `new` and `delete` operators with the debugging information turned on.

Example 8.59

```
#include "mystring.h"
#include "mystring.cpp"

int main()
{
   string::debug(trace::ON) ;
   string* ptr_string = new string("ABC") ;
   delete ptr_string ;

   return 0 ;
}
```

The output is:

```
operator new
Press a key...
char* constructor 09BA
Press a key...
Destructor 09BA
Press a key...
operator delete
Press a key...
```

■ Review Questions

1) Why would you want to overload a function?

2) What are the five steps that the compiler goes through in order to determine which of several overloaded functions it should call?

3) In what cases would you overload a class function as a member, and in what cases would you overload it as a nonmember?

4) Why would an overloaded member function return *this?

5) What is type-safe linkage, and why is it needed?

6) When and why should the overloaded assignment operator check for self-assignment?

7) What are the advantages and disadvantages of overloading an operator more than once so that it can accommodate all possible input argument types?

8) Why does an overloaded operator[]() return by reference?

9) How does the overloading of the increment and decrement operators differ in AT&T version 2.1 from version 2.0?

■ Exercise #1

Overload the unary operator ! for the string class as a member function so that it returns 'true' if the string pointed at by ptr is empty, 'false' otherwise. After this is working, overload it as a nonmember friend function.

■ Exercise #2

Modify the fraction class from Chapter 7, Exercise #1 so that add() is replaced by operator+(), sub() by operator-(), mult() by operator*(), div() by operator/(), and inc() by operator++().

The main() function should now be:

```
int main()
{
    fraction f1 , f2(2L , 0L) ;
    fraction f3(f2) ;
    f1.print() ;
    f2.print() ;
    f3.print() ;
    f3 = f3 + fraction(-5 , 4) ;
    f1 = f2 + f3 ;
    f1.print() ;
    f1 = f2 - f3 ;
    f1.print() ;
    f1 = f2 * f3 ;
```

```
        f1.print() ;
        (++(++f1)).print() ;
        f1 = f2 / f3 ;
        f1.print() ;

        return 0 ;
    }
```

Exercise #3

Overload the function call operator () for the string class to accept one argument of a constant string by reference. Have the function return the number of times the explicit input argument can be found within the implicit calling argument. For example, if the invoking string points to "AABBAA", then an explicit string pointing to "AA" would yield an answer of 2 and an explicit string pointing to "A" would yield an answer of 4.

Exercise #4

Revise the array class in Exercise #4 in Chapter 5 to take advantage of operator overloading.

Exercise #5

A complex number is written in the form: A + Bi, where A is the real part, B is the imaginary part, and i is defined to be the square root of -1.

Given the following skeleton declaration for the class complex:

```
class complex
{
    float real ;
    float imag ;

     public:
    // All member and nonmember functions
} ;
```

and the `main()` function:

```
int main ()
{
   complex c1 = 2.0 ;
   complex c2(1.2 , 3.4) ;
   complex c3 = c1 + 1.0 + c2 ;
   complex c4 ;
   c4 = c3 ;
   printf("c1 = %0.2f + %0.2fi\n" , c1.get_real(), c1.get_imag()) ;
   printf("c2 = %0.2f + %0.2fi\n" , c2.get_real(), c2.get_imag()) ;
   printf("c3 = %0.2f + %0.2fi\n" , c3.get_real(), c3.get_imag()) ;
   printf("c4 = %0.2f + %0.2fi\n" , c4.get_real(), c4.get_imag()) ;

   return 0 ;
}
```

and the output:

```
c1 = 2.00 + 0.00i
c2 = 1.20 + 3.40i
c3 = 4.20 + 3.40i
c4 = 4.20 + 3.40i
```

write the following functions for the class `complex`:

- A constructor function that can accommodate 0, 1 or 2 arguments. The default value for both arguments is 0.0. Use only the member initialization list.

- A copy constructor. Use only the member initialization list.

- An overloaded `operator+()`.

- An overloaded `operator=()` that also checks for self-assignment.

- Accessor functions to return the real and imaginary portions of the number.

Be sure to declare all of the member functions within the class definition, and define them outside the definition.

■ Exercise #6

Recall that you cannot allocate a 2-dimensional array from the heap at execution time because the compiler needs to know the number of columns. You can solve this dilemma by creating a class called `TwoDimensionalArray`. This class contains an array of pointers to integers (the length of which is equal to the number of rows), each element of which will point an array of integers (the length of which is equal to the number of columns).

The outline for the class is:

```
class TwoDimensionalArray
{
   // A pointer to an array of pointers to ints
   int** ptr ;

   // Number of rows and columns
   int rows , cols ;

      public:
   TwoDimensionalArray(int , int) ;
   ~TwoDimensionalArray() ;

   // This overloaded operator[]() function will return the address
   // contained in element 'i' of the array of pointers
   int* operator[](int i) const ;
} ;
```

Write the member functions for this class and a `main()` function to test the class.

■ Exercise #7

Using a long integer (4 bytes), the largest factorial that can be computed is that of 12 because the factorial of 13 (6,227,020,800) causes an overflow condition. However, you can still compute the factorial of larger numbers by writing a class that emulates very big numbers through the use of a string of characters.

Given the following `LongNumber` class definition:

```
class LongNumber
{
   unsigned length ;
   char* digit_ptr ;

      public:
   // All member and friend functions (declaration or
   // definition)
} ;
```

and the `main()` function:

```
int main()
{
   const int limit = 25;
   for(int i = 0 ; i <= limit ; ++i)
   {
     LongNumber LN(i) ;
     LN.sum() ;
     LN.factorial() ;
   }

   return 0 ;
}
```

copy the preceding code and write the member and nonmember functions for the class `LongNumber` that are designed to find the factorial of a number and the sum of all numbers up to and including a specific number. Be sure to use operator function overloading whenever you need to perform arithmetic operations, or compare numeric values, etc.

Note: The factorial of 25 is 15,511,210,043,330,985,984,000,000 and the sum of the numbers from 0 to 25 is 325.

■ Exercise #8

Given the following class:

```
class Date
{
   int month ;
   int day ;
   int year ;

      public:
   // All member and friend function declarations
   } ;
```

write the member and functions to read and write a date, increment a date by one day, compare two dates to see which one is greater, etc. Be sure to use operator overloading where applicable.

Notes

Notes

Chapter 9

Type conversions

Type conversions are an integral part of the C++ language, and provide you with the means by which you can convert, or cast, one type of data into another. With the introduction of user-defined types into the language, the number of possibilities for converting one type into another type increases from one to four. This chapter will explore in detail all four conversion methods.

Types of casts

In the C language there are two types of casts: implicit and explicit. The compiler will always perform an implicit cast whenever it must convert from one primitive type into another primitive type. For example, if you store a `float` into an `int`, the compiler is smart enough to throw away the fractional part and store the result into the `int`. If you store a `long` into a `double`, once again the compiler will perform the necessary conversion without your having to worry about it. On the other hand, you cannot store a `float` into a pointer type because a pointer is what's called a "derived type" and the compiler has no "rule" with which to do this. Similarly, in C++ there is no built-in "rule" with which the compiler can convert a primitive type into a user-defined type, and vice-versa.

Whenever a (non-reference) cast occurs in C or C++, it is important to remember that a *temporary* object is created that is used to complete the operation, whether that operation involves initialization, assignment, argument passing, etc. This temporary object is considered to be an 'rvalue', i.e., something that cannot be modified. On the other hand, in C++ you may cast into a reference type, in which case the result is considered to be an 'lvalue', i.e., something which can be modified. Of course, a cast into a *constant* reference is once again an 'rvalue'.

How casting is done

In C you know that when a cast must be explicitly written, it is enclosed within parentheses and treated as a unary operator, i.e., affecting the operand that immediately follows the cast. C++, however, provides a new style of casting (called function style) in which the *operand itself* may be written in parentheses. Generically speaking, this is what the two styles of casting look like:

Example 9.1

```
// C style
(type)variable

// Function style
type(variable)
```

For primitive types involving values or variables one method is just as good as the other. For example:

Example 9.2

```
(int)1.2 == int(1.2)

int number = 1 ;
(float)number == float(number)
```

Casting possibilities

As mentioned earlier, if you logically divide the data types in C++ into two categories, primitive (built-in) and user-defined (classes), then there are four ways to do casting:

- Primitive type to primitive type

- Primitive type to user-defined type

- User-defined type to primitive type

- User-defined type to user-defined type

Each of these types will be discussed in the following sections.

Primitive type to primitive type

The conversion of one primitive type to a different primitive type is handled automatically by the compiler based upon pre-determined rules. Essentially there are only two primitive types: 1) integral, and 2) floating point. The conversion from an integral type into a floating point type merely involves the appending of a zero fractional part, while the conversion from a floating point type into an integral type truncates the fractional part. This operation is handled in C++ exactly the same way it is handled in C.

Primitive type to user-defined type

You have already seen how to cast from a primitive type to a user-defined type by using a constructor function. For example, when an instance `in` of the class `integer` is created, and you want to initialize this instance with the number 1, the correct syntax is:

Example 9.3

```
integer in(1) ;
```

User-defined type to primitive type

Now the question is: how do you cast from a user-defined instance into some primitive type? That is, what does it mean to take an instance `in` of class `integer` and convert it into something as simple (primitive) as an `int`? To attempt such an operation in an initialization statement, you would write:

Example 9.4

```
class integer
{
   // Class members
} ;

integer in ;

// Implicit cast
int num = in ;

// C style cast
int num = (int)in ;

// Function style cast
int num = int(in) ;
```

It should come as no surprise to you that because a user-defined type is involved, the compiler has no idea how this should be done. Certainly a constructor function is *not* the answer because they do not exist for primitive types.

To solve this problem, the C++ language syntax provides the capability to write a class member function called a *conversion* function. Generically speaking, this function does a conversion *from* the type of the class to which it belongs *into* any other type (primitive or user-defined). However, it is almost always used to convert to some primitive type. The body of the function determines the value of the primitive type and returns it in the same fashion as any other function might return a value.

The rules for writing a conversion function are as follows:

■   The name of this function is the word `operator` followed by the type into which you want to do the conversion;

■   It must be a *member* (not friend) function of the class from which the conversion is to occur;

■   There is no explicit return type, because the function name itself implies the return type;

■   There are no input arguments to the function;

■ The function must return a value (usually having the same type as the name of the function itself);

■ The function probably should be declared as an accessor since it usually does not modify any class data members.

For example, within a class called `integer` you might have these declarations:

Example 9.5

```
class integer
{
    public:
// Convert from integer to int
operator int() const ;

// Convert from integer to double
operator double() const ;

// Convert from integer to const char*
operator const char*() const ;

// Convert from integer to class X
operator X() const ;
} ;
```

Note that if the conversion function is designed to convert the class into some pointer type, then the principle of data hiding can be violated because now you have provided the caller with the address of a private data member, thereby opening the possibility for a non-member function to modify the data member. Therefore, you should declare the return type of the function to be `const`. The same is true for returning by reference.

Perhaps you're wondering why you can't simply create and call an accessor function within the class if all you want to do is return the value of a private data member. The answer is you can, except that the conversion function obviates the need to explicitly write a member function name. Later in this chapter you will see how you can create a Boolean expression from a user-defined instance by the use of a conversion function.

First, let's consider the case where you have just one conversion function in a class. In this situation there is never any ambiguity as to what the compiler is supposed to do when converting from a class instance because it has just one function from which to choose. For example, this program casts from a user-defined type into type `int`.

Example 9.6

```
#include <stdio.h>

class integer
{
  int number ;

     public:
  integer(int = 0) ;
  operator int() const ;
} ;

inline integer::integer(int n) : number(n) {}

inline integer::operator int() const
{
  return number ;
}

int main()
{
  integer in(1) ;
  // Test implicit casting. The compiler looks for an
  // operator int() function to use implicitly
  printf("in = %d\n" , int(in)) ;

  return 0 ;
}
```

The output is:

```
in = 1
```

If you are going to have more than one conversion operator function for a given class, no promotions or conversions are considered by the compiler when determining which function should be called. Therefore, it is up to you to ensure that exact matches are always in effect when primitive types are involved, as shown in the following example.

Example 9.7

```c
#include <stdio.h>
class integer
{
    int number ;

        public:
    integer(int = 0) ;
    operator int() const ;
    operator float() const ;
} ;

inline integer::integer(int n) : number(n) {}

inline integer::operator int() const
{
    return number ;
}

inline integer::operator float() const
{
    return (float)number ;
}

int main()
{
    integer in(123) ;
    printf("in = %f\n" , float(in)) ;
    printf("in = %d\n" , int(in)) ;

    return 0 ;
}
```

The output is:

```
in = 123.000000
in = 123
```

Notice that in the following example even the slight change in the declaration of `f1` from `float` to `double` will cause a compilation error because the compiler doesn't know which operator conversion function to choose in order to convert from type `integer` into type `double`.

Example 9.8 *(Will not compile!)*

```
#include <stdio.h>

class integer
{
   int number ;
      public:

   integer(int = 0) ;
   operator int() const ;
   operator float() const ;
} ;

inline integer::integer(int n) : number(n) {}

inline integer::operator int() const
{
   return number ;
}

inline integer::operator float() const
{
   return (float)number ;
}

int main()
{
   integer in(123) ;
   printf("in = %f\n" , double(in)) ;
   printf("in = %d\n" , int(n)) ;

   return 0 ;
}
```

The compiler error message is:

```
Ambiguity between 'integer::operator int() const' and
'integer::operator float() const'
```

On the other hand, the following example now works because when the compiler is choosing between the `const char*` and the `float` to use when converting into a `double`, there is no ambiguity whatsoever.

Example 9.9

```
#include <stdio.h>

class integer
{
   int number ;

      public:
   integer(int = 0) ;
   operator const char*() const ;
   operator float() const ;
} ;

inline integer::integer(int n) : number(n) {}

inline integer::operator const char*() const
{
   return "A" ;
}

inline integer::operator float() const
{
   return (float)number ;
}

int main()
{
   integer in(123) ;
   printf("in = %f\n" , double(in)) ;
   printf("in = %s\n" , (const char*)in) ;

   return 0 ;
}
```

The output is:

```
in = 123.000000
in = A
```

User-defined type to user-defined type

Sometimes you want to be able to convert from one user-defined class into another user-defined class. Each class must then have a conversion function that outputs an instance of the other class. Because of this "circular" design, a forward declaration of one of the classes is required.

317

For example, suppose you have two classes, each of which maintains a date. The first maintains it as a Gregorian date, i.e., with two data fields: a month and a day. The second maintains it as an ordinal date, i.e., the absolute day number of the year. This program allows you to freely convert from one date format into the other. (Note that leap year is ignored.)

Example 9.10

```
#include <stdio.h>

class DayTable
{
   int days[12] ;

      public:
   DayTable() ;
   int operator[](int) const ;
} ;

DayTable::DayTable()
{
   int array[] =
   {
      31 , 28 , 31 , 30 , 31 , 30 ,
      31 , 31 , 30 , 31 , 30 , 31
   } ;

   for(int i = 0 ; i < 12 ; ++i)
      days[i] = array[i] ;
}

inline int DayTable::operator[](int n) const
{
   return days[n] ;
}

// Global instance of DayTable
DayTable table ;

// Forward declaration of Odate
class Odate ;
```

```
class Gdate
{
   int month , day ;

      public:
   Gdate(int = 0 , int = 0) ;
   operator Odate() const ;
   void print() ;
} ;

class Odate
{
   int days ;

      public:
   Odate(int = 0) ;
   operator Gdate() const ;
   void print() ;
} ;

inline Gdate::Gdate(int m , int d) : month(m) , day(d) {}

inline Odate::Odate(int n) : days(n) {}

Gdate::operator Odate() const
{
   int days = day ;
   for(int i = 0 ; i < month-1 ; ++i)
      days += table[i] ;
   return Odate(days) ;
}

Odate::operator Gdate() const
{
   int month = 1 ;
   int day = days ;
   for(int i = 0 ; day > table[i] ; ++i)
    {
      day -= table[i] ;
      ++month ;
    }
   return Gdate(month , day) ;
}

void Gdate::print()
{
   printf("Month = %d  Day = %d\n" , month , day) ;
}
```

```
void Odate::print()
{
   printf("Day number = %d\n" , days) ;
}

int main()
{
   Gdate Gd1(3 , 2) ;
   Odate Od1(Gd1) ;
   Od1.print() ;
   Gdate Gd2(Od1) ;
   Gd2.print() ;

   return 0 ;
}
```

The output is:

```
Day number = 61
Month = 3   Day = 2
```

Conversion functions used to emulate Boolean types

In C it's possible to take any primitive type (e.g., `int`, `long`, `char`, `float`) or pointer type and treat it as a Boolean value. In other words, the following example is valid code because `number` has an inherent Boolean value (false if zero, true if not zero).

Example 9.11

```
int number = 1 ;
if(number)
// Do something
```

However, in C++, for some class called `integer` and an instance called `in`, the following code will cause a compilation error because `in` is not a primitive type, and the compiler has no idea if `in` is 'true' or 'false'.

Example 9.12

```
integer in(1) ;
if(in)
// Do something
```

The same situation would occur if `in` were used as the first operand to the ternary operator, which requires a Boolean expression. However, this code can be made to work if you define a conversion function in the class. This function can then return whatever primitive value it wants, which will then become the value of the Boolean expression. Such a technique might be useful if you want to provide a more convenient way for the user of your class to check for the success or failure of a constructor function. In other words, you could have the constructor function set an error flag if it fails to do its job properly, and then have the conversion function return this flag whenever the user tests the instance that was just (presumably) created.

Note that if you define more than one conversion function that returns a primitive (Boolean) type, and attempt to use a class instance as a Boolean value, a compilation error will occur because the compiler has no way to determine which function to call.

In this example the `Gdate` class will perform a very simple validity check on its input arguments. If the test fails, an error flag will be set on for use by the conversion function.

Example 9.13

```
#include <stdio.h>

class DayTable
{
   int days[12] ;

      public:
   DayTable() ;
   int operator[](int) const ;
} ;
```

```
DayTable::DayTable()
{
   int array[] =
    {
       31 , 28 , 31 , 30 , 31 , 30
       31 , 31 , 30 , 31 , 30 , 31
    } ;
   for(int i = 0 ; i < 12 ; ++i)
       days[i] = array[i] ;
}

inline int DayTable::operator[](int n) const
{
   return days[n] ;
}

// Global instance of DayTable
DayTable table ;

class Gdate
{
   int month , day ;
   int error ;

      public:
   Gdate(int = 0 , int = 0) ;
   operator int() const ;
   void print() ;
} ;

inline
Gdate::Gdate(int m , int d) : error(0) , month(m) , day(d)
{
   if(m < 1 || m > 12 || d < 1 || d > table[m-1])
       error = 1 ;
}

Gdate::operator int() const
{
   return !error ;
}

void Gdate::print()
{
   printf("Month = %d  Day = %d\n" , month , day) ;
}
```

```
int main()
{
   printf("Enter a month and day: ") ;
   int r , month , day ;
   while((r = scanf("%d%d" , &month , &day)) != EOF)
    {
     if(r != 2)
        puts("Input error") ;
     else
      {
        Gdate date(month , day) ;
        if(date)
           date.print() ;
        else
           puts("Date error") ;
      }
     fflush(stdin) ;
     printf("Next month and day: ") ;
    }

   return 0 ;
}
```

A typical run would yield the following output:

```
Enter a month and day: 1 31
Month = 1   Day = 31
Next month and day: 1 32
Date error
Next month and day: 0 1
Date error
Next month and day: 12 31
Month = 12   Day = 31
Next month and day: ^Z
```

Avoid ambiguous situations

If you decide to use a conversion function, you must ensure that it does not create an ambiguous situation if you are also using overloaded operator functions.

The following example has both an overloaded addition operator and a conversion function. In main() the instance in3 is being initialized by adding the instance in1 to the number 3. Now the compiler does not know what to do. First, it could use implicit type conversion and the constructor function to convert the 3 to type integer, and then use this temporary instance as the second argument to the addition function. On the other hand, it could use the conversion function to change the instance in1 into type int, and then use the built-in addition operator to

323

add the resulting 1 and 3. Since it has no reason to give preference to one method over the other, it will yield a compilation error.

Example 9.14   *(Will not compile!)*

```
class integer
{
  int number ;
     public:

  integer(int = 0) ;
  operator int() const ;
  friend integer operator+(const integer& , const integer&) ;
} ;

integer::integer(int n) : number(n) {}

integer::operator int() const
{
  return number ;
}

integer operator+(const integer& in1 , const integer& in2)
{
  return in1.number + in2.number ;
}

int main()
{
  integer in1(1) , in2(2) , in3(in1 + 3) ;

  return 0 ;
}
```

The compiler error message is:

```
Ambiguity between 'operator +(const integer &,const integer &)'
and 'integer::operator int() const'
```

■ Review questions

1) What is the difference between a C style cast and a C++ style cast?

2) Why is a user-defined function needed to convert from a primitive type into a user-defined type, and vice-versa?

3) What is another method to convert from one class into another class?

4) When converting from one user-defined type into another user-defined type, why is a forward declaration required?

■ Exercise #1

Given the class:

```
class letter
{
   char character ;
      public:
   letter(char = '\0') ;
} ;
```

complete the class so that the user is able to write an `if(instance)` statement that checks to see whether the class got instantiated with a letter of the alphabet (upper or lower case). Be sure to test both the good and bad cases.

■ Exercise #2

Write a program that uses a conversion function to accommodate the following `main()` function. Do not use an overloaded `operator+()` function. The class `integer` has one data member of type `int`.

```
int main()
{
   integer in(1) ;
   printf("sum = %d\n" , 1 + in + 2) ;
   return 0 ;
}
```

The output should be:

```
sum = 4
```

■ Exercise #3

Rewrite Example 9.10 to use constructor functions instead of conversion functions.

■ Exercise #4

Write a class called `Fahrenheit` whose one data member reflects the temperature, and another class called `Celsius` whose one data member also reflects the temperature. Using conversion functions, provide the capability for an instance of one class to be converted into the type of the other class.

To convert from Celsius to Fahrenheit, the formula is:

Fahrenheit = Celsius x 9/5 + 32

and to convert from Fahrenheit to Celsius the formula is:

Celsius = 5/9 x (Fahrenheit - 32)

■ Exercise #5

Modify the fraction class from Chapter 7, Exercise #1 so that it now contains another data member called error. The constructor function must set error off if the denominator is not zero, and on if the denominator is zero. Then write a conversion function that returns 'true' if error is off, and 'false' if it is on. Finally, write a `main()` function that tests the enhanced class, as follows:

```
int main()
{
    fraction f1(6 , 0) ;
    if(!f1)
        puts("f1 is invalid") ;
    fracton f2(6 , 4) ;
    if(!f2)
        puts("f2 is invalid") ;

    return 0 ;
}
```

Notes

Notes

Notes

Chapter 10

Class inheritance

Inheritance is the process by which a derived class is created as the result of extending, or enhancing, an existing class. Stated differently, the derived class is inherited from a parent (or base) class. This capability saves you from having to "reinvent the wheel", because if a new class greatly resembles an existing class, then all of the properties of the existing class can be inherited into the new class, and any new members can then be added.

Why use inheritance?

Inheritance allows you to collect related classes into a hierarchy with the classes at the top serving as abstractions for those below. This implies that a derived class is a specialization of its parent class. In other words, the derived class "is a" type of base class, but with more detail added. For this reason, the relationship between a derived class and its base class is called an "is-a" relationship.

An example of inheritance

As an example of inheritance, in Chapter 8 you saw how a `string` class could be created and then utilize the capabilities of operator function overloading to make the class interface more intuitive. Now suppose you were to put this class into a library and announce its existence so that users could take advantage of it. But someone then says to you, "The class is fine, except that I want to overload the unary '-' as a member function so that it reverses the letters in the string and returns a new instance of the class. What should I do?". Your answer in this case would be for the user to derive a new class from the `string` class and add the new function. Then, when instantiations are made from the newly created class, all of the capabilities of the original class will still be there, plus the added capability of the new function. Since this newly created class is the `string` class with more features, the new class really "is a" kind of `string` class.

> ☞ The terms base class/derived class, or parent class/child class, are used to refer to the classes involved in the process of inheritance. The terms super class/sub class are not used because they are misleading in that the super class is the base class, and yet it is still "smaller" than the sub, or derived, class.

How to define a derived class

A singly inherited derived class is defined by writing:

- The keyword `class`;
- The name of the derived class;
- A single colon (:);
- The type of derivation (`private`, `protected`, or `public`);
- The name of the base, or parent, class;
- The remainder of the class definition.

For example, here is the definition of a class called `new_string` that is derived from class `string`. The overloaded `operator-()` function previously mentioned is declared.

Example 10.1

```
class new_string : public string
{
     public:
  // Reverse the letters
  new_string operator-() ;

  // Other function declarations
} ;
```

☞ A derived class is always at least as big as its parent class, so that an instance of the derived class *always* contains all of the members of its parent class. You cannot "subtract" anything from a parent class. However, *accessing* the inherited members is a different matter, and will be discussed shortly. A derived class can modify or enhance its inherited members by either adding new members or overriding (hiding) the definition of members that were inherited.

It is also important to understand the privileges that the derived class has insofar as access to members of its parent class are concerned. In other words, just because you happen to derive a class does *not* mean that you are automatically granted complete and unlimited access privileges to the members of the parent class. To understand this you must look at the different types of derivation and the effect of each one.

Private derivation

If no specific type of derivation is listed, then a private derivation is assumed (if you are using the keyword `class`; if you are using structures, then a public derivation is assumed). If a new class is derived *privately* from its parent class, then:

■ The *private* members inherited from the base class are *inaccessible* to new member functions in the derived class. This means that the creator of the base class has absolute control over the accessibility of these members, and there is no way that you can override this.

■ The *public* members inherited from the base class have *private* access privilege. In other words, they are treated as though they were declared as new private members of the derived class, so that new member functions can access them. However, if another private derivation occurs from this derived class, then per the first paragraph, these members are inaccessible to new member functions.

For example, in this program the base class has a private data member called `number`. The derived class inherits `number`, but cannot gain access to it in the function `derived::f()`. Therefore, this is an error and will not compile.

Example 10.2   *(Will not compile!)*

```
class base
{
     private:
   int number ;
} ;

class derived : private base
{
     public:
   void f ()
    {
      // private base member not accessible
      ++number ;
    }
} ;
```

The compiler error message is:

```
'base::number' is not accessible in function derived::f()
```

Now let's change the program so that `number` is public. Since public members of a base class are inherited as private in the derived class, the function `derived::f()` has no problem accessing it. However, when another class is derived from class `derived`, this new class inherits `number` but cannot access it. (This is essentially the same situation that was shown in Example 10.2.) So once again the program will fail to compile.

Example 10.3   *(Will not compile!)*

```
class base
{
     public:
   int number ;
} ;
```

```
class derived : private base
{
     public:
  void f ()
   {
      // Access to number is OK
      ++number ;
   }
} ;

class derived2 : private derived
{
     public:
  void g ()
   {
      // Access to number is prohibited
      ++number ;
   }
} ;
```

The compiler error message is:

```
'base::number' is not accessible in function derived2::g ()
```

Of course, if `derived2::g()` were to call upon `derived::f()`, there is no problem since `derived::f()` is public and inherited into `derived2` as private.

Example 10.4

```
class base
{
     public:
  int number ;
} ;

class derived : private base
{
     public:
  void f ()
   {
      // Access to number is OK
      ++number ;
   }
} ;
```

```
class derived2 : private derived
{
    public:
  void g()
   {
      // Access to derived::f() is OK
      f() ;
   }
} ;
```

But there's another way. In a private derivation, the class can selectively choose which public members are inherited as private or as public. This is done by writing an *access declaration*, which involves declaring the member in the public section of the derived class. Be sure, however, not to repeat the type of the member.

Here is Example 10.3 again, but now the member number has been inherited by the class derived as public. Therefore, it is then inherited by derived2 as private and may be accessed. This technique also works for functions. Just remember to leave off the parentheses when declaring the function name.

Example 10.5

```
class base
{
    public:
  int number ;
} ;

class derived : private base
{
    public:
  base::number ;
  void f()
   {
      // Access to number is OK
      ++number ;
   }
} ;

class derived2 : private derived
{
    public:
  void g()
   {
     // Access to number is OK
     ++number ;
   }
} ;
```

As you have just seen, private derivations are very restrictive in terms of accessibility of the base class members. Therefore, this type of derivation is rarely used. But there's another reason to avoid private derivations. Put simply, it fails to model an "is-a" relationship between the derived and base classes. In other words, every derived class should be a kind of base class, but in a private derivation, the compiler cannot implicitly cast from a derived type into a base type.

Public derivation

Public derivations are much more common than private derivations. In this situation:

- The *private* members inherited from the base class are *inaccessible* to new member functions in the derived class. (This is exactly the same as if a private derivation had occurred.)

- The *public* members inherited from the base class may be accessed by new member functions in the derived class and by instances of the derived class.

Here is Example 10.2 again, but now the derived class is inherited publicly. Nevertheless, it fails to compile because `number` is still inaccessible to `derived::f()`.

Example 10.6   *(Will not compile!)*

```
class base
{
     private:
   int number ;
} ;

class derived : public base
{
     public:
   void f ()
    {
      // Access to number is prohibited
      ++number ;
    }
} ;
```

The compiler error message is:

```
'base::number' is not accessible in function derived::f()
```

The *only* way for `derived::f()` to access `number` would be to make the data member `public` in the base class. Of course, this is a bad idea because it violates the principle of data hiding.

Protected access rights

In the preceding example, declaring the data member `number` as private is much too restrictive because clearly new member functions in a derived class need to gain access to it and (other data members) in order to perform some useful work. For example, consider the function to reverse the letters in a `string` object. How could this be done if the new member function could not access the pointer `ptr` to the string literal?

To solve this dilemma, the C++ syntax provides another access specification called `protected`. Here is how protected works:

■ In a *private* derivation the protected members inherited from the base class have *private* access privileges. Therefore, they may be accessed by new member functions and friends of the derived class.

■ In a *public* derivation the protected members inherited from the base class retain their protected status. They may be accessed by new member functions and friends of the derived class.

In both situations the new member functions and friends of the derived class have unrestricted access to protected members. However, insofar as *instances* of the derived class are concerned, protected and private are one and the same, so that direct access is always denied. Thus, you can see that the new category of `protected` provides a middle ground between `public` and `private` by granting access to new functions and friends of the derived class while still blocking out access by non-derived class member and friend functions.

As an illustration, here is Example 10.6 again, but now the access category of `number` has been changed to `protected`, and it compiles just fine.

Example 10.7

```
class base
{
     protected:
   int number ;
} ;

class derived : public base
{
     public:
   void f ()
    {
    // Access to number is OK
    ++number ;
    }
} ;
```

Protected derivation

In addition to doing private and public derivations, you may also do a protected derivation. In this situation:

■ The *private* members inherited from the base class are *inaccessible* to new member functions in the derived class. (This is exactly the same as if a private or public derivation had occurred.)

■ The *protected* members inherited from the base class have *protected* access privilege.

■ The *public* members inherited from the base class have *protected* access privilege.

Thus, the only difference between a public and a protected derivation is how the public members of the parent class are inherited. It is unlikely that you will ever have occasion to do this type of derivation.

Summary of access privileges

To summarize, if the designer of the base class wants no one, not even a derived class, to have access to a member, then that member should be made `private`. If the designer wants any derived class functions to have access to it, then that member should be made `protected`. If the designer wants to let everyone, including instances, have access to that member (usually a function), then that member should be made `public`.

The entire realm of derivation categories and who has access to what can be summarized in these four rules:

■ Regardless of the type of derivation (public or private) private members are inherited by the derived class, but *cannot* be accessed by a new member function of the derived class, and certainly not by instances of the derived class.

■ In a private derivation, the derived class inherits public and protected members as private. A new member function of the derived class can therefore access these members, but instances of the derived class may not. Also, any new member functions of any subsequently derived class may not gain access to these members because of the first rule.

■ In a public derivation, the derived class inherits public members as public, and protected members as protected. A new member function of the derived class may access the public and protected members of the base class, but instances of the derived class may access only the public members.

■ In a protected derivation, the derived class inherits public and protected members as protected. A new member function of the derived class may access the public and protected members of the base class, but instances of the derived class may access only the public members.

These rules can also be summarized by this table:

Table 10.1

Derivation type	Base class member	Access in derived class
private	private	(inaccessible)
	public	private
	protected	private
public	private	(inaccessible)
	public	public
	protected	protected
protected	private	(inaccessible)
	public	protected
	protected	protected

How to access base class members using a derived class instance

An instance of a derived class has complete access to the public members (usually functions) of the base class. Assuming that a member with the same name does not exist within the scope of the derived class, the member from the base class will automatically be used. Because there is no ambiguity involved in this situation, you do not need to use the scope resolution operator to refer to this base class member. However, you may do so.

In this program the function `base::get_number()` will be accessed twice. But there is a slight difference insofar as how it is reached. In the first call, the compiler will look at the scope of class `derived` to see if a function called `get_number()` exists. If not, it will then look at the scope of class `base`. In the second call, the compiler will look directly at the scope of the base class for `get_number()`.

Example 10.8

```
#include <stdio.h>

class base
{
    protected:
  int number ;

    public:
  base(int = 0) ;
  int get_number() const ;
} ;

inline base::base(int n) : number(n) {}

inline int base::get_number() const
{
  return number ;
}

class derived : public base
{
} ;

int main()
{
  derived d ;

  // First checks class derived, then class base
  printf("%d\n" , d.get_number()) ;

  // Goes directly to class base
  printf("%d\n" , d.base::get_number()) ;

  return 0 ;
}
```

The output is:

```
0
0
```

How to override (hide) base class member names

In addition to creating new members whose names are different than those inherited from the base class, a derived class may selectively override, or hide, existing names. This is done by declaring a member in the derived class with exactly the same name as that of a member from the base class.

This means that if an instance or member function of the *derived* class refers to a data member of the *base* class that has been overridden, the member from the *derived* class will be used by default. Since the derived class contains its base class, in order to "escape" from automatically referring to the member of the derived class and instead refer to the member from the *base* class, the base class name and scope resolution operator are required.

In the following example the derived class has overridden `base::number` with its own version of `number,` and overridden `base::get_number()` with a new function that returns the value of `number` plus one. Note that the first call to `get_number()` calls `derived::get_number()`, while the second calls `base::get_number()`.

Example 10.9

```
#include <stdio.h>

class base
{
    protected:
  int number ;

    public:
  base(int = 0) ;
  int get_number() const ;
} ;

inline base::base(int n) : number(n) {}

inline int base::get_number() const
{
    return number ;
}
```

```
class derived : public base
{
  int number ;

    public:
  derived(int = 1) ;
  int get_number() const ;
} ;

inline derived::derived(int n) : number(n) {}

inline int derived::get_number() const
{
  return number + 1 ;
}

int main()
{
  derived d ;

  // Calls derived::get_number()
  printf("%d\n" , d.get_number()) ;

  // Calls base::get_number()
  printf("%d\n" , d.base::get_number()) ;

  return 0 ;
}
```

The output is:

```
2
0
```

Summary of compiler lookup rules

In summary, using derived instances to access *function* members without the base class name and scope resolution operator, the compiler resolves the address by asking:

- Does the member have scope in the derived class? If so, use it; if not...

- Does the member have scope in the parent class? If so, use it; if not...

- Does the member have scope higher up in the hierarchy? If so, use it; if not, generate a compilation error. (Functions with the same name at file scope are not considered.)

Similarly, a function in a derived class resolves the address of a *data* member by asking:

- Does the member have scope in the function itself? If so, use it; if not...

- Does the member have (derived) class scope? If so, use it; if not...

- Does the member have scope in the parent class that is accessible? If so, use it; if not...

- Does the member have accessible scope higher up in the hierarchy? If so, use it; if not...

- Does the member exist at file scope? If so, use it; if not, generate a compilation error.

Of course, instances and member functions of the *base* class always refer to members from the *base* class since they know nothing about members of any derived classes which can only be defined in the future.

Hiding overloaded functions

Recall that function overloading only can occur with a single scope. That is, you *cannot* overload a base class function by redefining it in a derived class with a different argument list. The rationale behind this design is that if you override a function inherited from the base class, then there should be no danger of accidentally calling the base class version through the process of argument matching. In other words, if a base class function expects an `int` as an argument, and you hide it by redefining it to accept a `char*`, then calling the function using a derived instance with an `int` actual argument should cause a compilation error.

Here is an example proving that a function inherited from the base class is not examined under the rules of argument matching. It appears that the function call using an `int` as the actual argument would be a better match for the base class function that expects an `int`, rather than the derived class function that expects a `double`. But the derived class function is the one that gets called because it is the only one that the compiler knows about.

Example 10.10

```
#include <stdio.h>

class base
{
    public:
   void f(int n)
    {
        printf("n = %d\n" , n) ;
    }
} ;
```

```
class derived : public base
{
     public:
   void f(double n)
    {
       printf("n = %f\n" , n) ;
    }
} ;

int main()
{
   derived d ;
   d.f(1) ;

   return 0 ;
}
```

The output is:

```
n = 1.000000
```

Once again, even if there is no conceivable match within the scope of the derived class, the inherited members from the base class will not be examined. Therefore, this example will not compile.

Example 10.11   *(Will not compile!)*

```
#include <stdio.h>

class base
{
     public:
   void f(const char* ptr)
    {
       printf("ptr = %s\n" , ptr) ;
    }
} ;

class derived : public base
{
     public:
   void f(double n)
    {
       printf("n = %f\n" , n) ;
    }
} ;
```

```
int main()
{
  derived d ;
  d.f("A") ;

  return 0 ;
}
```

The compiler error message is:

```
'Cannot convert 'char *' to 'double'
```

However, don't forget that you can still access the hidden members from the base class by using the scope resolution operator with a derived class instance, as the following example shows.

Example 10.12

```
#include <stdio.h>

class base
{
    public:
  void f(const char* ptr)
   {
      printf("ptr = %s\n" , ptr) ;
   }
} ;

class derived : public base
{
    public:
  void f(double n)
   {
      printf("n = %f\n" , n) ;
   }
} ;

int main()
{
  derived d ;
  d.base::f("A") ;

  return 0 ;
}
```

The output is:

```
ptr = A
```

Constructor and destructor functions with derived classes

Recall that an instance of a derived class *always* contains the data members inherited from its base class. Therefore, it logically follows that whenever a derived class instance gets created, *two* constructor functions are needed to ensure the proper initialization of *all* of the data members of the instance. In other words, the constructor for the *base* class must somehow get control to do the initialization of *base* class members, and the constructor for the *derived* class must get control to initialize any new *derived* class data members.

Fortunately, the compiler takes care of this problem, and will *automatically* call both constructors. This happens because as soon as the derived class constructor gets control and establishes its formal arguments, the base class constructor will be called *immediately*, i.e., before the derived class initialization list is honored.

The only question now is, which base class constructor will be called? The answer is that if you fail to tell the compiler which one to call, it will attempt to invoke the default constructor (the one that can be called with no explicit arguments). Therefore, it is always a good idea to have a default constructor present in a base class. On the other hand, you may explicitly tell the compiler which base class constructor to call by using this syntax in the derived class's base/member initialization list:

■   The base class name (which is the name of the constructor function);

■   A list of arguments between parentheses, as in any "normal" function call. To explicitly invoke the base class default constructor, leave the argument list empty.

To repeat: because the initialization of any new *derived* class members may be dependent upon the proper initialization of the *base* class members, the base class constructor will *always* get called first. As you would expect, the destructor functions will get called in reverse order, i.e., derived class first, and base class last.

The following program shows how an argument can be passed into a base class constructor function, and traces the order of the calls to the constructor and destructor functions of both classes. Note that the derived instance d is being created with two integers. The first of these integers (a) is needed by the base class constructor to initialize base_number, while the second (b) is needed by the derived class in order to initialize derived_number.

Example 10.13

```
#include <stdio.h>

class base
{
    protected:
  int base_number ;

    public:
  base(int = 0) ;
  ~base() ;
  int get_base_number() const ;
} ;

inline base::base(int n) : base_number(n)
{
  puts("base constructor") ;
}

inline base::~base()
{
  puts("base destructor") ;
}

inline int base::get_base_number() const
{
  return base_number ;
}

class derived : public base
{
  int derived_number ;

    public:
  derived(int = 0 , int = 0) ;
  ~derived() ;
  int get_derived_number() const ;
} ;

inline derived::derived(int a , int b)
                : base(a) , derived_number(b)
{
  puts("derived constructor") ;
}

inline derived::~derived()
{
  puts("derived destructor") ;
}
```

```
inline int derived::get_derived_number() const
{
  return derived_number ;
}

int main()
{
  derived d(1 , 2) ;
  printf("d = (%d,%d)\n" , d.get_base_number() ,
                          d.get_derived_number()) ;

  return 0 ;
}
```

The output is:

```
base constructor
derived constructor
d = (1,2)
derived destructor
base destructor
```

☞ Caution: When you initialize base class data members, do *not* attempt to list them individually in the member initialization list of the derived class constructor. Their initialization is *not* the responsibility of the derived class, and in fact will cause a compilation error because the only items that can legally be written in a derived class initialization list are derived class data member names and base class constructor names.

You should also realize that base class constructor and destructor functions are unique in the sense that they are *not* inherited by the derived class. This simply means that if you create a derived class instance, then the proper constructor to handle that particular type of creation must exist within the derived class, not the base class. Stated another way, the compiler will *not* say, "Well, I can't find a constructor in the derived class with a formal argument list that matches the actual construction of the instance, so, like any other function, I will continue my search by looking to see if one exists in the scope of the base class."

Initialization of a derived instance with an existing derived instance

The initialization of a derived instance with an existing derived instance automatically invokes the copy constructor function in the derived class. Recall that if you fail to write one, then the compiler will supply one for you automatically.

Even if you write a copy constructor for the base class, and someone derives a new class from that base class and writes a copy constructor, then a potential problem exists because the compiler will *not* automatically invoke the copy constructor in the base class when the copy constructor in the derived class is invoked. Instead, the *default* constructor in the base class will get called.

The solution is to make an *explicit call* from the `derived` class copy constructor to the `base` class copy constructor. You do this by using the member initialization list to write the name of the `base` class constructor and, within parentheses, the same argument that the `derived` class copy constructor received. This is shown in the following program.

Example 10.14

```
#include <stdio.h>

class base
{
     protected:
   int base_number ;

     public:
   base(int = 0) ;
   base(const base&) ;
   ~base() ;
   int get_base_number() const ;
} ;

inline base::base(int n) : base_number(n)
{
   puts("base constructor") ;
}

inline base::base(const base& b) : base_number(b.base_number)
{
   puts("base copy constructor") ;
}

inline base::~base()
{
   puts("base destructor") ;
}

inline int base::get_base_number() const
{
   return base_number ;
}
```

```
class derived : public base
{
   int derived_number ;

      public:
   derived(int = 0 , int = 0) ;
   derived(const derived&) ;
   ~derived() ;
   int get_derived_number() const ;
} ;

inline derived::derived(int a , int b)
                 : base(a) , derived_number(b)
{
   puts("derived constructor") ;
}

inline derived::derived(const derived& d)
              : base(d) ,   // Note this call
                derived_number(d.derived_number)
{
   puts("derived copy constructor") ;
}

inline derived::~derived()
{
   puts("derived destructor") ;
}

inline int derived::get_derived_number() const
{
   return derived_number ;
}

int main()
{
   derived d1(1, 2) ;
   derived d2 = d1 ;
   printf("d2 = (%d,%d)\n" , d2.get_base_number() ,
                             d2.get_derived_number()) ;

   return 0 ;
}
```

The output is:

```
base constructor
derived constructor
base copy constructor
derived copy constructor
d2 = (1,2)
derived destructor
base destructor
derived destructor
base destructor
```

While making the call to the `base` class copy constructor, note that the object d is simply an *alias* for the object d1 (the existing instance) and that a cast occurs from a reference-to-derived into a reference-to-base. This is perfectly acceptable and normal code since the formal argument b in the `base` class copy constructor now is an alias for *only* the `base` class portion of the d1 instance.

Overloading the assignment operator for a derived class

The situation for the overloaded assignment operator in a derived class works in a fashion similar to that of the overloaded copy constructor. When you need to write an overloaded `operator=()` function in a derived class, it is your responsibility to make an *explicit call* to the overloaded `operator=()` in the base class. Unlike a constructor function, you have complete control over when this call is made. However, it makes sense to do it immediately so that the base portion of the derived object gets its data members assigned first, followed by the derived portion.

If the base class does not have an overloaded assignment operator, then the one supplied by the compiler will be called.

In the following program, Example 10.14 has been modified so that overloaded assignment operators exist in both the base and derived classes. Note the explicit call from the function `derived::operator=()` to the function `base::operator=()`.

Example 10.15

```c
#include <stdio.h>

class base
{
      protected:
    int base_number ;

      public:
    base(int = 0) ;
    base(const base&) ;
    ~base() ;
    int get_base_number() const ;
    base& operator=(const base&) ;
} ;

inline base::base(int n) : base_number(n)
{
    puts("base constructor") ;
}

inline base::base(const base& b) : base_number(b.base_number)
{
    puts("base copy constructor") ;
}

inline base::~base()
{
    puts("base destructor") ;
}

inline int base::get_base_number() const
{
    return base_number ;
}

inline base& base::operator=(const base& b)
{
    puts("base operator=") ;
    if(&b != this)
        base_number = b.base_number ;
    return *this ;
}
```

```
class derived : public base
{
  int derived_number ;

     public:
  derived(int = 0 , int = 0) ;
  derived(const derived&) ;
  ~derived() ;
  int get_derived_number() const ;
  derived& operator=(const derived&) ;
} ;

inline derived::derived(int a , int b)
                : base(a) , derived_number(b)
{
  puts("derived constructor") ;
}

inline derived::derived(const derived& d)
             : base(d) ,   // Note this call
               derived_number(d.derived_number)
{
  puts("derived copy constructor") ;
}

inline derived::~derived()
{
  puts("derived destructor") ;
}

inline int derived::get_derived_number() const
{
  return derived_number ;
}

inline derived& derived::operator=(const derived& d)
{
  puts("derived operator=") ;
  if(&d != this)
   {
     // Note this call
     base::operator=(d) ;
     derived_number = d.derived_number ;
   }
  return *this ;
}
```

```
int main()
{
  derived d1(1, 2) ;
  derived d2 ;
  d2 = d1 ;
  printf("d2 = (%d,%d)\n" , d2.get_base_number() ,
                            d2.get_derived_number()) ;

  return 0 ;
}
```

The output is:

```
base constructor
derived constructor
base constructor
derived constructor
derived operator=
base operator=
d2 = (1,2)
derived destructor
base destructor
derived destructor
base destructor
```

You might be interested in observing that the explicit call to the function `base::operator=()` was written using functional notation. If you want to use infix notation, you may use either of the following two methods:

Example 10.16

```
*(base*)this = d ;  // or
((base&)*this) = d ;
```

The first statement casts the derived pointer into a base pointer, and then dereferences the result to produce the base class portion of the invoking instance. Therefore, the base class `operator=()` will be called. The second statement achieves the same result, but in a more direct fashion, with the invoking instance itself now cast into a reference to the base class.

> ☞ If the derived class uses the functional notation to call the assignment operator in the base class, and this function is not explicitly written (i.e., generated automatically by the compiler), then Borland C++ will erroneously yield a compilation error.

Casting from 'derived' into 'base'

Casting from a derived class instance, pointer, or reference into a base class object of the same type presents no problem to the compiler. This was first mentioned in Example 10.14 when a reference-to-derived in the derived class copy constructor was passed into the base class copy constructor and received as a reference-to-base. It occurred again in Example 10.15. The reason is that since a derived class instance *always* contains a base class instance, when the cast occurs, the compiler simply "throws away", or ignores, the derived class portion of the instance that is being used, pointed at, or referred to.

In the following code a derived instance is used to initialize a base instance, after which a pointer-to-derived is used to initialize a pointer-to-base. After this has been done, b contains only the base class portion of the d object, and ptr_base "sees" only the base class portion of the derived object on the heap.

Example 10.17

```
derived d(1, 2) ;
base b = d ;

base* ptr_base = new derived ;
```

 In order for this cast to occur implicitly, a public derivation must have occurred. In other words, you cannot cast a derived class pointer into a base class pointer if a private or protected derivation had been done.

Casting from 'base' into 'derived'

On the other hand, if you attempt to cast from a base class instance, pointer, or reference into a derived class object of the same type, the compiler will complain because what you are trying to do now is put a smaller object (the base class) into a larger object (the derived class). This would mean that there is a "hole" left inside the derived object containing nothing (garbage). For this reason the compiler will not let you do it automatically.

In point of fact, what the compiler is looking for is a way in which it can convert a base class object into a derived class object. As with any other type of object that needs to be converted to a derived class, a constructor is required. What is unique about this particular constructor is that its one mandatory argument is a constant reference to a base class object. Optionally, you may specify additional arguments that will be used to initialize any additional derived class data members.

Why would you ever need to do this? One situation occurs when the derived class needs to call upon a friend function that was declared in the base class. If this friend function returns an instance of the base class, then the derived class now has a temporary base class instance with which it needs to do something, e.g., print, save, pass into another function. But such operations assume that a derived class instance will be used. Therefore, the conversion from base into derived needs to be made.

In the following program the class `integer` has overloaded the '+' operator as a binary friend to mean addition. Because there is no printing capability in this class, another class `integer_print` has been derived to add this feature. But note the compilation error that results:

Example 10.18   *(Will not compile!)*

```c
#include <stdio.h>

class integer
{
     protected:
   int number ;

     public:
   integer(int = 0) ;
   integer(const integer&) ;
   friend integer operator+(const integer& , const integer&) ;
} ;

inline integer::integer(int n) : number(n) {}

inline integer::integer(const integer& in) : number(in.number)
{}

inline integer operator+(const integer& in1 , const integer&
in2)
{
   return in1.number + in2.number ;
}

class integer_print : public integer
{
     public:
   integer_print(int = 0) ;
   void print() ;
} ;
```

```
inline integer_print::integer_print(int n)  :  integer(n)  {}

inline void integer_print::print()
{
   printf("number = %d\n" , number) ;
}

int main()
{
   integer_print ip1(1) , ip2(2) , ip3 = ip1 + ip2 ;
   ip3.print() ;

   return 0 ;
}
```

The compiler error message is:

```
Cannot convert 'integer' to 'integer_print' in function main()
```

The problem is that the output of the expression `ip1 + ip2` is of type `integer`, and the compiler cannot implicitly store an object of this type into the object `ip3` which is of type `integer_print`.

In the following program this problem has been fixed with the inclusion of a constructor in the class `integer_print` that accepts an `integer` by constant reference as its one formal argument. It then invokes the copy constructor in the `integer` class to initialize the base class portion of the new `integer_print` object.

Example 10.19

```
#include <stdio.h>

class integer
{
      protected:
   int number ;

      public:
   integer(int = 0) ;
   integer(const integer&) ;
   friend integer operator+(const integer& , const integer&) ;
} ;

inline integer::integer(int n) : number(n) {}

inline integer::integer(const integer& in) : number(in.number) {}
```

```
inline integer operator+(const integer& in1 , const integer& in2)
{
   return in1.number + in2.number ;
}

class integer_print : public integer
{
     public:
   integer_print(const integer&) ;
   integer_print(int = 0) ;
   void print() const ;
} ;

// New constructor
inline integer_print::integer_print(const integer& in)
                      : integer(in) {}

inline integer_print::integer_print(int n) : integer(n) {}

inline void integer_print::print() const
{
   printf("number = %d\n" , number) ;
}

int main()
{
   integer_print ip1(1) , ip2(2) , ip3 = ip1 + ip2 ;
   ip3.print() ;

   return 0 ;
}
```

The output is:

```
number = 3
```

☞ In the previous example, if the class `integer_print` had defined its own overloaded `operator+()`, then it would have been called to perform the add. But in this case if the compiler encounters an add operation in which one argument is type `integer` and the other type `integer_print`, it would fail to compile because of the ambiguity as to which function to invoke.

Static class data members

Recall that if a base class contains a static data member, then by definition *all* instances of that class share this one data member. Just like nonstatic data members, static members get inherited, so that an instance of a derived class also shares the static member defined in the base class. Of course, if a new member function in the derived class (static or nonstatic) wishes to access the inherited static data member, then the static data member must have been declared public or protected.

In Chapter 11 you see an example of inheritance of static data members.

Friend functions and inheritance

Bear in mind that individual classes do their own granting of friendship to whomever they like. There is really no connection between a derived class and its base class in this regard. This means that if a base class gives friendship to some class, and a class is then derived from this friend class, the latter class does *not* have implicit friendship from the base class.

Pointers to base and derived class instances

As you have already seen, pointers to base and derived class instances can be declared just like any other type of pointer. In terms of assignment, you can always assign a derived class pointer into a base class pointer because then the base class pointer will be pointing (only) to the base class portion of the derived object. However, the opposite is not true because if you attempt to store a base class pointer into a derived class pointer then the derived class pointer would, in theory, be pointing to data that it "thinks" it sees but in fact does not exist.

It should come as no surprise that you can always store the address of an instance into a pointer if the instance is the same type as that of the pointer. In other words, a base class pointer can always point to a base class instance, and a derived class pointer can always point to a derived class instance. The only time that a pointer may be used without its having to point to any instance is when a static member function is being called. In all other cases, the object being pointed at automatically becomes the invoking instance of the member function, and therefore has its address stored into the pointer variable `this`. (Remember: static member functions have no `this` pointer.)

When a pointer of type 'base' or 'derived' class is used to call a member function, and the function has been defined in *both* the base and derived classes, there is no ambiguity as to which version of the function will be called. The governing factor here is the *type of the pointer itself* (unless, of course, the function name has been explicitly qualified).

In the following program two pointers are declared, and each one is used to call the `identify()` function in its respective class. In addition, the derived class pointer may be used to call the `identify()` function in the base class provided that the function name is qualified with the base class name.

Example 10.20

```
#include <stdio.h>

class base
{
     public:
   void identify() ;
} ;

inline void base::identify()
{
   puts("I am the base class") ;
}

class derived : public base
{
     public:
   void identify() ;
} ;

inline void derived::identify()
{
   puts("I am the derived class") ;
}

int main()
{
   // Base class instance and pointer
   base* ptr_base = new base ;

   // Derived class instance and pointer
   derived* ptr_derived = new derived ;

   // Calls base::identify()
   ptr_base->identify() ;

   // Calls derived::identify()
   ptr_derived->identify() ;

   // Calls base::identify()
   ptr_derived->base::identify() ;

   delete ptr_base ;
   delete ptr_derived ;
```

```
        return 0 ;
    }
```

The output is:

```
I am the base class
I am the derived class
I am the base class
```

A base class pointer pointing to a derived class instance

Things become a lot more interesting when a *base* class pointer is used to store the address of a *derived* class object. Does this pose any problem for the compiler? No, because the pointer is, in reality, just pointing to the *base class portion* of the derived instance. (Remember: a derived class instance *always* contains a base class instance.)

Now suppose that the pointer is used to invoke a member function that is defined in the base class and overridden in the derived class. Which function will be called? The answer is that the member function that is within the scope of the *base* class will be used even though the pointer may be pointing to a *derived* class instance. Why? Because the compiler must generate an offset address for the function member at *compilation time*, even though the address of the instance stored in the pointer may be changed at *execution time*. Therefore, the compiler must say, "I know that the type of the pointer is 'base class', so I will generate an address relative to the start of some base class instance. If, at execution time, the instance to which the pointer points happens to be of type 'derived class', that's too bad because I will still call the function that is within the base class scope, and *not* the overridden function that is within the derived class scope."

This assertion is proven by the following program.

Example 10.21

```
#include <stdio.h>

class base
{
    public:
  void identify() ;
} ;
```

```
inline void base::identify()
{
   puts("I am the base class") ;
}

class derived : public base
{
      public:
   void identify() ;
} ;

inline void derived::identify()
{
   puts("I am the derived class") ;
}

int main()
{
   base* ptr_base = new derived ;

   // Calls base::identify()
   ptr_base->identify() ;

   delete ptr_base ;

   return 0 ;
}
```

The output is:

```
I am the base class
```

If this result troubles you, then your instincts are correct, because it serves no useful purpose to be "locked" into the base class world, even though the base class pointer can legitimately point a variety of derived class objects. This is especially troubling if you consider any kind of container object such as an array, linked list, queue, stack, etc., that might hold base class pointers as its data.

For example, suppose you are running a used car lot, and your inventory consists of a collection of "pointers" to the various cars on your lot. Someone then asks you to provide an inventory of all the cars present, so you then proceed to scan your collection of pointers and send some kind of identify message to each car, rightfully expecting that each car will identify itself in some unique fashion. Unfortunately, as things now stand, the only type of response that you will get back from all cars is, in effect, "I am a vehicle". Not very useful!

How we are going to "free" ourselves from this situation is the topic of the next chapter on virtual functions.

Do not use a base class pointer to point to an *array* of derived class objects. Performing pointer arithmetic on the pointer will not, in all probability, take you to the proper array element because the compiler will only be adding 'sizeof base' each time you add 1 to the pointer.

Multiple inheritance

Up to now the only type of inheritance has been single. That is, there has been only one base class from which the derived class has been inherited. But C++ also provides the capability to implement multiple inheritance, implying that a derived class has more than one parent or base class.

As an example, let's start by creating a class called `File` (stored in the file `file.h`) that will provide the basis of an inheritance whose purpose is to hide from the user the details of performing file input/output. This class can be abstracted by declaring a pointer to a `FILE` block, a constant representing the buffer size, and an error flag that will reflect the status of the file open operation. The only functions in the class are (1) a constructor function, (2) a destructor function, and (3) a conversion function that returns 'true' if the open succeeds and 'false' if it fails. No other functionality can be provided because it is not yet known if the class will be used for input or output file handling.

Example 10.22

```
#ifndef FILE_H
#define FILE_H

#include <stdio.h>

class File
{
        protected:
    FILE* ptr ;
    enum {size = 80} ;
    int error ;

        public:
    File() ;
    ~File() ;
    operator int() const ;
} ;

inline File::File() : error(0) {}
```

```
inline File::~File()
{
   fclose(ptr) ;
}

inline File::operator int() const
{
   return !error ;
}

#endif
```

From the class `File` we can now derive a class called `File_output` (stored in the file `file_out.h`) that will write records to a disk file. If the open operation should fail, then the error flag inherited from the `File` class will be turned on.

Example 10.23

```
#ifndef FILE_OUT_H
#define FILE_OUT_H

#include "file.h"
#include <stdio.h>
#include <string.h>

class File_output : virtual public File
{
      public:
   File_output(const char* = "") ;
   void write(const char*) ;
} ;

inline File_output::File_output(const char* name)
{
   if(strcmp(name , "") != 0)
      if((ptr = fopen(name , "w")) == 0)
         error = 1 ;
}

inline void File_output::write(const char* buffer)
{
   fputs(buffer , ptr) ;
}

#endif
```

Note that the inheritance was specified as `virtual`. This prevents the class `File` from being duplicated in any derived class that is itself inherited from two or more classes, each of which contains a `File` instance. The keyword `virtual` has nothing to do with virtual functions.

Here is a simple test of the derived class that will write several records to a disk file called OUTPUT.DAT.

Example 10.24

```cpp
#include "file_out.h"

#include <stdlib.h>

int main()
{
  File_output output("OUTPUT.DAT") ;
  if(!output)
   {
     puts("Can't open the file") ;
     exit(1) ;
   }

  const char* array[] =
   {
     "A rose by\n" ,
     "any other name\n" ,
     "is still a rose.\n"
    } ;

  const int size = sizeof(array) / sizeof(const char*) ;
  for(int i = 0 ; i < size ; ++i)
     output.write(array[i]) ;

  return 0 ;
}
```

Now let's derive a class called `File_input` (stored in the file `file_in.h`) from class `File` that will handle the reading of a disk file.

Example 10.25

```
#ifndef FILE_IN_H
#define FILE_IN_H

#include "file.h"
#include <stdio.h>
#include <string.h>

class File_input : virtual public File
{
   char buffer[size] ;

      public:
   File_input(const char* = "") ;
   const char* read() ;
   void display() ;
} ;

inline File_input::File_input(const char* name)
{
   if(strcmp(name , "") != 0)
     if((ptr = fopen(name , "r")) == 0)
        error = 1 ;
}

inline const char* File_input::read()
{
   return fgets(buffer , size , ptr) ;
}

inline void File_input::display()
{
   fputs(buffer , stdout) ;
}

#endif
```

Using this class, we can now read the disk file that was created in Example 10.24.

Example 10.26

```
#include <stdlib.h>
#include "file_in.h"

int main()
{
  File_input input("OUTPUT.DAT") ;
  if(!input)
   {
     puts("Can't open the file") ;
     exit(1) ;
   }

  while(input.read() != 0)
     input.display() ;

  return 0 ;
}
```

The output is:

```
A rose by
any other name
is still a rose.
```

Now let's take the final step and provide the capability to update a file. Since this involves both writing and reading, it makes sense to derive a new class called File_update (stored in the file file_up.h) from both File_output and File_input. The only new functionality is a rewind() function that will set the file position marker back to the beginning of the file. This class is an example of multiple inheritance since two base classes are being used.

Example 10.27

```
#ifndef UPDATE_H
#define UPDATE_H

#include "file_out.h"
#include "file_in.h"
#include <stdio.h>
#include <stdlib.h>

class File_update : public File_input , public File_output
{
     public:
   File_update(const char* = "") ;
   void rewind() ;
} ;

inline File_update::File_update(const char* name)
{
   if(strcmp(name , "") != 0)
     if((ptr = fopen(name , "w+")) == 0)
        error = 1 ;
}

inline void File_update::rewind()
{
   fseek(ptr , 0L , 0) ;
}

#endif
```

Now this class can be instantiated in order to create an output file, write some lines of data into it, rewind it, and read it. Of course, instead of simply reading the file, new information could have been written.

Example 10.28

```
#include "file_up.h"
#include <stdlib.h>

int main()
{
   File_update update("OUTPUT.DAT") ;
   if(!update)
    {
       puts("Can't open the file") ;
       exit(1) ;
    }

   const char* array[] =
    {
       "She sells\n" ,
       "C shells\n" ,
       "By the sea shore\n"
    } ;

   const int size = sizeof(array) / sizeof(const char*) ;
   for(int i = 0 ; i < size ; ++i)
       update.write(array[i]) ;

   update.rewind() ;

   while(update.read() != 0)
       update.display() ;

   return 0 ;
}
```

The output is:

```
She sells
C shells
By the sea shore
```

■ Review questions

1) What is the advantage of inheritance in C++?

2) What is the relationship between the base class and the derived class?

3) What are the two faces that a class shows?

4) Why is the access specifier protected needed?

5) What is the difference between a private, public, and protected derivation?

6) How does a base class receive its arguments in order to construct its members properly?

7) What happens if a derived class fails to explicitly provide arguments to the base class constructor?

8) How can the overloaded assignment operator in a derived class invoke the overloaded assignment operator in the base class?

9) Why can a base class pointer point to a derived class instance?

10) When using a base class pointer, why does it not matter that the pointer may be pointing to a derived class instance?

■ Exercise #1

Create a class called `person` that contains a pointer to a name, and a Social Security Number as a `long` integer. Write the constructor and destructor functions, and a function called `print()` that prints both data members.

Then, from class `person` derive a class called `hourly_employee` that contains new data members called `rate` and `hours`. In addition, derive a class called `salaried_employee` that contains a new data member called `salary`.

In the `main()` function create an instance of each class and call upon the respective `print()` function.

■ Exercise #2

Recall that the `string` class in Chapter 8 had two protected data members: `ptr` and `length`. Write a class called `reverse_string` (that is publicly derived from the `string` class) with the following member functions:

■ A default constructor function;

■ A copy constructor function;

■ A constructor function that takes a `const char*` as its one argument;

■ An overloaded assignment operator;

■ An overloaded `operator~()` that it reverses the characters pointed at by `ptr`, and returns a new `reverse_string` instance by value;

■ A conversion function that returns `ptr` .

The `main()` function is:

```
int main()
{
    reverse_string rs1("Monte") ;
    reverse_string rs2 ;
    rs2 = ~rs1 ;
    reverse_string rs3(~~rs1) ;
    puts(rs1) ;
    puts(rs2) ;
    puts(rs3) ;

    return 0 ;
}
```

The output should be:

```
Monte
etnoM
Monte
```

■ Exercise #3

Using the `fraction` class from Chapter 8, Exercise #2, derive a new class called `fraction_d` that can accommodate the following `main()` function:

```
int main()
{
    fraction_d f1(0 , 0) ;
    if(!f1)
      puts("f1 is invalid") ;

    fraction_d f2(6 , 4) , f3(2) ;
    fraction_d f4 = f2 + f3 ;
    fraction_d f5 ;
    if(!f2)
        puts("f2 is invalid") ;
    if(!f3)
        puts("f3 is invalid") ;
    if(!f4)
        puts("f4 is invalid") ;
    if(!f5)
        puts("f5 is invalid") ;
    f5 = f4 ;
    f5.reduce() ;
    printf("f5 = %ld/%ld\n" , f5.get_num() , f5.get_den()) ;

    return 0 ;
}
```

The output should be:

```
f1 is invalid
f5 = 7/2
```

■ **Exercise #4**

In Chapter 8 a case study was presented using the `string` class to demonstrate the concepts of name and operator function overloading. While the scheme presented works to provide an effective enhancement to strings in C, the implementation is inefficient because of the vast amount of heap management that is occurring. For example, when the copy constructor or overloaded assignment operator is called, the string literal to which the class's pointer (`ptr`) is pointing must be copied so that each instance has its own private resources on the heap. If this were not done, then two `string` instances would be pointing to the same heap space, and when the destructor functions get called, an attempt would be made to release the same heap space twice.

A better approach to handling the `string` class would be to use the concept of *referencing counting*. In this scheme it is perfectly permissible to have more than one `string` instance point to the same space on the heap. In other words, if two `string` instances are identical, then the string literals are also identical and may be shared by the two instances. Of course, this yields some very serious problems that must be addressed.

■ A new field (let's call it `ref_count`) must be added to each instantiation of the `string` class that maintains a count of how many instances are sharing the heap space. A brand new instantiation must set this `ref_count` to 1, while the copy constructor and overloaded assignment operator must increment `ref_count`.

■ The destructor function must decrement `ref_count` and, if it is zero, then (and only then) delete the heap space.

■ If the string literal is modified for any given instance, then obviously a new copy of the literal must be made to which the changes will be applied. Also, since the old string literal now has one less instance sharing it, its `ref_count` must be decremented by 1.

Let's call this new class `ref_string` and derive it from the `string` class. Thus, the definition for this class is:

```
class ref_string : public string
{
   int ref_count ;

    public:
   ref_string() ;
   ref_string(const char*) ;
   ref_string(const ref_string&) ;
   ref_string(const string&) ;
   ref_string& operator=(const ref_string&) ;
   ~ref_string() ;
   friend class wrapper ;
} ;
```

Each manager function must implicitly or explicitly interface with its corresponding function in the `string` class. Define the member functions, and test the class thoroughly before proceeding. Note that there is no need to do any initialization of the `ref_count` variable.

Once the class `ref_string` has been tested, it must then be "wrapped" inside another class that contains as its one data member (`ptr_rs`) a pointer to an instance of class `ref_string`. Let's call this class `wrapper`, which was granted friendship by the `ref_string` class. Now, if two instances of the `wrapper` class need to point to the same string literal, then it's just a matter of having both pointers point to same instance of class `ref_string`.

The definition for the `wrapper` class is:

```
class wrapper
{
    ref_string* ptr_rs ;
    // All private function declarations, if any

        public:
    wrapper() ;
    wrapper(const char*) ;
    wrapper(const wrapper&) ;
    wrapper& operator=(const wrapper&) ;
    wrapper& operator=(const char*) ;
    wrapper(const ref_string&) ;
    ~wrapper() ;
    wrapper& operator++() ;
    wrapper& operator--() ;
    wrapper& operator+=(const wrapper&) ;
    void print(const char*) ;
    friend wrapper operator+(const wrapper& , const wrapper&) ;
} ;
```

Now write the definitions for all of the member and friend functions in the `wrapper` class. The function `wrapper::print()` must display its input argument, the value of the string literal on the heap, and the value of `ref_count`. The non-manager functions of the class should invoke the corresponding functions in the `string` class. Note that all manipulations of the field `ref_count` should be done within the `wrapper` class, *not* the `ref_string` class.

Test your program with the following `main()` function:

```
int main()
{
    wrapper w1("E") ;
    w1.print("w1") ;
    wrapper w2(w1) ;
    w1.print("w1") ;
    w2.print("w2") ;
    w2 = w1 ;
    w1.print("w1") ;
    w2.print("w2") ;
    ++(++w1) ;
    --(--w2) ;
    w1.print("w1") ;
    w2.print("w2") ;
    w1 += w2 += w1 ;
    w1.print("w1") ;
    w2.print("w2") ;
    w1 = w2 = "N" ;
    w1.print("w1") ;
    w2.print("w2") ;

    return 0 ;
}
```

The output should be:

```
w1: "E" ref count = 1
w1: "E" ref count = 2
w2: "E" ref count = 2
w1: "E" ref count = 2
w2: "E" ref count = 2
w1: "G" ref count = 1
w2: "C" ref count = 1
w1: "GCG" ref count = 1
w2: "CG" ref count = 1
w1: "N" ref count = 2
w2: "N" ref count = 2
```

Notes

Notes

Chapter 11

Polymorphism in C++

The chapter covers how the concept of polymorphism is implemented in C++. The term itself simply means the ability to have different objects derived from a common class respond to the same command differently. The exact method for carrying out this command (or message) is not your concern; all you're worried about is that the end result is correct. This chapter will explain how C++ implements the concept of polymorphism using the virtual *keyword.*

Polymorphism in the real world

As an example of how polymorphism is used every day in the "real" world, a teacher in a classroom may point to each student and ask the question, "What is your name?", and rightfully expect a different response from each individual. In other words, the teacher wants to "iterate" across an array or list of students and send the same message ("What is your name?") to different objects (the students) and have each student "handle" the message differently. Similarly, you could call up several different pizza parlors on the phone and ask each of them to deliver a large pepperoni (no anchovies) to your home. Exactly how this "message" is carried out by each shop is not your concern. One shop may send it over by car, another by bicycle, or on foot. It really doesn't matter because all you're concerned about is that you have the pizza in your hands.

What is an object-oriented programming language?

For any computer language to call itself an object-oriented programming language (OOPL), it must contain three essential components:

- Data abstraction and encapsulation
- Inheritance
- Polymorphism

Data abstraction and encapsulation is the process of defining some new data type. This involves specifying the internal representation of that type along with the functions that are used to manipulate the type. This topic was introduced in Chapter 5.

Inheritance involves the creation of a new type from an existing type in some hierarchical fashion. This topic was covered in detail in Chapter 10.

Finally, the third component, polymorphism, is the topic of this chapter.

The problem with static binding

Recall from Chapter 10 that when you used a pointer of type *base* class, the only class members that could be referenced were those belonging to the base class, *even if this pointer pointed to a derived class object*. This is *not* polymorphism in action because the object being pointed at never received the message being sent. The reason is that the compiler only knows about the *type* of the pointer itself, and *nothing* about the object that the pointer will eventually point at during execution time. Therefore, the class member that is hard-coded is used to generate an offset address relative to the start of the *base* class. How could it be otherwise? The offset address of the member in the derived class probably will be different than the same member in the base class, but the compiler must choose one or the other. Because the compiler makes this choice, it is called "early (or static) binding" since the member that is referenced is "bound" to the type of the pointer being used.

Unfortunately, this method of coding is not very useful because the goal of an object-oriented programming language is to send a message to whatever instance happens to be pointed at by the pointer, *as opposed to the type of the pointer itself.* Why is this important? Because then you can control the content (an address) of the pointer at execution time, whereas the *type* of the pointer variable itself cannot be changed once it is hard-coded. In this fashion the instance itself can "figure out" what to do with the message and thereby implement the concept of polymorphism.

Therefore, in terms of C++, what is needed is a method to delay the choice of which member function (method) gets executed *until execution time.* Having such a method would imply that by using a single pointer and member function name, the same function call (message) can be sent to the instance that has its address stored in the pointer. If these instances implement the same function (method) differently, then *different* results can be obtained. Such a method is called "late (or dynamic) binding" because the compiler no longer makes the decision as to which function will get called.

Virtual functions

Fortunately, C++ has the tools built in to implement late binding. This is done by the use of a *virtual function.* Here is how it works:

> If a function in a base class definition is declared to be virtual, and is declared exactly the same way (including the return type) in one or more derived classes, then all calls to that function using pointers or references of type 'base class' will invoke the function that is specified by the object being pointed at, and *not* by the type of the pointer itself.

The keyword `virtual` is written before the return type (if any) of the function in the base class definition. It cannot appear outside a class definition. It is optional when declaring the same function in a derived class, although it's probably a good idea to write it for the sake of clearer documentation. In addition, even if the access category of a virtual function is public in the base class, and private in the derived class, the latter function is still callable via a pointer or reference of the base class type. It is through the use of virtual functions that C++ achieves the object-oriented goal of polymorphism.

As a very simple example of polymorphism, here is Example 10.21 again, but now the `identify()` function in the base class has been declared virtual. As a result, the `identify()` function in the *derived* class gets called.

Example 11.1

```
#include <stdio.h>

class base
{
    public:
  virtual void identify() ;
} ;

void base::identify()
{
  puts("I am the base class") ;
}

class derived : public base
{
    public:
  virtual void identify() ;
} ;

void derived::identify()
{
  puts("I am the derived class") ;
}

int main()
{
  base* ptr_base = new derived ;

  // Calls derived::identify()
  ptr_base->identify() ;

  delete ptr_base ;

  return 0 ;
}
```

The output is:

```
I am the derived class
```

In this program Example 11.1 is repeated, but now a reference to the base class is used instead of a pointer.

Example 11.2

```
#include <stdio.h>

class base
{
    public:
  virtual void identify() ;
} ;

void base::identify()
{
  puts("I am the base class") ;
}

class derived : public base
{
    public:
  virtual void identify() ;
} ;

void derived::identify()
{
  puts("I am the derived class") ;
}

int main()
{
  base& ref_base = *(new derived) ;

  // Calls derived::identify()
  ref_base.identify() ;

  delete &ref_base ;

  return 0 ;
}
```

The output is:

```
I am the derived class
```

☞ If a member function will be called as a result of static binding, then making it an inline function still has a potential benefit. However, if it will always be called as a result of dynamic binding, then making it inline provides no benefit whatsoever because the compiler does not know which function will eventually be called, and therefore cannot substitute the code.

A derived class may choose *not* to provide a new definition of a virtual function. This is perfectly acceptable. If the derived class then receives a call for this function, the message will be "passed up" to its parent class automatically, i.e., to the class from which the derived class was inherited.

In the following example the derived class has no method to handle an `identify()` message. Instead, it is passed up to the method `base::identify()`.

Example 11.3

```
#include <stdio.h>

class base
{
     public:
   virtual void identify() ;
} ;

void base::identify()
{
   puts("I am the base class") ;
}

class derived : public base
{
   // Nothing here
} ;

int main()
{
   base* ptr ;

   // Calls base::identify()
   ptr = new base ;
   ptr->identify() ;
   delete ptr ;

   // Calls base::identify() again
   ptr = new derived ;
   ptr->identify() ;
   delete ptr ;

   return 0 ;
}
```

The output is:

```
I am the base class
I am the base class
```

Virtual destructor functions

Recall that if instances are created at run time on the heap via the `new` operator, then their destructors are automatically called when you execute the `delete` statement to release the space occupied by the instance itself (as opposed to the space that a pointer data member may be pointing at on the heap). Because a derived class instance *always* contains a base class instance, it's necessary to invoke the destructors of *both* classes in order to ensure that all of the space on the heap is released.

Here is Example 11.1 again, but now a destructor function has been added to each class.

Example 11.4

```
#include <stdio.h>

class base
{
    public:
  virtual void identify() ;
  ~base() ;
} ;

void base::identify()
{
  puts("I am the base class") ;
}

base::~base()
{
  puts("base destructor") ;
}

class derived : public base
{
    public:
  virtual void identify() ;
  ~derived() ;
} ;

void derived::identify()
{
  puts("I am the derived class") ;
}
```

```
derived::~derived()
{
  puts("derived destructor") ;
}

int main()
{
  base* ptr_base = new derived ;

  // Calls derived::identify()
  ptr_base->identify() ;

  delete ptr_base ;

  return 0 ;
}
```

The output is:

```
I am the derived class
base destructor
```

Note that the destructor function for the derived class did *not* get called. This is obviously a program bug. The reason is that the pointer type was base so that the actual instance the pointer was pointing at became completely irrelevant insofar as determining which destructor function would be called. In other words, the destructor function of the base class is going to get called 100% of the time because of the early binding that the compiler performs.

To correct this problem, you must make the destructor function in the base class virtual. (Note that this "violates" the rule that states that virtual functions must have the same name, and destructors obviously do not have the same name because they are based upon their respective class names. Nevertheless, the compiler takes this into account, and simply ignores the name of the destructor.) Of course, when the destructor in the proper derived class gets called, the base class destructor will also get called since a derived class instance always contains a base class instance.

Here is a repeat of Example 11.4, but now the destructor function in the base class is virtual.

Example 11.5

```
#include <stdio.h>

class base
{
     public:
   virtual void identify() ;
   virtual ~base() ;
} ;

void base::identify()
{
   puts("I am the base class") ;
}

base::~base()
{
   puts("base destructor") ;
}

class derived : public base
{
     public:
   virtual void identify() ;
   virtual ~derived() ;
} ;

void derived::identify()
{
   puts("I am the derived class") ;
}

derived::~derived()
{
   puts("derived destructor") ;
}

int main()
{
   base* ptr_base = new derived ;

   // Calls derived::identify()
   ptr_base->identify() ;

   delete ptr_base ;

   return 0 ;
}
```

The output is:

```
I am the derived class
derived destructor
base destructor
```

How to use virtual functions to add specificity

Many times the designer of a base class will create only a skeleton, or shell, of a class with the intention that the derived classes will "fill in the holes". In other words, the base class is intended to be just an abstraction for something more specific that will follow. For example, as president of a car company, in your mind you may have an idea of a certain dream car that involves such features as length, height, weight, speed, miles per gallon, etc. The state of this car obviously is too "abstract" to start stamping out (instantiating) vehicles on some assembly line, so you would leave it up to your design engineers to fill in the details and provide specific values.

As an example of a class that defines a state but is still too abstract to do anything useful, here is a base class called `loan`. What kind of loan? It's too early to tell, but the member data and functions to do the work have been declared. Of course, if you attempt to use this base class, the output would be meaningless. (Shortly you will see a method that literally prevents you from instantiating the `loan` class.)

A loan is defined by the principal amount, the yearly interest rate, and the length of the loan in years. From these three variables you can compute the monthly payment. Exactly how this is to be done will be determined by the specific type of loan. That's why the function `compute()` is made virtual.

Here is the skeleton of the `loan` class (stored in the file `loan.h`).

Example 11.6

```
#ifndef LOAN_H
#define LOAN_H

#include <stdio.h>
#include <string.h>

class loan
{
    protected:
  double principal ;
  double yearly_rate ;
  int length_in_years ;
  double monthly_payment ;
  char* type ;

    public:
  loan(double , double , int , const char*) ;
  virtual ~loan() ;
  virtual void compute() = 0 ;
  double get_payment() const ;
  void display() ;
} ;

inline
loan::loan(double prin, double rate, int length ,const char* t)
                : principal(prin) ,
                  yearly_rate(rate) ,
                  length_in_years(length) ,
                  type(new char[strlen(t) + 1])
{
  strcpy(type , t) ;
}

inline loan::~loan()
{
  delete [] type ;
}

inline void loan::display()
{
  printf("\t%s\n" , type) ;
  printf("Principal = $%0.2f\n" , principal) ;
  printf("Rate = %0.2f%%\n" , yearly_rate * 100) ;
  printf("Length = %d\n" , length_in_years) ;
  printf("Payment = $%0.2f\n\n" , monthly_payment) ;
}
```

```
inline double loan::get_payment() const
{
   return monthly_payment ;
}

#endif
```

☞ **The signature of the** `compute()` **function has been modified to terminate with '= 0'. The meaning of this syntax will be discussed shortly.**

So now let's create some classes of specific loans and redefine the `compute()` function for each one. First, we'll assume that a simple interest loan is one in which the borrower will pay back the full amount in equal monthly payments consisting of both principal and interest. Even though the amount of the principal is being reduced each month, the interest being paid does not change. This is how such a loan might be implemented using a class called `simple_loan` (stored in the file `simple.h`):

Example 11.7

```
#ifndef SIMPLE_LOAN_H
#define SIMPLE_LOAN_H

#include "loan.h"

class simple_loan : public loan
{
     public:
   simple_loan(double , double , int) ;
   virtual void compute() ;
} ;

inline
simple_loan::simple_loan(double prin,double rate,int length)
             : loan(prin , rate , length , "Simple loan") {}

inline void simple_loan::compute()
{
   // P = Principal
   // R = Rate
   // L = Length
   // Monthly payment is:
   //    (P * (R * L + 1)) / (L * 12)
```

```
    double monthly_rate = yearly_rate / 12 ;
    int length_in_months = length_in_years * 12 ;
    monthly_payment =
          (principal * (monthly_rate * length_in_months + 1)) /
                      length_in_months ;
}

#endif
```

Next, a fully amortized loan is also one in which equal monthly payments are made. But now the interest is computed on the remaining principal balance, and the difference between the payment and the interest paid is applied toward paying off the principal. Since the remaining principal has been reduced, next month's interest payment will be slightly smaller while the principal reduction will be slightly larger. (This is the way most homes are financed today.) A class called `amortized_loan` (stored in the file `amort.h`) will provide this abstraction.

Example 11.8

```
#ifndef AMORTIZED_LOAN_H
#define AMORTIZED_LOAN_H

#include "loan.h"
#include <math.h>

class amortized_loan : public loan
{
     public:
   amortized_loan(double , double , int) ;
   virtual void compute() ;
} ;

inline
amortized_loan::amortized_loan(double prin , double rate ,
                                int length)
          : loan(prin , rate , length , "Amortized loan") {}

inline void amortized_loan::compute()
{
  // P = Principal
  // R = Rate
  // L = Length
  // Monthly payment is:
  //     (P * R * (1 + R)^L)) /
  //     ((1 + R)^L - 1)
```

```
      double monthly_rate = yearly_rate / 12 ;
      int length_in_months = length_in_years * 12 ;
      double temp = pow(1 + monthly_rate , length_in_months) ;
      monthly_payment = (principal * monthly_rate * temp) /
                        (temp - 1) ;
}

#endif
```

Now we can create some kind of container object, e.g., an array of pointers, that will be used to point to instances of the two specific types of loans. Let's assume that we're interested in a $100,000.00 loan, at 8.00% interest, for one year. Now it's just a matter of looping through the array and sending `compute()` and `display()` messages to each of our loans. Because the `compute()` function in the base class was declared to be `virtual`, the `compute()` function for the proper type of loan is guaranteed to gain control.

Here is the complete program:

Example 11.9

```
#include "loan.h"
#include "simple.h"
#include "amort.h"

int main()
{
  loan* portfolio[] =
  {
    new simple_loan(100000.0 , 0.08 , 1) ,
    new amortized_loan(100000.0 , 0.08 , 1)
  } ;

  const int size = sizeof(portfolio) / sizeof(loan*) ;
  for(int i = 0 ; i < size ; ++i)
  {
    portfolio[i] -> compute() ;
    portfolio[i] -> display() ;
  }

  for(i = 0 ; i < size ; ++i)
    delete portfolio[i] ;

  return 0 ;
}
```

The output is:

```
        Simple loan
Principal = $100000.00
Rate = 8.00%
Length = 1
Payment = $9000.00

        Amortized loan
Principal = $100000.00
Rate = 8.00%
Length = 1
Payment = $8698.84
```

Abstract base classes

Recall from the definition of the `loan` class that the `compute()` function was declared with the syntax '= 0'. The purpose of this syntax is to tell the compiler that the class should be construed as an *abstract base class*. The reason to do this is that the designer of a base class, while allowing for derivation to occur via protected data members and virtual functions, wants to prevent the user from actually creating an instance of the base class. The purpose of the base class `loan` was to serve only as a skeleton for the derived classes, which then supplied the specific type of loan computation.

To create an abstract base class, you must specify at least one *pure virtual function*. This is a function that is (1) declared to be virtual, and (2) has its "value" set to zero. A function is "set to zero" by following the argument list (and possibly the keyword `const`) with an '=' sign and a 0. A destructor function, even though it can be virtual, can never be made into a pure virtual function.

Thus, to make the `loan` class into an abstract base class, the `compute()` function was declared to be:

Example 11.10

```
virtual void compute() = 0 ;
```

There is nothing wrong with writing the actual definition of a pure virtual function. However, it should be obvious that it can be called only through the use of the base class name and the scope resolution operator (from within a derived class member function), or through an uninitialized base class pointer (not recommended). This just makes sense because to have it called "normally" via some instance of the class would violate the concept of an abstract base class.

The reason you might want to define it is to write some common code that would normally appear in all of the derived class functions. But for obvious reasons, you don't want to repeat this code in each individual function. Therefore, a good place to put it would be in the base class function and call it directly.

To prove that you are now unable to instantiate the base class `loan`, this program fails to compile.

Example 11.11   **(Will not compile!)**

```
#include "loan.h"

int main()
{
   loan unknown(100000.0 , .08 , 1 , "unknown") ;

   return 0 ;
}
```

The compiler error message is:

```
Cannot create instance of abstract class 'loan' in function
main()
```

☞ If a base class declares a pure virtual function, and a derived class does *not* provide a definition for that function, compilers based upon AT&T version 2.0 will complain with a fatal error. In AT&T version 2.1, however, a pure virtual function is inherited as such, so no redeclaration is needed. In this case the derived class is also an abstract base class.

☞ Borland 3.0 and 3.1 erroneously allow you to create an array of instances of the abstract base class type.

A container class

The problem with the previous implementation of the `loan` class is that it is the responsibility of the `main()` function to create some kind of container object to hold pointers to the various types of loans, and then iterate across the container before releasing the space that the loans occupy. This is not a good design because the user should not be concerned with such details. A better approach would be to isolate such tasks and store them into some kind of container object. The specific type of container object (array, linked list, queue, stack, etc.) is therefore hidden from the user, and rightly so. Should the implementation of this type of container be changed later, the user would not know it and not be affected by it.

Stated differently, all the `main()` function should have to do is instantiate some type of container object and pass it to the main function of some menu class that will provide the interactive interface to the user.

To get started, let's create a very generic container abstract base class called `abstract_container` (stored in the file `abs_cont.h`). It provides the functionality to add items (in the form of pointers to loans) and iterate across its members. Since the exact type of the container itself has yet to be determined, no data members can be stated.

Example 11.12

```
#ifndef ABS_CONT_H
#define ABS_CONT_H

#include "loan.h"

class abstract_container
{
     public:
   virtual void add(loan*) = 0 ;
   virtual void iterate() = 0 ;
   virtual ~abstract_container() {}
} ;

#endif
```

From this class we can derive another class called `array_container` that uses an array of pointers-to-loans to hold its members. The variable `index` is used to keep track of exactly how many loans are present. Note that the data member `portfolio` is of type 'pointer-to-pointer' because the number of loans that will be contained is unknown. The class then provides the specific virtual functions to add a loan and iterate across all loans.

Example 11.13

```
#ifndef ARR_CONT_H
#define ARR_CONT_H

#include "abs_cont.h"

class array_container : public abstract_container
{
  loan** portfolio ;
  int index ;

    public:
  array_container() ;
  virtual ~array_container() ;
  virtual void add(loan*) ;
  virtual void iterate() ;
} ;

inline
array_container::array_container() : index(0), portfolio(0) {}

#endif
```

Here are the definitions for the class `array_container`.

Example 11.14

```
// The file "arr.cpp"

#include "arr_cont.h"

void array_container::add(loan* p)
{
  loan** temp = new loan*[index + 1] ;
  for(int i = 0 ; i < index ; ++i)
     temp[i] = portfolio[i] ;
  temp[index++] = p ;
  delete [] portfolio ;
  portfolio = temp ;
}
```

```
void array_container::iterate()
{
   for(int i = 0 ; i < index ; ++i)
    {
      portfolio[i]->compute() ;
      portfolio[i]->display() ;
    }
}

array_container::~array_container()
{
   for(int i = 0 ; i < index ; ++i)
      delete portfolio[i] ;
   delete [] portfolio ;
}
```

Next, let's derive another class called `list_container` that uses a linked list to keep track of its members. This class is stored in the file `lst_cont.h`.

Example 11.15

```
#ifndef LST_CONT_H
#define LST_CONT_H

#include "abs_cont.h"

class node
{
   loan* ptr ;
   node* next ;
   node(loan*) ;
   ~node() ;
   friend class list_container ;
} ;

inline node::node(loan* p) : ptr(p) , next(0)  {}

inline node::~node()
{
   delete ptr ;
}

class list_container : public abstract_container
{
   node* head ;
   node* tail ;
      public:
```

```
      list_container() ;
      virtual ~list_container() ;
      virtual void add(loan*) ;
      virtual void iterate() ;
   } ;

   inline list_container::list_container() : head(0) , tail(0) {}

   #endif
```

Here are the definitions for the `list_container` class.

Example 11.16

```cpp
// The file "lst_cont.cpp"

#include "lst_cont.h"

void list_container::add(loan* p)
{
   node* temp = new node(p) ;
   if(!head)
      head = temp ;
   else
      tail->next = temp ;
   tail = temp ;
}

void list_container::iterate()
{
   node* temp = head ;
   while(temp)
    {
      temp->ptr->compute() ;
      temp->ptr->display() ;
      temp = temp->next ;
    }
}

list_container::~list_container()
{
   node* temp = head ;
   while(temp)
    {
      node* save = temp->next ;
      delete temp ;
      temp = save ;
    }
}
```

In order to make the program interactive, we need another class called menu that is responsible for obtaining the loan information from the user and calling upon the add() and iterate() functions of whatever container class it happens to be using. Note how the constructor function receives a reference to some container instance, and then uses this reference to initialize the reference data member ref_con. Of course, the exact type of the container instance is not known to the menu class, and it really does not care.

Example 11.17

```
#ifndef MENU_H
#define MENU_H

#include "abs_cont.h"

class menu
{
   abstract_container& ref_con ;

     public:
   menu(abstract_container&) ;
   void prompt() ;
   void choices() ;
   void add_simple() ;
   void add_amort() ;
} ;

inline menu::menu(abstract_container& c) : ref_con(c) {}

#endif
```

Here are the definitions for the menu class (stored in the file menu.cpp). Since ref_con is a reference to some container object, and the two functions container::add() and container::iterate() were made virtual, it is guaranteed that the proper function in either derived class will gain control. This is called a "using" relationship since the class menu is using the services of some container class. This type of relationship between classes is better than a "has-a" relationship because now the menu class does not literally contain an instance of either the array_container or list_container class. As a result, there is a looser coupling between the menu and the container classes. This is usually a good idea when doing object-oriented design.

Example 11.18

```
// The file "menu.cpp"

#include "menu.h"
#include <stdio.h>
#include <ctype.h>

void menu::prompt()
{
  choices() ;
  int ch ;
  while((ch = toupper(getchar())) != 'E')
   {
      switch(ch)
       {
          case 'S' : add_simple() ;
                     break ;
          case 'A' : add_amort() ;
                     break ;
          default : puts("Invalid response\n") ;
       }
      fflush(stdin) ;
      choices() ;
   }
  ref_con.iterate() ;
}

void menu::choices()
{
  puts("What is the type of loan?") ;
  puts("(S)imple") ;
  puts("(A)mortized") ;
  puts("(E)xit") ;
}

void menu::add_simple()
{
  puts("Enter the principal, rate, and length") ;
  double principal , rate ;
  int length ;
  int result = scanf("%lf%lf%d" , &principal , &rate , &length);
  if(result != 3)
      puts("Input error") ;
```

```
      else
       {
         loan* p = new simple_loan(principal , rate, length) ;
         ref_con.add(p) ;
       }
      fflush(stdin) ;
}

void menu::add_amort()
{
   puts("Enter the principal, rate, and length") ;
   double principal , rate ;
   int length ;
   int result =
         scanf("%lf%lf%d" , &principal , &rate , &length) ;
   if(result != 3)
      puts("Input error") ;
   else
    {
       loan* p = new amortized_loan(principal , rate , length) ;
       ref_con.add(p) ;
    }
   fflush(stdin) ;
}
```

At last we're ready to run a test on all of the classes. First, let's instantiate the container class that will use an array.

Example 11.19

```
#include "loan.h"
#include "simple.h"
#include "amort.h"
#include "arr_cont.h"
#include "menu.h"

#include "arr.cont.cpp"
#include "menu.cpp"

int main()
{
   array_container array ;
   menu request_array(array) ;
   request_array.prompt() ;

   return 0 ;
}
```

Next, let's instantiate the container class that will use a linked list.

Example 11.20

```
#include "loan.h"
#include "simple.h"
#include "amort.h"
#include "lst_cont.h"
#include "menu.h"

#include "lst_cont.cpp"
#include "menu.cpp"

int main()
{
   list_container list ;
   menu request_list(list) ;
   request_list.prompt() ;

   return 0 ;
}
```

If, for each type of loan, you entered a principal of $100,000.00, an interest rate of 8%, and a length of 1 year, then exit, the output would be:

```
      Simple loan
Principal = $100000.00
Rate = 8.00%
Length = 1
Simple loan: $9000.00

      Amortized loan
Principal = $100000.00
Rate = 8.00%
Length = 1
Amortized loan: $8698.84
```

Finite state machines

Another situation where virtual functions are useful is when you want to emulate finite state machines. These "machines" are nothing more than objects that take on different states depending upon the (possible) input values that they receive. In C++ each state can be represented by an instance of a derived class. The next state (derived class instance) to receive control is typically handled by a virtual function in the base class. This function determines what the next state should be and returns a pointer to that particular state. So that any derived class can return a pointer to any other derived class, the addresses of all of the different states (derived class instances) are maintained as static pointers of type 'base class' within the base class. This poses no problem since a base class pointer can point to a derived class instance.

In addition, note that the base class is simply an abstraction for the specific definition of the virtual function that the derived classes will supply. Therefore, there is no need to instantiate the base class, and the virtual function should be made into a pure virtual function so that an abstract base class is the result. In addition, this precludes the use of any non-static variables in base class that might take on different values for more than one instance of the base class.

A light bulb

As an example of a very simple finite state machine, let's consider a light bulb. It has only two states — on and off. If the "on" state gains control, it inherently knows that it should set the state of the light bulb to off; if the "off" state gains control, it sets the state of the light bulb to "on". The virtual function therefore returns a pointer to the opposite state. The abstraction of this light bulb (stored in the file `bulb.h`) is as follows:

Example 11.21

```
#ifndef BULB_H
#define BULB_H

class light_bulb
{
    protected:
  static light_bulb* ptr_off ;
  static light_bulb* ptr_on ;

    public:
  virtual light_bulb* change() = 0 ;
} ;

// State in which the light is off
class light_bulb_off : public light_bulb
{
    public:
  virtual light_bulb* change() ;
} ;
```

```
// State in which the light is on
class light_bulb_on : public light_bulb
{
    public:
  virtual light_bulb* change() ;
} ;

#endif
```

The definitions for this header file (stored in the file `bulb.cpp`) are as follows:

Example 11.22

```
// The file "bulb.cpp"

#include "bulb.h"
#include <stdio.h>

light_bulb* light_bulb_off::change()
{
  puts("The light is on") ;
  return ptr_on ;
}

light_bulb* light_bulb_on::change()
{
  puts("The light is off") ;
  return ptr_off ;
}

// Defines for static pointers
light_bulb* light_bulb::ptr_off = new light_bulb_off ;
light_bulb* light_bulb::ptr_on = new light_bulb_on ;
```

In order to specify the unique characteristics of a light bulb, such as an identification number, the maximum number of times it can be used, and a pointer to an instance that determines its current state, another class called `wrapper` must be created that contains a pointer to a light bulb as its key data member. This class can then have a function that uses the current state pointer to send a `change()` message, and have the address of the opposite state instance returned.

First, here is the header file for the `wrapper` class (stored in the file `wrapper.h`).

Example 11.23

```
#ifndef WRAPPER_H
#define WRAPPER_H

#include "random.h"
#include "bulb.h"

class wrapper
{
  static Random rn ;
  int bulb_number ;
  const int limit ;
  light_bulb* ptr_current_state ;

    public:
  wrapper() ;
  ~wrapper() ;
  void toggle() ;
} ;

inline wrapper::~wrapper()
{
  delete ptr_current_state ;
}

#endif
```

Here are the definitions for the wrapper class (stored in the file wrapper.cpp). The number of times that a light can be turned on will be random.

Example 11.24

```
// The file "wrapper.cpp"

#include "wrapper.h"
#include <stdio.h>

// Define for static member
Random wrapper::rn ;

wrapper::wrapper() : limit(rn.get_random(3) * 2 + 1) ,
                     ptr_current_state(new light_bulb_off)
{
  static int numb ;
  bulb_number = ++numb ;
}
```

```
void wrapper::toggle()
{
    printf("Light bulb #%d\n" , bulb_number) ;
    int counter = 0 ;
    while(counter++ < limit)
        ptr_current_state = ptr_current_state->change() ;
    puts("-------------------") ;
}
```

Next, to allow for a variable number of such `wrapper` objects, another class (called `room`) is needed that contains a pointer to an array of class `wrapper` . The constructor will prompt the use for the exact number of light bulbs, and then allocate this number from the heap space. Finally, an `activate()` function will toggle each light bulb on and off for the maximum number of times. When all light bulbs have "burned out", the program ends.

Example 11.25

```
#ifndef ROOM_H
#define ROOM_H

#include "wrapper.h"

class room
{
    wrapper* ptr_bulbs ;
    int index ;

        public:
    room() ;
    ~room() ;
    void activate() ;
} ;

inline room::~room()
{
    delete [] ptr_bulbs ;
}

#endif
```

Here are the definitions for the `room` class (stored in the file `room.cpp`):

Example 11.26

```
#include "room.h"
#include <stdio.h>

room::room()
{
  puts("How many bulbs? ") ;
  int r ;
  while((r = scanf("%d" , &index)) != 1 || r == EOF)
   {
     puts("Try it again: ") ;
     fflush(stdin) ;
   }
  ptr_bulbs = new wrapper[index] ;
}

void room::activate()
{
  for(int i = 0 ; i < index ; ++i)
    ptr_bulbs[i].toggle() ;
}
```

Here is the complete program, including a `main()` function that instantiates the `room` class and then activates all light bulbs.

Example 11.27

```
#include "bulb.h"
#include "wrapper.h"
#include "room.h"

#include "bulb.cpp"
#include "wrapper.cpp"
#include "room.cpp"

int main()
{
  room living ;
  living.activate() ;

  return 0 ;
}
```

A typical run would appear as:

```
How many bulbs?
2
Light bulb #1
The light is on
- - - - - - - - - - - - - - - - - -
Light bulb #2
The light is on
The light is off
The light is on
- - - - - - - - - - - - - - - - - -
```

Parsing text strings

Parsing problems are another good example of a finite state machine. Suppose our job is to parse an input sentence or phrase in order to extract and count the individual words. A word is considered to be any combination of letters, digits and underscores. As the characters are scanned, there are two states that the sentence passes through — either a word is in the process of being parsed, or it isn't.

If we are parsing a word, then the occurrence of a letter leaves us in the same state, and the occurrence of a non-letter means that the end of the word has just been found, so it's time to print the word and switch to the opposite state.

If we are not parsing a word, then the occurrence of a letter means that the start of a new word has been found, and the state should be switched, while the occurrence of a non-letter is simply ignored and the state remains unchanged.

Example 11.28

```
#include <stdio.h>
#include <ctype.h>
#include <string.h>

class phrase
{
    protected:
  static phrase* non_word_ptr ;
  static phrase* word_ptr ;
  static int counter ;
```

```
      public:
  static void set_counter() ;
  static int get_counter() ;
  virtual phrase* next(char) = 0 ;
} ;

inline void phrase::set_counter()
{
  counter = 0 ;
}

inline int phrase::get_counter()
{
  return counter ;
}

////////////////////////////////////

class non_word_state : public phrase
{
      public:
  virtual phrase* next(char ch) ;
} ;

phrase* non_word_state::next(char ch)
{
  // If a letter/digit is found, then it's the start of a
  // word. Add to the count of words and switch to the
  // word state
  if(isalnum(ch) != 0 || ch == '_')
   {
     printf("\"%c" , ch) ;
     ++counter ;
     return word_ptr ;
   }

  // Otherwise, we're just passing a non-letter/digit so
  // stay in this state
  return non_word_ptr ;
}

////////////////////////////////////

class word_state : public phrase
{
      public:
  virtual phrase* next(char ch) ;
} ;
```

```cpp
phrase* word_state::next(char ch)
{
   // If a letter/digit is found, then output it and stay
   // in this state
   if(isalnum(ch) != 0 || ch == '_')
    {
      putchar(ch) ;
      return word_ptr ;
    }

   // Otherwise, a non-letter/digit was found. End the
   // current word and switch to the non-word state
   printf("\"\n") ;
   return non_word_ptr ;
}

phrase* phrase::non_word_ptr = new non_word_state ;
phrase* phrase::word_ptr = new word_state ;
int phrase::counter ;

////////////////////////////////////////

class wrapper
{
   phrase* ptr_current_state ;
   enum { size = 128 } ;
   char buffer[size] ;
   void process() ;

      public:
   wrapper() ;
   ~wrapper() ;
   void prompt() ;
} ;

inline wrapper::wrapper()
{
   ptr_current_state = new non_word_state ;
}

inline wrapper::~wrapper()
{
   delete ptr_current_state ;
}
```

```
void wrapper::prompt()
{
   puts("Enter your text: ") ;
   while(fgets(buffer , size , stdin) != 0)
    {
      process() ;
      puts("\nNext text: ") ;
    }
}

void wrapper::process()
{
   phrase::set_counter() ;
   // Loop through the null byte
   for(int i = 0 ; i <= strlen(buffer) ; ++i)
    {
      char ch = buffer[i] ;
      ptr_current_state = ptr_current_state->next(ch) ;
    }

   // Print total number of words
   int total = phrase::get_counter() ;
   printf("\n%d word%s\n" ,total ,total == 1 ? "" : "s") ;
}

//////////////////////////////////////

int main()
{
   wrapper w ;
   w.prompt() ;

   return 0 ;
}
```

A typical run would appear as:

```
Enter your text:
The_answer is a C++ variable
"The_answer"
"is"
"a"
"C"
"variable"

5 words

Next text:

C
"C"

1 word

Next text:
^Z
```

How virtual functions work

In order to implement late binding, the compiler has to go through some extra steps whenever there is at least one virtual function within a class. First, it creates a table called the virtual function table, usually referred to as the 'vtbl'. This table contains the addresses of all of the virtual functions within the class. The first address occupies position 0, the next position 1, etc. For each derived class, the table is duplicated, and if a virtual function is redefined, then its address replaces the address of the corresponding function from the base class. Any new virtual functions are appended to the end of the table.

Whenever an instance of a class is created, the compiler reserves some extra bytes for use as a pointer to the 'vtbl'. This pointer is referred to as the 'vptr', or virtual pointer. It is automatically initialized to point to the 'vtbl' for the class to which it belongs. When you create a pointer of type base and store into it the address of a base or derived instance, and then execute a function using this pointer, the compiler will fetch the address pointed at by 'vptr' of the invoking instance (*this), offset this address by the index of the function in question (0 for f(), 1 for g()), fetch the address from the 'vtbl', and execute the function that this address points at.

Here is a program that does exactly this. The base class emulates two virtual functions, f() and g(). The derived class redefines only g().

Example 11.29

```
#include <stdio.h>

// B_PTR is a pointer to member function taking an integer and
// returning nothing
class base ;
typedef void(base::*B_PTR)(int) ;

// D_PTR is a pointer to member function taking an integer and
// returning nothing
class derived ;
typedef void(derived::*D_PTR)(int) ;

class base
{
     protected:
  // Array of pointers to member functions. One entry for each
  // virtual function in the base class. Made static so that all
  // instances are assured of sharing the same array. The array
  // is dimensioned 2. The "virtual" function takes an integer
  // and returns nothing
  static B_PTR base_vtbl[2] ;

     public:
  // A pointer to the virtual function array that will be
  // contained in each instance of the class. Made public so
  // that it can be accessed in main()
  B_PTR* vptr ;

  // Constructor to initialize vptr with the address of the
  // virtual function array
  base()
   {
     vptr = base_vtbl ;
   }

  // Two virtual functions now defined without the keyword
  // "virtual"
  void f(int n)
   {
     printf("base f() value %d\n" , n) ;
   }

  void g(int n)
   {
     printf("base g() value %d\n" , n) ;
   }
} ;
```

```
// Initialize the static array with the addresses of the
// virtual functions f() and g()
B_PTR base::base_vtbl[2] =
{
    &base::f ,   // & required
    &base::g
} ;

//////////////////////////////////

class derived : public base
{
      protected:
  // Array of pointers to functions
  static D_PTR derived_vtbl[2] ;

      public:
  // Constructor to initialize vptr to the address of the
  // virtual function array. Since the array has been
  // redefined, a cast is needed because a pointer to a
  // derived member function cannot implicitly be stored
  // into a pointer to a base member function
  derived()
   {
     vptr = (B_PTR*)derived_vtbl ;
   }

  // Only the function g() will be overridden in the derived
  // class
  void g(int n)
   {
     printf("derived g() value %d\n" , n) ;
   }
} ;

// Initialize the static array with the address of the
// functions base::f and derived::g
D_PTR derived::derived_vtbl[2] =
{
  &base::f ,
  &derived::g
} ;

//////////////////////////////////
```

```
int main()
{
   // Pointer of type base
   base* ptr ;

   // Create a base class instance
   ptr = new base ;

   // Emulate the call: ptr -> f() ;
   // First, create a pointer-to-function of class 'base'
   B_PTR ptr_function ;

   // Store the address of base::f into this pointer
   ptr_function = ptr -> vptr[0] ;

   // Using the instance pointed at by 'ptr', call the member
   // function whose address is contained in 'b_ptr'. Pass 1
   // as the actual argument
   (ptr ->* ptr_function) (1) ;

   // Emulate the call: ptr -> g() ;
   ptr_function = ptr -> vptr[1] ;
   (ptr ->* ptr_function) (2) ;

   // Release the instance space
   delete ptr ;

   // Create a derived class instance
   ptr = new derived ;

    // Emulate the call: ptr -> f() ;
   ptr_function = ptr -> vptr[0] ;
   (ptr ->* ptr_function) (3) ;

   // Emulate the call: ptr -> g() ;
   ptr_function = ptr -> vptr[1] ;
   (ptr ->* ptr_function) (4) ;

   // Release the instance space
   delete ptr ;

   return 0 ;
}
```

The output is:

```
base f() value 1
base g() value 2
base f() value 3
derived g() value 4
```

■ Review Questions

1) What problem arises without the use of a virtual function?

2) How does a virtual function solve this problem?

3) Why would you want to declare a destructor function as virtual?

4) Declaring a function virtual causes more memory to be allocated for each instance of the class in question. On the other hand, you have just seen the problem that arises when the destructor is *not* declared virtual. Question: Does this mean that you should *always* declare the destructor function in a base class as virtual, just on the chance that someone may inherit from it?

5) What is an abstract base class, and how do you create one?

6) Suppose a base class does not have a virtual function, and yet you still want to prevent the user of the class from instantiating it. How could you do this?

7) What is a 'using' relationship? Why is this better than a containing relationship?

■ Exercise #1

Given the following class:

```
class letter
{
     public:
   virtual void display(char) = 0 ;
} ;
```

derive three more classes called upper_case, lower_case, and error. The function upper_case::display() displays its input character argument in upper case. The function lower_case::display() displays its input character argument in lower case. The function error::display() simply sounds the alarm.

To test these classes, write a class called get_char that contains a pointer to a letter and a public function called get() that prompts the terminal operator to enter a letter of the alphabet. If the response is not a valid letter of the alphabet, instantiate the class error. Otherwise, instantiate the class whose display() function will output the letter in its opposite case. Then call upon the display() function. Continue in this fashion until the operator enters end-of-file.

In the main() function instantiate the class get_char and invoke the function get_char::get().

■ Exercise #2

Use object-oriented programming with a finite state machine approach to input a sentence and display only that part that is between double quotation marks.

■ Exercise #3

In Chapter 7 Exercise #10 you wrote a 2-dimensional cross-reference program that had to ignore all C and C++ style comments. There are four states: (1) process a word, (2) bypass a non-word, (3) process a C style comment, and (4) process a C++ style comment. Rewrite your program using a finite state machine approach.

■ Exercise #4

In Chapter 7 Exercise #4, you wrote a program to play the game "C Raps". Rewrite this program using a finite state machine approach.

■ Exercise #5

Modify Chapter 6, Exercise #5, so that the class `button` is just an abstraction for two specific kinds of buttons: (1) a button that, when pushed, designates which floor the elevator is to go to; and (2) a button that, when pushed, closes the doors and sets the elevator in motion. Obviously the `push()` function should be made into a pure virtual function.

■ Exercise #6

Write an abstract base class called `employee` that contains a pointer to a name, a social security number, and the respective accessor functions. It also contains a pure virtual function called `print()` whose task is to output the name and social security number.

Next, derive a class called `hourly` that adds a new data member called `wage`. Its `print()` function must print the name, social security number, and wage.

Next, derive another class called `salaried` that adds a new data member called `salary`. Its `print()` function must print the name, social security number, and salary.

In order to hold all employees, create a class called `roster` that is able to hold a variable number of employees (via a pointer to pointer to an `employee`, a linked list, etc.) Provide the capability to add an employee, delete an employee, and print the entire roster of employees. Do not allow a duplicate employee to be added (as determined by a duplicate social security number), and check that only existing employees are deleted.

In order to provide data to the program, write member functions to prompt the user of the class interactively for the various fields.

■ Exercise #7

Write a class called `budget` that contains the following abstraction:

```
class budget
{
    protected:
  double gross_income ;
  loan* ptr_loan ;
  double net_income ;

    public:
    // All public functions
} ;
```

The class must provide the functionality to compute the `net_income` for the month (`gross_income` minus the loan payment).

Next, create a class called `finances` that contains the following abstraction:

```
class finances
{
  double income ;
  budget* budget_ptr ;
  // All function declarations
} ;
```

The functions of the class must provide the capability to prompt the user for the monthly gross income, the type of loan, and the terms of the loan. After this information has been entered, instantiate the proper type of loan from the heap and pass the resulting address and the gross income to the constructor of the `budget` class. The instance itself of the `budget` class comes from the heap space. Now you can compute the net income using the pointer `budget_ptr` to the `budget` class.

The `main()` function should be:

```
int main()
{
  finances the_budget ;
  the_budget.income_info() ;
  the_budget.loan_info() ;

  return 0 ;
}
```

Notes

Notes

Notes

Chapter 12

Stream output

C++ provides a new way to perform input and output operations, called iostream *methods. While the capabilities of the stdio library, such as printf() and scanf(), are still available, you should now get into the habit of using the new methods in your programs.*

Why switch to something new?

Perhaps you are wondering about the justification for abandoning the stdio library and switching to something new. There are several good reasons for doing so:

■ The `iostream` library closely resembles the concepts that you have already learned in regard to instantiation and message passing. That is, every input or output operation consists of (1) an object, (2) a message to that object, and (3) optional parameters with the message.

For example, to display a piece of information to the screen, you would send a message to the screen object. The data itself would be the parameter. This technique also allows you to send multiple messages to the same object using the concept of function chaining that you learned in Chapter 7.

■ While `printf()` and the rest of the functions in the `stdio` library can handle primitive types just fine, it is completely self-contained, and cannot be modified to accommodate user-defined types. On the other hand, the input/output streams in C++ are extensible, so that the input or output of an instance of some class can be written *exactly* that same way as that for a primitive type. How this feature can be implemented is discussed later in this chapter.

■ The functions `scanf()` and `printf()` are very error-prone. You have to remember that if you're printing an `int`, then the conversion mask must be `%d`, and if you're printing a `long`, then it must be `%ld`. If you make a mistake, then you may get incorrect output. Fortunately, this problem goes away when you use `iostream` methods because the argument type itself determines how it is to appear.

■ Finally, in Chapter 16 you will see how `iostream` methods are required in a function template in which the type of arguments must remain generic. This precludes the use of `scanf()` and `printf()` in which the types are "hard-coded" by the very nature of a conversion specification.

C++ input/output classes

The C++ input/output mechanism(provided with C++ compilers that support at least AT&T release 2.0) is comprised of a series of classes that have been created to handle the problem of sending and receiving data. Here is a brief description of these classes:

■ The `streambuf` class provides memory for a buffer along with class methods for filling the buffer, accessing buffer contents, flushing the buffer, and managing the buffer memory. It handles the most primitive functions for streams on a first-in-first-out basis.

■ The `filebuf` class is derived from class `streambuf` and extends it by providing basic file operations.

■ The `strstreambuf` class is derived from class `streambuf` and is designed to handle memory buffers.

- The `ios` class represents general properties of a stream, such as whether it's open for reading and whether it is a binary or a text stream, and it includes a pointer member to a `streambuf` class.

- The `ostream` class derives from the `ios` class and provides output methods. That is, it formats the data you send to an output device so that it appears in the way you expect.

- The `istream` class also derives from the `ios` class and provides input methods. That is, it accepts data from an input device in the way you expect.

- The `iostream` class is based on the `istream` and `ostream` class and thus inherits both input and output methods.

The definitions of these classes are found in the file `iostream.h`. Therefore, in any C++ program that you write in which you want to use `iostream` methods, you must have the statement:

Example 12.1

```
#include <iostream.h>
```

in order to provide the compiler with the public interface to the various classes.

Instances of the class `ostream`

Of course, classes in and of themselves do you no good unless you subsequently create instances, or objects, of those classes. Fortunately, this has already been done for you at global scope, so that these objects are immediately available for you to use. Here is a list of the objects to which you can send messages:

- The `cout` object corresponds to the standard output stream. By default, this stream is associated with the standard output device, typically a monitor. `cout` is an instantiation of the class `ostream`.

- The `cerr` object corresponds to the standard error stream, which you can use for displaying error messages. By default, this stream is associated with the standard output device, typically a monitor, and the stream is unbuffered. That means information is sent directly to the screen without waiting for a buffer to fill or for a newline character.

- The `clog` object also corresponds to the standard error stream. By default, this stream is associated with the standard output device, typically a monitor, and the stream is buffered.

Stated in another way, your terminal screen is an object in the real world. This object has a state and a public interface. By sending both mutator and accessor messages to this object, you can effectively perform all of the same operations that you now do using the output functions provided in the `stdio` library.

> ☞ To be 100% correct, the three output instances are instantiations of the class ostream withassign, which has been derived from class ostream. This class has overloaded the assignment operator to allow a pointer to a filebuf object to be assigned to it, thereby attaching each output instance to an output file.

How to do simple output using the insertion operator

To repeat what was stated above, the global instance cout of class ostream is used to initiate all output operations to the monitor. In the class ostream, the function you will use the most often is the overloaded bitwise left-shift operator. It has been given a special name — the insertion operator. The name "insertion" comes from the fact that you are "inserting" items into an output buffer, as represented by the object cout.

Within the class ostream the operator '<<' (left-shift) has been overloaded many times as a binary member function. The one implicit argument is, of course, the invoking instance (the instance cout), and the one explicit argument is the data item that you wish to output. If you were to peek inside the file iostream.h, then you would see many declarations for this overloaded function within the ostream class, such as:

Example 12.2

```
ostream& operator<<(/* 1 explicit argument */) ;
```

While you could certainly use this overloaded operator in its functional notation, there is really no reason to do so. In other words, you should get into the habit of using infix notation. Note also the return type of ostream&. This allows successive calls to the insertion operator to be chained together, since each implementation terminates by returning *this. (Recall that function chaining was discussed in Chapter 7.)

More specifically, the function operator<<() has been overloaded to accommodate these types:

- unsigned char
- signed char
- unsigned short int
- short int
- int
- unsigned int
- long
- unsigned long

426

- float
- double
- long double
- const signed char*
- const unsigned char*
- void*
- streambuf*
- ostream& (*) (ostream&)

These are essentially all of the types that `printf()` can accept. The last item is designed to accommodate a *manipulator function*. The topic of manipulator functions will be covered in more detail in Chapter 14.

Here is a simple example using the insertion operator and function chaining. Three different types of data are output to the screen, but this presents no problem whatsoever to the compiler since it will automatically invoke the proper insertion operator function using the rules of function overloading that were discussed in Chapter 8.

Example 12.3

```
#include <iostream.h>

int main()
{
   int number = 65 ;
   cout << "number = " << number << "\n" ;

   char ch = 'A' ;
   cout << "ch = " << ch << "\n" ;

   float money = 56.87 ;
   cout << "money = " << money << "\n" ;

   return 0 ;
}
```

The output is:

```
number = 65
ch = A
money = 56.869999
```

Be aware of precedence

As you know, one of the rules involved with overloading a built-in operator is that you *cannot* change its precedence. That is, you're "stuck" with the order that is inherent in the precedence of C++ operators. Since the left-shift operator has lower precedence than the arithmetic operators, statements such as:

Example 12.4

```
cout << 1 + 2 ;
cout << 2 * 3 ;
cout << ++number ;
```

pose no problem because the arithmetic is done first. However, a fragment such as:

Example 12.5

```
int x = 123 ;
cout << x ? 1 : 0 ;
```

will output the number 123 instead of the number 1 because the output line is interpreted as:

Example 12.6

```
int x = 123 ;
(cout << x) ? 1 : 0 ;
```

since the left-shift operator has *higher precedence* than the conditional operator. Then the conditional operator is executed, but the result doesn't do anything useful. If the number 1 is to be output (since the numeric value 123 has the Boolean value 'true'), then parentheses are needed around the entire conditional operator:

Example 12.7

```
int x = 123 ;
cout << (x ? 1 : 0) ;
```

Bit format flags

Now think about a `printf()` function call. It usually consists of a control string argument and, optionally, a list of expressions to be output. The control string contains literals which will be output exactly as shown, and conversion specifications that indicate exactly how an expression from the list of expressions is to appear. Each conversion specification starts with a % and ends with a conversion character, e.g., %d or %i for decimal format, %c for character format, %s for a string, etc. Between the start and end you may enter various flags, the field width, base formatting, justification, floating point precision, and so forth. Each conversion specification stands on its own; there is no connection to any other one.

Now, however, we're working with an object (cout) that has some state, and it's this state that governs how the data will appear on the screen. For example, if the state of coutis set to 'hex', then all integer output will appear in hexadecimal. If the state of cout is set to left-justify, then all fields from now on will appear left-justified.

Most of the states of the cout object are represented by a long (protected) field inherited from the class ios. Since each state is a binary representation of some 'on' or 'off 'condition, all it needs is one bit. Therefore, this long integer can uniquely represent at most 32 different binary conditions. For example, the output state of decimal is either on or off. Similarly, the state of left-justification is either on or off.

The value for each binary state is represented by a constant value in an unnamed public enumerated type within the class ios. No two fields of this type have the same bit on. Using a mutator function, these bits are then bitwise ORed into the long integer that reflects the state of the cout object.

Each binary value also has a name associated with it that you may reference. The complete list of all enumerated values is shown below. Don't forget that because these names exist within the class ios, the name of this class must be specified in conjunction with the scope resolution operator (::) to unambiguously access a specific value. These are the names and values that Borland C++ uses:

TABLE 12.1

Name	Value	Meaning
ios::skipws	0x0001	Skip whitespace on input
ios::left	0x0002	Left-justification of output
ios::right	0x0004	Right-justification of output
ios::internal	0x0008	Pad after sign or base indicator
ios::dec	0x0010	Show integers in decimal format
ios::oct	0x0020	Show integers in octal format
ios::hex	0x0040	Show integers in hexadecimal format
ios::showbase	0x0080	Show the base for octal and hex numbers
ios::showpoint	0x0100	Show the decimal point for all floats
ios::uppercase	0x0200	Show uppercase hex numbers
ios::showpos	0x0400	Show + for positive numbers
ios::scientific	0x0800	Show exponential notation on floats
ios::fixed	0x1000	Show fixed decimal output on floats
ios::unitbuf	0x2000	Flush all streams after insertion
ios::stdio	0x4000	Flush stdout and stderr after insertion

Different C++ compilers will handle these values differently. For Borland C++, it will turn on the skipws and unitbuf bits at the start of each program. All other bits will be off.

How to turn on the bit format flags

In order to change the state of the cout object, you must be able to change the bits that represent its state. Within the class ios there are several mutator member functions provided that allow this to be done. The first of these functions is called setf(). Remember: to call it, you must first specify the instance name, cout, the dot operator, and then the function name. Thus, you would write:

Example 12.8

```
cout.setf( /* arguments */ ) ;
```

The function setf() has been overloaded to accept either one or two arguments. In both cases, the first argument specifies which bits are to be turned ON.

For example, to turn on the ios::showpos bit, you would code:

Example 12.9

```
cout.setf(ios::showpos) ;
```

The function `setf()` works by bitwise ORing its first argument with the existing values, thereby leaving any other bits undisturbed. This means that it's possible to turn on more than one bit with just one call to `setf()` by using an expression for the first argument that contains several bits ORed together.

For example, to turn on the `ios::showpos` and the `ios::uppercase` bits, you would code:

Example 12.10

```
cout.setf(ios::showpos | ios::uppercase) ;
```

Unfortunately, ambiguous situations can arise. For example, from a logical perspective, you should never set the state of the `cout` object to say that output should appear in decimal *and* in hexadecimal *and* in octal. But there is nothing to prevent you from specifying this.

To help you guard against this possibility, the function `setf()` has another version that you may use. In this case it takes two arguments. The first is identical to what we have already been using, i.e., those bits that are to be turned on. But the second argument specifies those bits that are first to be turned off. Thus, for example, before specifying that output is to appear in octal, you can easily specify that the decimal and hexadecimal bits are to be turned off first. To do this, you would code:

Example 12.11

```
cout.setf(ios::oct , ios::dec | ios::oct | ios::hex) ;
```

Note that even though the `ios::oct` bit is to be set on, it is still mandatory that you specify it in the second argument. The reason is that the bit to be turned on is the result of doing a bitwise AND of the first and second arguments.

How to turn off the bit format flags

In order to turn bits off directly, you may use the mutator member function `unsetf()`. This function takes exactly one argument: the bit pattern to be turned off. Thus, to turn off the bit `ios::showpos`, you would code:

Example 12.12

```
cout.unsetf(ios::showpos) ;
```

Like setf(), more than one bit at a time can be turned off by ORing the enumerated values together in the argument field. For example, to turn off the ios::showpos and ios::uppercase bits, you would code:

Example 12.13

```
cout.unsetf(ios::showpos | ios::uppercase) ;
```

How to access the bit format flags as a group

Because the field in the class ios that represents the bit settings is protected, you cannot access it directly. However, there is a public accessor member function in the class ios called flags() that will return this field to you as a long integer. In addition, if you provide a long integer as an argument to flags(), then the existing value will be returned to you *after* your argument is used to provide a new setting for the field.

In this example the initial value of the bit settings is returned and printed in uppercase hexadecimal notation.

Example 12.14

```
#include <iostream.h>

int main()
{
  long value = cout.flags() ;
  cout.setf(ios::uppercase) ;
  cout.setf(ios:: hex , ios::dec | ios::oct | ios::hex) ;
  cout << "Initial value = " << value << "\n" ;

  return 0 ;
}
```

The output is:

```
Initial value = 2001
```

How to display integers in the proper base

Output formatting is important because you want to have complete flexibility in the manner in which your data appears. Let's start with the base in which integers will be shown. In a `printf()` function call, you have 3 choices: decimal, octal and hex. A decimal output can be obtained by using a conversion specification of `%d` or `%i`, an octal by using `%o`, and hex by using `%x` or `%X`. (How to emulate lower vs. upper case will be discussed later.) There are 3 bits in the enumerated values shown in Table 12.1 that control the base setting:

TABLE 12.2

Name	Value	Meaning
ios::dec	0x0010	Show integers in decimal format
ios::oct	0x0020	Show integers in octal format
ios::hex	0x0040	Show integers in hexadecimal format

To guarantee that decimal output is used, you must turn on the bit `ios::dec`, and *ensure that the remaining 2 bits are turned off.* The same reasoning applies to octal and hex output.

The interesting aspect about the output base setting is that in Borland C++ all three bits shown in Table 12.2 are initially off. Therefore, the logical question is, which base will be used? The answer is that Borland (and probably other C++ compilers) will default to decimal output. Remember: once the base has been set, it stays set for all future integers unless it is subsequently changed.

Recall from Example 12.11 the form of the `setf()` function that you must use in order to turn on one of the 3 base setting bits and ensure that the other 2 bits are off. Since the second argument entails a lot of coding on your part, the `iostream` library has conveniently provided a `static const` variable that is the bitwise OR of the 3 base setting bits. This variable is called `ios::basefield`, and has the following definition:

Example 12.15

```
// Declaration in the class ios
static const long basefield ;

// Definition
const long ios::basefield = ios::dec | ios::oct | ios::hex ;
```

The following example runs a test on all 3 base settings.

Example 12.16

```
#include <iostream.h>

int main()
{
   int x = 65 ;

   cout << "Decimal: " << x << "\n" ;

   cout.setf(ios::oct , ios::basefield) ;
   cout << "Octal: " << x << "\n" ;

   cout.setf(ios::hex , ios::basefield) ;
   cout << "Hex: " << x << "\n" ;

   cout.setf(ios::dec , ios::basefield) ;
   cout << "Decimal: " << x << "\n" ;

   return 0 ;
}
```

The output is:

```
Decimal: 65
Octal: 101
Hex: 41
Decimal: 65
```

How to show the base setting of integers

In a `printf()` function call, the use of the flag # causes the base of an octal or hexadecimal number to appear (0 and 0x, respectively). The same effect can be achieved in C++ by setting on the bit `ios::showbase`. To revert back to not showing the base setting, use the `unsetf()` function.

TABLE 12.3

Name	Value	Meaning
ios::showbase	0x0080	Show the base for octal and hex numbers

Here is Example 12.16 again, but now with the `ios::showbase` bit turned on.

Example 12.17

```cpp
#include <iostream.h>

int main()
{
   int x = 65 ;
   cout.setf(ios::showbase) ;
   cout << "Decimal: " << x << "\n" ;

   cout.setf(ios::oct , ios::basefield) ;
   cout << "Octal: " << x << "\n" ;

   cout.setf(ios::hex , ios::basefield) ;
   cout << "Hex: " << x << "\n" ;

   cout.setf(ios::dec , ios::basefield) ;
   cout << "Decimal: " << x << "\n" ;

   return 0 ;
}
```

The output is:

```
Decimal: 65
Octal: 0101
Hex: 0x41
Decimal: 65
```

How to display the sign of an integer

Note that on positive decimal output, a '+' sign is assumed, but by default will not appear. In a `printf()` function call, you can force the '+' sign to appear if you use the flag '+'. In C++, if you want this sign to appear, you must turn on the bit `ios::showpos`. (Of course, if the number is negative, the '-' sign will always appear.) To revert back to not showing the '+' sign, use the `unsetf()` function.

TABLE 12.4

Name	Value	Meaning
ios::showpos	0x0400	Show + for positive numbers

Here is Example 12.17 again, but now with the `ios::showpos` bit turned on.

Example 12.18

```
#include <iostream.h>

int main()
{
   int x = 65 ;
   cout.setf(ios::showbase) ;
   cout.setf(ios::showpos) ;

   cout << "Decimal: " << x << "\n" ;

   cout.setf(ios::oct , ios::basefield) ;
   cout << "Octal: " << x << "\n" ;

   cout.setf(ios::hex , ios::basefield) ;
   cout << "Hex: " << x << "\n" ;

   cout.setf(ios::dec , ios::basefield) ;
   cout << "Decimal: " << x << "\n" ;

   return 0 ;
}
```

The output is:

```
Decimal: +65
Octal: 0101
Hex: 0x41
Decimal: +65
```

☞ There is no bit available with which to emulate the 'blank' flag in a `printf()` statement. This flag causes a blank to appear in the sign position of a positive number.

How to display output in uppercase

There is one other option you can employ with hexadecimal numbers. By default any hex digit, as well as the 'x' in the base, appears in lowercase. The same rule applies to the 'e' when printing in scientific notation. In a `printf()` function call, you would code a capital 'X' to obtain hex digits in uppercase, or a capital 'E' to show the 'E' in scientific notation in uppercase. In C++ if you want to see uppercase, turn on the bit `ios::uppercase`. To revert back to lowercase, use the `unsetf()` function.

TABLE 12.5

Name	Value	Meaning
ios::uppercase	0x0200	Show uppercase hex numbers

The following example prints the hex number 'abc' in hexadecimal, and shows the base setting and all hex digits in uppercase.

Example 12.19

```
#include <iostream.h>

int main()
{
   cout.setf(ios::uppercase | ios::showbase) ;
   cout.setf(ios::hex , ios::basefield) ;
   cout << 0xabc << "\n" ;

   return 0 ;
}
```

The output is:

```
0XABC
```

How to output a character

If you want to display a character, there is no problem since the compiler will use argument matching to invoke the operator insertion that expects a char as its one explicit argument. If you want to display a character as some other type, e.g., an integer, then you must provide an explicit cast.

Example 12.20

```
#include <iostream.h>

int main()
{
    char ch = 'A' ;
    cout << "char: " << ch << "\n" ;
    cout << "int: " << int(ch) << "\n" ;

    return 0 ;
}
```

The output is:

```
char: A
int: 65
```

In addition to using the insertion operator to output a character, the member function called `put()` provides a way to guarantee that any value gets shown in its character format (Think of the C function `putchar()`.) This function also returns the invoking instance by reference, so it can be chained to a subsequent function call.

Example 12.21

```
#include <iostream.h>

int main()
{
    char ch1 = 'A' ;
    cout.put(ch1) << "\n" ;
    int ch2 = 66 ;
    cout.put(ch2) << "\n" ;
    float ch3 = 67.0 ;
    cout.put(ch3) << "\n" ;

    return 0 ;
}
```

The output is:

```
A
B
C
```

How to set the field width

The field width in C++ works in a similar manner to that of C. If the total number of characters needed for output is less than the specified width, then the extra spaces will be filled with the current fill character. If the number of characters is greater than the specified width, then the width is "expanded" to accommodate the entire field. (In C the fill character in a `printf()` function call can only be either a zero or a space; in C++ it can be any character you desire. This topic is discussed next.)

If no width is ever specified, then the default value of zero is assumed (just as it is in C). To change the field width, use the member function `width()` with one argument: the width value itself. Then the next field to be output will use this value.

For example, this program prints the number 1 right-justified and preceded by 19 blanks.

Example 12.22

```
#include <iostream.h>

int main()
{
   int x = 1 ;
   cout.width(20) ;
   cout << x << " is the answer\n" ;

   return 0 ;
}
```

The output is (b represents a blank):

```
bbbbbbbbbbbbbbbbbbb1 is the answer
```

Something should strike you as odd about the preceding example. If the state of the `cout` object was set to contain a field width of 20, then why wasn't this state used when it came time to output the string literal `" is the answer\n"`? In other words, why wasn't the string literal also output in a 20-position field right-justified? The answer is that *the width specification only applies to the next field to be output*. After the width has been "used", it reverts back to its default value of zero.

In addition to setting the field width, the `width()` function also returns the value of the width as it existed prior to the function call. If you wish to return this value and make no modification to it, then call the `width()` function with no argument specified.

Borland C++ and the `width()` function

Under version 3.0 (and prior) of Borland C++, the field width specification does *not* apply to any character fields that are output. Most other C++ compilers honor the width setting for a character. However, for Borland this does *not* mean that the width reverts back to zero merely upon encountering a character field. Instead, the current width setting is deferred until the next non-character field that is encountered.

Without explicitly saying so, the implication is that character fields are not affected by the current width setting. It's interesting to note that the AT&T spec on the subject says nothing about making an exception for character fields. Note that this behavior has been changed in Borland C++ version 3.1 so that the current width setting does indeed pertain to a character field.

Here is a test of this situation.

Example 12.23

```
#include <iostream.h>

int main()
{
   cout.width(20) ;
   cout << 'A' << " is first\n" ;

   return 0 ;
}
```

The output in Borland 3.0 is:

```
Abbbbbbbbbbbbis first
```

whereas the output in Borland 3.1 is:

```
bbbbbbbbbbbbbbbbbbbA is first
```

Therefore, in Borland C++ 3.0, if you need to output a character in some specified field width, the best you can do is to fill all but one of the spaces with blanks before the character itself. (Also, see Chapter 14 for a solution using a manipulator.)

How to specify the fill character

If the total number of characters needed to display a field is less than the current field width, the extra output spaces will be filled with the current fill character. In a `printf()` function call, the default fill character is a blank, and you only have the option to change it to a zero.

In C++, however, you now have the option for *any* character to serve as the fill character. As before, the default is a blank. The member function `fill()` is used to specify a new fill character. Once it is specified, it remains as the fill character unless it is subsequently changed. The function takes a single argument: the new fill character, and returns the previous fill character. As with `width()`, it may be called with no actual argument if you merely want to return the previous fill character. Also, it is possible to fill a field on the right with *any* character, including zero.

Example 12.24

```
#include <iostream.h>

int main()
{
   cout.width(5) ;
   cout.fill('0') ;
   cout << 1 << "\n" ;

   cout.width(5) ;
   cout.fill('*') ;
   cout << 23 << "\n" ;

   return 0 ;
}
```

The output is:

```
00001
***23
```

How to specify field justification

In a `print()` function call, whenever a field is output, the data is always right-justified. If you want to left-justify a field, you must use the '-' formatting flag.

In the `iostream` library there are 3 bits which are used to specify the field justification:

TABLE 12.6

Name	Value	Meaning
ios::left	0x0002	Left-justification of output
ios::right	0x0004	Right-justification of output
ios::internal	0x0008	Pad after sign or base indicator

If no bit is ever specified, then the justification defaults to right. As with the integer base setting the base, if one of the bits is on you must ensure that the remaining 2 bits are off. To this end, the field called `ios::adjustfield` has been defined with all 3 justification bits turned on.

Example 12.25

```
// Declaration in the class ios
static const long adjustfield ;

// Definition
const
long ios::adjustfield = ios::left | ios::right | ios::internal ;
```

The following example prints a number using all 3 justifications. The justification `ios::internal` means that padding with the fill character, if any, will occur after the base of the number has been shown (for octal and hexadecimal numbers) and before the number itself. This is also true if a sign for the number is shown, i.e., the padding will occur between the sign and the number itself.

Example 12.26

```
#include <iostream.h>

int main()
{
   int x = 65 ;
   cout.fill('*') ;
   cout.setf(ios::showpos) ;

   cout.setf(ios::left , ios::adjustfield) ;
   cout.width(5) ;
   cout << x << "\n" ;
```

```
    cout.setf(ios::right , ios::adjustfield) ;
    cout.width(5) ;
    cout << x << "\n" ;

    cout.setf(ios::internal , ios::adjustfield) ;
    cout.width(5) ;
    cout << x << "\n" ;

    return 0 ;
}
```

The output is:

```
+65**
**+65
+**65
```

How to format floating point numbers

Floating point numbers are output in C++ just like any other type of number.
However, the formatting is certainly different, and default values are not the same as
you would get from using a `printf()` function call. Our goal then is to emulate the
`%f` and `%e` conversion specifications.

In the following example some floating point constants are output with no special
formatting:

Example 12.27

```
#include <iostream.h>

int main()
{
    cout << 1.23456789 << "\n" ;
    cout << 4.00 << "\n" ;
    cout << 5.678E2 << "\n" ;
    cout << 0.0 << "\n" ;

    return 0 ;
}
```

The output is:

```
1.234568
4
567.8
0
```

For the first constant, note that no more than 6 positions after the decimal point were shown. In the second case, not only do the trailing zeroes *not* show, but even the decimal point does not appear. In the third case, the number prints in fixed point notation despite being keyed in scientific notation. In the final case, even though the value is zero, at least one significant digit will always appear.

If you really want to emulate how the `printf()` function works, you first need to turn on the bit `ios::showpoint`. This will cause the output to show 6 positions after the decimal point. To revert back to the default value, use the function `unsetf()` to turn it off.

TABLE 12.7

Name	Value	Meaning
ios::showpoint	0x0100	Show the decimal point for all floats

Here is the previous example with the `ios::showpoint` bit now turned on.

Example 12.28

```cpp
#include <iostream.h>

int main()
{
   cout.setf(ios::showpoint) ;

   cout << 1.23456789 << "\n" ;
   cout << 4.00 << "\n" ;
   cout << 5.678E2 << "\n" ;
   cout << 0.0 << "\n" ;

   return 0 ;
}
```

The output is:

```
1.234568
4.000000
567.800000
0.000000
```

The next step is to override the default of 6 decimal positions. To do this, use the member function `precision()` in which the one argument is the number of decimal positions to be shown. If it is called without an argument, it merely returns the current value of the precision and does not alter it. The default precision is 0.

Here is the previous example again with the precision now set to 2.

Example 12.29

```cpp
#include <iostream.h>

int main()
{
   cout.setf(ios::showpoint) ;
   cout.precision(2) ;

   cout << 1.23456789 << "\n" ;
   cout << 4.00 << "\n" ;
   cout << 5.678E2 << "\n" ;
   cout << 0.0 << "\n" ;

   return 0 ;
}
```

The output is:

```
1.23
4.00
567.80
0.00
```

☞ Borland C++ versions 3.0 and 3.1 treat a precision of 0 as though it were 6. This is an acknowledged bug.

Sometimes the program will decide to show your floating output in scientific, rather than fixed, notation. To guarantee that all output is shown in either fixed decimal or scientific notation, use the following bits:

TABLE 12.8

Name	Value	Meaning
ios::scientific	0x0800	Show exponential notation on floats
ios::fixed	0x1000	Show fixed decimal output on floats

If neither bit is turned on, then the compiler emulates the `%g` conversion specification in a `printf()` function call. Also, there is a constant called `ios:floatfield` that is the value of these two bits ORed together, and should be used as the second argument in a `setf()` function call.

Example 12.30

```
// Declaration in the class ios
static const long floatfield ;

// Definition
const long ios::floatfield = ios::scientific | ios::fixed ;
```

Here is Example 12.29 again, now with both notations used.

Example 12.31

```
#include <iostream.h>

int main()
{
   cout.setf(ios::showpoint) ;
   cout.precision(2) ;

   // Guarantee fixed decimal
   cout.setf(ios::fixed , ios::floatfield) ;
   cout << 1.23456789 << "\n" ;
   cout << 4.00 << "\n" ;
   cout << 5.678E2<< "\n" ;
   cout << 0.0 << "\n\n" ;
```

```
    // Guarantee scientific
    cout.setf(ios::scientific , ios::floatfield) ;
    cout << 1.23456789 << "\n" ;
    cout << 4.00 << "\n" ;
    cout << 5.678E2<< "\n" ;
    cout << 0.0 << "\n" ;

    return 0 ;
}
```

The output is:

```
1.23
4.00
567.80
0.00

1.23e+00
4.00e+00
5.68e+02
0.00e+00
```

How to print an address

The address of a variable (or instance of a class) can be generated by using the address operator (&). Because the address operator can be applied to a wide variety of types (both built-in and user-defined), the type of argument can theoretically be 'pointer-to-int' or 'pointer-to-float' or even 'pointer-to-my-class-type'. To accommodate all of these various types, the class `ostream` contains an operator insertion function to handle *all* such argument types. The one explicit argument to this function is declared as type `void*` which, according to the rules of argument matching, is acceptable to the compiler as a "match" for any pointer type.

In Borland C++, this address is always shown in 16-bit (2 byte) or 32-bit (4 byte) hexadecimal form.

Example 12.32

```
#include <iostream.h>

int main()
{
   int x = 0 ;
   cout << "&x = " << &x << "\n" ;

   return 0 ;
}
```

The output is:

```
&x = 0xfff4
```

Of course, the actual address on your computer will probably be different.

Note that in the case of a string literal, which is type `char[]`, or a pointer-to-a-character, which is type `char*`, the class `ostream` contains an operator insertion function accepting type `const char*` that matches the actual argument exactly (after a trivial conversion). This is fine if your intent is to print the literal to which the pointer is pointing. However, if you wish to print the content of the pointer variable itself, i.e., the address of the first character being pointed at, then you must cast this address into a `void*` type.

Example 12.33

```
#include <iostream.h>

int main()
{
   const char* ptr = "C++" ;
   cout << ptr << "\n" ;
   cout << (void*)ptr << "\n" ;

   return 0 ;
}
```

The output is:

```
C++
0x00aa
```

How a memory address is stored

Since the 8086 microprocessor chip uses only 16-bit addressing, the highest address possible is 65,535. This obviously is insufficient to handle the addresses on a computer with 1MB of RAM. What is really needed is a 20-bit address. Therefore, the address is divided between 2 hardware registers, the first called the *segment register*, and the second called the *offset register*. A segment is a 64K region of RAM that starts on an even multiple of 16 bytes. The location of any byte within a segment is determined by the offset. Thus, the physical 20-bit address of any specific byte within the computer is determined by shifting the segment address left 4 bits (1 hex digit, or a value of 16) and adding the offset value. The resulting address is usually shown in "segment:offset" form, just like the %p conversion specification in a printf() function call.

Here is a program that prints an address in 'segment:offset' form. The header file dos.h is needed here.

Example 12.34

```
#include <iostream.h>
#include <dos.h>

int main()
{
   int x ;
   cout << "&x = " << FP_SEG(&x) << ":" << FP_OFF(&x) << "\n" ;

   return 0 ;
}
```

The output is:

```
&x = 2372:65524
```

Binary output

It's possible to take any internal representation of a C++ type and output it as though it were just an array of characters. That is, whatever the bit representation of the type is in memory, that pattern will be written to the output device with no formatting performed. In C this is accomplished with the function fwrite(). In C++ the name of the function is write(). This function takes 2 arguments: (1) The address of the data to be output, and (2) the number of bytes to be written. Note that in the case of a string, the null byte is treated just like any other byte.

Because the function `write()` is declared to accept an argument of type `const char*`, if the item you wish to print is not of this type, then its address must be cast.

For example, this program writes the first 3 bytes of a string to the screen.

Example 12.35

```
#include <iostream.h>

int main()
{
    char buffer[] = "ABCDE" ;
    cout.write(buffer , 3) ;
    cout << "\n" ;

    return 0 ;
}
```

The output is:

```
ABC
```

This program writes 3 hexadecimal numbers to the screen. Note the cast from `int*` to `char*`.

Example 12.36

```
#include <iostream.h>

int main()
{
    int array[] = { 0x41 , 0x42 , 0x43 } ;
    cout.write((char*)array , sizeof(array)) ;
    cout << "\n" ;

    return 0 ;
}
```

The output is:

```
A B C
```

How to output to a memory buffer

In C you can send output to a memory buffer of type `char*` instead of to the screen by using the function `sprintf()`, where the first argument specifies the address of the buffer area where the data is to be stored. Here is an example:

Example 12.37

```
#include <stdio.h>

int main(void)
{
   char buffer[80] ;
   int x = 65 ;
   sprintf(buffer, "x = %d", x) ;
   printf("buffer = \"%s\"\n" , buffer) ;

   return 0 ;
}
```

The output is:

```
buffer = "x = 65"
```

In order to accomplish the same result in C++ you must first include the header file `strstream.h`. This file contains the definition of the class `ostrstream`, which you then use to create some instance. At the time of creation, you must provide two arguments: (1) the address of the buffer where the data is to be written, and (2) the maximum size of this buffer (which normally is the `sizeof` the buffer).

After this has been done, the instance `output` is used where you would normally use `cout`. All of the data is thus sent to the `buffer` area. If you subsequently want to send this `buffer` area to the screen, don't forget to append a null byte to make the `buffer` a legitimate string object. If you subsequently wish to place more output into this buffer area starting back at character position 0, you must use the (inherited) member function `seekp()` with an argument of 0.

Example 12.38

```
#include <iostream.h>
#include <strstream.h>

int main()
{
   char buffer[80] ;
   ostrstream output(buffer , sizeof buffer);

   int number = 65 ;
   output << "number = " << number << '\0' ;
   cout << '\"' << buffer << '\"' << "\n" ;

   output.seekp(0) ;
   output << "A new buffer stream " << "of characters" << '\0' ;
   cout << '\"' << buffer << '\"' << "\n" ;

   return 0 ;
}
```

The output is:

```
"number = 65"
"A new buffer stream of characters"
```

The instances `cerr` and `clog`

In addition to the instance `cout`, C++ provides you with two other instances of the class `ostream` called `cerr` and `clog`. They are used for any error messages that you may wish to direct to the terminal operator. The output of `cerr` is unbuffered, while the output of `clog` is buffered. Although the output of both instances will normally be shown on the screen, if redirection is used, say to a printer or disk file, then the results of `cout` will be redirected while the results of `cerr` and `clog` will continue to be shown on the screen.

Example 12.39

```
#include <iostream.h>

int main()
{
  cout << "Output of cout\n" ;
  cerr << "Output of cerr\n" ;
  clog << "Output of clog\n" ;

  return 0 ;
}
```

After running this program, redirect the output to the printer or to a disk file.

The function `flush()`

If, at any time, you want to explicitly flush the output buffer, you may do so by calling the member function `flush()`. For screen output, this is not necessary since all output is flushed automatically. However, in the case where one disk file is being copied to another, you may have to flush the output buffer prior to rewinding the output file for continued use.

Example 12.40

```
#include <iostream.h>

int main()
{
  cout << "Good-bye world\n" ;
  cout.flush() ;

  return 0 ;
}

The output is:

Good-bye world
```

☞ The function flush() does not have anything to do with flushing the *input* buffer.

How to overload the insertion operator

As noted at the start of this chapter, one of the features of the I/O stream classes provided in C++ is the capability to overload the insertion operator so that it can be used with instances of user-defined classes. In other words, the goal is to be able to output instances of user-defined types just as though they were instances of primitive types. This can be done because the insertion operator, which has already been overloaded by the ostream class, may be overloaded again by you so that you may then use the instance cout in the normal fashion. Certainly, if you failed to overload the operator, the compiler would have no idea what to do except generate a compilation error.

The general formats for the function declaration and definition are:

Example 12.41

```
// Declaration
friend ostream& operator<<(ostream& , const X&) ;

// Definition
ostream& operator<<(ostream& stream , const X& obj)
{
   // Output fields of the object using 'obj' and the dot
   // operator. Then...
   return stream ;
}
```

Since you want this function to be invoked by the instance cout and *not* by an instance of the user-defined class x, it *must* be declared as a binary friend of the class x. The first argument is a reference to the first argument of the function call (usually cout), and is returned by reference so that function calls can be chained together. The second argument must be an instance of the user-defined class x, and should be passed in by constant reference.

Here is a complete example that uses the complex class to add two numbers together. Then the overloaded operator<<() friend function is used to display all three numbers.

Example 12.42

```
#include <iostream.h>

class complex
{
   double real , imag ;

      public:
   complex(double = 0.0 , double = 0.0) ;
   friend complex operator+(const complex& , const complex&) ;
   friend ostream& operator<<(ostream& , const complex&) ;
} ;

inline
complex::complex(double r , double i) : real(r) , imag(i) {}

complex operator+(const complex& c1 , const complex& c2)
{
   return complex(c1.real + c2.real , c1.imag + c2.imag) ;
}

ostream& operator<<(ostream& stream , const complex& c)
{
   return stream << c.real << (c.imag < 0 ? "" : "+")
                 << c.imag << "i" ;
}

int main()
{
   complex c1(3 , -4) , c2(2) ;
   complex c3 = c1 + c2 ;
   cout << "c1 = " << c1 << "\n" ;
   cout << "c2 = " << c2 << "\n" ;
   cout << "c3 = " << c3 << "\n" ;

   return 0 ;
}
```

The output is:

```
c1 = 3-4i
c2 = 2+0i
c3 = 5-4i
```

Commingling stdio and iostream output

As a general rule, you should not commingle `stdio` and `iostream` output. The reason is that they flush their buffers at different times, so that the order of the output cannot be guaranteed. However, if you are determined to do so, then you must first call the static function `ios::sync_with_stdio()` that will coordinate the two output systems.

■ Exercise #1

Write a class called `display` that contains the methods to print an integer in these four ways:

- ■ Decimal within a field width of 10 with leading blanks

- ■ Hexadecimal within a field width of 10 with leading asterisks and with the base and uppercase of the number shown

- ■ Octal within a field width of 10 with leading carets and with the base of the number shown

- ■ Character within single quotes. However, if the number represents a non-printable character (as determined by the `ctype.h` library function `isprint()`), then output the word NON-PRINTABLE instead of the character itself.

Then write a `main()` function that creates an instance of the class and calls upon each class function using the internally generated numbers 0 through 50.

For example, the output for the numbers 31 and 32 would be:

```
DEC -        31
HEX - ******0X1F
OCT - ^^^^^^^037
CHR - Non-printable

DEC -        32
HEX - ******0X20
OCT - ^^^^^^^040
CHR - ' '
```

■ Exercise #2

Given the following class definition:

```
class mult_table
{
    int base ;
    void title_line() const ;
    void body() const ;
```

```
      public:
   mult_table(int) ;
   void display() const
   {
   title() ;
   body() ;
   }
} ;
```

and the `main()` function:

```
int main()
{
   const int start = 2 ;
   const int end = 10 ;

   for(int base = start ; base <= end ; ++base)
   {
      mult_table table = base ;
      table.display() ;
   }

   return 0 ;
}
```

write the member functions `title()` and `body()` that display the title and body, respectively, of a multiplication table of size `base`. All entries must align on the units position. Have the `main()` function use an instance of the class to generate tables for all bases in the range 2 through 10, inclusive.

For example, the multiplication table for the base 5 should appear as:

```
      MULTIPLICATION TABLE FOR BASE 5

            0     1     2     3     4

  0         0     0     0     0     0
  1         0     1     2     3     4
  2         0     2     4    11    13
  3         0     3    11    14    22
  4         0     4    13    22    31
```

■ Exercise #3

From the `string` class in Chapter 8, derive a new class called `print_string` and give it the capability to output a `string` instance by overloading the insertion operator. Be sure to display both the string literal and the length. At the very minimum, your `main()` function should appear as follows:

```
int main()
{
    print_string ps1 , ps2("C++") ;
    cout << ps1 << endl ;
    cout << ps2 << endl ;

    return 0 ;
}
```

■ Exercise #4

In Example 12.42 each output line contains a commingling of the two types of insertion operators, i.e., member of the class ostream and friend of the class complex. Rewrite one of the output lines completely in functional notation.

Notes

Chapter 13

Stream input

In addition to being able to use classes to control output, C++ stream I/O classes also handle all input. Just as output consists of a stream of characters being sent to some device, input consists of characters coming in from some device and being translated into their proper defined type. Unlike output, the realm of possibilities for "formatting" simply does not exist when inputting data.

The instance `cin`

As noted in Chapter 12, the class `istream`, which is derived from the class `ios`, controls the input handling functions. The global instance that you use is called `cin`. Think of `cin` as being the keyboard object, from which you will be extracting data (the terminal operator's input).

 As was the case with the three output instances, `cin` is actually an instance of the class `istream_withassign`.

How to do simple input using the extraction operator

The function you will use the most often to read input from the keyboard is called the *extraction* operator. Note that it is the overloaded right-shift operator, whereas the insertion function `operator<<()` in Chapter 12 is the overloaded left-shift operator. Within the class `istream` it has been overloaded many times as a binary member function. Thus, it is declared as:

Example 13.1

```
istream& operator>>(/* 1 explicit argument */) ;
```

The name "extraction" comes from the fact that you are "extracting" (taking) data from the input stream. The argument to this function is the variable name that you wish to contain the input data. Note that all such overloaded functions ignore leading whitespace characters from the keyboard, and terminate upon encountering a whitespace character within the data.

More specifically, the extraction operator function has been overloaded to accommodate these types:

- unsigned char*
- signed char*
- unsigned char&
- signed char&
- unsigned short int&
- short int&
- int&
- unsigned int&
- long&
- unsigned long&
- float&

- ■ double&
- ■ long double&
- ■ streambuf*
- ■ istream& (*) (istream&)

For example, to input an integer using infix notation, you would code:

Example 13.2

```
int number ;
cin >> number ;
```

Note that unlike `scanf()`, there is no need to use the address operator (for a non-array type), nor is there a need to specify any type of conversion specification. That is, the function "knows" that you want to do integer input because it matches the type of variable `number` (`int` in this case) to the corresponding overloaded `operator>>()` function that takes an `int` by reference as its one formal argument. As you learned in Chapter 2, the reference type allows the function to modify the actual argument (`number`).

For example, this program inputs a decimal number, a character and a float, and then echoes them back.

Example 13.3

```
#include <iostream.h>

int main()
{
   cout << "Enter a number: " ;
   int number ;
   cin >> number ;
   cout << "You entered: " << number << "\n" ;

   cout << "Enter a character: " ;
   char ch ;
   cin >> ch ;
   cout << "You entered: " << ch << "\n" ;

   cout << "Enter a float: " ;
   float fl ;
   cin >> fl ;
   cout << "You entered: " << fl << "\n" ;

   return 0 ;
}
```

A typical run of the program would yield:

```
Enter a number: 23
You entered: 23
Enter a character: A
You entered A
Enter a float: 1.2
You entered: 1.2
```

Note: In this and future examples, the terminal operator's input is <u>underlined</u> to differentiate it from the program's output.

The extraction operator, like the insertion operator, can be chained together so that you have to write the cin instance only once.

Example 13.4

```
#include <iostream.h>

int main()
{
   cout << "Enter a number, character, and float: " ;
   int number ;
   char ch ;
   float fl ;
   cin >> number >> ch >> fl ;
   cout << "You entered: " << number << " and "
        << ch << " and " << fl << "\n" ;

   return 0 ;
}
```

A typical run of the program would yield:

```
Enter a number, character, and float:  23A1.2
You entered: 23 and A and 1.2

Enter a number, character, and float: 23 A 1.2
You entered: 23 and A and 1.2

Enter a number, character, and float: 23 A1.2
You entered: 23 and A and 1.2

Enter a number, character, and float: 23 A 1 .2
You entered: 23 and A and 1
```

Integer input

Recall from the discussion on output in chapter 12 that the base setting for integer output is, by default, decimal. This setting can, of course, be changed by using the `setf()` function.

In a similar manner, the default base setting for integer input is decimal. This means that for any integral variable, only valid integer data is acceptable, and any attempt to violate this rule will cause an error condition to occur. For example, entering A12 for an integer value will cause an error. However, entering 12A will cause the number 12 to be stored into the integer, and the letter A to remain in the input stream buffer, so that this is not necessarily an error condition; it depends on what you do next.

Even though the default input base setting is decimal, it is still possible to override this default if you wish to input either an octal or hexadecimal number. This can be done by explicitly entering the base of these numbers, i.e., 0 for octal and 0x (or 0X) for hex. This is analogous in C to writing `scanf()` with a conversion specification of `"%i"`.

Example 13.5

```
#include <iostream.h>

int main()
{
    cout << "Enter a number: " ;
    int number ;
    cin >> number ;
    cout << "You entered: " << number << "\n" ;

    return 0 ;
}
```

A typical run of the program would yield:

```
Enter a number: 20
You entered: 20

Enter a number: 024
You entered: 20

Enter a number: 0x14
You entered: 20
```

However, note what happens when the input base setting is *explicitly* set to decimal via a setf() function call. In this case only *decimal input* is allowed. This is analogous in C to writing scanf() with a conversion specification of "%d". Here is Example 13.5 again, but with the base setting explicitly specified.

Example 13.6

```
#include <iostream.h>

int main()
{
   cin.setf(ios::dec , ios::basefield) ;
   cout << "Enter a number: " ;
   int number ;
   cin >> number ;
   cout << "You entered: " << number << "\n" ;

   return 0 ;
}
```

A typical run of the program would yield:

```
Enter a number: 20
You entered: 20

Enter a number: 024
You entered: 24

Enter a number: 0x14
You entered: 0
```

In a similar manner, you can hard-code the program to accept octal or hexadecimal input values by turning on the ios::oct or ios::hex bit, respectively. In this situation the terminal operator no longer needs to explicitly enter the base setting for the number (0 for octal and 0x for hexadecimal). Essentially, this is how the %o and %x conversion specifications in a scanf() function call can be emulated.

Character input

The simplest way to read in a character is to use the extraction function operator>>(). As mentioned earlier, all leading whitespace characters are bypassed, and the first non-whitespace character is fetched.

In the following example, enter 2 non-whitespace characters interspersed with lots of blanks and tabs. Then press <ENTER>. Regardless of the whitespace that you may have entered, only the 2 non-whitespace characters will be stored.

Example 13.7

```
#include <iostream.h>

int main()
{
   cout << "Enter 2 characters: " ;
   char ch1 , ch2 ;
   cin >> ch1 >> ch2 ;
   cout << "You entered: " << "'" << ch1 << "'"
        << " and " << "'" << ch2 << "'" << "\n" ;

   return 0 ;
}
```

A typical run of the program would yield:

```
Enter 2 characters: ___a b___
You entered: 'a' and 'b'
```

Another way to read characters is provided by the member function `get()`. It takes a single argument — the character itself, and returns a reference to the invoking instance so that the function calls can be chained together. The difference between `operator>>()` and `get()` is that `get()` will honor any and all whitespace characters.

Here is the previous example now using `get()` instead of `operator>>()`.

Example 13.8

```
#include <iostream.h>

int main()
{
   cout << "Enter 2 characters: " ;
   char ch1 , ch2 ;
   cin.get(ch1).get(ch2) ;
   cout << "You entered: " << "'" << ch1 << "'"
        << " and " << "'" << ch2 << "'" << "\n" ;

   return 0 ;
}
```

A typical run of the program would yield:

```
Enter 2 characters: a b
You entered: 'a' and ' '

Enter 2 characters:  a b
You entered: ' ' and 'a'
```

The `get()` function has also been overloaded so that it can take no input argument (just like `getchar()` in C). In this form it returns a value of type `int`, which represents the character just read, or the `EOF` constant if either (a) end-of-file was detected, or (b) no character could be read. Because the return type is `int`, no chaining of this form of `get()` is possible.

In the following example `get()` is used to read in a character, after which a check for end-of-file is made. Because the variable `ch` must be defined as type `int`, don't forget the cast in order to display it as a character.

Example 13.9

```cpp
#include <iostream.h>

int main()
{
   cout << "Enter a character: " ;
   int ch = cin.get() ;
   if(ch != EOF)
      cout << "You entered: " << "'" << (char)ch << "'" << "\n" ;
   else
      cout << "End-of-file\n" ;

   return 0 ;
}
```

A typical run of the program would yield:

```
Enter a character: a
You entered: 'a'

Enter a character: ^z
You entered: End-of-file
```

String input

Strings may also be entered using the extraction operator. Don't forget that leading whitespace is bypassed, and the first whitespace encountered terminates the input. This acts just like the function `scanf()` with the conversion specification `"%s"`.

Example 13.10

```
#include <iostream.h>

int main()
{
   cout << "Enter a string: " ;
   const int max = 128 ;
   char string[max] ;
   cin >> string ;
   cout << "Your string: " << '\"' << string << '\"' << "\n" ;

   return 0 ;
}
```

A typical run of the program would yield:

```
Enter a string:    Hello world
Your string: "Hello"
```

But just like `scanf()`, you could have a program hang or crash if the operator enters more characters than can safely be accommodated by the string array. To guard against this disaster, you may set the width of the input stream to physically limit the number of characters that can be stored. This is done by using the member function `width()` in conjunction with the `cin` instance. The result is that only the number of characters (less 1) specified by the argument to `width()` will be extracted from the input stream; the remaining characters are left alone. Of course, the first whitespace character encountered will still terminate the input. And don't forget — just like the `width()` function used for output, the input `width()` function only applies to the next item to be input.

For example, in the following program the terminal operator can input any number of characters, but only the first 9 will be stored into the buffer area.

Example 13.11

```
#include <iostream.h>

int main()
{
  const int max = 10 ;
  cout << "Enter a string no longer than " << max - 1
       << " characters\n" ;
  cin.width(max) ;
  char string[max] ;
  cin >> string ;
  cout << "You entered: " << '\"' << string << '\"' << "\n" ;

  return 0 ;
}
```

A typical run of the program would yield:

```
Enter a string no longer than 9 characters
ThisIsALongString
You entered: "ThisIsALo"
```

Another way to read in strings is to use the member function get(). In this form it takes 3 arguments.

■   The first argument is the address of the string area;

■   The second argument is the maximum number of characters (less 1) that will be stored into your buffer area;

■   The third argument specifies the terminating character (the one that will stop the transfer of characters from the system buffer into your string array). This third argument defaults to the value '\n', which is the <ENTER> key. Note, however, that if it is changed to some other character, then the <ENTER> key must still be pressed for the input action to cease.

Note the similarity to the C function fgets(). The advantage to using get() as opposed to operator>>() is that now both leading whitespace and embedded whitespace are retained as part of the string value.

Example 13.12

```
#include <iostream.h>

int main()
{
  const int max = 10 ;
  cout << "Enter a string no longer than " << max - 1
       << " characters\n" ;
  char string[max] ;
  cin.get(string , max) ;
  cout << "Your string: " << '\"' << string << '\"' << "\n" ;

  return 0 ;
}
```

A typical run of the program would yield:

```
Enter a string:    Hello world
Your string: "   Hello "
```

A slight variation on using the function get() to read a string is the function getline(). The only difference is that getline() extracts the newline character ('\n') from the system input buffer, whereas get() leaves it alone (and, presumably, must then be flushed by you before you attempt to read another string).

The member function gcount()

It's also possible to find out exactly how many characters were extracted from the system input buffer after a get() or getline() operation. The member function gcount() returns this value.

Here is the previous example with a call to gcount().

Example 13.13

```
#include <iostream.h>

int main()
{
    const int max = 10 ;
    cout << "Enter a string no longer than " << max - 1
         << " characters\n" ;
    char string[max] ;
    cin.get(string , max) ;
    cout << "Your string: " << '\"' << string << '\"' << "\n" ;
    cout << "You extracted " << cin.gcount()
         << "characters\n" ;

    return 0 ;
}
```

A typical run of the program would yield:

```
Enter a string: Hello
Your string: "Hello"
You extracted 5 characters
```

Now the example has been changed so that the function get line () is used instead of get (). Note that one extra character (the newline) is now being extracted from the system input buffer.

Example 13.14

```
#include <iostream.h>

int main()
{
    const int max = 10 ;
    cout << "Enter a string no longer than " << max - 1
         << " characters\n" ;
    char string[max] ;
    cin.getline(string , max) ;
    cout << "Your string: " << '\"' << string << '\"' << "\n" ;
    cout << "You extracted " << cin.gcount()
         << "characters\n" ;

    return 0 ;
}
```

A typical run of the program would yield:

```
Enter a string: Hello
Your string: "Hello"
You extracted 6 characters
```

How to check for end-of-file

When reading data from the keyboard or a file, you must always be on guard for the occurrence of an end-of-file mark. For example, in C you usually examine the return value `scanf()` and `getchar()` for the value `EOF`, and the return value of `gets()` and `fgets()` for `NULL`.

From the keyboard different key combinations are used to create an end-of-file condition, depending upon the operating system that you are using. In DOS, it's <CTRL>Z or function key <F6>, while Unix uses <CTRL>D.

Since the `cin` is just an instance of class `istream`, which is inherited from class `ios`, one of its data members reflects whether or not it is in an end-of-file condition. This condition can be tested by you with the accessor function `ios::eof()`. This function will return 'true' if `cin` is in an end-of-file condition, 'false' if it is not.

Normally data is obtained within a `while` loop, with the loop continuing to execute as long as end-of-file is *not* detected. This situation could be coded like this:

Example 13.15

```cpp
#include <iostream.h>

int main()
{
  cout << "Enter a number: " ;
  int num ;
  cin >> num ;
  while(!cin.eof())
   {
     cout << "You entered: " << num << "\n" ;
     cout << "\nNext number: " ;
     cin >> num ;
   }
  cout << "End-of-file\n" ;

  return 0 ;
}
```

A typical run of the program would yield:

```
Enter a number: 12
You entered: 12

Next number: 34
You entered: 34

Next number: ^Z
End-of-file
```

However, the previous program can be simplified. Since the extraction operator returns a reference to the invoking object itself (`cin`), this object can be used as the invoking object for the `eof()` member function call. Notice how the read and check for end-of-file have been combined to form the Boolean condition of the `while` loop.

Thus, Example 13.15 can be revised to look like:

Example 13.16

```cpp
#include <iostream.h>

int main()
{
  cout << "Enter a number: " ;
  int num ;
  while(!(cin >> num).eof())
   {
      cout << "You entered: " << num << "\n" ;
      cout << "\nNext number: " ;
   }
  cout << "End-of-file\n" ;

  return 0 ;
}
```

The output is the same as that of Example 13.15.

How to check for errors

Unfortunately, we live in an imperfect world. People don't smile, cars crash, checks bounce, and data entry operators don't always do what they're supposed to do. This means that as a programmer, you must be responsible for making your code as "operator-proof" as possible. In other words, no matter what the user may enter as "data", your program must capture it and successfully trap all error conditions to avoid such catastrophes as "garbage in, garbage out", aborts, hangs, endless loops, etc.

When expecting character or string input, there's not too much that can go wrong, other than array overflow, which has already been covered. But with numeric data, such as integers, floats and doubles, only certain keystrokes in a prescribed order are considered to be valid. For example, when you expect a decimal integer to be input, the user may enter a sign (+ or -) followed by the digits 0 through 9. An entry of A12 is obviously invalid. An entry such as 12A, however, is considered to be the number 12, with the "invalid" character 'A' serving to terminate the numeric portion of the input stream. In addition, any whitespace character terminates a numeric entry, and all leading whitespace characters are bypassed automatically.

The condition of the cin instance is represented by a collection of enumerated values in the class ios, as follows:

TABLE 13.1

Name	Value	Meaning
ios::goodbit	0x0000	Good condition, all bits off
ios::eofbit	0x0001	End-of-file detected
ios::failbit	0x0002	Last input operation failed
ios::badbit	0x0004	Invalid operation attempted
ios::hardfail	0x0080	Unrecoverable error

These bits are stored in a protected integer, and may be accessed by using the function rdstate(). However, it's much more convenient to test the cin instance by using any of the following four accessor functions:

TABLE 13.2

Function	Returns true if:
ios::good()	All bits off
ios::eof()	ios::eofbit is on
ios::fail()	ios::fail or ios::bad or ios::hardfail is on
ios::bad()	ios::badbit or ios::hardfail is on

Another way to check for an input error is to use the overloaded function operator! (Boolean 'not') on the instance cin. This operator will return 'true' if an error occurred, 'false' otherwise. Similarly, testing the instance cin itself as a Boolean value will return 'true' if the input was good, 'false' otherwise. (How this technique works was discussed in Chapter 9.)

The following program is designed to test the `cin` instance in every possible way. Recall from Chapter 12 that the parentheses surrounding the ternary operator are mandatory.

Example 13.17

```
#include <iostream.h>

int main()
{
   cout << "Enter a number: " ;
   int number ;
   cin >> number ;

   cout << "eof() = " << (cin.eof() ? "True\n" : "False\n") ;
   cout << "good() = " << (cin.good() ? "True\n" : "False\n") ;
   cout << "fail() = " << (cin.fail() ? "True\n" : "False\n") ;
   cout << "bad() = " << (cin.bad() ? "True\n" : "False\n") ;
   cout << "if(!cin) = " << (!cin ? "True\n" : "False\n") ;
   cout << "if(cin) = " << (cin ? "True\n" : "False\n") ;

   return 0 ;
}
```

This is a test of valid numeric input:

```
Enter a number: 65
eof() = False
good() = True
fail() = False
bad() = False
if(!cin) = False
if(cin) = True
```

This is a test of invalid input:

```
Enter a number: Garbage
eof() = False
good() = False
fail() = True
bad() = False
if(!cin) = True
if(cin) = False
```

This is a test of end-of-file:

```
Enter a number: ^Z
eof() = True
good() = False
fail() = True
bad() = False
if(!cin) = True
if(cin) = False
```

How to flush the input stream buffer

The next problem is how to eliminate any and all "garbage" characters from the input stream. But there is something that you must do first. The problem is that when an error occurs, the status of the input stream is changed from 'good' to 'fail' and *no more characters can be read until the status is reset to 'good'*. To do this, you must call upon the member function `ios::clear()` with no arguments (the default argument is 0, which means "set the status of the stream to 'good'").

The following function FLUSH() (declared in the file `manips.h` and defined in the file `manips.cpp`) shows one way to flush the input stream buffer. Note the function's return type of `istream&`. While it is not being used in this example, this function is actually a manipulator, and will be discussed in more detail in the next chapter. For now, it will be used as a simple function call with the return value ignored.

Example 13.18

```cpp
#include <iostream.h>

// Declaration
istream& FLUSH(istream&) ;

// Definition
istream& FLUSH(istream& stream)
{
   if(stream.rdbuf()->in_avail() > 0)
   {
      stream.clear() ;
      stream.ignore(256 , '\n') ;
   }
   return stream ;
}
```

Thus, an "operator-proof" program that loops while reading numbers and checking for end-of-file and garbage input might resemble this:

Example 13.19

```
#include <iostream.h>
#include "manips.h"

#include "manips.cpp"

int main()
{
   cout << "\nEnter a number: " ;
   int number ;
   while(!(cin >> number).eof())
    {
      // Test for a bad number
      if(!cin)
         cerr << "Input error!\n" ;

      // Process a good number
      else
         cout << "You entered: " << number << "\n" ;

      // Clear out the input buffer
      FLUSH(cin) ;

      cout << "\nNext number: " ;
    }
   cout << "\nEnd of file\n" ;

   return 0 ;
}
```

A typical run of the program would yield:

```
Enter a number: 12
You entered: 12

Next number: a
Input error!

Next number: 34^Z
You entered: 34

Next number: 5 6
You entered: 5
```

```
Next number: ^Z
End of file
```

One note about the logic of this program. If two *valid* numbers are entered before the operator presses <ENTER>, then only the first number will be processed; the second will be flushed. You may or may not want this to happen, depending upon your design philosophy.

Binary input

In Chapter 12 you learned how to write data using the function `write()` so that its internal representation was preserved on the output device. In a similar fashion, the function `read()` can be used to read in this data from an input device.

In the following program the keyboard will be used to read in characters. Of course, in most other cases you would want to read from a disk file.

Example 13.20

```
#include <iostream.h>

int main()
{
    const int size = 3 ;
    char buffer[size + 1] ;
    cout << "Enter " << size << " characters: " ;
    cin.read(buffer , size) ;
    buffer[size] = '\0' ;
    cout << "buffer: " << '\"' << buffer << '\"' << "\n" ;

    return 0 ;
}
```

A typical run of the program would yield:

```
Enter 3 characters: ABC
buffer: "ABC"
```

How to input from a memory buffer

In C you can read input from a memory buffer of type `char*` instead of from the keyboard by using the function `sscanf()`, where the first argument specifies the address of the buffer area from which the data is to be read. For example:

Example 13.21

```
#include <stdio.h>

int main(void)
{
   char buffer[] = "ABC 1.234 5" ;
   char string[100] ;
   float f ;
   int n ;

   sscanf(buffer , "%s%f%d" , string , &f , &n) ;
   printf("string = %c%s%c\n" , '\"' , string , '\"') ;
   printf("float = %f\n" , f) ;
   printf("int = %d\n" , n) ;

   return 0 ;
}
```

The output is:

```
string = "ABC"
float = 1.234000
int = 5
```

In order to accomplish the same result in C++ you must first include the header file `strstream.h`. (Note: DOS only honors the first 8 characters of the file name.) This file contains the definition of the class `istrstream`, which you then use to create some instance. At the time of creation, you must provide two arguments: (1) the address of the buffer from which the data is to be read, and (2) the maximum size of this buffer (which normally is the `sizeof` the buffer). For example,

Example 13.22

```
char buffer[80] ;
istrstream input(buffer , sizeof buffer) ;
```

After this has been done, the instance `input` is used where you would normally use `cin`. All of the data is thus read from the `buffer` area. If you subsequently wish to read this buffer area starting back at character position 0, you must use the (inherited) member function `seekg()` with an argument of 0.

Example 13.23

```
#include <iostream.h>
#include <strstream.h>

int main()
{
   char buffer[] = "ABC 1.234 5" ;
   char string[100] ;
   float f ;
   int n ;

   istrstream input(buffer , sizeof buffer) ;

   input >> string >> f >> n ;
   cout << "string = " << '\"' << string << '\"' << "\n" ;
   cout << "float = " << f << "\n" ;
   cout << "int = " << n << "\n" ;

   // Let's do it again
   input.seekg(0) ;
   input >> string >> f >> n ;
   cout << "string = " << '\"' << string << '\"' << "\n" ;
   cout << "float = " << f << "\n" ;
   cout << "int = " << n << "\n" ;

   return 0 ;
}
```

The output is:

```
string = "ABC"
float = 1.234000
int = 5
string = "ABC"
float = 1.234000
int = 5
```

If you wish to do both input and output using a memory buffer, one way is to create an instance of the class strstream, but with no arguments. When the instance both is used, data is stored in an internal buffer area. The extraction operator may then be used with the instance to read from this buffer area. In addition, the function rdbuf() returns the address of the buffer area.

Example 13.24

```
#include <iostream.h>
#include <strstream.h>

int main()
{
  strstream both ;

  // Put data into the internal buffer
  both << "ABC" << " " << 1.234 << " " << 5 << '\0' ;

  // The data so far:
  cout << both.rdbuf() << "\n" ;

  // Don't forget this
  both.seekg(0) ;

  // Extract data from 'buffer'
  char string[100] ;
  float f ;
  long n ;
  both >> string >> f >> n ;

  // Verify the data
  cout << "string = " << '\"' << string << '\"' << "\n" ;
  cout << "float = " << f << "\n" ;
  cout << "long = " << n << "\n" ;

  return 0 ;
}
```

The output is:

```
ABC 1.234 5
string = "ABC"
float = 1.234
long = 5
```

If you wish to create your own buffer area, then you may do so provided that you open the internal file in both input and output modes (see Chapter 15 on file I/O for more information on file modes).

Example 13.25

```
#include <iostream.h>
#include <strstream.h>

int main()
{
   char buffer[100] ;
   strstream both(buffer , sizeof buffer , ios::in | ios::out) ;

   // Put data into 'buffer'
   both << "ABC" << " " << 1.234 << " " << 5 << '\0' ;

   // The data so far:
   cout << buffer << "\n" ;

   // Don't forget this
   both.seekg(0) ;

   // Extract data from 'buffer'
   char string[100] ;
   float f ;
   int n ;
   both >> string >> f >> n ;

   // Verify the data
   cout << "string = " << '\"' << string << '\"' << "\n" ;
   cout << "float = " << f << "\n" ;
   cout << "int = " << n << "\n" ;

   return 0 ;
}
```

The output is:

```
ABC 1.234 5
string = "ABC"
float = 1.234
long = 5
```

The function `tie()`

Chapter 12 talked about the function `ostream::flush()` which causes everything in the output buffer to be sent to the output device. In point of fact, you probably will never need to use this function for several reasons. First, recall that the bit `ios::unitbuf` in the class `ios` is on by default. This causes all output streams to be flushed automatically whenever there is data in them. Second, the stream `ostream` is "tied" to the stream `istream` by the function call:

Example 13.26

```
cin.tie(&cout) ;
```

This statement has already been executed for you, and means that whenever the operator needs to enter some data from the keyboard, any prompting information in the output stream is guaranteed to appear on the terminal screen. To "untie" these streams, you may call the `tie()` function with a value of zero.

Therefore, if you really want to avoid flushing the output stream, you must (a) turn off the bit `ios::unitbuf`, and (b) untie the streams.

In this example, the prompt does *not* appear before the operator must enter a number.

Example 13.27

```
#include <iostream.h>

int main()
{
  cout.unsetf(ios::unitbuf) ;
  cin.tie(0) ;

  cout << "Enter a number: " ;
  int number ;
  cin >> number ;
  cout << "You entered: " << number << "\n" ;

  return 0 ;
}
```

A typical run of the program would yield:

```
12
Enter a number: You entered: 12
```

Note that the prompt did not appear until after the number was entered. Now let's add the `flush()` function so that the prompt again appears.

Example 13.28

```
#include <iostream.h>

int main()
{
  cout.unsetf(ios::unitbuf) ;
  cin.tie(0) ;

  cout << "Enter a number: " ;
  cout.flush() ;
  int number ;
  cin >> number ;
  cout << "You entered: " << number << "\n" ;

  return 0 ;
}
```

A typical run of the program would yield:

```
Enter a number: 12
You entered: 12
```

How to overload the extraction operator

In Chapter 12 you saw how the insertion operator could be overloaded for a user-defined class. In a similar fashion, the extraction operator can also be overloaded so that instances of a class can be input just like the primitive types.

The general formats for the function declaration and definition for some generic class x are:

Example 13.29

```
// Declaration
friend istream& operator>>(istream& , X&) ;

// Definition
istream& operator>>(istream& stream , X& obj)
{
  // Input into the fields of the object using 'obj' and the dot
  // operator. Then...
  return stream ;
}
```

The first argument must be a reference to the class istream, and the second must be a reference to an instance of the user-defined class.

Here is an Example 12.41 enhanced so that both the extraction and the insertion operators have been overloaded.

Example 13.30

```
#include <iostream.h>

class complex
{
   double real , imag ;

      public:
   complex(double = 0.0 , double = 0.0) ;
   friend complex operator+(const complex& ,
                            const complex&) ;
   friend istream& operator>>(istream& , complex&) ;
   friend ostream& operator<<(ostream& , const complex&) ;
} ;

inline
complex::complex(double r, double i) : real(r) , imag(i) {}

complex operator+(const complex& c1 , const complex& c2)
{
   return complex(c1.real + c2.real , c1.imag + c2.imag) ;
}

istream& operator>>(istream& stream , complex& c)
{
   return stream >> c.real >> c.imag ;
}

ostream& operator<<(ostream& stream , const complex& c)
{
   return stream << c.real << (c.imag < 0 ? "" : "+")
                 << c.imag << "i" ;
}

int main()
{
   cout << "Enter the data for 2 complex numbers\n" ;
   complex c1 , c2 ;
   cin >> c1 >> c2 ;
   if (!cin)
      cerr << "Input error\n" ;
```

```
     else
     {
       complex c3 = c1 + c2 ;
       cout << "c1 = " << c1 << "\n" ;
       cout << "c2 = " << c2 << "\n" ;
       cout << "c3 = " << c3 << "\n" ;
     }

     return 0 ;
}
```

A typical run of the program would yield:

```
Enter the data for 2 complex numbers
3 -4 2 1
c1 = 3-4i
c2 = 2+1i
c3 = 5-3i

Enter the data for 2 complex numbers
3 4 2 A
Input error
```

How to inherit from class `istream`

As with any user-defined class, the class `istream` may serve as the base for any class which needs to extend or enhance its capabilities. In order to instantiate the derived class, its constructor must receive a pointer to a `filebuf` object (declared in the header file `fstream.h`) which must be passed on to the base class. The `filebuf` object must be instantiated with the low-level I/O handle number. In this case, the keyboard is number 0.

One reason to inherit from class istream would be to add unbuffered input capability. That is, the ability to strike a key and have the program resume execution without having to press the <ENTER> key. Since this is now handled by the DOS functions `getch()` and `getche()`, it's just a matter of adding member functions to emulate these DOS functions.

Example 13.31

```
#include <fstream.h>
#include <conio.h>

class istream_unbuff : public istream
{
      public:
   istream_unbuff(filebuf*) ;
   int getche() ;
   int getch() ;
} ;

istream_unbuff::istream_unbuff(filebuf* p) : istream(p) {}

int istream_unbuff::getche()
{
   return ::getche() ;
}

int istream_unbuff::getch()
{
   return ::getch() ;
}

int main()
{
   // Instantiate the class
   const int size = 256 ;
   char buffer[size] ;
   filebuf* ptr = new filebuf(0) ;
   istream_unbuff cin_unbuff(ptr) ;

   // Test unbuffered input with echo
   int ch ;
   cout << "Enter some characters\n" ;
   while((ch = cin_unbuff.getche()) != '\r')
      cout << (char)ch ;
   cout << "\n" ;

   // Test unbuffered input without echo
   char pass[size] = "" ;
   int i = 0 ;
   cout << "Enter a password\n" ;
   while((ch = cin_unbuff.getch()) != '\r')
    {
      pass[i++] = ch ;
      cout.put('*').flush() ;
    }
```

```
    pass[i] = '\0' ;
    cout << "\n" << pass << "\n" ;

    return 0 ;
}
```

A typical run would produce:

```
Enter some characters
TThhiiss_ iiss_ aa_ tteesstt<ENTER>
Enter a password
***<ENTER>
007
```

Exercise #1

Modify Exercise #1 in Chapter 12 so that the number that is displayed is obtained from the terminal operator (as an int) instead of being hard-coded. Be sure to check for:

- End-of-file (which terminates the program)
- Valid numeric input
- A number in the range 0 through 255, inclusive

Exercise #2

Write a class called format that contains member functions to prompt the user for:

- A floating point number
- The number of positions after the decimal point
- The width of the field
- Left or right justification
- The fill character
- Fixed or scientific output

Check all responses for numerics (if appropriate) and valid data. Then call another member function that will output the number between angle brackets (<>) according to all of the specifications. In the main program, use a while loop so that many tests can be run. Terminate the program when end-of-file is encountered.

■ Exercise #3

A class called `mortgage` has the following definition:

```
class mortgage
{
      private:
    double principal ;          // Principal amount of loan
    double interest ;           // Yearly interest rate of loan
    unsigned length ;           // Length of loan in years
    double payment ;            // Computed monthly payment

      public:
    void compute() ;            // Compute the monthly payment
    friend istream& operator>>  // Input a mortgage
        (istream& , mortgage&) ;
    friend ostream& operator<<  // Output a mortgage
        (ostream& , const mortgage&) ;
} ;
```

Write the implementation of the member and friend functions:

- ■ The function `operator>>()` gets the 3 input values.

- ■ The function `mortgage::compute()` computes the monthly payment which, on a fully amortized loan, is given by the equation:

  $$(P * R * (1 + R)^L) / ((1 + R)^L - 1)$$

  where: P = the principal, R = the *monthly* interest rate, L = the length of the loan in *months*. Write your own exponentiation routine, or use `pow()`.

- ■ The function `operator<<()` prints the monthly payment in fixed decimal, showing exactly 2 decimal positions. It then prints the complete amortization schedule. This should consist of 5 columns of data:

  1) The payment number, starting at 1

  2) The beginning principal balance

  3) The amount of the payment that is applied toward paying off the interest due that month

  4) The amount of the payment that is applied toward paying off the principal

  5) The new principal balance

Be sure to show a grand total for the interest and principal amounts paid. Verify your answer by adding these two amounts and comparing the sum against the monthly payment multiplied by the number of months in the loan.

The `main()` function looks like:

```
int main()
{
   mortgage loan ;
   while(!(cin >> loan).eof())
   {
     if(!cin)
        cerr << "Input error\n" ;
     else
     {
        loan.compute() ;
        cout << loan ;
     }
     cin >> FLUSH ;
   }
   return 0 ;
}
```

■ Exercise #4

Modify Chapter 12, Exercise 3 so that the user can interactively enter string instances from the keyboard. Overload the extraction operator to do this. At the very minimum, your `main()` function should be:

```
int main()
{
   print_string ps1 , ps2 ;
   cout << "Enter two strings: " ;
   cin >> ps1 >> ps2 ;
   cout << ps1 << endl ;
   cout << ps2 << endl ;

   return 0 ;
}
```

Notes

Notes

Chapter 14

Manipulator functions

Manipulator functions provide you with the capability to facilitate and encapsulate the formatting you must do with the input and output streams. Up to now all such formatting has been painstakingly tedious and very error-prone. That is now about to change.

The problem with formatting

You have probably noticed by now that the elimination of conversion specifications ("%d", "%c", etc.) found in the scanf() and printf() functions in C causes you to do a lot of extra coding to accomplish the same end result using the iostream methods. For example, to output a number in hexadecimal, the specification "%x" does the job in a printf() statement, but using the function setf() supplied with the iostream library you have to write:

Example 14.1

```
cout.setf(ios::hex , ios::basefield) ;
```

Certainly this constitutes a lot of keystrokes on your part, and that's just one of several possible formatting statements that you might need.

Fortunately, the input and output stream classes provide the capability to eliminate much of this tedious coding, as well as a method to combine the setting of the stream state with the actual output (or input) of the data itself. This method uses what is called a *manipulator*. The term comes from the fact that a manipulator does just what it implies — it manipulates, or changes, the state of the I/O stream.

In the same sense that a call of a function causes that function to do any number of individual tasks the programmer may specify, a manipulator is also a function that modifies the stream state. The input and output classes come with some manipulators already built in, and a nice feature is that you can easily define your own.

The format for a manipulator function

Because of the way in which a manipulator function is called, it must conform to a predefined standard. This standard dictates that the function must take as an argument an instance of ostream by reference (assuming an output manipulator), and return an instance of ostream by reference. To allow the chaining of manipulator functions (with other calls to the insertion operator), the function must terminate by returning its input argument. Note that manipulator functions are *global* functions, not class member functions.

Therefore, the complete definition for writing an output manipulator function is:

Example 14.2

```
ostream& manipulator(ostream& stream)
{
  // your code here using 'stream'
  return stream ;
}
```

In a similar fashion, all input manipulators have the format:

Example 14.3

```
istream& manipulator(istream& stream)
{
  // your code here using 'stream'
  return stream ;
}
```

Manipulator functions are "called" by an operator insertion (or extraction) function that receives the address of the manipulator as an argument. Therefore, when it is written, the manipulator must *not* use parentheses. (This is explained in more detail later in this chapter.) Of course, they may also be defined as inline functions.

Some simple manipulator functions

As a test of an output manipulator function, here is a program that creates a manipulator function called `set()` that sets the field width to 5 and the fill character to an "*".

Example 14.4

```
#include <iostream.h>

ostream& set(ostream& stream)
{
  stream.width(5) ;
  stream.fill('*') ;
  return stream ;
}
```

```
int main()
{
   cout << set << 23 << '\n' ;

   return 0 ;
}
```

The output is:

```
***23
```

Note that it's certainly possible to use a manipulator as a "normal" function by calling it directly, but then the chaining aspect is lost, and two statements are now needed. For example, the previous program could have been written:

Example 14.5

```
#include <iostream.h>

ostream& set(ostream& stream)
{
   stream.width(5) ;
   stream.fill('*') ;
   return stream ;
}

int main()
{
   set(cout) ;
   cout << 23 << '\n' ;

   return 0 ;
}
```

The output is:

```
***23
```

The problem, of course, is that the "flow" of the cout statement now has been lost.

As an example of an input manipulator, in Chapter 13 the function FLUSH() was defined (in Example 13.18) to clear the system input buffer of extraneous characters. Because the function takes an istream object by reference, and returns an istream object by reference, it can be used as a manipulator function:

Example 14.6

```
cin >> FLUSH ;
```

The ability to create custom manipulators allows you to eliminate the need to write the `setf()` function every time the state of the output stream must be changed. For example, if you wish to turn on left or right justification, it's easy to create manipulators for these tasks. Note that the `FLUSH()` manipulator and the ones that follow are declared in the file `manips.h` and defined in the file `manips.cpp` (Appendix C).

Example 14.7

```
// Declaration
ostream& LEFT(ostream&) ;

// Definition
ostream& LEFT(ostream& stream)
{
   stream.setf(ios::left , ios::adjustfield) ;
   return stream ;
}

// Declaration
ostream& RIGHT(ostream&) ;

// Definition
ostream& RIGHT(ostream& stream)
{
   stream.setf(ios::right , ios::adjustfield) ;
   return stream ;
}
```

Another use of a manipulator would be to ensure that all money amounts appear right-justified, fixed-decimal, with 2 decimal points. Note that this manipulator uses the services of yet another manipulator.

Example 14.8

```
// Declaration
ostream& MONEY(ostream&) ;

// Definition
ostream& MONEY(ostream& stream)
{
   stream << RIGHT ;
   stream.setf(ios::fixed , ios::floatfield) ;
   stream.setf(ios::showpoint) ;
   stream.precision(2) ;
   return stream ;
}
```

Here is a program that prompts for a name and a money amount, and then prints the name left-justified, and the amount right-justified.

Example 14.9

```
#include <iostream.h>
#include "manips.h"

#include "manips.cpp"

int main()
{
   const int max = 256 ;
   cout << "Enter a name and amount: " ;
   char name[max] ;
   while(!cin.getline(name , max).eof())
    {
      float amount ;
      cin >> amount ;
      if(!cin)
         cerr << "Input error\n" ;
      else
       {
         cout.width(20) ;
         cout << LEFT << name ;
         cout.width(10) ;
         cout << MONEY << amount << '\n' ;
       }
      cin >> FLUSH ;
      cout << "Next data set: " ;
    }
```

```
      return 0 ;
}
```

If you entered the name Humpty Dumpty, pressed <ENTER>, then entered the amount 34.567, the output would be:

```
Humpty Dumptybbbbbbbbbbbbbbbb34.57
```

where b represents a space.

Built-in manipulators with no arguments

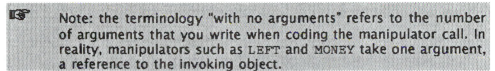

Note: the terminology "with no arguments" refers to the number of arguments that you write when coding the manipulator call. In reality, manipulators such as LEFT and MONEY take one argument, a reference to the invoking object.

Because some output (and input) stream operations are done so frequently, the `iostream` library includes some pre-defined manipulators to handle these operations.

The manipulator `endl`

For example, the manipulator `endl` (read: "end line") is designed to output a new line character and flush the output buffer. You may use this at any time in place of `'\n'`.

Example 14.10

```
#include <iostream.h>

int main()
{
   cout << 1 << endl << 2 << endl ;

   return 0 ;
}
```

The output is:

```
1
2
```

The manipulators `dec`, `oct` and `hex`

The manipulators `dec`, `oct` and `hex` work for both input and output operations, and set the stream state to either decimal, octal, or hexadecimal, respectively. For example:

Example 14.11

```
// Set the output state to decimal
cout << dec ;
// Set the output state to octal
cout << oct ;
// Set the output state to hex
cout << hex ;

// Set the input state to decimal
cin >> dec ;
// Set the input state to octal
cin >> oct ;
// Set the input state to hex
cin >> hex ;
```

Here is a test in which a hexadecimal number is input and then displayed in octal.

Example 14.12

```
#include <iostream.h>

int main()
{
  cout << "Input a hex number: " ;
  int number ;
  cin >> hex >> number ;
  cout << "The number in hex is " << hex << number << endl ;
  cout << "The number in octal is " << oct << number << endl ;

  return 0 ;
}
```

If you enter the number `ff`, you would see:

```
The number in hex is ff
The number in octal is 377
```

The manipulator `ws`

Recall that when using the function `get()` or `getline()` with 3 arguments to read in a string, both leading and embedded whitespace are retained. If you want to *bypass* the leading whitespace, and still *retain* the embedded whitespace, then use the input manipulator `ws`. Note, however, that it is effective only for the next input operation, after which another `get()` or `getline()` would *retain* leading whitespace.

Example 14.13

```
#include <iostream.h>

const int length = 100 ;

int main()
{
   cout << "Enter a string: " ;
   cin >> ws ;
   char string[length] ;
   cin.get(string , length) ;
   cout << "Your string: " << '\"' << string << '\"' << endl ;

   return 0 ;
}
```

If you entered some spaces, the string "I like manipulators", then pressed <ENTER>, the output would be:

```
Your string: "I like manipulators"
```

The manipulator `ends`

Another built-in manipulator that takes no argument is called `ends`. This causes a null character to be output, and is useful for objects of type `strstream`.

Here is Example 12.37 again, this time using `endl` and `ends`.

Example 14.14

```
#include <iostream.h>
#include <strstream.h>

int main()
{
  int number = 123 ;
  char buffer[80] ;

  ostrstream output(buffer , sizeof buffer);

  output << "number = " << number << ends ;
  cout << '\"' << buffer << '\"' << endl ;

  output.seekp(0) ;
  output << "A new buffer stream " << "of characters" << ends ;
  cout << '\"' << buffer << '\"' << endl ;

  return 0 ;
}
```

The output is:

```
"number = 123"
"A new buffer stream of characters"
```

The manipulator `flush`

The last manipulator that takes no input argument is called `flush`. This is exactly the same as the `ostream` member function `flush()`, and causes the stream associated with the output instance to be completely emptied. The function itself is nothing more than:

Example 14.15

```
ostream& flush(ostream& stream)
{
  return stream.flush() ;
}
```

Here is Example 13.29 again, but now using the `flush` manipulator.

Example 14.16

```
#include <iostream.h>

int main()
{
   cout.unsetf(ios::unitbuf) ;
   cin.tie(0) ;

   cout << "Enter a number: " << flush ;
   int number ;
   cin >> number ;
   cout << "You entered: " << number << endl ;

   return 0 ;
}
```

How a manipulator works

As stated above, manipulators really are functions, but recall that when you write the name of a function *without* writing parentheses, the compiler generates the *address* of that function. Therefore, in the following statement there are no direct function calls occurring, so the left-to-right order of items to be output when sending data to the `cout` instance can be guaranteed. This means that when you write a statement such as:

Example 14.17

```
cout << arg1 << manipulator << arg2 ;
```

you are absolutely assured that first `arg1` will be sent, followed by the `manipulator` "item", and finally `arg2`.

In the case of a manipulator function, since we're supplying the address of a function, that takes as its one argument a reference to `cout` and returns a reference, the compiler will look for an overloaded `operator<<()` function that conforms to this scheme.

Now, if you have a pointer-to-function variable, then you may execute the function itself by "dereferencing" that variable and enclosing the entire expression within parentheses. Since `*this` always refers to the invoking instance of any nonstatic member function call, in this case it's the object `cout`, which is passed to the manipulator function as an actual argument. Finally, since the manipulator function itself returns a reference to cout, this reference must, in turn, be passed back to the original statement to allow the function chaining to occur.

This is how the insertion function to accommodate manipulators is written:

Example 14.18

```
ostream& ostream::operator<< (ostream& (*ptr)(ostream&))
{
   return (*ptr)(*this) ;
}
```

Built-in manipulators with 1 argument

It is possible to write a manipulator with one actual argument. The call (assuming output) would appear as:

Example 14.19

```
cout << manipulator(arg) ;
```

However, to differentiate this syntax from a "regular" function call, such a manipulator requires special handling by the compiler. To do this, a separate header file called `iomanip.h` *must* be included with each program that uses such a manipulator, whether that manipulator is built-in or user-defined. In Borland C++ the file `iomanip.h` automatically includes the file `iostream.h`, but this may not be true for all C++ compilers.

The manipulator `setw`

Perhaps the most frequently used manipulator that takes an argument is `setw()`. Like its counterpart, the member function `ios::width()`, it is used to set the field width *for the next output item only*. The one argument is, of course, the field width itself.

This example uses a manipulator to set the field width to 5.

Example 14.20

```
#include <iostream.h>
#include <iomanip.h>

int main()
{
   cout << setw(5) << 1 << endl ;
   cout << setw(5) << 23 << endl ;

   return 0 ;
}
```

The output is:

```
bbbb1
bbb23
```

where b represents a blank.

The manipulator `setfill`

Another frequently used manipulator is the one that sets the fill character. It is called setfill() and, as you would expect, the 1 argument is the fill character itself.

This example uses manipulators to set the field width and fill character.

Example 14.21

```
#include <iostream.h>
#include <iomanip.h>

int main()
{
   cout << setw(5) << setfill('0') << 1 << endl ;
   cout << setw(5) << setfill('*') << 23 << endl ;

   return 0 ;
}
```

The output is:

```
00001
***23
```

Misc. manipulators

The other built-in manipulators that take a single argument are:

- resetiosflags(long flag) -- turns off the bits specified in flag (input and output)

- setbase(int base) -- sets the output base to decimal if base is 0 or 10; to octal if base is 8; to hexadecimal if base is 16 (output)

- setiosflags(long flag) -- turns on the bits specified in flag (input and output)

- setprecision(int prec) -- sets the number of digits displayed after the decimal point to prec (output)

How to create a manipulator with 1 argument (int or long)

Let's just see how the manipulator taking one argument is coded. There is a slight difference between those manipulators that take either an int or a long as the one formal argument. Don't forget to include the file iomanip.h.

Assuming that the one argument is an int or a long, the generic form of an output manipulator is:

Example 14.22

```
ostream& manipulator(ostream& stream , type arg)
{
   // your code here using arg
   return stream ;
}
```

where type is either int or long, and arg is the formal argument name.

Next, you must include this code:

Example 14.23

```
OMANIP(type) manipulator(type arg)
{
   return OMANIP(type) (manipulator , arg) ;
}
```

where OMANIP is a class defined in the file iomanip.h.

For example, here is a manipulator called `set` that sets the field width to whatever the argument happens to be, and also sets the fill character to an '*'.

Example 14.24

```
#include <iostream.h>
#include <iomanip.h>

ostream& set(ostream& stream , int length)
{
   return stream << setw(length) << setfill('*') ;
}

OMANIP(int) set(int length)
{
   return OMANIP(int) (set , length) ;
}

int main()
{
   cout << set(7) << 123 << endl ;
   cout << set(5) << 45 << endl ;

 return 0 ;
}
```

The output is:

```
****123
***45
```

Here is another manipulator that is designed to tab to an absolute column position on some output device. This is useful when you need to do column alignment of data. If the tab position is less than the current file position marker, then a newline is performed.

Example 14.25

```
      // Declaration
      ostream& TAB(ostream& , long) ;
      OMANIP(long) TAB(long) ;

      // Definition
      ostream& TAB(ostream& stream , long col)
      {
        long here = stream.tellp() ;
        if(col < here)
         {
            stream << endl ;
            here = 0L ;
         }
        return stream << setw(col-here) << " " ;
      }

      OMANIP(long) TAB(long col)
      {
          return OMANIP(long) (TAB , col) ;
      }
```

> ☞ **For this manipulator to work properly, the built-in manipulator
> `endl` has been overridden in the file `manips.h` with one that
> does the identical task but also sets the stream file position
> marker to zero.**

As a test of this manipulator, the following program creates an array of employees
and then outputs the names, ages, and incomes in column format.

Example 14.26

```
      #include <iostream.h>
      #include <iomanip.h>
      #include <string.h>
      #include "manips.h"

      #include "manips.cpp"

      class person
      {
        char* name ;
        int age ;
        float income ;

          public:
```

```
   person(const char* = "" , int = 0 , float = 0.0) ;
   ~person() ;
   friend ostream& operator<<(ostream& , const person&) ;
} ;

inline person::person(const char* n , int a , float i)
              : age(a) , income(i)
{
  name = new char[strlen(n) + 1] ;
  strcpy(name , n) ;
}

inline person::~person()
{
  delete [] name ;
}

ostream& operator<<(ostream& stream , const person& p)
{
  stream.seekp(0L) ;
  stream << p.name ;
  stream << TAB(20) << p.age ;
  stream << MONEY ;
  stream << TAB(30) << p.income ;
  stream << endl ;
  return stream ;
}

int main()
{
  person staff[] =
   {
     person("John Doe" , 21 , 34566.67) ,
     person("Mary Jones" , 23 , 35700.33)
     person("Pat Lowry" , 20 , 33100.10)
   } ;

  const int size = sizeof(staff) / sizeof(person) ;
  for(int i = 0 ; i < size ; ++i)
     cout << staff[i] ;

  return 0 ;
}
```

The output is:

```
John Doe          21        34566.67
Mary Jones        23        35700.33
Pat Lowry         20        33100.10
```

How to create a manipulator with 1 argument (not `int` nor `long`)

If you wish to create a manipulator using a type other than `int` or `long`, then you must include the following statement:

Example 14.27

```
IOMANIPdeclare(type) ;
```

before the declaration or definition of the manipulator itself, where `type` is either `char`, `float`, `double`, etc. If the type is a pointer, then it must be `typedef`'ed before using, e.g.,

Example 14.28

```
typedef const void* P ;
IOMANIPdeclare(P) ;
```

Here is Example 14.24 again, but now the fill character is variable and the field width is fixed.

Example 14.29

```
#include <iostream.h>
#include <iomanip.h>

IOMANIPdeclare(char) ;

ostream& set(ostream& stream , char ch)
{
   return stream << setw(7) << setfill(ch) ;
}

OMANIP(char) set(char ch)
{
   return OMANIP(char) (set , ch) ;
}
```

```
int main()
{
   cout << set('*') << 123 << endl ;
   cout << set('$') << 45 << endl ;

   return 0 ;
}
```

The output is:

```
****123
$$$$$45
```

Example 12.33 showed how to print an address in 'segment:offset' form using the functions `FP_SEG()` and `FP_OFF()` which are declared in the header file `dos.h`. Instead of going to the trouble of writing several lines of code to accomplish this, a manipulator works much better. Here is a manipulator called `ADDRESS()` that does the same thing.

Example 14.30

```
// Declaration
typedef const void* P ;
IOMANIPdeclare(P) ;
ostream& ADDRESS(ostream& , P) ;
OMANIP(P) ADDRESS(P) ;

// Definition
ostream& ADDRESS(ostream& stream , P add)
{
   char oldfill = stream.fill() ;
   stream << setfill('0') ;
   long save = stream.flags() ;
   stream.setf(ios::right , ios::adjustfield) ;
   stream
#if defined __COMPACT__ || \
       defined __LARGE__  || \
       defined __HUGE__
   << setw(5) << FP_SEG(add)
#endif
   << ':' << setw(5) << FP_OFF(add) ;
   stream << setfill(oldfill) ;
   stream.flags(save) ;
   return stream ;
}
```

Here is a test of the ADDRESS() manipulator in which the address of an integer is printed.

Example 14.31

```
#include <iostream.h>
#include <iomanip.h>
#include "manips.h"

#include "manips.cpp"

int main()
{
   int number ;

   cout << "Address of number in segment:offset form is"
        << ADDRESS(&number) << endl ;

   return 0 ;
}
```

The output is:

```
Address of number in segment:offset form is :65524
```

As another example of where a manipulator is very useful, recall from Chapter 12 that Borland C++ version 3.0 does *not* honor the current width setting when outputting a character. Here is a repeat of Example 12.23 in which this is proven:

Example 14.32

```
#include <iostream.h>

int main()
{
   cout.width(20) ;
   cout << 'A' << " is first\n" ;

   return 0 ;
}
```

The output of this program in Borland version 3.0 is:

```
Abbbbbbbbbbbis first
```

If, however, you pass the character to a manipulator, then you can solve the problem by having the manipulator convert the character into a string, which will then be honored by the current width setting. This is done by the manipulator CHAR.

Example 14.33

```
// Declaration
IOMANIPdeclare(char) ;
ostream& CHAR(ostream& , char) ;
OMANIP(char) CHAR(char) ;

// Definition
ostream& CHAR(ostream& stream , char ch)
{
   char buff[2] ;
   buff[0] = ch ;
   buff[1] = '\0' ;
   return stream << buff ;
}

OMANIP(char) CHAR(char ch)
{
   return OMANIP(char) (CHAR , ch) ;
}
```

Here is a test in which a character constant and character variable are printed.

Example 14.34

```
#include <iostream.h>
#include <iomanip.h>
#include "manips.h"

#include "manips.cpp"

int main()
{
   cout << setw(20) << CHAR('A') << "is first\n" ;

   return 0 ;
}
```

The output is:

bbbbbbbbbbbbbbbbbbbA is first

where b is a blank.

How a manipulator with 1 argument works

A manipulator that is written with one explicit argument works by having the preprocessor replace the function call with a temporary unnamed instance of a class. When this instance is output with the insertion operator, an overloaded insertion operator that was granted friendship by the class then takes control and invokes another function that performs the actual work.

This can be illustrated by the following example that is designed to emulate how the setw() manipulator works. When the expression setw(5) is evaluated, it returns a temporary instance of the class Omanip_int. This instance contains an int and a pointer to a function returning an ostream by reference and taking two arguments — an ostream by reference and an int . When the instance is actually output, the friend function in the class Omanip_int gains control and executes the function _setw(), which ultimately sets the proper width value.

Example 14.35

```
#include <iostream.h>

class Omanip_int
{
   int i ;
   ostream& (*ptr)(ostream& , int) ;

      public:
   Omanip_int(int , ostream& (*) (ostream& , int)) ;
   friend ostream& operator<<(ostream&, const Omanip_int&) ;
} ;

Omanip_int::Omanip_int(int x , ostream& (*p) (ostream& , int))
         : i(x) , ptr(p) {}

ostream& operator<<(ostream& stream , const Omanip_int& a)
{
   return (*a.ptr)(stream , a.i) ;
}

ostream& _setw(ostream& stream , int x)
{
   stream.width(x) ;
   return stream ;
}
```

```
Omanip_int setw(int i)
{
   return Omanip_int(i , _setw) ;
}

int main()
{
   cout << setw(5) << 123 << endl ;

   return 0 ;
}
```

The output is:

```
bb123
```

whre b represents a blank

How to create manipulators with 2 or more arguments

There are no built-in manipulators taking 2 arguments. However, you can easily build your own. For example, suppose you wish to write a manipulator whose purpose is to output a line consisting of a variable number of any given character. This means that the manipulator requires two arguments: (1) the number of characters to be output, and (2) the character itself.

The first thing you must do is to package the arguments into a structure object. Here it is called args.

Example 14.36

```
struct args
{
   char ch ;
   int number ;
} ;
```

Next, the name of the structure becomes the type that is used in the IOMANIPdeclare declaration.

Example 14.37

```
IOMANIPdeclare(args) ;
```

Next, write the manipulator function as though it were taking just one argument. This argument is of the type of the structure. The name of manipulator here is `fill`. It loops the requisite number of times and outputs the character.

Example 14.38

```
ostream& fill(ostream& stream , args a)
{
   for(int i = 0 ; i < a.number ; ++i)
      stream << a.ch ;
   return stream ;
}
```

Finally, write the OMANIP macro shown in Example 14.23. Note that the arguments are listed individually, and the body of the macro creates an instance of the structure and assigns the input values to it

Example 14.39

```
OMANIP(args) fill(char ch , int number)
{
   args a ;
   a.ch = ch ;
   a.number = number ;
   return OMANIP(args)(fill , a) ;
}
```

Here is the complete program.

Example 14.40

```cpp
#include <iostream.h>
#include <iomanip.h>
#include "manips.h"

#include "manips.cpp"

struct args
{
   char ch ;
   int number ;
} ;

IOMANIPdeclare(tag) ;

ostream& fill(ostream& stream , args a)
{
   for(int i = 0 ; i < a.number ; ++i)
      stream << a.ch ;
   return stream ;
}

OMANIP(args) fill(char ch , int number)
{
   args a ;
   a.ch = ch ;
   a.number = number ;
   return OMANIP(args)(fill , a) ;
}

int main()
{
   cout << "How many characters? " ;
   int number ;
   while(!(cin >> number).eof())
    {
      if(cin.fail())
         cout << "Invalid entry\n" ;
      else
       {
         cout << "Enter the character: " ;
         char ch ;
         cin >> FLUSH ;
         cin.get(ch) ;
         cout << fill(ch , number) << endl ;
       }
      cin >> FLUSH ;
```

```
            cout << "How many characters? " ;
        }

    return 0 ;
}
```

A typical run would produce:

```
How many characters: 10
Enter the character: A
AAAAAAAAAA
How many characters? ^Z
```

■ Exercise #1

Create two output manipulators called UPPERCASE and LOWERCASE that cause hexadecimal numbers and floating point scientific numbers to be shown first using upper-case letters and then lower-case letters, respectively. Then write a program to test these manipulators.

■ Exercise #2

Create an output manipulator called LINES that takes an integer input argument specifying the number of new-line characters ('\n') to be output. In other words, if you want to output three blank lines, you would code:

```
    cout << LINES(3) ;
```

■ Exercise #3

In C you may display the first n characters of a string by including a decimal point and the value for n in the format string. For example:

```
    printf("%.3s\n" , "ABCDEFG") ;
```

will display:

```
    ABC
```

Write a manipulator that can emulate this feature. This manipulator must take two arguments: the address of the string to be printed, and an integer representing the number of characters to be displayed.

Chapter 14 Manipulators

■ Exercise #4

Write a manipulator that takes one argument of type `long`, and emulates the blank flag in a `printf()` function call. That is, the manipulator should output the number preceded by a blank if it is greater than or equal to zero, and precede it with a minus sign if it is less than zero.

■ Exercise #5

Write a manipulator that takes one argument of type `long`. The manipulator must output this number with commas inserted in the appropriate positions.

■ Exercise #6

Write a manipulator that takes 3 arguments — a string and two characters. The manipulator must output the string while substituting the second character every time it encounters the first character.

■ Exercise #7

Write a manipulator that takes one argument of type `int` and outputs the binary representation of this number.

■ Exercise #8

Write a manipulator called ALARM that sounds the alarm ('\a') 10 times. Then modify the manipulator so that it takes one argument of type `int` and sounds the alarm the appropriate number of times.

Notes

Notes

Chapter 15

File input/output

File input/output in C++ using AT&T version 2.0 stream methods gives you the capability to perform these three operations: (1) read a file, (2) write a file, and (3) both read and write a file. To do this, the operations associated with keyboard input and screen output have been enhanced to accommodate any legitimate file device.

File input/output classes

To handle file I/O, special classes have already been defined for you. They are:

■   ifstream (derived from istream). This is used whenever you wish to read a file.

■   ofstream (derived from ostream). This is used whenever you wish to write a file.

■   fstream (derived from iostream). This is used whenever you wish to update a file.

To use any of these classes, you must have the following include statement in your program:

Example 15.1

```
#include <fstream.h>
```

This #include automatically includes the header file iostream.h.

Creating instances of the classes

There are no pre-defined instances of these classes comparable to cin and cout. Therefore, the first step in using file I/O is to create an instance of the appropriate class. For example:

Example 15.2

```
ifstream in ;        // Input instance
ofstream out ;       // Output instance
fstream in_out ;     // Update instance
```

Now you may use the instance in in conjunction with all of the member functions of class istream, the instance out with the member functions of class ostream, and the instance in_out with the member functions of both istream and ostream.

Opening a file

The first step in using a file instance is to open a disk file. In any computer language this means establishing a communication link between your code and the external file. Each of the three file I/O classes provides the member function open() to do this. The declarations for these open() functions are as follows:

Example 15.3

```
void ifstream::open(const char* name ,
                    int m = ios::in ,
                    int prot = filebuf::openprot) ;

void ofstream::open(const char* name ,
                    int m = ios::out ,
                    int prot = filebuf::openprot) ;

void fstream::open(const char* name ,
                   int m ,
                   int prot = filebuf::openprot) ;
```

The first argument is the external file name passed in as a constant string literal. This is analogous to the first argument that you would use in C with `fopen()`. (Note: if you hard-code a file name under DOS and need to specify a path, don't forget to write two backslashes (\\) to yield one.)

The second argument is the file mode, and is analogous to the second argument of `fopen()`. All file modes come from a public enumerated type in the class `ios`. There are eight possible modes, as follows:

TABLE 15.1

Name	Meaning
ios::in	Input mode. (Default for input file)
ios::out	Output mode. (Default for output file)
ios::app	Append to an output file rather than update an existing record
ios::ate	Position file marker at end of file instead of beginning
ios::trunc	Delete file if it exists and re-create it
ios::nocreate	File must exist, otherwise open fails (output only)
ios::noreplace	File must not exist, otherwise open fails (output only)
ios::binary	Binary mode; default is text

Note that for an `istream` (input) instance, the default mode is `ios::in`, and for an `ostream` instance (output), the default mode is `ios::out`. However, for an `fstream` (input/output) instance, there is no default mode, so it is up to you to explicitly provide one. Obviously, if you need to specify more than one mode, they may be bitwise ORed together.

The third argument is the file access. Under Borland C++ the possible values are:

TABLE 15.2

Value	Meaning
0	Default
1	Read-only file
2	Hidden file
4	System file
8	Archive bit set

For example, this is how the aforementioned three instances might be used to open some files:

Example 15.4

```
in.open("INPUT") ;
out.open("OUTPUT") ;
in_out.open("UPDATE" , ios::in | ios::out) ;
```

An alternate method of executing the open function is to call the constructor with the same argument(s) that you would use for the `open()`. Thus, instead of creating the instance and then explicitly calling the `open()` function, you can combine these two steps by writing:

Example 15.5

```
ifstream in("INPUT") ;
ofstream out("OUTPUT") ;
fstream in_out("UPDATE", ios::in | ios::out) ;
```

Checking for open failure

Of course, you should always check the result of an open operation to ensure that it succeeded. This check is virtually the same as the check for the failure of an input operation from the keyboard. The following table shows the various possibilities that exist for checking for success or failure after doing an open on some instance called `file`.

TABLE 15.3

Test	Success	Failure
if(file)	true	false
if(!file)	false	true
if(file.good())	true	false
if(!file.good())	false	true
if(file.fail())	false	true
if(!file.fail())	true	false

Closing a file

When you are done using the file, the member function `close()` in all three classes taking no arguments will close it. This function is called automatically by the destructor for the class, but you may explicitly call it if you wish.

A simple example of write, append and read

Let's start with a simple program that accepts string input from the user and writes it to a disk file called OUTPUT.

Example 15.6

```
#include <fstream.h>
#include <stdlib.h>

const int max = 256 ;

int main()
{
   ofstream out("OUTPUT") ;
   if(!out)
    {
      cerr << "Open failed\n" ;
      exit(1) ;
    }
```

```
      cout << "Enter a line of data: " ;
      char buffer[max] ;
      while(!cin.getline(buffer , max).eof())
       {
          out << buffer << endl ;
          cout << "Next line: " ;
       }
      return 0 ;
}
```

A typical run might be:

```
Enter a line of data: This is<ENTER>
Next line: a test<ENTER>
Next line: ^Z
```

Now let's give the user a chance to append more records to the file. Note that the mode of the file is ios::out | ios::app (although ios::app by itself would still have worked).

Example 15.7

```
#include <fstream.h>
#include <stdlib.h>

const int max = 256 ;

int main()
{
   ofstream out("OUTPUT" , ios::out | ios::app) ;
   if (!out)
    {
       cerr << "Open failed\n" ;
       exit(1) ;
    }

   cout << "Enter a line of data: " ;
   char buffer[max] ;
   while(!cin.getline(buffer , max).eof())
    {
       out << buffer << endl ;
       cout << "Next line: " ;
    }

   return 0 ;
}
```

A typical run might be:

```
Enter a line of data: Some more<ENTER>
Next line: data<ENTER>
Next line: ^Z
```

The mode `ios::noreplace` ensures that the file does not already exist when being opened. As a test of the open failure code, let's try to open the file with this mode specified.

Example 15.8

```cpp
#include <fstream.h>
#include <stdlib.h>

const int max = 256 ;

int main()
{
   ofstream out("OUTPUT" ,
                ios::out | ios::app | ios::noreplace) ;
   if(!out)
    {
      cerr << "Open failed\n" ;
      exit(1) ;
    }

   cout << "Enter a line of data: " ;
   char buffer[max] ;
   while(!cin.getline(buffer , max).eof())
    {
      out << buffer << endl ;
      cout << "Next line: " ;
    }

   return 0 ;
}
```

The output is:

```
Open failed
```

Finally, this program numbers and prints the records that were just written.

Example 15.9

```
#include <fstream.h>
#include <stdlib.h>

const int max = 256 ;

int main()
{
   ifstream in("OUTPUT") ;
   if(!in)
    {
       cerr << "Open failed\n" ;
       exit(1) ;
    }

   int rec = 0 ;
   char buffer[max] ;
   while(!in.getline(buffer , max).eof())
       cout << "Record #" << ++rec << ": " << buffer << endl ;

   return 0 ;
}
```

The output is:

```
Record #1: This is
Record #2: a test
Record #3: Some more
Record #4: data
```

The file position markers

So that the file I/O classes can keep track of where in a file the data is to be written to and read from, they establish what is called a "file position marker" (fpm). In Borland C++ this marker has been typedef'ed as a `long` integer representing an offset value from the beginning of the file. In point of fact, there are two such markers, one for reading, and one for writing.

Changing the file position markers

The classes `istream` and `ostream` each have a member function that allows you to change these markers. In `istream` it's called `seekg()` and in `ostream` it's called `seekp()`. The function `seekg()` is associated with the file's "get or read" pointer, and the function `seekp()` with the file's "put or write" pointer. The declarations for these two functions are as follows:

Example 15.10

```
// Class istream
istream& seekg(streampos) ;
istream& seekg(streamoff , ios::seek_dir) ;

// Class ostream
ostream& seekp(streampos) ;
ostream& seekp(streamoff , ios::seek_dir) ;
```

where `streampos` and `streamoff` represent `long` integers, and `seek_dir` is a public enumerated type defined as follows:

Example 15.11

```
enum seek_dir {beg , cur , end} ;
```

Note that each function has been overloaded. If the 1-argument form of the function is used, then the argument is the offset from the beginning of the file. If the 2-argument form is used, then the first argument is the offset number of bytes (positive or negative) from the absolute `seek_dir` position. For example, a call to `seekg()` with a single argument of 0L causes the file to rewind and data to be read starting with the first record. A call with the first argument of 0L and the second of `ios::end` places the file position marker on the end-of-file byte.

Reading the file position markers

To find out the positions of these markers at any time, once again each class has an appropriate member function. In `istream` it's called `tellg()`, and in `ostream` it's called `tellp()`. They are declared as follows:

Example 15.12

```
// Class istream
streampos tellg() ;

// Class ostream
streampos tellp() ;
```

The first character of a record is deemed to be in position 0. Note that for a file opened in text mode (the default), a newline character is actually stored as 2 characters: a newline ('\n') and a carriage return ('\r'). In binary mode, only a newline is stored (as would be the case in Unix).

To illustrate the file position marker in action, we will use an instance of the class fstream so that both output and input operations can be performed. After each record is read and printed, the file position marker (fpm) is displayed.

Example 15.13

```
#include <fstream.h>
#include <stdlib.h>

const int max = 256 ;

int main()
{
   fstream in_out("UPDATE" , ios::in | ios::out | ios::trunc) ;
   if(!in_out)
    {
      cerr << "Open failed\n" ;
      exit(1) ;
    }

   cout << "Enter a line of data: " ;
   char buffer[max] ;
   while(!cin.getline(buffer , max).eof())
    {
      in_out << buffer << endl ;
      cout << "Next line: " ;
    }

   // Flush the output buffer
   in_out << flush ;

   // Return to the start of the file
   in_out.seekg(0L) ;

   // Read and print the records, and show the file position
   // marker
   int rec = 0 ;

   while(!in_out.getline(buffer , max).eof())
    {
      cout << "Record #" << ++rec  << ": " << buffer << endl ;
      cout << "fpm = " << in_out.tellg() << endl ;
    }
```

```
      return 0 ;
}
```

A typical run might be:

```
Enter a line of data: A<ENTER>
Next line: test<ENTER>
Next line: ^Z
Record #1: A
fpm = 3
Record #2: test
fpm = 9
```

Let's repeat this example using a binary file just to see the difference in the file position marker.

Example 15.14

```cpp
#include <fstream.h>
#include <stdlib.h>

const int max = 256 ;

int main()
{
   fstream in_out("UPDATE" ,
               ios::in | ios::out | ios::trunc | ios::binary ) ;
   if(!in_out)
    {
      cerr << "Open failed\n" ;
      exit(1) ;
    }

   cout << "Enter a line of data: " ;
   char buffer[max] ;
   while(!cin.getline(buffer , max).eof())
    {
      in_out << buffer << endl ;
      cout << "Next line: " ;
    }

   // Flush the output buffer
   in_out << flush ;

   // Return to the start of the file
   in_out.seekg(0L) ;
```

```
    // Read and print the records, and show the file position
    // marker
    int rec = 0 ;
    while(!in_out.getline(buffer , max).eof())
     {
      cout << "Record #" << ++rec  << ": " << buffer << endl ;
      cout << "fpm = " << in_out.tellg() << endl ;
     }
    return 0 ;
}
```

A typical run might be:

```
Enter a line of data: A<ENTER>
Next line: test<ENTER>
Next line: ^Z
Record #1: A
fpm = 2
Record #2: test
fpm = 7
```

Using the line printer

The line printer is just another output file insofar as DOS is concerned. To redirect output to a printer from within your program, use the predefined name prn, as shown in the following example:

Example 15.15

```
#include <fstream.h>
#include <stdlib.h>

int main()
{
   ofstream printer("prn") ;
   if(!printer)
    {
       cerr << "Can't open the printer\n" ;
       exit(1) ;
    }
   printer << "This line appears on the printer\n" ;

   return 0 ;
}
```

The actual condition of the printer (device time out, selected, out of paper, etc.) must be tested by the function `biosprint()` which is prototyped in the file `bios.h`.

How to alternate screen and printer output

Suppose you wish to toggle your output between the screen and the line printer. One way to do it would be to create a global instance, say POUT, of the class `ofstream` and tie it to the printer. Then create a manipulator called PRINTER to return this instance, as well as a manipulator called SCREEN to return the global instance `cout`.

This program will run a test by toggling the output back and forth between the screen and the printer.

Example 15.16

```
#include <fstream.h>

// Global instance tied to the printer
ofstream POUT("prn") ;

// Manipulator to change the invoking instance to the printer
ostream& PRINTER(ostream&)
{
   return POUT ;
}

// Manipulator to change the invoking instance to the screen
ostream& SCREEN(ostream&)
{
   return cout ;
}

int main()
{
   cout << "To the screen\n"
        << PRINTER << "To the printer\n"
        << SCREEN << "And back to the screen\n" ;

   return 0 ;
}
```

Another way to toggle output between the screen and the printer (or a disk file) is to create an instance of the second output device and then use a pointer-to-`ostream` to point to the proper instance that is to receive the output.

In this program the output will once again be toggled between the screen and the printer.

Example 15.17

```
#include <fstream.h>
#include <stdlib.h>

int main()
{
  // Pointer to ostream
  ostream* output ;

  // Printer instance
  ofstream printer("prn") ;

  // Output a message to the printer
  output = &printer ;
  *output << "To the printer\n" ;

  // Set up to go back to the screen
  output = &cout ;

  // Output a message to the screen
  *output << "To the screen\n" ;

  return 0 ;
}
```

Finally, here is another method to accomplish the same result.

Example 15.18

```
#include <fstream.h>

const int print_handle = 4 ;

int main()
{
  filebuf f(print_handle) ;
  streambuf* old = cout.rdbuf() ;
  cout = &f ;
  cout << "To the printer\n" ;
  cout = old ;
  cout << "To the screen\n" ;

  return 0 ;
}
```

How to hide file I/O from the user

The details of how file I/O is handled can be encapsulated and hidden from the user by the creation of a class. Then all the user would have to do is instantiate the class and use the member and friend functions.

In the following example notice how an instance of the student class is used as one of the arguments to the overloaded insertion and extraction operators of the in_out class.

Example 15.19

```
#include <fstream.h>
#include <string.h>

// A manipulator to output the GPA
ostream& show_gpa(ostream& stream)
{
   stream.setf(ios::showpoint) ;
   stream.setf(ios::fixed , ios::adjustfield) ;
   stream.precision(2) ;
   return stream ;
}

// A typical student record
class student
{
   enum {size = 25} ;
   char name[size] ;
   int age ;
   float gpa ;

      public:
   student(const char* = "" , int = 0 , float = 0.0) ;
   friend ostream& operator<<(ostream& , const student&) ;
} ;

// Constructor
inline student::student(const char* n , int a , float g)
                  : age(a) , gpa(g)
{
   strcpy(name , n) ;
}
```

```
// Output a student
ostream& operator<<(ostream& stream , const student& stu)
{
   stream << "Name: " << stu.name << endl ;
   stream << "Age: " << stu.age << endl ;
   stream << "GPA: " << show_gpa << stu.gpa << endl ;
   return stream ;
}

// A class that encapsulates the details of doing file I/O
class in_out
{
   fstream file ;
     public:

   in_out() ;
   void operator!() ;
   friend in_out& operator<<(in_out& , const student&) ;
   friend in_out& operator>>(in_out& , student&) ;
} ;

// Constructor
inline in_out::in_out()
{
   file.open("FILE" , ios::in | ios::out | ios::binary) ;
}

// Operator ! means to rewind the file
inline void in_out::operator!()
{
   file << flush ;
   file.seekg(0L) ;
}

// Friend function to write a student to disk
in_out& operator<<(in_out& io , const student& stu)
{
   io.file.write((char*)&stu , sizeof stu) ;
   return io ;
}

// Friend function to read a student from disk
in_out& operator>>(in_out& io , student& stu)
{
   io.file.read((char*)&stu , sizeof stu) ;
   return io ;
}
```

```
int main()
{
  // Instance of I/O class
  in_out IO ;

  // Array of students
  student array[] =
   {
      student("Bob Williams" , 17 , 3.40) ,
      student("Kimberley Johnson" , 16 , 3.75) ,
      student("Julie Fletcher" , 18 , 2.95)
   } ;

  // Compute size of the array
  const int size = sizeof(array) / sizeof(student) ;

  // Output all students to disk
  for(int i = 0 ; i < size ; ++i)
     IO << array[i] ;

  // Rewind the file
  !IO ;

  // Read and print all students
  for(i = 0 ; i < size ; ++i)
   {
      student pupil ;
      IO >> pupil ;
      cout << pupil << endl ;
   }

  return 0 ;
}
```

The output is:

```
Name: Bob Williams
Age: 17
GPA: 3.40

Name: Kimberley Johnson
Age: 16
GPA: 3.75

Name: Julie Fletcher
Age: 18
GPA: 2.95
```

■ Exercise #1

Given the following class definition:

```
class file
{
   fstream in_out ;

      public:
   int open(int argc , char* argv[]) ;
   void read() ;
   void write() ;
   void beginning() ;
   void end() ;
   void print() ;
   void close() ;
} ;
```

write the definitions of the member functions so that the user of the class has complete flexibility as to the name of the external file to be manipulated, and modes to be used. All such variables are entered from the DOS command line. The first argument is the disk file name, and the remaining arguments represent the various open modes, exactly as specified by the enumerated types.

■ Exercise #2

Modify your final answer to Chapter 7, Exercise #11 so that instead of processing a single line of text, you will read and process a complete disk file, showing both the line and column where unique words occur. To do this, make the following changes:

■ The program prompts for the name of a C++ program file as its input. For testing purposes, enter the file name con in order to take all of your input from the keyboard.

■ Do not create an array of class one_words. In the class all_words. Instead, use a *linked list* that is always kept in strict ascending sequence. Obviously, this means that there no longer is a need for a separate sort routine. Such a linked list might have this class declaration:

```
class one_word
{
   friend class all_words ;
   char* word ;
   long* position ;
   int counter ;
   one_word* next ;
} ;
```

■ The final test data for your program should be the program source code itself. Be sure to process the *entire* file before printing the cross-reference listing. In other words, do *not* process and print one line at a time.

■   Also run a small test using keyboard input (file `cin`).

■   Obviously you should print but not process comments in your program. The parser class should now be handling this. To ensure that this part of your program is working properly, include this function at the end of your program:

```
void DummyFunction()
{
    /*  comment1  */
    int live_data1 ;
    //  comment2
    int live_data2 ;
    /*  comment3  //
       comment3 (cont.)  */
    int live_data3 ;
    //  comment4   /*  comment4 (cont.)
    int live_data4 ; /* comment5 */
}
```

■ Exercise #3

Modify Example 15.19 so that the `student` class uses a pointer instead of a fixed size array to represent the name.

Notes

Notes

Chapter 16

Function templates

Function templates provide you with the capability to write a single function that is a skeleton, or template, for a family of similar functions. In this function at least one formal argument is generic. This function template becomes a "real" function with "real" types when and only when it needs to be invoked, or its address taken.

What's wrong with function overloading?

In Chapter 8 you learned a great deal about how to overload functions in C++ and the benefits you may achieve from doing so. The chief advantage is that it relieves someone who is using your functions from having to know about different names for various functions (either at global or class scope) that essentially do the same task. Unfortunately, overloaded functions, while a vast improvement over what's available in C, aren't the ultimate solution to the problem that is inherent when writing functions that are similar in their behavior.

To see why, here is a function called `max()` that returns the greater of its two input arguments. Of course, it has to be continually overloaded in order to accommodate the various types of arguments that can conceivably be used to invoke it.

Example 16.1

```cpp
#include <iostream.h>

int max(int x , int y)
{
   return (x > y) ? x : y ;
}

long max(long x , long y)
{
   return (x > y) ? x : y ;
}

double max(double x , double y)
{
   return (x > y) ? x : y ;
}

char max(char x , char y)
{
   return (x > y) ? x : y ;
}
```

```
int main()
{
   cout << max(1 , 2) << endl ;
   cout << max(4L , 3L) << endl ;
   cout << max(5.62 , 3.48) << endl ;
   cout << max('A' , 'a') << endl ;

   return 0 ;
}
```

The output is:

```
2
4
5.62
a
```

☞   You must be using a compiler that supports AT&T version 3.0 in order to compile the examples shown in this chapter and in Chapter 17.

Even though function overloading has been used, the problem with this example is that there is still too much repetitious coding. In other words, each function is doing essentially the same thing — returning the greater of its two input arguments. Now, instead of your having to write many similar max() functions, wouldn't it be nice to be able to write just *one* max() function that returns the greater of its two input arguments and can accommodate almost *any* type of input argument?

Why not use a macro?

Certainly you can write a macro to "solve" this problem, but what you lose is the ability to ensure that you are not comparing arguments of different types. That is, if your intent is to guarantee that both arguments are the same type, then a macro does not work because this program compiles and executes just fine. In addition, macros are handled by the preprocessor which makes debugging more difficult. Note also how easy it is to make a mistake when writing a macro, such as forgetting a set of parentheses.

Example 16.2

```
#include <iostream.h>

#define max(x , y) \
(((x) > (y)) ? (x) : (y))

int main()
{
   cout << max(1 , 2.98) << endl ;
   cout << max('A' , 3L) << endl ;

   return 0 ;
}
```

The output is:

```
2.98
65
```

How a function template solves the problem

A *function template* solves the problem by allowing you to write just *one* function that serves as a skeleton, or template, for a family of functions whose tasks are all similar. At the same time, full type checking is carried out.

This function template does not specify the actual type(s) of the arguments that the function accepts; instead, it uses a generic, or parameterized, type as a "place holder" until you determine the specific type(s). This choice occurs implicitly when you make a call to the function or take the function's address. At this time the compiler infers the type of the actual argument(s), and then proceeds to *instantiate* the function with the actual type(s) by replacing the generic type(s) that you specified. For each new type(s) that you code, a different function, called a *template function*, will be instantiated.

☞ The term *function template* refers to the generic function that you write. The term *template function* refers to a function template that has been instantiated by the compiler and thus has had its generic type(s) replaced by specific type(s).

How to write a function template

A function template should be written at the start of your program in the global area, or you may place it into a header file. All function templates start with a template declaration. This is its syntax:

- The C++ keyword `template`

- A left angle bracket (<)

- A list of generic types, each one separated by a comma. A generic type consists of two parts:

  - The keyword `class` (Note: this usage of word `class` has nothing to do with the keyword `class` to create a user-defined type.)

  - A variable that represents some generic type, and will be used whenever this type needs to be written in the function definition. Typically the name `T` is used (as in Template), but any valid C++ name will do.

- A right angle bracket (>).

After the template declaration, you continue with the function definition itself, preceded by any of the normal modifiers, e.g., `inline`, `extern`, `static`, etc.

These function templates must be available to the compiler when the call to the function is encountered, so that they usually are stored in a header file that is included with the source code. If several modules instantiate identical functions, then by default the linker will *not* deem this to be a duplicate function definition. Of course, if you were to compile the function template before doing any instantiations, it may very well compile successfully. However, when doing an instantiation, the compiler will look for other error conditions, such as performing bitwise operations on floating point numbers.

> ☞ The formal argument list for a function template must use, at least once, *all* of the parameterized types that were specified between the angle brackets. Merely using the type as the return type of the function is not good enough.

For example, here is the definition for a function template called `max()` that takes two generic types, each of which is called `T`, and returns the greater of the two input values.

Example 16.3

```
#include <iostream.h>

template <class T> const T& max(const T& a , const T& b)
{
    return (a > b) ? a : b ;
}

int main()
{
    cout << max(5 , 6) << endl ;
    cout << max('B' , 'A') << endl ;
    cout << max(1.2 , 3.4) << endl ;
    cout << max(8 , 7) << endl ;

    return 0 ;
}
```

The output is:

```
6
B
3.4
8
```

Each of the first three `max()` function calls causes a template function to be instantiated, first with an `int`, then with a `char`, and then with a `double`. Note that the last call using two integers does *not* cause another instantiation to occur because this call can use the instantiated function that was generated as a result of the first call that also uses two integers.

Note also that the actual arguments are being received by *constant reference*. The keyword `const` is used so that constants may be passed (you may not be able to create a non-`const` reference to a constant), and a reference is used in case the actual arguments are user-defined types.

In addition, you cannot instantiate the function template with *different* types. For example, this program will not compile because the first argument is an `int` and the second is a `double`.

☞ Borland C++ will also perform an instantiation if it encounters a function declaration in which the modifiers for the return type and argument types are identical to that of any function template within the source program.

Example 16.4   ***(Will not compile!)***

```
#include <iostream.h>

template <class T> const T& max(const T& a , const T& b)
{
   return (a > b) ? a : b ;
}

int main()
{
   cout << max(5 , 6.1) << endl ;

   return 0 ;
}
```

The compiler error message is:

```
Could not find a match for 'max(int,double)'
```

You are telling the compiler that T really is type int, and then you are telling it that T really is type double. Since T can't possibly represent both types, the call is flagged as an error. Later in this chapter you will see how more than one argument type can be accommodated.

Overloading a function template

Sometimes a function template just can't handle all of the possible instantiations that you might want to do. Either the program will not compile or, if it does, the wrong answer may be obtained. In this case you must overload the function template by declaring the function and specifying fixed argument types, just as you would with any other overloaded function. Pointers are a good example of where you need to overload a function template because they always consist of two parts: the pointer itself and the object to which it points. And, as you know, pointers always need special handling.

Consider the max() function template called with string literals.

Example 16.5 *(Will not compile!)*

```
#include <iostream.h>

template <class T> const T& max(const T& a , const T& b)
{
   return (a > b) ? a : b ;
}

int main()
{
   cout << max("A" , "B") << endl ;

   return 0 ;
}
```

The compiler error message is:

```
Could not find a match for 'max(char *,char *)'
```

In this case the Borland compiler refuses to perform an instantiation since it will not convert a `char[]` to a `const char[]&`. And even if it did perform the conversion, the function would then be comparing the addresses of the strings, not the string values themselves.

To fix the problem, you need an overloaded `max()` function that is specifically designed to accommodate strings. There is no problem insofar as the compiler is concerned in having this new function coexist with a function template. So this is what the revised example looks like:

Example 16.6

```
#include <iostream.h>
#include <string.h>

const char* max(const char* a , const char* b)
{
   return strcmp(a , b) > 0 ? a : b ;
}

template <class T> const T& max(const T& a , const T& b)
{
   return (a > b) ? a : b ;
}
```

```
int main()
{
    cout << max("A" , "B") << endl ;

    return 0 ;
}
```

The output is:

```
B
```

Avoid default function arguments

Some C++ compilers do not allow default function arguments to be used in a function template. To see why, consider the following example:

Example 16.7

```
#include <iostream.h>

template <class T>
void f(T x , T y = 0)
{
    cout << "x = " << x << " y = " << y << endl ;
}

int main()
{
    f(1.2) ;

    return 0 ;
}
```

The output is:

```
x = 1.2 y = 1.113841e-316
```

(and Borland version 3.1 hangs the computer)

The call to the function `f()` is illegal because it is a call to `f(1.2 , 0)` and there is no version of `f()` that takes a `double` and an `int`. It is essentially the same as Example 16.4.

Commingling parameterized and fixed types

If a function template needs arguments other than parameterized types, there is no problem in simply specifying these fixed argument types just as you would in any other function declaration.

For example, suppose you want to write a function that prints an array. The first argument is the (generic) type of the array, while the second is the length of the array specified as a constant integer.

Example 16.8

```
#include <iostream.h>
template <class T> void print(T* ptr , const int length)
{
   for(int i = 0 ; i < length ; ++i)
      cout << ptr[i] << endl ;
   cout << endl ;
}

int main()
{
   int int_array[] = {1 , 2 , 3 , 4 , 5} ;
   const int int_size = sizeof(int_array) / sizeof(int) ;
   print(int_array , int_size) ;
   double double_array[] = {2.3 , 6.43 , 9.85} ;
   const int double_size = sizeof(double_array)/sizeof(double) ;
   print(double_array , double_size) ;

   return 0 ;
}
```

The output is:

```
1
2
3
4
5
2.3
6.43
9.85
```

How the argument type is determined

How does the compiler determine the type(s) of a function template's arguments based upon the actual arguments? It does this by inferring the type of the parameterized argument(s) by matching it with the actual function argument(s). Then, any modifiers (e.g., pointers or references) are stripped away, and what's left is the actual type. The return type of the function is never considered in this process.

Take another look at Example 16.8. The first instantiation of the function `print()` uses an `int*` type as the first actual argument. Therefore `T*` is equated to an `int*`. By "canceling" both asterisks, you are left with `T` representing an `int`. Similarly, for the second instantiation `T` is equated to a `double`.

Here is another program that uses a function template whose task is to return the largest value from an array of values. The function needs two input arguments: a pointer to the array and the number of elements in the array.

Example 16.9

```cpp
#include <iostream.h>

template <class T> T largest(T* ptr , const int size)
{
    T answer = ptr[0] ;
    for(int i = 1 ; i < size ; ++i)
        if(ptr[i] > answer)
            answer = ptr[i] ;
    return answer ;
}

int main()
{
    int int_array[] = { 4 , 7 , -3 , 32 , 0 } ;
    const int int_size = sizeof(int_array) / sizeof(int) ;
    cout << "Largest int is "
         << largest(int_array , int_size) << endl ;
    double double_array[] = { -4.52 , 21.9 , 7.43 } ;
    const int double_size = sizeof(double_array)/sizeof(double) ;
    cout << "Largest double is "
         << largest(double_array , double_size) << endl ;

    return 0 ;
}
```

The output is:

```
Largest int is 32
Largest double is 21.9
```

For the first function call to `largest()`, the type of the first argument is `int*`. Therefore, type `T*` is replaced by `int*`, the two asterisks are stripped away, and `T` is equated to an `int`. Note that the first function argument had to be `T*` instead of `T` since the return type is `T`. If the first argument had been type `T`, then you would be attempting to return a value of type `int*` instead of type `int`.

Argument matching rules — trivial conversions

When a function template has *not* been overloaded and the compiler attempts to find a match between the actual arguments and the formal arguments of a function template, it may or may not do trivial conversions, e.g., cast an `int` into a `const int`, or a `char*` into a `const char*`. The Annotated C++ Reference Manual (ARM) by Ellis and Stroustrup calls for no trivial conversions to be made, but the X3J16 Technical Committee is considering a proposal to provide full argument matching capability. In the meantime, you can expect different behavior from different compilers.

Therefore, it is up to you to ensure that an exact match occurs. For example, this program does not compile in Borland C++ because the function template is looking for a `const int` as its second argument, whereas the actual argument is just an `int`.

Example 16.10   ***(Will not compile!)***

```
template <class T> void f(T , const int) {}

int main()
{
   int x = 1 ;
   f(1 , x) ;

   return 0 ;
}
```

The compiler error message is::

```
Could not find a match for 'f(int,int)'
```

Similarly, in the following program the Borland compiler will not convert a `char*` type into a `const char*`.

Example 16.11   **(Will not compile!)**

```
template <class T> void f(T , const char*) {}

int main()
{
    f(1 , "A") ;
    return 0 ;
}
```

The compiler error message is:

```
Could not find a match for 'f(int,char *)'
```

However, Borland treats conversions into references as exact matches, so the following example compiles just fine.

Example 16.12

```
template <class T> void f(T , int&) {}

int main()
{
    int x = 0 ;
    f(1 , x) ;

    return 0 ;
}
```

Another place to go wrong is to assume that a function that has been instantiated from a function template will be examined *under the normal rules of argument matching*. This is not presently the situation, as illustrated by the following program. The compiler complains that it cannot find a match for `max(char , int)` on the second call. This is correct because (1) the function template cannot accommodate two different types (`char` and `int`), and (2) the existing instantiation of `max(int , int)` as a result of the first call does not constitute an exact match.

Example 16.13   *(Will not compile!)*

```
#include <iostream.h>

template <class T> const T& max(const T& a , const T& b)
{
  return (a > b) ? a : b ;
}

int main()
{
  cout << max(5 , 6) << endl ;
  cout << max('A' , 1) << endl ;

  return 0 ;
}
```

The compiler error message is:

```
Could not find a match for 'max(char,int)'
```

One way around the preceding problem is to declare (not define) a function that:

■ Can satisfy the function call using the normal argument matching rules;

■ Has arguments and a return type that are explicitly specified, while any modifiers to the arguments match exactly those of the function template.

In the following example a function declaration taking two arguments, each of which is type const int&, satisfies the second call to max() with a char and an int. But what about the function *definition* that the linker will insist upon finding? In this case the compiler is smart enough to use, as the definition for the second call, the template function that was instantiated as a result of the first call to max().

Example 16.14

```
#include <iostream.h>

template <class T> const T& max(const T& a , const T& b)
{
  return (a > b) ? a : b ;
}

// Declaration to satisfy (char , int)
const int& max(const int& , const int&) ;
```

```
int main()
{
  cout << max(5 , 6) << endl ;
  cout << max('A' , 1) << endl ;

  return 0 ;
}
```

The output is:

```
6
65
```

Earlier it was pointed out that the mere presence of a function declaration is enough to cause the compiler to do an instantiation. This is now the case when the first function call to `max()` is removed. In essence, the compiler is saying, "I'm happy that you have provided a function *declaration* taking two integers by constant reference that I can use to satisfy the call to max() using a `char` and an `int`. However, I know that the linker will need a function *definition* that can accommodate these argument types. It could come from a library file, or it could come from the program itself. But just to be on the safe side, if it cannot be found in either place, I will generate a template function definition that takes two integers by constant reference."

That's why the following program compiles and links just fine using Borland C++. Other compilers may yield a linker error message.

Example 16.15

```
#include <iostream.h>

template <class T> const T& max(const T& a , const T& b)
{
  return (a > b) ? a : b ;
}

// Declaration to satisfy (char , int)
const int& max(const int& , const int&) ;

int main()
{
  cout << max('A' , 1) << endl ;

  return 0 ;
}
```

The output is:

```
65
```

On the other hand, Borland C++ will perform a trivial conversion (e.g., int to const int and char* to const char*) on actual arguments in an attempt to match a template function that has already been instantiated. For example, this program compiles successfully because the first call to max() generates the template function max(const int, const int) while the second call converts the integer z into a const int. If the first call were not present, then the program would fail to compile.

Example 16.16

```cpp
#include <iostream.h>

template <class T> const T& max(const T& a , const T& b)
{
    return (a > b) ? a : b ;
}

int main()
{
    const int x = 1 , y = 2 ;

    // Generates this function: max(const int , const int)
    cout << max(x , y) << endl ;

    int z = 3 ;
    // Uses previously defined function by converting int to
    // const int
    cout << max(x , z) << endl ;

    return 0 ;
}
```

The output is:

```
2
3
```

☞ As noted earlier, different C++ compilers are likely to yield different results when performing argument matching and when linking object files, so the last several examples may not work with a compiler other than Borland.

Argument matching rules — the 3-step process

When a function template has been overloaded with at least one function having the same name but with specific argument types, there are three steps that the compiler goes through in an attempt to obtain a match with the arguments of a function call. These steps are:

■ Examine all of the overloaded functions for an exact match (no promotions or conversions are done, but some compilers may do trivial conversions).

■ Examine the function template to see if an instantiation can occur.

■ Re-examine the overloaded functions and use promotions and conversions in an attempt to find an unambiguous match.

Let's start with this program that overloads f() to accept an integer argument. Because the actual argument is an int and an overloaded function exists whose formal argument is an int, an exact match has occurred and the function template is never examined.

Example 16.17

```
#include <iostream.h>

template <class T> void f(T*)
{
   cout << "template function\n" ;
}

void f(int)
{
   cout << "int function\n" ;
}

int main()
{
   f(1) ;

   return 0 ;
}
```

The output is:

```
int function
```

Next, the call to the function has been changed to a char* object. Now there is no match with the overloaded function, and the function template is examined. Since there is no problem matching `char*` with `T*` (after which `T` becomes a `char`), the function template is used to do the instantiation.

Example 16.18

```
#include <iostream.h>

template <class T> void f(T*)
{
   cout << "template function\n" ;
}

void f(int)
{
   cout << "int function\n" ;
}

int main()
{
   f("ABC") ;

   return 0 ;
}
```

The output is:

```
template function
```

Now let's change the actual argument again to a `double`. There is no exact match with the overloaded function, and no template function can be instantiated because there is no way in which `T*` can be equated with a `double` (what would `T` then become?). Rule #3 says to re-examine the overloaded function, and since a `double` can be converted into an `int`, this is what happens.

Example 16.19

```
#include <iostream.h>

template <class T> void f(T*)
{
   cout << "template function\n" ;
}

void f(int)
{
   cout << "int function\n" ;
}
```

```
int main()
{
   f(1.2) ;

   return 0 ;
}
```

The output is:

```
int function
```

Finally, let's add another overloaded function to the previous example, this time accepting a `float`. Now all of the rules fail, even #3, because the compiler does not know which overloaded function to call.

Example 16.20

```
#include <iostream.h>

template <class T> void f(T*)
{
   cout << "template function\n" ;
}

void f(int)
{
   cout << "int function\n" ;
}

void f(float)
{
   cout << "float function\n" ;
}

int main()
{
   f(1.2) ;

   return 0 ;
}
```

The compiler error message is::

```
Ambiguity between 'f(float)' and f(int)'
```

Multiple parameterized types

A function template may contain more than one parameterized type. In this case you must use unique names for each type, and each type must be used at least once in the formal argument list.

In the following example function `f()` takes two arguments of (possibly) different types, displays them, and returns nothing. By the way, note how nicely the `iostream` methods fit into a template function since you no longer need (nor could you use) a `printf()` conversion specification that designates the type of the argument being output.

Example 16.21

```
#include <iostream.h>

template <class T , class U>
void print(const T& a , const U& b)
{
   cout << "First = " << a << endl ;
   cout << "Second = " << b << endl ;
}

int main()
{
   print(1 , 2.3) ;
   print('A' , 5L) ;

   return 0 ;
}
```

The output is:

```
First = 1
Second = 2.3
First = A
Second = 5
```

Instantiating a function template with a class instance

If you wish to instantiate a function template using an instance of some user-defined class, there is no problem unless the function uses operations on its arguments that are invalid for the class. For example, the `max()` function uses the "greater than" (>)

operator to compare the two arguments. Therefore, any instantiation that uses a class will insist that the class overload the "greater than" operator. In addition, the function returns the greater of the two values, and if this value is to be output like any primitive type, then the insertion operator must also be overloaded.

This program illustrates these points by using instances of the string class to instantiate the function template. Note that the string class has both the "greater than" and the insertion operator overloaded.

Example 16.22

```
#include <iostream.h>
#include "mystring.h"

#include "mystring.cpp"

template <class T>
const T& max(const T& a , const T& b)
{
   return (a > b) ? a : b ;
}

int main()
{
   string s1("A") , s2("a") , s3("B") ;
   cout << max(s1 , s2) << endl ;
   cout << max(s3 , s1) << endl ;
   cout << max(s3 , s2) << endl ;

   return 0 ;
}
```

The output is:

```
a
B
a
```

■ Review Questions

1) What is a function template, and why would you ever need one?

2) How do you tell the compiler that a function is a template?

3) How does the compiler infer the type(s) of the function arguments when a call to that function is made?

4) Why would you need to overload a function template?

5)   What is wrong with the following template declarations?

```
<class T> T f(T arg) {}
template <T> T f(T arg) {}
template <class T> T f() {}
template <class T , class T> T f(T arg) {}
template <class T , class U> void f(T arg) {}
template <class T , U> void f(T arg1 , U arg2) {}
```

■ Exercise #1

Write a function template called `swap()` that swaps the contents of its two input arguments. Test this function by using several different instantiations of primitive types. Then create a user-defined type (e.g., a complex number) and apply the `swap()` function to this type.

■ Exercise #2

Using your `swap()` function, write a function template that takes as its two arguments a parameterized type representing a pointer to an array and an `int` representing the length of the array. The function must bubble sort the array into ascending sequence and then print the array.

■ Exercise #3

Write a function template called `count()` that accepts three arguments: a parameterized type representing a pointer to an array, the length of the array, and some value of the array type. Count the number of occurrences of the value within the array and return the resulting count. Instantiate the function using several different types.

■ Exercise #4

Modify Exercise #3 so that a string can be searched for the number of occurrences of a specified substring.

Notes

Notes

Notes

Chapter 17

Class templates

In addition to function templates, C++ also supports the concept of class templates. By definition, a class template is a class definition that describes a family of related classes. The philosophy is essentially the same as that of function templates, i.e., the ability to create a class (or structure) that contains one or more types that are generic, or parameterized.

How to define a class template

A class template is defined in a manner similar to that of a function template. You start by writing a template declaration followed by the class definition:

Example 17.1

```
template <class T>
class test
{
   // data and functions
} ;
```

Of course, you may have more than one parameterized type between the angle brackets. You then proceed to write the class definition as you normally would, but you would then use the parameterized type T instead of a known primitive or user-define type.

Note that the name of a non-parameterized class and a parameterized class are *not* the same. In other words, whenever you need to write the class name, e.g., in front of the scope resolution operator, you must tell the compiler that you're referring to a *template class*, not a non-template class. You do this by writing the class name followed by the parameterized type name between angle brackets.

For example, assuming that the parameterized type name is T, then whenever you need to refer to the parameterized class name test within or outside the class definition of test, you must write:

Example 17.2

```
test<T>
```

Note, however, that is *not* done when you are writing a constructor or destructor function name because in this context the name test is being used as a function, not class, name.

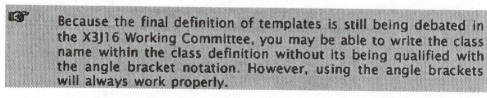

☞ Because the final definition of templates is still being debated in the X3J16 Working Committee, you may be able to write the class name within the class definition without its being qualified with the angle bracket notation. However, using the angle brackets will always work properly.

For example, here is the definition of a class template whose one private data member `number` is a parameterized type. Note that no default function arguments are used since this is invalid syntax to some C++ compilers, as mentioned in the previous chapter.

Example 17.3

```cpp
#include <iostream.h>

template <class T>
class test
{
  T number ;

    public:
// Default constructor
test() : number(0) {}

// Constructor taking a value
test(T n) : number(n) {}

// Copy constructor
test(const test<T>& t) : number(t.number) {}

// Destructor
~test() {}

// Assignment operator
test<T>& operator=(const test<T>& t)
 {
    number = t.number ;
    return *this ;
 }

// Insertion operator
friend ostream& operator<<(ostream& stream ,const test<T>& t)
 {
    return stream << t.number ;
 }
} ;
```

Here is the previous example with the member functions (and friend function) defined outside the class definition. Because all of the class member functions are automatically template functions, the template declaration must be repeated for each function.

Example 17.4

```
#include <iostream.h>

template <class T>
class test
{
   T number ;

      public:
   test() ;
   test(T) ;
   test(const test<T>&) ;
   ~test() ;
   test<T>& operator=(const test<T>&) ;
   friend ostream& operator<<(ostream& , const test<T>&) ;
} ;

// Default constructor
template <class T>
test<T>::test() : number(0) {}

// Constructor taking a value
template <class T>
test<T>::test(T n) : number(n) {}

// Copy constructor
template <class T>
test<T>::test(const test<T>& t) : number(t.number) {}

// Destructor
template <class T>
test<T>::~test() {}

// Assignment operator
template <class T>
test<T>& test<T>::operator=(const test<T>& t)
{
   number = t.number ;
   return *this ;
}

// Insertion operator
template <class T>
ostream& operator<<(ostream& stream , const test<T>& t)
{
   return stream << t.number ;
}
```

How to instantiate a class template

After the class template has been defined, you may instantiate the class by using a specific primitive or user-defined type to replace the parameterized type. To do this, you must enclose the specific type between angle brackets and insert this expression immediately after the class name. For example:

Example 17.5

```
// Instantiate 'test' with an int
test<int> t1 ;

//Instantiate 'test' with a long
test<long> t2(123456789L) ;

// Instantiate 'test' with a double
typedef test<double> test_double ;
test_double t3(4.59) ;
```

When this happens, it causes the following instantiations to occur:

■ All class static and non-static member functions;

■ All class static data members;

■ The instance itself, either in the stack, heap or global space.

Within the class's functions and static declarations, the parameterized type is replaced by actual type. Of course, performing such instantiations using different types will cause separate copies of the member functions and static definitions to occur.

You may now use the instance names t1, t2 and t3 as you normally would to call upon the member functions. Note that test<int>, test<long> and test<double> are completely separate class names, and instances of these three classes may not be commingled in statements, e.g., assignment.

Here is a complete program that uses the class template.

Example 17.6

```
#include <iostream.h>

template <class T>
class test
{
  T number ;

    public:
  test() ;
  test(T) ;
  test(const test<T>&) ;
  ~test() ;
  test<T>& operator=(const test<T>&) ;
  friend ostream& operator<<(ostream& , const test<T>&) ;
} ;

// Default constructor
template <class T>
test<T>::test() : number(0) {}

// Constructor taking a value
template <class T>
test<T>::test(T n) : number(n) {}

// Copy constructor
template <class T>
test<T>::test(const test<T>& t) : number(t.number) {}

// Destructor
template <class T>
test<T>::~test() {}

// Assignment operator
template <class T>
test<T>& test<T>::operator=(const test<T>& t)
{
  number = t.number ;
  return *this ;
}

// Insertion operator
template <class T>
ostream& operator<<(ostream& stream , const test<T>& t)
{
  return stream << t.number ;
}
```

```
int main()
{
   test<int> t1(1) ;
   cout << t1 << endl ;

   test<int> t2(t1) ;
   cout << t2 << endl ;

   test<int> t3 ;
   t3 = t2 ;
   cout << t3 << endl ;

   test<long> t4(123456789L) ;
   cout << t4 << endl ;

   return 0 ;
}
```

The output is:

```
1
1
1
123456789
```

Specializing a member function

Sometimes a class member function cannot accommodate all of the types that would normally be used to instantiate the class. This is the same problem that occurred in Chapter 16 when an instantiation was attempted using a string literal, and it's the same problem here.

For instance, suppose that in Example 17.6 the class `test` gets instantiated with a string literal so that the instantiation might appear as:

Example 17.7

```
// Instantiate 'test' with a string
test<char*> str("Test string") ;
cout << str << endl ;
```

Obviously the class is not set up to handle instantiations of a string literal because there is no heap allocation occurring in the constructor and overloaded assignment operator functions, nor is there any provision to delete a string from the heap in the destructor function.

To solve this dilemma, you may specialize any class member function with one that is customized to a specific type. To do this, simply write the member function for a specific type by writing a specific type name (instead of naming the parameterized type) between the angle brackets.

For example, to accommodate a string instantiation of the class, Example 17.6 would now appear as:

Example 17.8

```cpp
#include <iostream.h>
#include <string.h>

template <class T>
class test
{
  T number ;

    public:
  test() ;
  test(T) ;
  test(const test<T>&) ;
  ~test() ;
  test<T>& operator=(const test<T>&) ;
  friend ostream& operator<<(ostream& , const test<T>&) ;
} ;

// Parameterized default constructor
template <class T>
test<T>::test() : number(0) {}

// Default constructor for a char*
test<char*>::test() : number(new char[1])
{
  number[0] = '\0' ;
}

// Parameterized constructor taking a value
template <class T>
test<T>::test(T n) : number(n) {}

// Constructor for a char*
test<char*>::test(char* s) : number(new char[strlen(s)+1])
{
  strcpy(number , s) ;
}

// Parameterized copy constructor
template <class T>
test<T>::test(const test<T>& t) : number(t.number) {}
```

```cpp
// Copy constructor for a char*
test<char*>::test(const test<char*>& s)
{
  number = new char[strlen(s.number) + 1] ;
  strcpy(number , s.number) ;
}

// Parameterized destructor
template <class T>
test<T>::~test() {}
// Destructor for a char*
test<char*>::~test()
{
  delete [] number ;
}

// Parameterized assignment operator
template <class T>
test<T>& test<T>::operator=(const test<T>& t)
{
  number = t.number ;
  return *this ;
}

// Assignment operator for a char*
test<char*>& test<char*>::operator=(const test<char*>& s)
{
  if(&s != this)
   {
     delete [] number ;
     number = new char[strlen(s.number) + 1] ;
     strcpy(number , s.number) ;
   }
  return *this ;
}

// Parameterized insertion operator that is always used
template <class T>
ostream& operator<<(ostream& stream , const test<T>& t)
{
  return stream << t.number ;
}

int main()
{
  test<char*> s1("Test string") ;
  test<char*> s2(s1) ;
  test<char*> s3 ;
  s3 = s2 ;
  cout << s1 << endl ;
  cout << s2 << endl ;
  cout << s3 << endl ;
```

```
      return 0 ;
}
```

The output is:

```
Test string
Test string
Test string
```

It should be obvious that doing all these function specializations is quite a lot of work! But there is a much better way. After all, didn't we define a `string` class in Chapter 8 with all of the capabilities of initialization, assignment, etc? So the proper approach is to simply instantiate the `test` class with the type `string`.

Example 17.9

```
#include <iostream.h>
#include "mystring.h"
#include "mystring.cpp"

template <class T>
class test
{
  T number ;

    public:
  test() ;
  test(T) ;
  test(const test<T>&) ;
  ~test() ;
  test<T>& operator=(const test<T>&) ;
  friend ostream& operator<<(ostream& , const test<T>&) ;
} ;

// Parameterized default constructor
template <class T>
test<T>::test() : number(0) {}

// Parameterized constructor taking a value
template <class T>
test<T>::test(T n) : number(n) {}

// Parameterized copy constructor
template <class T>
test<T>::test(const test<T>& t) : number(t.number) {}

// Parameterized destructor
template <class T>
test<T>::~test() {}
```

```
// Parameterized assignment operator
template <class T>
test<T>& test<T>::operator=(const test<T>& t)
{
  number = t.number ;
  return *this ;
}

// Parameterized insertion operator that is always used
template <class T>
ostream& operator<<(ostream& stream , const test<T>& t)
{
  return stream << t.number ;
}

int main()
{
  test<string> s1("Test string") ;
  test<string> s2(s1) ;
  test<string> s3 ;
  s3 = s2 ;
  cout << s1 << endl ;
  cout << s2 << endl ;
  cout << s3 << endl ;

  return 0 ;
}
```

The output is:

```
Test string
Test string
Test string
```

How to define static data members

In order to define the static data members of a class template, you must once again use the template declaration preceding the static definition. Because the class template will presumably be instantiated with different types, each instantiation will have its own unique copy of the static member(s).

First, here is a case where the static is a primitive type. Note the qualification of the data member number with the parameterized class name A<T> in the definition.

Example 17.10

```
template <class T>
class A
{
   static int number ;
} ;

template <class T>
int A<T>::number = 0 ;
```

On the other hand, the type of the static may be that of the parameterized type itself.

Example 17.11

```
template <class T>
class A
{
   static T number ;
} ;

template <class T>
T A<T>::number(0) ;
```

The problem with Example 17.11 is that different instantiations of class A may need to initialize the static data member differently. In other words, if you instantiate class A with an int, then you may want the value of number to be a certain value. On the other hand, if you instantiate with a double, then you may want the value of number to be something else.

To solve this problem, you may provide specific definitions that will take precedence over any template definition. Note that if more than one template static definition is provided, then the template declaration is still written just once inside the class definition.

For example, suppose that for an instantiation with an int you want to take the default value of zero, but for an instantiation of a double you want the static member to have the value 1.23. Here is the complete program to do this.

Example 17.12

```
#include <iostream.h>

template <class T>
class A
{
   static T number ;

      public:
   static T get_number() ;
} ;

// Generic static definition
template <class T> T A<T>::number = 0 ;

// Specific static definition for a double
double A<double>::number = 1.23 ;

template <class T>
T A<T>::get_number()
{
   return number ;
}

int main()
{
   // Instantiate with an 'int'
   cout << A<int>::get_number() << endl ;

   // Instantiate with a 'double'
   cout << A<double>::get_number() << endl ;

   return 0 ;
}
```

The output is:

```
0
1.23
```

☞ **This example will not compile under Borland C++ version 3.0, but is OK under version 3.1.**

The type of a static data member may be that of another class. In the following example an instance of class template A is used as a static data member of the class template B. Note that the two classes can be instantiated with different types, so the template declaration for class B needs to take two different parameterized types.

Example 17.13

```
#include <iostream.h>
#pragma option -Jgd

template <class T>
class A
{
  T n ;
    public:
  A(T = 0) ;
  friend ostream& operator<<(ostream& , const A<T>&) ;
} ;

template <class T>
A<T>::A(T x) : n(x) {}

template <class T>
ostream& operator<<(ostream& stream , const A<T>& a)
{
  return stream << a.n ;
}

template <class T , class U>
class B
{
  U f ;
  static A<T> number ;

    public:
  B(U = 0.0) ;
  static void print_number() ;
  void print_f() ;
} ;

// static definition
template <class T , class U>
A<T> B<T , U>::number ;

template <class T , class U>
B<T , U>::B(U x) : f(x) {}

template <class T , class U>
void B<T , U>::print_number()
{
  cout << "number = " << number << endl ;
}
```

```
template <class T , class U>
void B<T , U>::print_f()
{
   cout << "f = " << f << endl ;
}

int main()
{
   B<int , double> b = 2.3 ;
   B<int , double>::print_number() ;
   b.print_f() ;

   return 0 ;
}
```

The output is:

```
number = 0 ;
f = 2.3
```

☞ **This example will compile under Borland C++ version 3.0. However, under version 3.1 a `pragma` compiler directive is needed.**

To avoid having to use the #`pragma` directive in the previous example, you may declare the static member to be a pointer, and initialize it in the constructor function.

Example 17.14

```
#include <iostream.h>

template <class T>
class A
{
   T n ;

      public:
   A(T = 0) ;
   friend ostream& operator<<(ostream& , const A<T>&) ;
} ;

template <class T>
A<T>::A(T x) : n(x) {}
```

```
template <class T>
ostream& operator<<(ostream& stream , const A<T>& a)
{
   return stream << a.n ;
}

template <class T , class U>
class B
{
   U f ;
   static A<T>* number ;

      public:
   B(U = 0.0) ;
   static void print_number() ;
   void print_f() ;
} ;

// static definition
template <class T , class U>
A<T>* B<T , U>::number ;

template <class T , class U>
B<T , U>::B(U x) : f(x)
{
   *number = 0 ;
}

template <class T , class U>
void B<T , U>::print_number()
{
   cout << "number = " << *number << endl ;
}

template <class T , class U>
void B<T , U>::print_f()
{
   cout << "f = " << f << endl ;
}

int main()
{
   B<int , double> b = 2.3 ;
   B<int , double>::print_number() ;
   b.print_f() ;

   return 0 ;
}
```

The output is:

```
number = 0 ;
f = 2.3
```

How a class template grants friendship

If a class template wishes to grant friendship to another class template, it may do so provided that the friend class name is qualified with the parameterized type. For example, a class representing a node of some generic type needs to give friendship to a linked list class, because the list class needs to have access to the private members of the node class. This is the skeleton of how it is done:

Example 17.15

```
template <class T>
class node
{
   T data ;
   node* next ;
   node(T) ;
   friend class list<T> ;
} ;

template <class T>
class list
{
   // Data and functions for the class
} ;

int main()
{
   list<int> mylist ;
   // etc.
   return 0 ;
}
```

How to inherit from a class template

There is no problem if you want to inherit from a class template. In this case the derived class is also a class template. Don't forget to specify the parameterized type when you write the base class name in the derived class definition.

For example, suppose you have a class template with some generic type for a data member. The class has the usual constructor functions and an overloaded `operator+()` function that adds two instances of itself together. Then you wish to derive a new class with the added capability to display the data member. This is how it would appear.

Example 17.16

```
#include <iostream.h>

template <class T>
class A
{
     protected:
   T number ;

     public:
   A() ;
   A(T) ;
   A(const A<T>&) ;
   friend A<T> operator+(const A<T>& , const A<T>&) ;
} ;

// Default constructor
template <class T>
A<T>::A() : number(0) {}

// Constructor for the parameterized type T
template <class T>
A<T>::A(T n) : number(n) {}

// Copy constructor
template <class T>
A<T>::A(const A<T>& a) : number(a.number) {}

// Addition operator
template <class T>
A<T> operator+(const A<T>& a1 , const A<T>& a2)
{
   return a1.number + a2.number ;
}

/////////////////////////////////
```

```
// Derived class
template <class T>
class B : public A<T>
{
     public:
   B() ;
   B(T) ;
   B(const A<T>&) ;
   void print() ;
} ;

// Default constructor
template <class T>
B<T>::B() : A<T>(0) {}

// Constructor taking parameterized type T
template <class T>
B<T>::B(T n) : A<T>(n) {}

// Constructor taking base class type
template <class T>
B<T>::B(const A<T>& a) : A<T>(a) {}

// Printing function
template <class T>
void B<T>::print()
{
   cout << "number = " << number << endl ;
}

int main()
{
   B<int> n1 = 1 , n2 = 2 , n3 = n1 + n2 ;
   n3.print() ;

   B<double> n4 = 3.1 , n5 = 5.62 , n6 = n4 + n5 ;
   n6.print() ;

   return 0 ;
}
```

The output is:

```
number = 3
number = 8.72
```

Class templates with non-type arguments

Unlike function templates, a class template declaration may also contain fixed type names, such as int, float, char*, etc. If desired, each type may then be followed by an argument name. A parameterized type name is still also valid.

When you instantiate the class, you must write the actual value that will be stored into the argument name within the template declaration. This value must be known by the compiler. That is, it cannot be computed at execution time. In addition, the ARM calls for an exact match on the actual value specified and the type of the value within the template declaration. However, Borland C++ allows for a trivial conversion to be done.

For example, here is a class template that emulates an array of some primitive type. The dimension of the array is specified as one of the arguments within the template declaration.

Example 17.17

```cpp
#include <iostream.h>

template <class T , int n>
class array
{
  T* ptr ;
  int size ;

    public:
  array() ;
  array(const array<T , n>& a) ;
  const array<T , n>& operator=(const array<T , n>&) ;
  T& operator[](int) ;
  ~array() ;
  friend ostream&
  operator<<(ostream& stream , const array<T , n>& a)
   {
     for(int i = 0 ; i < a.size ; ++i)
       stream << '[' << i << ']' << " = " << a.ptr[i]
              << endl ;
     return stream ;
   }
} ;
```

```
// Default constructor
template <class T , int n>
array<T , n>::array() : size(n) , ptr(new T[size])
{
   for(int i = 0 ; i < size ; ++i)
     ptr[i] = 0 ;
}

// Copy constructor
template <class T , int n>
array<T , n>::array(const array<T , n>& a) : size(a.size) ,
                                             ptr(new T[size])
{
   for(int i = 0 ; i < size ; ++i)
     ptr[i] = a.ptr[i] ;
}

// Assignment operator
template <class T , int n>
const array<T , n>&
array<T , n>::operator=(const array<T , n>& a)
{
   if(&a != this)
    {
      delete [] ptr ;
      ptr = new T[size = a.size] ;
      for(int i = 0 ; i < size ; ++i)
         ptr[i] = a.ptr[i] ;
    }
   return *this ;
}

// Subscript operator
template <class T , int n>
T& array<T , n>::operator[](int x)
{
   return ptr[x] ;
}

// Destructor
template <class T , int n>
array<T , n>::~array()
{
   delete [] ptr ;
}
```

```
int main()
{
   const int dim = 5 ;

   array<int , dim> a1 ;
   a1[0] = 1 ;
   a1[1] = 2 ;
   cout << a1 << endl ;

   array<double , dim - 3> a2 ;
   for(int i = 0 ; i < dim - 3 ; ++i)
      a2[i] = i + 3.4 ;
   cout << a2 << endl ;

   return 0 ;
}
```

The output is:

```
[0] = 1
[1] = 2
[2] = 0
[3] = 0
[4] = 0

[0] = 3.4
[1] = 4.4
```

☞ This example will not compile under Borland C++ unless the friend function is defined within the class definition. Also, Borland version 3.1 erroneously gives a warning message about unreachable code in function `main()`.

How to instantiate a class with a template class

It's quite possible to instantiate a class using a type that is itself a template class. But you must be very careful how you write the instantiation.

For example, in the following program the class template `generic_type` abstracts some generic type of data, and provides a public interface. Next, the class template `array` abstracts some generic array type. When you instantiate the `array` class, you decide to do so using the `generic_type` class that has been specialized with type `int`. This is how it might look:

Example 17.18   *(Will not compile!)*

```
template <class T>
class generic_type
{
  T data ;
  // Public interface
} ;

template <class T>
class array
{
  T* ptr  ;
  int length ;
  // Public interface
} ;

int main()
{
  array<generic_type<int>> arr ;

  return 0 ;
}
```

The compiler error messages are:

```
, expected in function main()
Type name expected in function main()
```

While not very informative, the error messages point to the line where the instantiation is being performed. If you look closely, you will see that the compiler has encountered two right angle brackets next to each other, and thus interprets them to be the token '>>', or the right-shift operator. Of course, this is not what you intended to write. Therefore, it is your responsibility to separate these two angle brackets with a least one white space character, such as a blank.

Finally, to send you on your way into the world of C++ and class templates, here is a very unusual way to compute a factorial value.

Example 17.19

```
#include <iostream.h>

template <long i>
class Fact : private Fact<i - 1>
{
     public:
   long eval()
    {
        return i * Fact<i - 1>::eval() ;
    }
} ;

class Fact<0L>
{
     public:
   long eval()
    {
        return 1L ;
    }
} ;

int main()
{
   Fact<10L> f ;
   cout << f.eval() << endl ;

   return 0 ;
}
```

The output is:

```
3628800
```

■ Review Questions

1) What is a class template, and why would you ever need one?

2) How do you tell the compiler that a class is a template?

3) Why would you need to specialize a member function of a class template?

4) How is a static member of a class template defined?

5) How do you inherit from a class template?

■ Exercise #1

Write a template array class that emulates an array of whatever the parameterized type is. Instantiate and test the class using integers and doubles. Be sure to include all of the manager functions, a function to add two arrays together, and a function to sort the array.

■ Exercise #2

Write a template array class that handles a queue list of items. Use a linked list. Include member functions to add an item, remove an item, determine if the queue is empty, and display the list.

■ Exercise #3

Given the following class template definition that represents a pointer type:

```
template <class T> class pointer
{
   T* ptr ;
   int length ;

     public:
   pointer(int = 0) ;
   ~pointer() ;
   T& operator*() ;
   T& operator[](int) const ;
   friend T* operator+(const pointer<T>& , int) ;
   friend T* operator+(int , const pointer<T>&) ;
} ;
```

write the member and friend function definitions.

If the value of the constructor argument is not specified, or is zero, then assume this represents an uninitialized pointer. Otherwise, allocate the requested amount of space on the heap and initialize it to zero. Whenever the pointer is dereferenced (either with the asterisk or bracket notation), ensure that the pointer is pointing to space on the heap.

Then write a `main()` function that creates several pointers, some initialized and others not initialized. Test the class by attempting to dereference the pointers.

■ Exercise #4

Write a class template called `node` that contains a data item of some generic type and a pointer to another `node` item. Then write a class template called `list` containing functions that create a linked list of `node` items and display them. Test the `list` class by instantiating it with several different primitive types.

■ Exercise #5

Modify Exercise #4 so that the linked list can accommodate a user-defined type.

Notes

Notes

Notes

Chapter 18

Exception handling

Exception handling in C++ provides a better method by which the caller of a function can be informed that some error condition has occurred. Previous methods proved to be inadequate because of the semantics of the language itself, and the inability of the function to know what the caller wanted to do after the error had been detected. You will now see how exception handling can solve these problems.

What is the problem?

As mentioned, without exception handling there are inherent problems in how a function can inform the caller that some error condition has occurred. For example, suppose a function is designed to take two `long` integers as its arguments, and return the quotient as a type `double`.

Example 18.1

```cpp
#include <iostream.h>
#include <iomanip.h>
#include "manips.h"

#include "manips.cpp"

double divide(long dividend , long divisor)
{
   return (double)dividend / divisor ;
}

int main()
{
   cout << "Enter a dividend and a divisor: " ;
   long dividend , divisor ;
   while(!(cin >> dividend >> divisor).eof())
    {
      if(cin.good())
         cout << dividend << '/' << divisor << " = " << MONEY
                << divide(dividend , divisor) << endl ;
      else
         cerr << "Input error\n" ;
      cin >> FLUSH ;
      cout << "Next dividend and divisor: " ;
    }
   return 0 ;
}
```

The output for a typical run would be:

```
Enter a dividend and a divisor: 7 4
7/4 = 1.75
Next dividend and divisor: 7 A
Input error
Next dividend and divisor: 7 0
7/0 = inf
Next dividend and divisor: ^Z
```

☞ To compile the examples in this chapter, you need a compiler that supports exception handling, specifically the keywords `throw`, `catch` and `try`.

The preceding example works just fine unless the function `divide()` gets called with a divisor equal to zero. In this case the Watcom compiler outputs the message "inf", meaning "infinity", and keeps on processing. Borland, on the other hand, says that a "floating point error: Divide by 0" has occurred, and aborts the program. In either case, the result is not good.

To solve this problem, the function `divide()` could be revised to check for a zero divisor and, if detected, abort the program.

Example 18.2

```cpp
#include <iostream.h>
#include <iomanip.h>
#include <stdlib.h>
#include "manips.h"

#include "manips.cpp"

double divide(long dividend , long divisor)
{
   if(divisor == 0L)
    {
      cerr << "Division by zero\n" ;
      exit(1) ;
    }
   return (double)dividend / divisor ;
}

int main()
{
   cout << "Enter a dividend and a divisor: " ;
   long dividend , divisor ;
   while(!(cin >> dividend >> divisor).eof())
    {
      if(cin.good())
         cout << dividend << '/' << divisor << " = " << MONEY
                << divide(dividend , divisor) << endl ;
      else
         cerr << "Input error\n" ;
      cin >> FLUSH ;
      cout << "Next dividend and divisor: " ;
    }

   return 0 ;
}
```

The output for a typical run would be:

```
Enter a dividend and a divisor: 7 4
7/4 = 1.75
Next dividend and divisor: 7 A
Input error
Next dividend and divisor: 7 0
Division by zero
```

This is certainly not a very elegant solution to the problem. After all, the function divide() has now determined that *it* knows what the caller wants to do whenever a divisor of zero is encountered, i.e., exit from the program. But what if the user doesn't want to exit? Suppose the user really wants to retain control and provide some kind of recovery technique and continue to prompt the user for more input. Now what?

In this situation the function divide() cannot perform an exit() call, but instead must return control to the caller. But the syntax of the language still demands that an object of type double be returned from the function, so that the question now becomes, what should be returned, and how could this signify to the caller that a zero divisor had been detected? This situation is fairly typical since the function knows how to detect an error, but not how to process it. On the other hand, the caller knows how to process the error, but not how to detect it.

The only possible escape from this dilemma is to return some kind of pseudo value for which the caller must make a special check. The problem now is to determine which double value constitutes a pseudo value, since they are all legitimate return values. And even then there is no guarantee that the caller will make this check or do it correctly.

How to throw an exception

Exception handling solves this problem by providing a more elegant way to exit from the function, regardless of the function's return type, and let the caller retain control. This is done by having the function *throw* an exception. The syntax to do this is as follows:

Example 18.3

```
throw expression ;
```

where `expression` is any valid C++ expression. The word `throw` is a keyword. For example, if the `divide()` function wants to, it could throw the offending divisor back to the caller this way:

Example 18.4

```
double divide(long dividend , long divisor)
{
   if(divisor == 0L)
      throw divisor ;
   return (double)dividend / divisor ;
}
```

On the other hand, it could throw an error message:

Example 18.5

```
double divide(long dividend , long divisor)
{
   if(divisor == 0L)
      throw "Division by zero" ;
   return (double)dividend / divisor ;
}
```

It's important to note that the type of the expression being thrown has nothing to do with the return type of the function itself.

How to catch an exception

In order for the calling routine to recognize the various types of exceptions that are being thrown, it must first invoke the function within the context of a `try` block or any function called from within a `try` block. The word `try` is a keyword. A `try` block is written as follows:

Example 18.6

```
try
{
   // Call the function
}
```

Note that even if there is only one statement that comprises the `try` block, the braces are still needed.

Immediately following the `try` block you must write one or more handlers that can *catch* the exception being thrown. A handler has this syntax:

Example 18.7

```
catch( /* 1 formal argument */ )
{
  // Process the exception
}
```

The word `catch` is a keyword. Note that an exception handler (also known as a `catch` block) can appear *only* after a `try` block or another exception handler. There can be no intervening statements. The parentheses contain a declaration that is used in a fashion similar to that of a function declaration.

An exception handler that accepts some type `T`, `const T`, `T&`, or `const T&` is a match for a throw expression if that expression matches the type exactly or with a trivial conversion. Promotions and standard conversion are not tried. Also, the type of the throw expression may be that of a class derived from type `T`, assuming that `T` is an accessible base. Finally, the type of the throw expression may be a pointer type that can be converted to `T` by standard pointer conversion.

The process of throwing and catching an exception entails searching the exception handlers after the `try` block for the first one that can be invoked. After the handler has finished its processing, all remaining handlers are automatically skipped and execution of the program resumes normally with the first statement after the last handler. Although it may be complicated to read, an exception handler may itself contain a `try` block followed by its own exception handlers.

For example, here is a repeat of Example 18.2 in which a message is thrown by the `divide()` function. Note how the program continues to execute after the division by zero is thrown and caught.

Example 18.8

```cpp
#include <iostream.h>
#include <iomanip.h>
#include "manips.h"

#include "manips.cpp"

double divide(long dividend , long divisor)
{
   if(divisor == 0L)
      throw "Division by zero" ;
   return (double)dividend / divisor ;
}

int main()
{
   cout << "Enter a dividend and a divisor: " ;
   long dividend , divisor ;
   while(!(cin >> dividend >> divisor).eof())
    {
      if(cin.good())
       {
         try
          {
            cout << dividend << '/' << divisor << " = " << MONEY
                   << divide(dividend , divisor) << endl ;
         } // end try block
         catch(const char* message)
          {
            cerr << message << endl ;
         } // end catch block
       }
      else
         cerr << "Input error\n" ;
      cin >> FLUSH ;
      cout << "Next dividend and divisor: " ;
    }

   return 0 ;
}
```

The output for a typical run would be:

```
Enter a dividend and a divisor: 7 4
7/4 = 1.75
Next dividend and divisor: 7 A
Input error
Next dividend and divisor: 7 0
Division by zero
Next dividend and divisor: ^Z
```

Uncaught exceptions

What if there is no handler to catch the exception being thrown? In this case a special function called `terminate()` will be called and a run-time error message will be displayed. Then the program will automatically be terminated. This is essentially the same situation that occurred in Example 18.2, but in this case it's the user now taking the responsibility for aborting the program by not explicitly providing a handler for a possible error condition.

Example 18.8 has now been changed so that only a type `int` can be caught. Since a string literal is being thrown, the exception cannot be caught, and the program aborts.

Example 18.9

```cpp
#include <iostream.h>
#include <iomanip.h>
#include "manips.h"

#include "manips.cpp"

double divide(long dividend , long divisor)
{
   if(divisor == 0L)
      throw "Division by zero" ;
   return (double)dividend / divisor ;
}
```

```
int main()
{
   cout << "Enter a dividend and a divisor: " ;
   long dividend , divisor ;
   while(!(cin >> dividend >> divisor).eof())
    {
       if(cin.good())
        {

           try
            {
               cout << dividend << '/' << divisor << " = " << MONEY
                    << divide(dividend , divisor) << endl ;
            }  // end try block
           catch(int x)
            {
               cerr << x << endl ;
            }  // end catch block
        }
       else
           cerr << "Input error\n" ;
       cin >> FLUSH ;
       cout << "Next dividend and divisor: " ;
    }

   return 0 ;
}
```

The output for a typical run would be:

```
Enter a dividend and a divisor: 7 4
7/4 = 1.75
Next dividend and divisor: 7 A
Input error
Next dividend and divisor: 7 0
No handler for thrown object!
```

Rather than let an abort occur, you can provide a function that can serve as a default when an exception is thrown but not caught. To do this, you must call the set_terminate() function (prototyped in the file except.h) and provide an argument that is a pointer to your own termination function. The latter function must take no arguments and return nothing. This is done in the following example:

Example 18.10

```cpp
#include <iostream.h>
#include <iomanip.h>
#include <except.h>
#include "manips.h"

#include "manips.cpp"

double divide(long dividend , long divisor)
{
   if(divisor == 0L)
      throw "Division by zero" ;
   return (double)dividend / divisor ;
}

void my_terminate()
{
   cerr << "Uncaught exception!\n" ;
}

int main()
{
   set_terminate(my_terminate) ;
   cout << "Enter a dividend and a divisor: " ;
   long dividend , divisor ;
   while(!(cin >> dividend >> divisor).eof())
    {
      if(cin.good())
       {
         try
          {
            cout << dividend << '/' << divisor << " = " << MONEY
                   << divide(dividend , divisor) << endl ;
          } // end try block
         catch(int x)
          {
            cerr << x << endl ;
          } // end catch block
       }
      else
         cerr << "Input error\n" ;
      cin >> FLUSH ;
      cout << "Next dividend and divisor: " ;
    }

   return 0 ;
}
```

The output for a typical run would be:

```
Enter a dividend and a divisor: 7 4
7/4 = 1.75
Next dividend and divisor: 7 A
Input error
Next dividend and divisor: 7 0
Uncaught exception!
```

Exception specifications

Typically the user of a function is only aware of the function's prototype, i.e., the number and types of the arguments that the function expects to receive, and the type of argument (if any) that will be returned. But if the user is supposed to write exception handlers to accommodate all of the exceptions that the function may throw, then obviously the types of the thrown expressions must also be known.

To solve this problem, a function declaration (or definition, if it replaces the declaration) may include *exception specifications* that provide this information. These specifications appear immediately after the parenthesized list of formal arguments (and before the base/member initialization list when writing a constructor function), and take this form:

Example 18.11

```
throw(type1 , type2 , /* etc. */ ) ;
```

where `type1`, `type2`, etc., represent the types of the expressions that can appear in a `throw` statement. If both a declaration and its definition are written, then the exception specification must appear in both places. If an exception specification has no types whatsoever written between the parentheses, then it promises not to throw any exceptions.

Here is a repeat of Example 18.8 with an exception specification shown in the declaration of the `divide()` function, and the function itself moved after the `main()` function.

Example 18.12

```
#include <iostream.h>
#include <iomanip.h>
#include "manips.h"

#include "manips.cpp"

double divide(long dividend , long divisor) throw(const char*) ;

int main()
{
   cout << "Enter a dividend and a divisor: " ;
   long dividend , divisor ;
   while(!(cin >> dividend >> divisor).eof())
    {
      if(cin.good())
       {
         try
          {
            cout << dividend << '/' << divisor << " = " << MONEY
                   << divide(dividend , divisor) << endl ;
         } // end try block
         catch(const char* message)
          {
            cerr << message << endl ;
         } // end catch block
       }
      else
         cerr << "Input error\n" ;
      cin >> FLUSH ;
      cout << "Next dividend and divisor: " ;
    }

   return 0 ;
}

double divide(long dividend , long divisor) throw(const char*)
{
   if(divisor == 0L)
      throw "Division by zero" ;
   return (double)dividend / divisor ;
}
```

The output for a typical run would be:

```
Enter a dividend and a divisor: 7 4
7/4 = 1.75
Next dividend and divisor: 7 A
Input error
Next dividend and divisor: 7 0
Division by zero
Next dividend and divisor: ^Z
```

If the function throws an exception that has not been specified, the function
`unexpected()` will automatically get executed. This function will cause the program
to terminate.

Example 18.13

```cpp
#include <iostream.h>
#include <iomanip.h>
#include "manips.h"

#include "manips.cpp"

double divide(long dividend , long divisor) throw(const char*) ;

int main()
{
  cout << "Enter a dividend and a divisor: " ;
  long dividend , divisor ;
  while(!(cin >> dividend >> divisor).eof())
   {
     if(cin.good())
       {
         try
          {
            cout << dividend << '/' << divisor << " = " << MONEY
                 << divide(dividend , divisor) << endl ;
          }  // end try block
         catch(const char* message)
          {
            cerr << message << endl ;
          }  // end catch block
       }
     else
        cerr << "Input error\n" ;
     cin >> FLUSH ;
     cout << "Next dividend and divisor: " ;
   }
```

```
      return 0 ;
}

double divide(long dividend , long divisor) throw(const char*)
{
   if(divisor == 0L)
      throw divisor ;
   return (double)dividend / divisor ;
}
```

The output for a typical run would be:

```
Enter a dividend and a divisor: 7 4
7/4 = 1.75
Next dividend and divisor: 7 A
Input error
Next dividend and divisor: 7 0
violation of function exception specification!
```

If you wish to trap this condition, you may call the function set_unexpected() with an argument that is the address of your own function that takes no arguments and returns nothing. The function set_unexpected() is prototyped in the file except.h.

Example 18.14

```
#include <iostream.h>
#include <iomanip.h>
#include <except.h>
#include "manips.h"

#include "manips.cpp"

double divide(long dividend , long divisor) throw(const char*) ;

void my_unexpected()
{
   cerr << "Unexpected exception!\n" ;
}
```

```
int main()
{
   set_unexpected(my_unexpected) ;
   cout << "Enter a dividend and a divisor: " ;
   long dividend , divisor ;
   while(!(cin >> dividend >> divisor).eof())
    {
       if(cin.good())
        {
          try
           {
             cout << dividend << '/' << divisor << " = " << MONEY
                     << divide(dividend , divisor) << endl ;
          } // end try block
          catch(const char* message)
           {
             cerr << message << endl ;
          } // end catch block
        }
       else
          cerr << "Input error\n" ;
       cin >> FLUSH ;
       cout << "Next dividend and divisor: " ;
    }

   return 0 ;
}

double divide(long dividend , long divisor) throw(const char*)
{
   if(divisor == 0L)
      throw divisor ;
   return (double)dividend / divisor ;
}
```

The output for a typical run would be:

```
Enter a dividend and a divisor: 7 4
7/4 = 1.75
Next dividend and divisor: 7 A
Input error
Next dividend and divisor: 7 0
Unexpected exception!
```

How to throw more than one value

Suppose that when an error is detected you wish to throw more than one value. To do this, these values must be encapsulated within an instance of some class whose data members can then represent the values being thrown.

For example, let's create a class called `throw_error` that consists of two long integers. When the `divide()` function detects a divisor of zero, it can then instantiate a temporary instance of `throw_error` with both the dividend and the divisor. In order to catch this exception, a `catch` block must be written that can receive an instance of `throw_error` by constant reference. Using accessor functions, the individual data members can then be displayed. (Of course, you may choose to write a structure rather than a class so that the data members have public access, thereby negating the need to use accessor functions.)

Example 18.15

```cpp
#include <iostream.h>
#include <iomanip.h>
#include "manips.h"

#include "manips.cpp"

class throw_error
{
   long dividend , divisor ;

      public:
   throw_error(long a , long b) : dividend(a) , divisor(b) {}

   long get_dividend() const
    {
      return dividend ;
    }

   long get_divisor() const
    {
      return divisor ;
    }
} ;

double divide(long dividend , long divisor) throw(throw_error)
{
   if(divisor == 0L)
      throw throw_error(dividend , divisor) ;
   return (double)dividend / divisor ;
}
```

```
int main()
{
   cout << "Enter a dividend and a divisor: " ;
   long dividend , divisor ;
   while(!(cin >> dividend >> divisor).eof())
    {
       if(cin.good())
        {
           try
            {
               cout << dividend << '/' << divisor << " = " << MONEY
                       << divide(dividend , divisor) << endl ;
           }  // end try block
           catch(const throw_error& error)
            {
               cerr << "Error!\n" ;
               cerr << "\tDividend = " << error.get_dividend()
                       << endl ;
               cerr << "\tDivisor = " << error.get_divisor()
                       << endl;
           }  // end catch block
        }
       else
          cerr << "Input error\n" ;
       cin >> FLUSH ;
       cout << "Next dividend and divisor: " ;
    }

   return 0 ;
}
```

The output for a typical run would be:

```
Enter a dividend and a divisor: 7 4
7/4 = 1.75
Next dividend and divisor: 7 A
Input error
Next dividend and divisor: 7 0
Error!
    Dividend = 7
    Divisor = 0
Next dividend and divisor: ^Z
```

Unwinding the stack

It is certainly possible that just prior to an exception being thrown, one or more user-defined types have already been instantiated. Furthermore, let's assume that the constructor function for these types has allocated private resources on the heap.

So when the exception is thrown, what happens to these resources as the instances go out of scope? The answer is that the stack is automatically "unwound", and the destructor function is guaranteed to be called, thereby negating the possibility of memory leakage. (This scheme does not apply to memory that was allocated in a function other than a constructor function. In this case the pointer to the heap space would have to be thrown so that the catch block can release the memory.)

To prove this, a non-temporary instance of the class throw_error will be instantiated and thrown if the divisor is equal to zero. The class itself has been enhanced to trace the calls to the constructor and destructor functions.

Example 18.16

```cpp
#include <iostream.h>
#include <iomanip.h>
#include "manips.h"

#include "manips.cpp"

class throw_error
{
   long dividend , divisor ;

     public:
   throw_error(long a = 0L , long b = 0L) : dividend(a) ,
                                            divisor(b)
    {
      cout << "Def constructor\n" ;
    }

   throw_error(const throw_error& x) : dividend(x.dividend) ,
                                       divisor(x.divisor)
    {
      cout << "Copy constructor\n" ;
    }

   ~throw_error()
    {
      cout << "Destructor\n" ;
    }

   long get_dividend() const
    {
      return dividend ;
    }
```

```
      long get_divisor() const
       {
         return divisor ;
       }
   } ;

   double divide(long dividend , long divisor) throw(throw_error)
   {
      if(divisor == 0L)
       {
         throw_error te(dividend , divisor) ;
         throw te;
       }
      return (double)dividend / divisor ;
   }

   int main()
   {
      cout << "Enter a dividend and a divisor: " ;
      long dividend , divisor ;
      while(!(cin >> dividend >> divisor).eof())
       {
         if(cin.good())
          {
            try
             {
               cout << dividend << '/' << divisor << " = " << MONEY
                       << divide(dividend , divisor) << endl ;
             }  // end try block
            catch(const throw_error& error)
             {
               cerr << "Error!\n" ;
               cerr << "\tDividend = " << error.get_dividend()
                       << endl ;
               cerr << "\tDivisor = " << error.get_divisor()
                       << endl ;
             }  // end catch block
          }
         else
            cerr << "Input error\n" ;
         cin >> FLUSH ;
         cout << "Next dividend and divisor: " ;
       }

      return 0 ;
   }
```

The output for a typical run would be:

```
Enter a dividend and a divisor: 7 4
7/4 = 1.75
Next dividend and divisor: 7 A
Input error
Next dividend and divisor: 7 0
Def constructor
Copy constructor
Destructor
Error!
    Dividend = 7
    Divisor = 0
Destructor
Next dividend and divisor: ^Z
```

Throwing an exception from a class

The following example shows how class functions can use exception handling to detect catastrophic errors. In the following example there are two such errors present: (1) the constructor function detects that no more heap space is available, and (2) the overloaded `operator[]()` function detects an invalid index. In both cases an exception is thrown. If you wish to emulate the first error, then it is just a matter of uncommenting the statement in the constructor function that sets the member `ptr` to zero.

Example 18.17

```cpp
#include <iostream.h>
#include <string.h>
#include "manips.h"

#include "manips.cpp"

class array
{
   long* ptr ;
   long size ;

      public:
   array(long = 1L) throw(const char*) ;
   ~array() ;
   long& operator[](long) throw(long) ;
   friend ostream& operator<<(ostream& , const array&) ;
} ;
```

```
array::array(long n) throw(const char*) : size(n) ,
                                           ptr(new long[size])

{
   // ptr = 0 ;  // Emulate out-of-heap-space condition
   if(ptr == 0)
      throw("Out of heap space!") ;
   for(long i = 0 ; i < size ; ++i)
      ptr[i] = 0L ;
}

array::~array()
{
   delete [] ptr ;
}

long& array::operator[](long x) throw(long)
{
   if(x < 0 || x >= size)
      throw x ;
   return ptr[x] ;
}

ostream& operator<<(ostream& stream , const array& a)
{
   cout << "The array:\n" ;
   for(long i = 0 ; i < a.size ; ++i)
      stream << '[' << i << ']' << "  " << a.ptr[i] << endl ;
   return stream ;
}

int main()
{
   cout << "How long is the array? " ;
   long length ;
   while(!(cin >> length).eof())
    {
      if(cin.good())
       {
          try
           {
              array a(length) ;
              cout << "Enter an index and a value: " ;
              cin >> FLUSH ;
              long index , value ;
              while(!(cin >> index >> value).eof())
               {
                  if(cin.good())
                   {
                      a[index] = value ;
                      cout << a << endl ;
                   }
```

```
                    else
                        cerr << "Input error\n" ;

                    cin >> FLUSH ;
                    cout << "Next index and value: " ;
                }
            } // end try block
            catch(const char* message)
            {
                cerr << message << endl ;
            }

            catch(long x)
            {
                cerr << "Invalid index: " << x << endl ; }
            }
        else
            cerr << "Input error\n" ;
        cin >> FLUSH ;
        cout << "Next array length: " ;
    }

    return 0 ;
}
```

The output for a typical run would be:

```
How long is the array: X
Input error
Next array length: 3
Enter an index and a value: 2 X
Input error
Next index and value: 2 101
The array:
[0]  0
[1]  1
[2] 101

Next index and value: 3 56
Invalid index: 3
Next array length: ^Z
```

If you now uncommented the line in the constructor, the output would be:

```
How long is the array: 3
Out of heap space!
Next array length: ^Z
```

Segregating the `try` and `catch` blocks

Writing a program that contains `try` and `catch` blocks tends to produce somewhat awkward looking code, as the previous examples have shown. A better approach would be to isolate the `try` and `catch` blocks in the `main()` function, while the rest of the program is contained in other functions. Of course, to continue execution after an exception is thrown, the `try` and `catch` blocks must be coded within the context of some kind of loop. This loop must continue to execute as long as the end-of-file condition has not yet been encountered.

Here Example 18.17 has been changed to isolate the `try` and `catch` blocks.

Example 18.18

```
#include <iostream.h>
#include <string.h>
#include "manips.h"

#include "manips.cpp"

class array
{
  long* ptr ;
  long size ;

    public:
  array(long = 1L) throw(const char*) ;
  ~array() ;
  long& operator[](long) throw(long) ;
  friend ostream& operator<<(ostream& , const array&) ;
} ;

array::array(long n) throw(const char*) : size(n) ,
                                          ptr(new long[size])
{
  // ptr = 0 ;  // Emulate out-of-heap-space condition
  if(ptr == 0)
    throw("Out of heap space!") ;
  for(long i = 0 ; i < size ; ++i)
    ptr[i] = 0L ;
}

array::~array()
{
  delete [] ptr ;
}
```

```
long& array::operator[](long x)  throw(long)
{
   if(x < 0 || x >= size)
      throw x ;
   return ptr[x] ;
}

ostream& operator<<(ostream& stream , const array& a)
{
   cout << "The array:\n" ;
   for(long i = 0 ; i < a.size ; ++i)
      stream << '[' << i << ']' << "  " << a.ptr[i] << endl ;
   return stream ;
}

void my_main(int&) ;

int main()
{
   int done = 0 ;
   while(!done)
    {
       try
        {
           my_main(done) ;
        }
       catch(const char* message)
        {
           cerr << message << endl ;
        }
       catch(long x)
        {
           cerr << "Invalid index: " << x << endl ;
        }
    }

   return 0 ;
}

void my_main(int& done)
{
   cout << "How long is the array? " ;
   long length ;
   while(!(cin >> length).eof())
    {
       if(cin.good())
        {
           array a(length) ;
           cout << "Enter an index and a value: " ;
           cin >> FLUSH ;
           long index , value ;
```

```
      while(!(cin >> index >> value).eof())
       {
          if(cin.good())
           {
             a[index] = value ;
             cout << a << endl ;
           }
          else
             cerr << "Input error\n" ;

          cin >> FLUSH ;
          cout << "Next index and value: " ;
       }
    }
    else
       cerr << "Input error\n" ;
    cin >> FLUSH ;
    cout << "Next array length: " ;
   }

 done = 1 ;
}
```

The output is the same as that of Example 18.17

Review Questions

1) What is the purpose of exception handling?

2) What error recovery techniques are available without exception handling?

3) What is meant by "throwing an exception"?

4) What is a `try` block?

5) What is meant by "catching" an exception?

6) What is a `catch` block?

7) What is an "exception specification"?

Exercise #1

Write a global function that takes an integer as its one formal argument and does a table look-up on an array of elements, each of which consists of an integer and a string. If there is an exact match on the integer input, then the function returns the string verbiage of the number itself, e.g., "one" for 1, "five" for 5, etc. If the number cannot be found in the array, then throw an exception.

■ Exercise #2

Modify the `fraction` class from Chapter 8, Exercise 2, so that a denominator of zero causes an exception to be thrown.

■ Exercise #3

Modify Example 18.15 so that the `throw_error` class is a class template.

Notes

Notes

Notes

Appendix A

C++ precedence chart

Symbol	Description	Associativity
literal this () for grouping name ::	Primary expressions	
. -> [] () () ++ --	direct member access indirect member access subscripting function call function-style cast postfix postfix	Left to right
sizeof ++ -- ~ ! - + & * new new [] delete delete []	size of prefix prefix one's complement not unary minus unary plus address of dereference allocate single instance allocate array of instances delete single instance delete array of instances	Right to left
()	C-style cast	Right to left

.* ->*	pointer-to-member selection pointer-to-member selection	Left to right
* / %	multiply divide modulus	Left to right
+ -	add subtract	Left to right
<< >>	shift left shift right	Left to right
< <= > >=	less than less than or equal to greater than greater than or equal to	Left to right
== !=	equal not equal	Left to right
&	bitwise AND	Left to right
^	bitwise exclusive OR	Left to right
|	bitwise inclusive OR	Left to right
&&	logical AND	Left to right
||	logical OR	Left to right
? :	conditional expression	Left to right
= *= /= %= += -= <<= >>= &= |= ^=	assignment multiply and assign divide and assign modulus and assign add and assign subtract and assign shift left and assign shift right and assign bitwise AND and assign inclusive OR and assign exclusive OR and assign	Right to left
,	comma	Left to right

Appendix B

The files `mystring.h` and `mystring.cpp`

```cpp
// The file "mystring.h"

#ifndef MYSTRING_H
#define MYSTRING_H

#include <stdio.h>
#include <string.h>
#include <stdlib.h>
#include <ctype.h>
#include "trace.h"

class ostream ;

class string
{
    private:
  static trace tracer ;
  void copy(const char*) ;
  void copy(char) ;
  void copy(int) ;
  void release() ;
  void concat(const char* , const char*) ;

    protected:
  int length ;
  char* ptr ;

    public:
  static void debug(trace::STATUS = trace::OFF) ;
  int get_length() const ;
  string() ;
  string(const char*) ;
  string(char) ;
  string(const string&) ;
  string(int) ;
  ~string() ;
  void print(const char* = "") const ;
  string& operator=(const string&) ;
  string& operator+=(const string&) ;
```

```
        string operator+() const ;
        friend string operator+(const string& , const string&) ;
        friend string operator+(const string& , const char*) ;
        friend string operator+(const char* , const string&) ;
        friend string operator+(const string& , char) ;
        friend string operator+(char , const string&) ;
        friend int operator==(const string& , const string&) ;
        friend int operator!=(const string& , const string&) ; friend
        int operator<(const string& , const string&) ;
        friend int operator>(const string& , const string&) ; friend
        int operator<=(const string& , const string&) ;
        friend int operator>=(const string& , const string&) ;
        friend ostream& operator<<(ostream& , const string&) ;
        char& operator[](int) const ;
        friend char* operator+(const string& , int) ;
        friend char* operator+(int , const string&) ;
        int operator()(const string& , int) const ;
        string& operator++() ;
        string& operator--() ;
        string operator++(int) ;
        string operator--(int) ;
        static void* operator new(size_t) ;
        static void operator delete(void*) ;
    } ;

    inline void string::copy(const char* s)
    {
       length = strlen(s) ;
       ptr = new char[length + 1] ;
       strcpy(ptr , s) ;
    }

    inline void string::copy(char ch)
    {
       length = 1 ;
       ptr = new char[2] ;
       ptr[0] = ch ;
       ptr[1] = '\0' ;
    }

    inline void string::copy(int len)
    {
       length = len ;
       ptr = new char[length + 1] ;
       ptr[0] = '\0' ;
    }

    inline void string::release()
    {
       delete [] ptr ;
    }
```

```cpp
inline void string::concat(const char* s1 , const char* s2)
{
   char* temp = new char[strlen(s1) + strlen(s2) + 1] ;
   strcpy(temp , s1) ;
   strcat(temp , s2) ;
   release() ;
   copy(temp) ;
   delete [] temp ;
}

inline void string::debug(trace::STATUS t)
{
   tracer.change(t) ;
}

inline int string::get_length() const
{
   return length ;
}

inline string::string()
{
   tracer.dump("Default constructor" , this) ;
   copy("") ;
}

inline string::string(const char* s)
{
   tracer.dump("char* constructor" , this) ;
   copy(s) ;
}

inline string::string(char ch)
{
   tracer.dump("char constructor" , this) ;
   copy(ch) ;
}

inline string::string(int len)
{
   tracer.dump("int constructor" , this) ;
   copy(len < 0 ? 0 : len) ;
}

inline string::string(const string& s)
{
   tracer.dump("Copy constructor" , this) ; copy(s.ptr) ;
}
```

```cpp
inline string::~string()
{
   tracer.dump("Destructor" , this) ; release() ;
}

inline void string::print(const char* name) const
{
   tracer.dump("Heap address" , ptr) ;
   printf("%s: \"%s\" %d\n" , name , ptr , length) ;
}

inline string& string::operator=(const string& s)
{
   tracer.dump("operator=()" , this) ;
   // Check for self-assignment
   if(&s == this)
      tracer.dump("Self-assignment" , this) ;
   else if(length != s.length)
   {
      release() ;
      copy(s.ptr) ;
   }
   else
      strcpy(ptr , s.ptr) ;

   return *this ;
}

inline string operator+(const string& s1 , const string& s2)
{
   string::tracer.dump("binary operator+(string,string)") ;
   string new_string(s1.length + s2.length) ;
   new_string.concat(s1.ptr , s2.ptr) ;
   return new_string ;
}

inline string operator+(const string& s1 , const char* str)
{
   string::tracer.dump("binary operator+(string,char*)") ;
   string new_string(s1.length + (int)strlen(str)) ;
   new_string.concat(s1.ptr , str) ;
   return new_string ;
}

inline string operator+(const char* str , const string& s1)
{
   string::tracer.dump("binary operator+(char*,string)") ;
   string new_string((int)strlen(str) + s1.length) ;
   new_string.concat(str , s1.ptr) ;
   return new_string ;
}
```

```cpp
inline string operator+(const string& s1 , char ch)
{
   string::tracer.dump("binary operator+(string,char)") ;
   char buffer[2] ;
   buffer[0] = ch ;
   buffer[1] = '\0' ;
   return s1 + buffer ;
}

inline string operator+(char ch , const string& s1)
{
   string::tracer.dump("binary operator+(char,string)") ;
   char buffer[2] ;
   buffer[0] = ch ;
   buffer[1] = '\0' ;
   return buffer + s1 ;
}

inline string& string::operator+=(const string& s)
{
   tracer.dump("operator+=()\n") ;
   return *this = *this + s ;
}

inline int operator==(const string& s1, const string& s2)
{
   string::tracer.dump("operator==()\n") ;
   return (!strcmp(s1.ptr,s2.ptr)) ;
}

inline int operator!=(const string& s1, const string& s2)
{
   string::tracer.dump("operator!=()\n") ;
   return (strcmp(s1.ptr,s2.ptr)) ;
}

inline int operator<(const string& s1, const string& s2)
{
   string::tracer.dump("operator<()\n") ;
   return (strcmp(s1.ptr,s2.ptr) < 0) ;
}

inline int operator>(const string& s1, const string& s2)
{
   string::tracer.dump("operator>()\n") ;
   return (strcmp(s1.ptr,s2.ptr) > 0) ;
}
```

```cpp
inline int operator<=(const string& s1, const string& s2)
{
   string::tracer.dump("operator<=()\n") ;
   return (strcmp(s1.ptr,s2.ptr) <= 0) ;
}

inline int operator>=(const string& s1, const string& s2)
{
   string::tracer.dump("operator>=()\n") ;
   return (strcmp(s1.ptr,s2.ptr) >= 0) ;
}

inline ostream& operator<<(ostream& stream , const string& s)
{
   return stream << s.ptr ;
}

inline char* operator+(const string& s , int i)
{
   string::tracer.dump("operator+(s , i)\n") ;
   return &s[i] ;
}

inline char* operator+(int i , const string& s)
{
   string::tracer.dump("operator+(i , s)\n") ;
   return &s[i] ;
}

inline int string::operator()(const string& s , int len) const
{
   tracer.dump("operator()()\n") ;
   return !strncmp(ptr , s.ptr , len) ;
}

#endif

// The file "mystring.cpp"

#include "mystring.h"

// OFF passed to constructor in static definition
trace string::tracer = trace::OFF ;

string string::operator+() const
{
   tracer.dump("unary operator+()\n") ;
   string new_string = *this ;
   for(int i = 0 ; i < length ; ++i)
      new_string.ptr[i] = toupper(new_string.ptr[i]) ;
   return new_string ;
}
```

```cpp
char& string::operator[](int index) const
{
   tracer.dump("operator[]()\n") ;
   if(index < 0 || index >= length)
   {
      putchar('\a') ;
      static char dummy ;
      dummy = '\0' ;
      return dummy ;
   }
   return ptr[index] ;
}

string& string::operator++()
{
   tracer.dump("operator++()" , this) ;
   for(int i = 0 ; i < length ; ++i)
      ++ptr[i] ;
   return *this ;
}

string& string::operator--()
{
   tracer.dump("operator--()" , this) ;
   for(int i = 0 ; i < length ; ++i)
      --ptr[i] ;
   return *this ;
}

string string::operator++(int)
{
   tracer.dump("operator++(int)" , this) ;
   string temp(*this) ;
   ++(*this) ;
   return temp ;
}

string string::operator--(int)
{
   tracer.dump("operator--(int)" , this) ;
   string temp(*this) ;
      --(*this) ;
   return temp ;
}
```

```cpp
void* string::operator new(size_t size)
{
   tracer.dump("operator new") ;
   void* temp = new char[size] ;
   if(temp == 0)
      puts("Out of heap space") ;
   return temp ;
}

void string::operator delete(void* p)
{
   tracer.dump("operator delete") ;
   delete p ;
}
```

Appendix C

The files `manips.h` and `manips.cpp`

```cpp
// The file "manips.h"

#ifndef MANIPS_H
#define MANIPS_H

#include <iostream.h>
#include <iomanip.h>
#include <dos.h>

ostream& endl(ostream&) ;
istream& FLUSH(istream&) ;
ostream& LEFT(ostream&) ;
ostream& RIGHT(ostream&) ;
ostream& MONEY(ostream&) ;

ostream& TAB(ostream& , long) ;
OMANIP(long) TAB(long) ;

typedef const void* P ;
IOMANIPdeclare(P) ;
ostream& ADDRESS(ostream& , P) ;
OMANIP(P) ADDRESS(P) ;

IOMANIPdeclare(char) ;
ostream& CHAR(ostream& , char) ;
OMANIP(char) CHAR(char) ;

#endif

// The file "manips.cpp"

#include "manips.h"

ostream& endl(ostream& stream)
{
   stream << "\n" << flush ;
   stream.seekp(0L) ;
   return stream ;
}
```

```
istream& FLUSH(istream& stream)
{
   stream.clear() ;
   int ch ;
   while((ch = cin.get()) != '\n' && ch != EOF) {}
   stream.clear() ;
   return stream ;
}

ostream& LEFT(ostream& stream)
{
   stream.setf(ios::left , ios::adjustfield) ;
   return stream ;
}

ostream& RIGHT(ostream& stream)
{
   stream.setf(ios::right , ios::adjustfield) ;
   return stream ;
}

ostream& MONEY(ostream& stream)
{
   stream << RIGHT ;
   stream.setf(ios::fixed , ios::floatfield) ;
   stream.setf(ios::showpoint) ;
   stream.precision(2) ;
   return stream ;
}

ostream& TAB(ostream& stream , long col)
{
   long here = stream.tellp() ;
   if(col < here)
   {
      stream << endl ;
      stream.seekp(0L) ;
      here = 0L ;
   }
   return stream << setw(col - here) << " " ;
}

OMANIP(long) TAB(long col)
{
   return OMANIP(long) (TAB , col) ;
}
```

```
ostream& ADDRESS(ostream& stream , P add)
{
   char oldfill = stream.fill() ;
   stream << setfill('0') ;
   long save = stream.flags() ;
   stream.setf(ios::right , ios::adjustfield) ;
   stream
#if defined __COMPACT__ || \
    defined __LARGE__ || \
    defined __HUGE__
   << setw(5) << FP_SEG(add)
#endif
   << ':' << setw(5) << FP_OFF(add) ;
   stream << setfill(oldfill) ;
   stream.flags(save) ;
   return stream ;
}

OMANIP(P) ADDRESS(P add)
{
   return OMANIP(P) (ADDRESS , add) ;
}

IOMANIPdeclare(char) ;

ostream& CHAR(ostream& stream , char ch)
{
   char buff[] = " " ;
   buff[0] = ch ;
   return stream << buff ;
}

OMANIP(char) CHAR(char ch)
{
   return OMANIP(char) (CHAR , ch) ;
}
```

Appendix D

Bibliography

AT&T Library Manual, C++ Stream Library, 1989

Atkinson, Lee and Atkinson, Mark, Using Borland C++, Que Corporation, 1991

Barkakati, Naba, Object-Oriented Programming In C++, Sams Publishing, 1991

Becker, Pete, Template notes

Berry, John, C++ Programming, Howard W Sams & Company, 1988

Borland C++ 3.0 Programmer's Guide

Budd, Timothy, An Introduction To Object-Oriented Programming, Addison-Wesley Publishing Company, 1991

Cargill, Tom, C++ Programming Style, Addison-Wesley Publishing Company, 1992

Chirlian, Paul M, Programming in C++, Merrill Publishing Company, 1990

Coplien, James O, Advanced C++, Addison-Wesley Publishing Company, 1992

Davis, Stephen R, Hands-On Turbo C++, Addison-Wesley Publishing Company, 1991

Dewhurst, Stephen C and Stark, Kathy T, Programming in C++, Prentice Hall, 1989

Eckel, Bruce, Using C++, Osborne McGraw-Hill, 1989

Eckel, Bruce, C++ Inside & Out, Osborne McGraw-Hill, 1993

Ellis, Margaret A and Stroustrup, Bjarne, The Annotated C++ Reference Manual, Addison-Wesley Publishing Company, 1990

Flamig, Bryan, Turbo C++, A Self-Teaching Guide, John Wiley & Sons, 1991

Gorlen, Keith E and Orlow, Sanford M and Plexico, Perry, Data Abstraction and Object-oriented Programming in C++, John Wiley & Sons, Inc., 1990

Graham, Neill, Learning C++, McGraw-Hill, 1991

Harbison, Samuel P and Steele Jr, Guy L, C: A Reference Manual (third edition), Prentice Hall, 1991

Horstmann, Cay S, Mastering C++, John Wiley & Sons, Inc., 1991

Ladd, Scott Robert, C++ Techniques & Applications, M&T Books, 1990

Lippman, Stanley, C++ Primer (2nd edition), Addison-Wesley Publishing Company, 1991

Lucas, Paul J, The C++ Programmer's Handbook, Prentice Hall, 1992

Mancl, Dennis, "Inline functions in C++", The C++ Report, February 1990

Meyers, Scott, Effective C++, Addison-Wesley Publishing Company, 1992

Murray, Robert, "The C++ Puzzle", The C++ Report, September, 1991

Murray, Robert, C++ Strategies and Tactics, Addison-Wesley Publishing Company, 1993

Pappas, Chris H and Murray, III, William H, Turbo C++ Professional Handbook, Osborne McGraw-Hill, 1990

Perry, Greg, Moving From C To C++, Sams Publishing, 1992

Plum, Thomas and Saks, Dan, C++ Programming Guidelines, Plum Hall, Inc., 1991

Pohl, Ira C, C++ for C Programmers, The Benjamin/Cummings Publishing Company, 1989

Prata, Stephen, C++ Primer Plus, Waite Group Press, 1991

Saks, Dan, "Standard C++: A Status Report", Supplement to Dr, Dobb's Journal, December, 1992

Schildt, Herbert, Turbo C/C++ The Complete Reference, Osborne McGraw-Hill, 1990

Schildt, Herbert, Using Turbo C++, Osborne McGraw-Hill, 1990

Shapiro, Jonathan S, A C++ Toolkit, Prentice Hall, 1991

Skinner, M T, The Advanced C++ Book, Silicon Press, 1992

Stevens, Al, Teach Yourself C++, MIS: Press, 1990

Stroustrup, Bjarne, The C++ Programming Language (Second Edition), Addison-Wesley Publishing Company, 1991

Weiner, Richard S & Pinson, Lewis J, The C++ Workbook, Addison-Wesley Publishing Company, 1990

Weiner, Richard S & Pinson, Lewis J, An Introduction to Object-Oriented Programming and C++, Addison-Wesley Publishing Company, 1988

Weiskamp, Keith & Flamig, Bryan, The Complete C++ Primer, Academic Press, 1990

Weiskamp, Keith and Heiny, Loren and Flamig, Bryan, Object-Oriented Programming with Turbo C++, John Wiley & Sons, Inc., 1991

K

L

M